Twilight Warriors

Twilight Warriors

Covert Air Operations against the USSR

Curtis Peebles

Naval Institute Press

ANNAPOLIS, MARYLAND

Naval Institute Press
291 Wood Road
Annapolis, MD 21402

Library of Congress Cataloging-in-Publication Data
Peebles, Curtis.
    Twilight warriors : covert air operations against the USSR / Curtis Peebles.
    p. cm.
    Includes bibliographical references and index.
    ISBN 1-59114-660-7 (hardcover)
    1. United States–Military relations–Soviet Union. 2. Soviet Union–Military
relations–United States. 3. United States–Military relations–Communist countries.
4. Communist countries–Military relations–United States. 5. Aerial reconnaissance,
American–Soviet Union. 6. Espionage, American–Soviet Union. 7. Subversive
activities–Soviet Union. 8. Intelligence service–United States–History–20th century.
9. United States–Foreign relations–1945–1989. 10. Cold War. I. Title.
    E183.8.S65P444 2005
    327.1273'047'09045–dc22
                                                        2005009671
Printed in the United States of America on acid-free paper ⊗

12 11 10 09 08 07 06 05   1 2 3 4 5

Contents

Preface

When the Cold War started, the United States undertook covert operations against the Soviet Union and its allies. The ultimate goal of these operations was to subvert these Communist governments and to so weaken them that they could no longer remain in power. Other efforts were directed to collecting intelligence, particularly any indications that a Soviet attack was about to begin. Should such a war break out, the resistance movements that Western intelligence agencies sought to establish could disrupt the attack. Covert operations were also seen as filling more limited roles. They could be used as a means to divert Communist attention or to overthrow leftist governments in the third world. They could be viewed as a middle course between doing nothing when U.S. interests were threatened and committing large numbers of troops.

This twilight struggle was fought within the heart of the USSR's new empire, in humid jungles, in scientific meetings, on tour buses, and on the polar ice cap or some other isolated, barren place on earth. The warriors who fought these secret battles were equally varied. Some were men fighting for the liberation of their homelands from Communist oppression. Theirs was a battle fought with no hope of survival, which they accepted because they could not do otherwise. Some were military personnel who undertook behind-the-lines combat operations. Others were perfectly ordinary people who volunteered to serve their countries in secret ways. They were tourists and businessmen, professors and students, scientists and engineers, politicians and chess players. They ran great risks without rewards, but by keeping their eyes open, and asking the right questions of the right people, they could discover some of the Soviet bloc's greatest secrets.

Many of these covert operations relied on pilots and aircrews capable of flying missions where extraordinary risks were simply part of the job. They were Americans and foreigners, civilians and military. Their missions sometimes involved flying airliners at treetop altitudes, at night, to drop agents and supplies deep inside Communist territory. They might find themselves flying passengers and cargo to and from short, rugged dirt strips built on the side of a mountain, making dozens of such takeoffs and landings each day. At other times, they would be flying combat missions, striking ground targets, convoys, and troop concentrations. The most extraordinary was the mission of a small group of Air Force crews. They were to rescue downed bomber crews from deep inside the Soviet Union following the outbreak of World War III.

Despite their worldwide scale, these U.S. covert operations attracted little public attention. Communist governments would announce that agents had been captured or executed, that operations had been uncovered, or that aircraft had been shot down. American officials would issue denials, ridiculing the Communist claims. Throughout the 1950s, both press and public tended to accept their denials. Not until the failed Bay of Pigs invasion did the public realize that the U.S. government did, indeed, undertake covert operations, and did lie about it. The debate over such covert operations would grow during the 1960s. This would lead to the controversy over the secret war in Laos, and the role Air America played in that conflict.

With the Cold War's end, the release of once-secret documents from U.S., Russian, Chinese, Eastern European, and other countries' archives has filled in many of the historical blanks of this era. This information includes details of the "technical collection" means developed during the Cold War, including the U-2 overflights and the Corona reconnaissance satellite. In contrast, covert operations have remained sensitive. Some operations still remain unacknowledged, even after half a century. The CIA officers who participated must still remain nameless or are identified by pseudonyms. Significant unknowns still remain about these operations. Often the primary sources are not official documents but, rather, the published recollections of those involved.

Today, at the beginning of the twenty-first century, the Cold War seems to be a part of some remote era. This is not only because of the passage of time, but also because these events are now on the other side of the great historical divide of September 11, 2001. It is hard for us to put ourselves into that time. To those who planned and undertook these missions, the need was clear. The West and the Soviet bloc were in a desperate struggle, and they saw the stakes as nothing less than survival itself.

Acknowledgments

My thanks go to the people and organizations who provided help along the way, including, but not limited to, Len LeSchack and the other veterans of Operation Coldfeet, Intermountain Aviation, and Air America; John Wright and his film crew; Evergreen International Aviation and its B-17 crew; Dr. Raymond L. Puffer and the staff of the Edwards AFB History Office; Frederick A. Johnsen; R. W. Koch; Peter W. Merlin; Meg Simmonds and John Parkinson of Eon Productions; Joel Carpenter; Sue Henderson; the National Security Archives; and the San Diego Aerospace Museum.

Acronyms and Abbreviations

ADIZ	Air Defense Identification Zone
AEC	Atomic Energy Commission
AFB	Air Force Base
ANG	Air National Guard
ARCS	Air Resupply and Communications Service
ARCW	Air Resupply and Communications Wing
ARG	Air Rescue Group
ARS	Air Rescue Squadron
BOA	Boun Oum Airways
CAT	Civil Air Transport
CCRAK	Covert, Clandestine, and Related Activities—Korea
CCTS	Combat Crew Training Squadron
CIA	Central Intelligence Agency
CIG	Central Intelligence Group
CNAC	China National Aviation Corporation
DCI	Director of Central Intelligence
DCS	Domestic Contact Service
DDP	Deputy Director for Plans
DIA	Defense Intelligence Agency
DMZ	Demilitarized Zone
DOD	Department of Defense
ECM	Electronic Countermeasures

FAA	Federal Aviation Administration
FAC	Forward Air Controller
FAR	Royal Laotian Army
FEAF	Far East Air Force
FEC	Far East Command
GDR	German Democratic Republic
ICBM	Intercontinental Ballistic Missile
JACK	Joint Advisory Commission- Korea
JCS	Joint Chiefs of Staff
JTAG	Joint Technical Advisory Group
KGB	Committee of State Security
MACV	Military Assistance Command, Vietnam
MATS	Military Air Transport Service
MGB	Ministry of State Security
MVD	Ministry of the Interior
NAS	Naval Air Station
NKGB	People's Commissariat of State Security
NP8/9	North Pole Soviet Ice Stations
NSAM	National Security Action Memorandum
NSC	National Security Council
NTS	National Labor Alliance
NVN	North Vietnam
ONI	Office of Naval Intelligence
ONR	Office of Naval Research
OPC	Office of Policy Coordination
OPLAN	Operational Plan
OSI	Office of Scientific Intelligence
OSO	Office of Special Operations
OSS	Office of Strategic Services
OUN	Organization of Ukrainian Nationalists
PDO	Parachute Dispatch Officer
PLA	Peoples Liberation Army (Chinese)
POW	Prisoner of War

RAF	Royal Air Force
SAC	Strategic Air Command
SAFE	Selected Areas for Evasion
SAM	Special Air Mission (chapter 3)
	Surface-to-Air Missile (chapter 6)
SARP	Strategic Aircrew Recovery Program
SIS	Secret Intelligence Service
SOE	Special Operations Executive
SOG	Studies and Observation Group
SSPL	Sacred Sword of the Patriots League
TACAN	Tactical Air Navigation
TLO	Tactical Liaison Office
UB	Polish Secret Police
UN	United Nations
USNS	U.S. Naval Service
USSR	Union of Soviet Socialist Republics
VC	Viet Cong
VFF	Volunteer Freedom Fighters for Religious and Political Resistance
WEI	Western Enterprises Incorporated
WIGMO	Western International Ground Maintenance Organization
WiN	Freedom and Independence

Twilight Warriors

Introduction

With the end of World War II in 1945, the United States found itself in conflict with the Union of Soviet Socialist Republics (USSR). This struggle was neither peace nor war, and one in which the United States had little experience to draw upon. The Soviet Union was an entirely new kind of state, born of conspiracy. Vladimir Lenin created the Bolsheviks not as a mass party in the Western tradition, but as a small, tightly disciplined covert organization, for the dual purpose of overthrowing the government of Czarist Russia and eliminating any potential rivals to Lenin's total control.

Following the Communist seizure of power in November 1917, Lenin maintained this subversive and conspiratorial outlook. He attempted unsuccessfully to foment Communist revolutions within Germany and Eastern Europe. Within the USSR, the secret police and Red Army sought to destroy internal enemies, both real and imagined. The USSR emerged from the revolution and civil war as a state that saw itself surrounded by hostile capitalist countries and threatened from within by class enemies, spies, and saboteurs. Lenin died in 1924, and his successor, Joseph Stalin, expanded both foreign covert action and mass terror at home to deal with these enemies.

The primary means of Soviet covert action from the 1920s and into the 1940s were foreign Communist parties. Ostensibly independent, they were actually extensions of the Soviet government. Stalin dictated their policies, while "Moscow Gold" paid for one-third to one-half of each party's yearly expenses. The foreign Communist parties, and the front organizations, newspapers, intellectuals, writers, and unions they controlled, provided both overt and covert support for Soviet policies. This included spreading pro-Soviet propaganda, influencing public opinion, and organizing demonstrations and strikes. The foreign Communist parties also served Soviet espionage activities. To learn of capitalist plots, party members were recruited as spies. By the start of World War II, the Soviets had willing, ideologically motivated agents in the highest reaches of the U.S. and British government, military, and industrial agencies.

In contrast, the United States had only limited experience with intelligence activities. Unlike European countries, the United States had no specialized peace-time foreign intelligence service. The limited intelligence collection and analysis was fragmented, handled as it was among the State Department and armed services. Even these efforts were beset by rivalries and political hostility. When Secretary of State Henry L. Stimson learned in 1929 that the United States was breaking other nations' codes, he announced, "Gentlemen do not read each other's mail," and closed down the operation. The disaster of Pearl Harbor was a direct result of the weaknesses of U.S. intelligence efforts. It was not until 13 June 1942 that the first specialized U.S. foreign intelligence agency, Office of Strategic Services (OSS), was established.

During World War II, resistance groups proved to be valuable sources of intelligence in Occupied Europe and Nazi Germany. The French Resistance was the most famous, but it was by no means the only such group. In Italy, partisans had supplied tactical intelligence directly from the German headquarters in Rome, and were later responsible for the liberation of every major city in Northern Italy. In Poland, the Home Army supplied intelligence on German V-2 rocket tests, and was even able to recover a crashed missile. These resistance movements were supported by massive airdrops of arms, supplies, and personnel from the OSS, as well as the British Secret Intelligence Service (SIS) and the Special Operations Executive (SOE). Such covert activities were integrated into overt military operations, and assisted the advance of Allied troops through Western Europe.

With the end of the war, however, President Harry S Truman closed down the OSS on 20 September 1945. Despite this, Truman clearly saw the need for a civilian peacetime intelligence service, and on 22 January 1946, he established the Central Intelligence Group (CIG), with Rear Adm. Sidney W. Souers as the first Director of Central Intelligence (DCI). The CIG was hobbled from the start. President Truman saw its goals as limited to producing a summary of important intelligence. The CIG had a small staff, and lacked the political clout to make an impact in Washington.

The CIG's shortcomings were soon apparent even to Truman, and he accepted the need for a sizable operational agency. This was to be part of a complete reorganization of the military services. In September 1947, the National Security Act established the Department of Defense (DOD), made the Air Force an independent service, created the National Security Council (NSC), and set up the Central Intelligence Agency (CIA). Despite its improved status, the CIA still suffered from many of the same weaknesses as the old CIG.

While U.S. intelligence efforts were fragmented and underfunded, the USSR had emerged from World War II with greatly expanded influence and power. Following the defeat of Nazi Germany, the Soviets had gained occupation zones in Germany and Austria. The USSR had also installed Communist-dominated coalition governments throughout Eastern Europe. Covert activities were a central instrument in the rule of this expanded empire. Soviet advisers, through the local Communists, controlled the police, rigged elections, and purged non-Communist parties.

In spite of these gains, Stalin seemed intent in the months following the end of the war to extend Soviet power beyond its traditional sphere of influence. Territorial demands were made against Turkey and Iran, while a pro-Communist guerrilla movement flared up in Greece. These threatened to extend Soviet control into the eastern Mediterranean and the Near East. In May 1945, with the end of the war in Europe, foreign Communist parties abandoned their wartime alliance with the capitalist nations, and now attacked them as fascists and enemies of peace. In France and Italy, the Communist parties were part of coalition governments, and had significant popular support, raising the possibility of Western Europe also going Communist. Within the USSR, Stalin tightened ideological controls and began a campaign against Western ideas.

By early 1947, the situation in Turkey and Greece had become critical, while in Western Europe the economy was on the verge of collapse. On 12 March,

Truman announced in a speech before Congress that the United States would resist Communist attempts to extend its power and influence. Although the establishment of the Truman Doctrine is seen today as the formal start of the Cold War, the Soviets at the time did not see it as such. They believed that the United States was too divided for the policy to be effective. Their attitude changed with the June 1947 announcement of the Marshall Plan for European economic reconstruction. Although the West saw Soviet control of Eastern Europe as being total, the Soviets themselves saw it as fragile. Non-Communist opposition parties still had considerable support in Eastern Europe, especially in Czechoslovakia. The influx of Western capital into Eastern Europe thus threatened Soviet domination, and the Marshall Plan was seen as but the prelude to establishment of an anti-Soviet Western bloc.

In July, the Soviets walked out of the Marshall Plan meeting in Paris, thus forcing the Eastern European satellites to reject Western aid. The coalition governments in Eastern Europe were transformed over the following months into Stalinist "people's democracies," Soviet art and culture were purged of Western influences, and foreign Communist parties were mobilized to subvert and disrupt the Marshall Plan. Soon after, violent demonstrations by militant Communist unions broke out in France and Italy. The police had to use force to put them down. The division of Europe between East and West was now official, and the Cold War was formally joined.

War with the USSR now seemed a real and immediate possibility. The turning point came in Czechoslovakia. Of the Eastern European satellites, it had the greatest degree of independence. On 20 February 1948, the non-Communist parties resigned from the government, hoping to force new elections. Klement Gottwald, the prime minister and Communist Party chairman, did not dissolve the government, but formed a National Front government of Communist and fellow travelers. Self-appointed "action committees" undertook wholesale nationalizations and intimidated non-Communist opposition.

The brazenness of the Communist coup in Czechoslovakia shocked Gen. Lucius D. Clay, the U.S. military governor in Germany. In the aftermath of the coup, Clay's fears continued to grow. During Allied Control Commission meetings on 26 February and 2 March 1948, the Soviet representatives launched into violent verbal attacks on the Western allies. These attacks were thoroughly prepared, unprovoked, and were often unrelated to the meetings. General Clay put his fears into words in a 5 March cable to Washington. The cable, addressed to the director of Army intelligence, Lt. Gen. Steven J. Chamberlin, read:

> For many months, based on logical analysis, I have felt and held that war was unlikely for at least ten years. Within the last few weeks, I have felt a subtle change in Soviet attitude which I cannot define but which now gives me a feeling that it may come with dramatic suddenness. I cannot support this change in my own thinking with any data or outward evidence in relationships other than to describe it as a feeling of a new tenseness in every Soviet individual with whom we have official relations. I am unable to submit any official report in the absence of supporting data but my feeling is real. You may advise the Chief of Staff of this for whatever it may be worth if you feel it is advisable.

Clay's "war warning" shocked official Washington. Pearl Harbor was still fresh in the minds of both military and political leaders alike. That evening, Secretary of the Army Kenneth C. Royall asked a surprised Atomic Energy Commission Chairman David E. Lilienthal how long it would take to get a certain number of "eggs" (i.e., A-bombs) to the Mediterranean. Events in the following days did little to ease the fears of war.

Finland was the next target for a Soviet-backed coup. Once part of the Czarist Russian empire, Finland had gained its independence following the revolution. During World War II, it had been allied with Nazi Germany. Finland had retained its independence after the war's end, but was obliged to follow the Soviet's lead in foreign policy. On 9 March 1948 Communist "flying squads" had gone to Helsinki newspapers, warning them not to print any anti-Soviet statements. This was similar to the tactics used during the Czechoslovakian coup the month before. The coup attempt failed on 19 March, when Yrjo Leino, the Communist Minister of the Interior (which had control of the police and internal security) warned General Sihvo, Chief of the General Staff, of the plot. General Sihvo put the Finnish Army on alert, and brought loyal troops into Helsinki.

The day after the Finnish coup attempt failed, the entire Soviet delegation walked out of the Allied Control Commission. Starting on 26 March, the Soviets embarked on a deception effort to make it appear they were building up forces for an invasion of Western Europe. The U.S. Air Force and some of the Scandinavian armed forces were put on alert. In fact, these Soviet efforts were the buildup to an attempt to force the West to accept Moscow's terms for a German settlement. These included reparations, demilitarization, an occupation policy similar to that imposed on Eastern Europe, and a halt to Western moves to set up a separate, independent West Germany. The means would be the "regulation" of Western access to Berlin.

On 1 April 1948, the Soviets announced that no military trains would be allowed to go to and from Berlin unless they had first been inspected. All Western military and civilian personnel would also have to submit documentation and allow their belonging to be inspected. These demands were deemed unacceptable by the Western allies, and both U.S. and British train commanders refused Soviet inspection demands. The Soviets responded by preventing the trains from crossing through their zone, and Berlin was blockaded. In response, General Clay directed Lt. Gen. Curtis E. LeMay, commander, U.S. Air Forces in Europe, to begin an airlift into Berlin to keep the military garrisons supplied. The "Little Lift," as the effort became known, was short-term. The Soviets dropped their blockade on 10 April, and normal train traffic resumed.

The Soviets were satisfied by the results of their initial blockade. A 17 April 1948 report to Moscow stated, "Our control and restrictive measures have dealt a strong blow at the prestige of the Americans and British in Germany." The report noted the Little Lift, but dismissed it by saying: "Clay's attempts to create 'an airlift' connecting Berlin with the Western zones have proved futile. . . . The Americans have admitted that idea would be too expensive."

The Western allies also drew conclusions from the Soviet efforts. These were seen by the allies as an attempt to force the West out of Berlin, and they were determined not to accept such a retreat, as this would have devastating political and military consequences. They would also press forward with establishment of an independent West Germany, whatever the risks. The stage had now been set, and the preliminaries completed. The struggle that ensued was to last four decades, and would decide the fate and future of humanity.

I

Eastern Europe and the USSR

1

Spies and Anti-Soviet
Resistance Groups

We must recruit men who are intelligent but appear to be stupid; who seem to be dull but are strong in heart; men who are agile, vigorous, hardy, and brave; well-versed in lowly matters and able to endure hunger, cold, filth, and humiliation.

— Sun Tzu, *The Art of War*

As relations continued to deteriorate, the pressure for intelligence on Soviet activity grew to a near panic. However, Western intelligence had few sources on the Soviet Union at the time. The displaced persons camps scattered across the continent provided some information. Their populations included Eastern Europeans and Russians who had been brought to Nazi Germany as forced labor, individuals fleeing Communist rule, and Soviet personnel who had escaped to the West. Other sources were German intelligence officers who had escaped to the Western occupation zones at the war's end, and collaborators and war criminals fleeing Soviet revenge. All had no place to go, and many had information to trade.

The West's need for information on the USSR was quickly exploited by the unscrupulous. "Paper mills," many of which were run by émigré groups, and fabricators prospered during the early postwar years, selling a mixture of valid intelligence, overt material, propaganda, and outright forgeries. They quickly learned that Western intelligence agencies accepted uncritically any information on the USSR, at times attempting to outbid each other to obtain it.

The volume of material from the paper mills was astonishing. A CIA officer estimated in 1952 that more than half of the intelligence received on Soviet bloc countries was from paper mills. Efforts to detect and neutralize the material proved difficult. Analysts had little valid "control" information that could be used to test the paper mill intelligence. It wasted the time of large numbers of CIA officers, skewed U.S. estimates, and resulted in the small amount of solid intelligence on the USSR being drowned in a flood of fiction.

Tracking the Soviet A-Bomb

A more reliable window into Soviet activities came from occupied Germany. The postwar chaos had allowed both sides to acquire large numbers of local German agents at a small cost in money, cigarettes, and coffee. The data they provided included the locations and activities of Soviet military units; Soviet exploitation of German industry; banking and trade transactions; and the political situation within the Soviet occupation zone. Soviet security measures were also still relatively weak in the initial months of the occupation.

One part of the U.S. and British intelligence efforts in occupied Germany involved tracking the Soviet A-bomb program. One of the first successes came in June 1945 when the British SIS learned that Dr. Nikolaus Riehl and six of his research team, who had worked on refining uranium for the German atomic bomb program, had been taken to the USSR. By the end of the year, more than a hundred technicians had been grouped around a few German atomic scientists. In addition to Riehl, these scientists included Professor Gustav Hertz, a Nobel Prize winner who discovered the gaseous diffusion method of enriching uranium; Professor Adolf Thiessen, the director of the Kaiser Wilhelm Institute for Physical Chemistry; Baron Manfred von Ardenne, an expert on cyclotrons used to enrich uranium; Professor Max Vollmer, an outstanding physical chemist; and Dr. Hans Born, who had worked on the biophysics of radiation. In early 1946, a group of German nuclear reactor scientists was assembled under Dr. Heinz Pose.

By February 1946, the CIG received a report from an agent in the Soviet zone that von Ardenne's cyclotron group had been sent to the Crimea in the summer of 1945, and then established in October in one of the small towns located between Anaklia and Poti on the eastern shore of the Black Sea. Another agent confirmed that von Ardenne, along with Thiessen, Hertz, and Vollmer, were at the Black Sea coast between Sukhumi and Poti. The agent reported that they had not done any work up to the beginning of November 1945, as the housing and laboratories were still under construction. The locations of Born's group of biophysicists and those of the groups under Riehl and Pose were unknown.

Some of the refugees in the Western zones were German engineers and scientists who were, as a later account put it, "willing to sell information on their unloved masters." One of these was a chemical engineer who had worked at the former I. G. Farben plant at Bitterfeld in the Soviet zone. After reaching West Berlin in December 1946, he told U.S. intelligence agents that the plant "had started in the past few weeks producing 500 kilograms per day of metallic calcium. Boxes of the chemical are sent by truck every afternoon to Berlin, labeled to Zaporozhe on the Dnieper. Calcium is believed to be used as a slowing agent in processes connected with the production of atomic explosive." By mid-January 1947, the production of metallic calcium at Bitterfeld was confirmed, and the amount and purity of the material was such that it could be for use only in refining uranium.

Dr. Adolf Krebs provided additional information on the Soviet A-bomb program. He had been among the Germans approached to work in the research effort by the Soviets. As part of their recruitment process, he had been taken to Moscow in early 1947 for a series of interviews. One of these had been with Dr. Riehl, and had taken place at Elektrostal, a town some thirty-nine miles east of Moscow where a crucible steel plant was located. Dr. Krebs declined the position and returned to the Soviet zone. He then quickly fled to the West, fearing Soviet reprisals for turning down their job. Dr. Krebs told U.S. Army interrogators that Dr. Riehl was refining "uranium on a production scale using a new process which utilized electric furnaces."

The British checked out Dr. Krebs's report and found that Dr. Riehl's former secretary had told an agent that Dr. Riehl's last letter to her, dated 7 October 1946, had been postmarked from Elektrostal rather than the cover address of "Post Box 1037P, Main Post Office, Moscow." When the British files were searched for any mention of Elektrostal, a report stating that three train carloads of uranium ore had been sent from the Joachimstal mines in Czechoslovakia to

Elektrostal was found. This circumstantial evidence indicated that Elektrostal was the site of the Soviet Union's uranium metal plant, rather than that of a small-scale research effort.

The CIA and the British agencies each recruited sources at Bitterfeld. The CIA source provided documentation that three railroad cars of metallic calcium had been shipped to "Elektrostahl Moskau" on 26 July 1947, while the British agent provided monthly shipping statistics on a box-by-box basis, product analysis, and changes in Soviet specifications and requirements as they occurred. The thirty tons per month of metallic calcium that Bitterfeld was producing was enough to manufacture sixty tons of uranium metal. This was the final proof that the uranium metal plant was at Elektrostal, and that full-scale production was under way.

Dr. Krebs also provided information on the other groups of German scientists in the USSR. He reported that the Hertz group was working on the separation of uranium isotopes at Sukhumi on the Black Sea coast. The von Ardenne and Thiessen groups were also there, confirming the two agent reports. Dr. Vollmer and several assistants were working on heavy water production techniques at Sukhumi. Dr. Krebs had also heard that the area east of the Ural Mountains had been surveyed in May and June of 1945 for its suitability for reactor construction. He thought the Pose group was somewhere in this area.

The key issue in trying to understand the Soviet nuclear program was uranium production. The data Western intelligence had been able to gather indicated this was a bottleneck to the early production of a Soviet A-bomb. The "Summary Report of the Status of the Russian Nuclear Energy Program," dated 1 June 1947, reflected this belief, stating that the "indication from metallic calcium production . . . appears to be the construction of two plutonium producing reactors . . . with 500 megawatts of total power." The report continued, however:

It is particularly significant that a project of this size cannot be supported by the estimated reserves of uranium ore available to the Russians . . . 514 tons uranium oxide already available and 2,200 tons of uranium in reserves. . . . The best information indicates that this program is not proceeding well, and in fact uranium metal appears to have been produced in insufficient quantity to operate more than a very small pilot reactor, such as that first operated in this country in December 1942. Thus, if it is assumed in the worst case that Russian progress from this date will proceed at a rate comparable to that of the American project . . . then to produce a single bomb, January 1950 represents the absolute lower limit.

U.S. and British intelligence also discovered that intercepted letters from the German scientists to friends, relatives, and former coworkers in East Germany were a valuable source, allowing Allied intelligence to track their locations, activities, and movements. These letters, eventually numbering in the hundreds, soon proved far more effective than trying to penetrate facilities like Bitterfeld. The Soviets tried closing off any leaks of information by strictly censoring the letters, and, without exception, having them carry the Moscow cover address. However, some details still slipped through.

A March 1947 letter from Mrs. Blobel (Dr. Riehl's secretary), mailed from the Moscow cover address, indicated that biophysicists Born and Karl Zimmer, as well as the Riehl group, were all living thirty-nine miles from Moscow. This was obviously Elektrostal. In addition to finally pinning down the location of the Born group, which had been unknown, the letter indicated the structure of Soviet nuclear research. The processing of uranium ore and the study of biological effects were at Elektrostal; the experimental and theoretical work conducted by the other groups was located at the Black Sea.

In 1948, German ex-prisoners of war (POWs) who had been held in the USSR began to return to West Germany. They had been used as forced laborers to rebuild war-damaged factories, power and communications facilities, urban areas, and military bases. Among the early returnees were several POWs who had built two nuclear institutes in the Black Sea area. One of the institutes, under the direction of Professor Hertz, was located near the village of Agudzeri, while the other was near Sinop.

Even as data were slowly being assembled on the Soviet nuclear program, the belief that it would be many years before the USSR could build an A-bomb had become an article of faith. As a result, U.S. Air Force and Atomic Energy Commission efforts to develop a capability to detect a Soviet nuclear test met opposition from scientists who saw no immediate need for it. Despite this, WB-29 weather planes were modified with scoops to collect radioactive fallout. On 3 September 1949, a WB-29 flying from Japan to Alaska picked up significant levels of radioactivity. Twenty days later, after an intensive sampling and analysis effort, the White House press secretary made a brief announcement that the Soviets had tested an A-bomb. From the fallout, the United States was able to reconstruct the design of the Soviet A-bomb and discovered it was identical in design to that of the "Fat Man" weapon dropped on Nagasaki. Sonic data from ground stations also pinpointed the test site as being in Soviet Central Asia.

The intercepted letters continued to be a valuable source after the Soviet test. The U.S. Army Security Agency intercepted most of the letters, while British intelligence services carried out the analysis. Study of the letters indicated there were seven groups of German atomic scientists. The Riehl group was still at Elektrostal, and the Hertz group remained at Agudzeri, while the von Ardenne and Thiessen groups were both nearby at Sinop. The Vollmer group had left Agudzeri and was now near Moscow. A returning German who had worked on electronic development confirmed they were working on heavy water production. Of the other two groups, the location of Pose's reactor specialists had still not been identified, whereas Dr. Born's group of biophysicists had left Elektrostal in 1948 for an unknown destination.

The two missing groups' locations were discovered through small bits of information that individually were insignificant, but when assembled gave a surprisingly clear picture. The first step was to identify which individuals were in each of the seven groups. This was done by such methods as correlating letters from different persons who mentioned the same event, such as the death of a small child while playing with matches. Thus, names of the members of the Pose and Born groups were known, even though their location was not.

Locating the Pose group was a relatively straightforward task. The group's letters indicated to U.S. intelligence analysts that Moscow was a two-and-a-half-hour train trip away, there was good swimming at a nearby river, and a lot of construction activity was under way in new suburbs nearby. From a study of maps and railroad timetables, the Maloyaroslavets area to the southwest of Moscow was suggested as a possible location. British analysts added several other clues, such as that there was a large market town a half-hour bus ride away. Railroad timetables showed that the Obnino station was two and a half hours from Moscow. This was also where the road and railroad both crossed the Protva River on their way to the fair-sized town of Maloyaroslavets, which was about nine miles away. A bus would take about a half hour to travel between the two towns. Some ten other sites were examined but later eliminated for various reasons, such as being either a large town or not near a river. Obnino was the only site that fit, and the Pose group was finally located.

Finding the Born group's new location, in contrast, was a long, involved puzzle. The British Directorate of Scientific Intelligence noted in 1951 that letters from the Born group described topography, scenery, weather, and temperatures suggestive of the Urals. So much of the letters' content dealt with weather conditions that the British decided to use this to further pin down the location, comparing the weather as described on a specific day to Soviet weather maps and marking those areas with matching conditions. The single area common to all the reports was a section of the Urals some one to two hundred miles to the north and south of Sverdlovsk. The northern area seemed to be slightly more probable.

The British then used an intercepted letter from a man named Rintelen, who described a train trip from Sukhumi to the location of the Born group. As with all such letters, it was tightly censored, and no cities were named. The letter read:

> After the first long train journey, we had an opportunity on the 10th of December from morning till evening to buy warm clothes, travel by underground and bus, and sit in good cafes. . . . In the evening we traveled on again and arrived on the 12th of December in the next large town from here. The following evening we traveled a further five hours by train and on the 14th of December we arrived here after a two-hour bus journey.

The first city was obviously Moscow, as it was the only Soviet city then that had a subway. The British checked the schedules of trains departing Moscow for the Urals on the evening of 10 December. Three trains left for the city of

Perm (then named Molotov), which was on the west side of the northern Urals. However, when the analysts looked at the schedules of trains leaving Perm, they found there was no destination that was both five hours away from Perm *and* had a departure time that would have required Rintelen to lay over a day. Kizel was five hours away, but Rintelen could have caught a train the same day. Nor would a layover have been required had Rintelen been traveling to the eastern Urals to the north of Sverdlovsk.

Thus, by the process of elimination, it was concluded that Sverdlovsk had to be the large town near the Born group's location. Three trains left Moscow on the evening of 10 December, and all arrived at Sverdlovsk on the evening of 12 December. Again checking the train schedules, the British found three trains left Sverdlovsk in the early to mid-afternoon (thus requiring a layover by Rintelen). Two trains went to Kamyshlov, but although the trip took five hours, this town was well east of the Urals, and was therefore ruled out for geographical reasons. The other afternoon train departed Sverdlovsk at 2:30 P.M. going south and arrived five hours later at Kyshtym, in the south central Urals. Allowing for the two-hour bus ride, the British located the Born group within twenty miles of Kyshtym. This was the location of the reactor that produced the plutonium for the first Soviet A-bomb, so having a biophysics group near the site was logical.

Tracking the German atomic scientists was not the only activity being undertaken by Western intelligence services. Because a Soviet attack on Western Europe seemed a real possibility, many in the CIA and SIS believed that the West had to covertly establish World War II–style agent networks and resistance groups within the USSR and its allies.

The Great Game Resumed—Early British Covert Action

In the late-nineteenth century, Britain and Czarist Russia had been rivals in the "Great Game" on India's North-West Frontier. After the Russian Revolution, Lenin and his successors saw the British Empire as the primary external threat to the USSR during the interwar years. The USSR supplied money to the British Communist Party and front groups, and spread propaganda in labor unions and the British military. Although these actions had limited effects on British society, they created a self-fulfilling climate of hostility. The SIS saw the Soviet Union as its primary intelligence target from the end of World War I until the mid-1930s, when attention shifted to Nazi Germany. With the end of World War II, the Great Game between Britain and Russia resumed. The first round in this renewed struggle was played out in the forests of the Baltic states. It was here that the SIS launched its first postwar covert operation.

The Baltic states of Latvia, Lithuania, and Estonia had originally been part of the Czarist Russian empire. Following the Russian Revolution, they became independent countries until June 1940, when they were forcibly merged with the USSR as part of the Nazi-Soviet Nonaggression Pact. Stalin subjected their populations to terror and deportation during the next year, sending—as "enemies of the people"—about 2 percent of the people of Latvia and Lithuania and 4 percent of Estonia on a long journey by cattle car to camps in Siberia and Central Asia.

On 22 June 1941, Nazi Germany launched its invasion of the USSR, quickly driving the Soviets out of the Baltic states. Not surprisingly, the Germans were viewed as liberators, and volunteers from the Baltic states joined the German forces, including SS divisions who fought on the Eastern Front. When the tide of war turned in the USSR's favor, these units fled west to escape Soviet revenge. Within the Baltic states, guerrilla movements began to be organized. Called the "forest brothers," they intended to resist the reincorporation of their countries into the Soviet Union.

The return of the Red Army to the region in September 1944 brought a resumption of the prewar terror and deportations. The People's Commissariat of State Security (NKGB) primarily carried out the anti-guerrilla effort. Georgi Martynov, an NKGB officer who participated in anti-guerrilla operations, recalled one action in Latvia. A group of "leftovers," as they were called, had been located in a forest near a small farm where they received food and water. Three ranks of soldiers encircled the area, sealing off all escape. Then the circles of NKGB troops slowly moved inward, until they would come face-to-face with the guerrillas. When the circle closed up, however, no traces of the guerrillas could be found.

The NKGB troops searched the area, and in an old barn near the farm they found a large trap door in the floor—the entrance to a large underground bunker. One of the Soviets ordered those inside to surrender, warning that if they did not, the NKGB troops would attack with grenades. A voice from inside the bunker agreed to surrender, but only if the Soviets pulled back about 200 yards from the barn and waited for them to come out. The Soviets accepted the condition, and withdrew. A half hour passed without anyone leaving the barn, then, without warning, the Latvians in the loft opened fire with automatics, machine guns, and even mortars.

The NKGB troops suffered casualties before they could take cover and return fire. The Latvians then ceased fire, the barn doors opened, and thirty to forty women and children rushed out. The NKGB colonel in charge of the operation ordered the troops to cease fire, and to allow them to pass through the Soviet lines. The NKGB troops saw a group of Latvian men following behind the women and children. The Soviet troops opened fire, trying to split the two groups, but both ran back into the barn. The Latvians refused the Soviet calls to surrender, saying that either they would leave with their families or the Soviets would have to kill them all.

The NKGB troops closed to within about thirty yards of the barn, so that none of the Latvians could escape as night fell. After a long, nerve-racking wait, the Latvians again opened fire—heavy, but disorganized—which the NKGB troops returned. Martynov recalled that the noise was unbelievable, from both the gunfire and the cracks as bullets hit tree trunks and branches. Suddenly, the barn exploded into a huge fire. Without a command, the NKGB troops stopped firing. A lone figure staggered out of the fire. Badly burned and unable to see in the darkness, he ran straight into the arms of the NKGB troops. He was the sole survivor. After the fire had died down, the bunker was examined, and more than 150 bodies were found. The survivor was not executed, as he was needed as a witness.

The Baltic states had been a window into the USSR in the 1920s and 1930s for the SIS. As the end of World War II neared, senior SIS official Harry Carr began planning the rebuilding of the prewar agent networks in the Baltic states, with the goal of penetrating the USSR. Just before May 1945, Carr provided radio sets for two agents being infiltrated into Latvia by an émigré group. The agreement was that the agents would share with the SIS the intelligence they collected.

On the night of 15 October 1945, four more Latvian agents were to be landed from an SIS speedboat. The infiltration went wrong when the boat overturned as it neared the coast. The four agents swam ashore, but most of their equipment was lost. They were able to recover at least one radio, however, and the team's operator reported their safe arrival to the SIS. However, their infiltration did not go undetected. The agents' equipment was discovered washed up on a beach the following morning by a border patrol. A search for the agents was mounted, and they were all captured within a few weeks.

Maj. Janis Lukasevics, a thirty-five-year-old NKGB counterintelligence officer, suggested using the captured Latvians to send false information to the SIS. The Soviets referred to this as an "operational game." Major Lukasevics's proposal was approved, but by this time the captured agents had been too badly tortured to be of any use. The long period without radio contact with the agents was also a difficulty. Major Lukasevics finally arranged the release from prison of another captured radio operator named Augusts Bergmanis, who had agreed to cooperate.

In March 1946, with Major Lukasevics beside him, Bergmanis began transmitting, using the captured SIS radio and codebooks. He informed the suspicious SIS that he was a guerrilla who had been given the radio and codes by the agents shortly before they were captured. It took some time before Bergmanis was finally accepted. Soviet intelligence, now renamed the Ministry of State Security (MGB), was in a position to counter SIS attempts to set up spy networks within the Baltic states.

The next move in the Soviets' operational game came in August 1946, when two Latvian SIS agents, Rihards Zande and Eriks Tomsons, were successfully landed. Zande began to have trouble with his radio, however, and in November, the SIS station in Stockholm advised him to contact Bergmanis. The meeting took place, and Zande told Tomsons, "I am satisfied that Bergmanis is not under MGB control." Major Lukasevics wanted to embark on a large-scale deception operation, but the MGB leadership feared that if Zande and Tomsons remained free, SIS activities would expand. In March 1947, Bergmanis radioed a message to London—"Great disaster. Zande and Tomsons arrested. I've escaped but fear Zande's interrogation. All activities have stopped. Will contact you when safe." The operational game was put on hold, pending a decision by the MGB leadership on how to proceed.

Plausible Deniability

By the spring of 1948, the United States was also considering offensive action to weaken the Soviet Union from within. George Kennan, the head of the State Department planning staff, proposed establishment of a permanent covert action group. On 18 June, President Harry Truman signed NSC document NSC 10/2, which ordered the creation of a CIA office for

> propaganda; economic warfare; preventive direct action, including sabotage, anti-sabotage, demolition and evacuation measures; subversion against hostile states, including assistance to underground resistance movements, guerrillas and refugee liberation groups, and support of indigenous anti-Communist elements in threatened countries of the free world.

NSC 10/2 also said that these covert actions were to be "so planned and executed that any U.S. Government responsibility for them is not evident to unauthorized persons and that if uncovered the U.S. Government can plausibly disclaim any responsibility for them." Such "plausible deniability" was seen as a critical requirement. Peacetime support of sabotage, subversion, and resistance movements would be an act of war. The hand of the United States could not be seen. Although the United States was willing to provide guidance, money, and support, it would have to be within limits. Unlike the operations of the OSS during World War II, direct use of Western forces was out of the question.

Less than two weeks later, on the night of 24–25 June 1948, the Soviets halted all rail, road, and canal traffic to West Berlin. With surface transport cut off, and a U.S. airlift effort not seen as a threat, the Soviets thought they could force the West to accept Soviet policies on Germany. General Clay and other

Western officials believed that the Berlin Blockade was intended to force the Western powers out of the city. Gen. Curtis E. LeMay, commander, U.S. Air Forces in Europe, was ordered to fly food into the city on 26 June 1948. This was to supply both the Western military garrisons and the civilian population of West Berlin.

On 20 August 1948, with the Berlin Airlift under way for nearly two months, President Truman approved NSC 20, which authorized guerrilla operations against the USSR and its Eastern European satellites. To carry out these activities, the Office of Policy Coordination (OPC) was established on 1 September 1948. On paper, the OPC was part of the CIA, but the reality was more complex. Its director, Frank Wisner, former OSS station chief in Romania, was appointed by the secretary of state, and took his orders from the State Department and the Department of Defense. The OPC also operated separately from the CIA's Office of Special Operations (OSO), which had responsibility for setting up spy networks.

The OPC was to provide support to the various nationalist and anti-Soviet resistance movements inside the USSR and Eastern Europe. The strongest resis-tance was in the Ukraine, which had suffered the brunt of Stalin's terror in the 1930s. The two resistance groups were the Organization of Ukrainian Nation-alists (OUN)—which, in 1947, made the exaggerated claim to have 100,000 partisans under arms—and its rival, the National Labor Alliance (NTS)—which was an émigré social-democratic group favored by the CIA.

Assessments as to the potential of these groups varied. The preface to NSC 20, written by Kennan, declared optimistically that although "it is not our peacetime aim to overthrow the Soviet Government," covert action could create "circumstances and situations" that would make it difficult for the "present Soviet leaders . . . to retain their power in Russia." This was called "rolling back" the USSR.

The Joint Intelligence Committee was more circumspect. They concluded that it was "extremely doubtful that the forces of resistance within the Soviet orbit would effectively assert themselves unless and until they received guidance and material support from the West, and saw hope for early liberation by Western forces." The DCI, Adm. Roscoe H. Hillenkoetter, also had his doubts, saying that Soviet émigré groups were "highly unstable and undependable, split by personal rivalries and ideological differences, and primarily concerned with developing a position for themselves in the Western world." More important, these groups had been targeted by the Soviets since the revolution for infiltration and deception operations.

The CIA and military soon agreed that agents should be established at strategic locations deep within the USSR. They were to provide early warning of any Soviet preparations for an attack on the United States or Western Europe. These agents could not carry their radio equipment overland; they would have to be parachuted into the heart of the USSR.

The First Agent Airdrops

During the fall of 1948, two Ukrainian couriers were able to escape overland from the USSR. They had been sent by the leadership of one of the resistance movements in hopes of promoting Ukrainian independence and gaining American support for the resistance efforts. The CIA selected them to be the first agents air-dropped into the USSR, and the pair underwent ten months of intensive training to serve as radio operators and intelligence collectors. Although the Berlin Blockade ended on 11 May 1949, the panicky belief that war with the USSR could break out at any time remained as strong as ever.

While the Ukrainians were completing their training, the CIA made preparations for their return. The CIA operated several unmarked C-47s, which had been used for short-range missions into Eastern Europe. To maintain plausible deniability, Czech and Hungarian pilots—stateless persons with no visible connections with the U.S. government—flew the missions.

The missions into the USSR would require better maintenance than what had been obtained in the past, a secure airfield, and specialized flight planning. CIA official Harry Rositzke met with the Air Force chief of intelligence to make the arrangements, and told him about the CIA's facilities, what target areas they wanted to cover, and what the operation would need in the way of ground support. The Air Force officer immediately agreed, and together they wrote a classified cable to the Ninth Air Force Headquarters in West Germany. The Air

Force support of the agent drops, Rositzke recalled three decades later, "was the least bureaucratic and most quickly coordinated project" that he knew of. The agent drops were very closely held, they were never cleared with the State Department, and the secretary of state was not told of the missions until the early 1950s.

Finally, on 5 September 1949, the two Ukrainians boarded the C-47 that was to take them back to the USSR. In addition to a heavy parachute, each had strapped to his waist a small suitcase containing a radio. The C-47 pilots were two Czech airmen who had flown for the Royal Air Force (RAF) during the Battle of Britain. The plane took off from an airfield in the American sector of West Germany. The plane climbed to five thousand feet and headed east. It crossed the East German border, then flew on across Poland. Soviet radar sites detected the intruder, but no attempts were made by the Soviets to intercept the plane.

The C-47 reached the Ukraine, and the Czech copilot went back into the aft fuselage to get the two agents ready for the drop. They were in high spirits, both loudly singing a partisan song: "Belt after belt, on into battle, Ukrainian insurgents never retreat." As the C-47 neared the drop zone, the pilot slowly reduced altitude, descending to six hundred feet. At a signal from the copilot, the two agents jumped, one after the other, into the moonless night, and on into battle. The C-47 climbed, then turned west and flew a more southerly route back to the airfield. Four days later, the two agents radioed that they had arrived safely.

This first agent airdrop was the start of a four-year program. The agents operated individually or as two-man teams. They were recruited from the displaced persons camps that were scattered across Western Europe, from among Soviet military defectors, and from among individuals sponsored by émigré groups. The majority were from the minority groups within the Soviet Union, which included individuals from the Baltic states, as well as Ukrainians, Armenians, and Georgians. Once a promising candidate was spotted, he was asked whether he would be interested in undertaking a mission into the USSR.

Those who agreed were taken to a safe house for further interrogation and assessment. The potential agent was also subjected to medical and psychological tests, as well as hostile interrogations and lie detector tests. The individual's complete life history was examined—every place he had lived, everything he had done, and every person who could recognize him in the USSR. The case officers who would train him made the final decision.

The agents volunteered for different reasons. Some were fighting for the freedom of their homelands; others acted for personal reasons, to avenge the suffering inflicted by the purges on their families or villages. All were young, fit, single, and highly motivated. All realized that the odds were against them. All knew they were about to undertake a long-term mission from which there was little possibility of escape and a high probability of death.

Those individuals selected as agents then underwent nearly a year of training in parachute jumps, radio repair, coding and decoding messages, aircraft recognition, photography, and other elements of spy "tradecraft" they would need. The agents were also briefed on trolley fares and the price of bread, new Russian slang, and the vast numbers of rules and restrictions that governed every aspect of a Soviet citizen's life and work.

The agent's "legend," which was a false life history, such as jobs and residences, to hide the agent's time in the West, was also worked out and memorized. The agent had to be able to talk easily about his past activities, current plans, and future. Thus, the legend was based on those elements of the agent's own experiences that could be safely used, and had to be supported by false documents. Every Soviet citizen had to carry an internal passport, which was the basic identity document. It was valid for five years, and was different for each of the Soviet republics. A labor book, which listed every place a person had worked, with each entry signed by the different factory managers, was also required. An agent might also need a work or transit permit, which also could be different in various areas, or a Communist Party book.

The production of forged documents was a difficult task. They had to have both the shoddy appearance of Soviet paper and the right "feel." The rubber stamps used had to appear worn and to look as if they had been stamped in rapid succession, and at different times. Police and MGB personnel had seen thousands of legitimate documents, so no flaw was too small. The CIA initially had to use forged internal passports produced by the Nazi German intelligence services during World War II, because it was not able to copy the printing process for Soviet documents until 1951. The blank documents then had to be filled out with false names, birth dates, addresses, workplaces, landlords, factory managers, and the like. The forged signatures of the correct issuing officials were needed, using the right inks.

To make it difficult to uncover the forgeries, the CIA took advantage of the wide-scale destruction of Soviet records during the war. Thus, the agents were "born" in villages that had been destroyed, then "lived" in apartments and "worked" in factories that had been bombed-out during the war. Both the agent's legend and documents were intended to stand up against casual questions from Soviet citizens, such as during a job interview, or a routine police document check, such as were made at railway stations. Should an agent be subjected to a serious MGB interrogation, however, it was understood that he would quickly be exposed.

When the agent's training was complete and the documents were ready, the final preparations were made. The agent wore clothing of Soviet or East German manufacture. He also carried for barter or bribery several watches and U.S. five-dollar bills, which were available to Soviet troops in East Germany. The agent's radio was in his suitcase. In the final briefing before the drop, the agent was given a danger signal. If the agent was captured, he was to insert this into a radio message to let the CIA know he was under MGB control. The agent was also offered an "L-pill," which was a glass capsule that contained cyanide. The agent would bite down to break the glass, then take a deep breath and hold it. He would lose consciousness in about thirty seconds, and death would soon follow.

Valuable—The Secret Invasion of Albania

A month after the CIA air-dropped its first two agents inside the USSR, the SIS embarked on an effort to create a resistance movement in Albania to overthrow the Communist government of Enver Hoxha. Albania was providing a safe haven for Communist guerrillas trying to overthrow the pro-Western Greek government. A resistance movement would carry the civil war to Albania, making it impossible to continue this support.

Albania was also seen as isolated and weak. In June 1948, the Yugoslavian Communist leader, Marshal Tito, had split with Moscow over Stalin's high-handed attempts to infiltrate his government. Tito had dominated Albania before the split with Moscow. After the split, Hoxha and the MGB purged the pro-Yugoslav elements in the Albanian party, including the interior minister, Koci Xoxe, who was shot in July 1949 after a show trial. Bordered by Yugoslavia and Greece, Albania was cut off from direct land contact with the USSR, while the purges left it internally divided, with Hoxha and the Communists seen as having little popular support. The SIS believed that the Albanian government would not be able to suppress an internal uprising.

British Prime Minister Clement Attlee gave the go-ahead in March 1949 for the operation, code-named "Valuable." The first group of thirty Albanians was recruited from displaced persons camps in Italy, and was taken to Malta. After the Communist takeover, the Albanians had been forced to flee, and they were eager for revenge. The SIS, working with the OPC, also created an anti-Communist government-in-exile, the "Committee for Free Albania," to unite the feuding royalist, social democrat, and independent factions, as well as to provide plausible deniability. After reaching Malta, the group was trained in the use of small arms and explosives, long-distance running, map reading, radio procedures, and beach landings. There were doubts about these recruits. One of the British trainers said many years later that they were "hardly the commando type," and there was not a natural leader among them.

The first SIS landing was made on the night of 3–4 October 1949. The nine Albanians, dubbed "pixies" by the British, were transported to the coast in a schooner and then rowed ashore. They were armed with German machine guns and carried ammunition, food, water, propaganda leaflets, photos of the different émigré leaders, and two heavy radio sets. To hide SIS involvement, the British boat crew did not accompany them inland and left as soon as the Albanians were ashore.

The nine Albanians headed inland, moving by night and spending the day in caves. After two days, they split up, with each of the two groups taking a radio set. Soon after, one of the groups was ambushed. Three of the pixies were killed in the firefight, and a fourth one disappeared. The second group learned of the attack from a friendly villager. They also learned that several days before their landing, Albanian troops had moved into the area, sealing off the coastal area. Villages were alerted, and shepherds were ordered to report any suspicious travelers.

The remaining five pixies moved on, trying to recruit friends, relatives, and others whom they trusted to form resistance groups. They gave out the leaflets and photos and tried to impress the villagers with the level of backing they were getting from the British and Americans. Their reception was mixed—the local villagers were interested in what they had to say and were willing to fight against the Communist government. They were not impressed, however, by merely five guerrillas, without a British officer. The villagers asked, "Why are there just five of you?" and "Why have you not brought us arms?" because they wanted to see an open commitment by the United States and Britain to overthrow the Communist government. Only then would the villagers take the guerrillas seriously. The five pixies decided to head for the Greek border, to report the popular feelings. One of the group members was killed in an ambush, but the other four made it safely across the border.

A second group of eleven Albanians was landed on 10 October 1949. They were not able to recruit any local resistance groups, and the people they contacted were later arrested, tortured, and executed. All eleven pixies were able to reach the Greek border safely. The Albanians had known of the landings beforehand, as well as their general location. Robert Low, the OPC officer who had worked with the SIS during the early planning, said later, "It was obvious that there was a leak somewhere. The Communists just knew too much about these people we were sending in." Several meetings were held to pinpoint the leak, but it was not possible to identify the source.

These two landings were followed in 1950 by several more, followed by cross-border missions later in the year in which the pixies walked into southern Albania from Greece. The results were more disappointing than those of the October 1949 missions. The villagers were afraid to help the pixies because the Albanian police arrested anyone they contacted, along with their relatives. It was much harder for the pixies to move around, and losses were high. Morale in the Malta training camp dropped because the effort was seen as hopeless. Low later noted that "we had to ask ourselves how long we could go on dropping these young men into the bag."

BGFiend—The OPC Airdrops into Albania

Despite the continuing setbacks in Albania, the OPC remained optimistic that "we had only to shake the trees and the ripe plums would fall." Wisner told his staff that Albania was to be a "clinical test" of the West's ability to roll back Communist rule in Eastern Europe. Albania was to be the start, a probe to find a fissure that could then be expanded.

The CIA's initial estimate, made in December 1949, was far less positive. It noted that "Overt opposition against the regime exists in the country, but as yet it is largely uncoordinated and its effectiveness is an unknown quantity. Albanian exile groups must overcome their mutual jealousies before they can exert any significant pressure against the Communist regime." The CIA further concluded that

> A combination of factors makes any overthrow of the pro-Soviet Albanian regime unlikely this winter . . . . the pro-Soviet Communists directing the Albanian regime, with the active support and assistance of the USSR, seem able to avert any likelihood of a successful internal revolt in the near future.

During the spring of 1950, OPC began preparing its own guerrilla force, under the code name "BGFiend." (CIA code names used a two-letter prefix.) The cover for the resistance group was as a labor battalion, which were units of Eastern European displaced persons attached to U.S. occupation forces to carry out road repairs, rubble clearance, and similar tasks. The Albanian unit, "Company 4000," would appear to be another of these units. The Committee for Free Albania recruited the potential agents. Halil Nerguti, who was among those selected, later explained that not volunteering had never entered his mind. He understood the risks, and that the Communists would retaliate against members of his family, but to fight against the Communists meant self-respect and dignity for him.

The first group of forty-nine recruits arrived at their barracks outside Munich, West Germany, on 8 June 1950. As with the Albanians recruited by the British a year before, there were shortcomings in the quality of these recruits. Medical examinations showed several had serious illnesses. The rest were tough, but not officer material, with many being illiterate. During the summer, the members of Company 4000 underwent basic military training. The unit's U.S. commanders, who would be selecting the individuals to be sent on the first mission, were also studying the company. Complicating the situation was feuding between the émigré factions. This caused tension among the émigrés, as well as between the Albanians and the Americans.

The scale of the OPC operations would be far larger than the British had been able to support. Another difference was in how the guerrillas would be sent into Albania. The SIS had used landings and cross-border operations from Greece. These were limited to southern Albania, where the social democratic resistance forces were concentrated. The royalists, who were backing King Zog, were strongest in central Albania, east of the capital of Tirana, whereas the tribes in the north supported the independents. To reach these areas overland would require a hike of several weeks. The OPC decided to parachute them into the areas where they were to operate.

The SIS handled recruitment of the pilots who would make the drops. In charge were Harold Perkins, who had run secret operations in Poland during World War II, and Roman Rudkowski, an ex-Polish air force colonel who had parachuted into Poland in 1944. They chose six Poles who had flown for the RAF, and offered them jobs flying for the CIA. The Poles understood the risks. One of the pilots said later,

> We all fully accepted the fact that no one would protect us if we were caught. That was the deal. The Americans explained it all quite simply, and they gave us cyanide pills just in case. All our clothing and equipment were made in Eastern Europe. They even gave us Russian watches. Of course, the Communists would have known where we came from, but we were stateless and they could never have proved it. We would not have caused the West any great embarrassment.

The flights would use a black-painted C-54, the military version of the DC-4 airliner. The plane's crew would be the pilot, copilot, navigator, radioman, and jumpmaster, who would connect the static lines of the Albanians' parachutes and give them the signal to jump when the plane was over the drop zone. The Poles were sent to the U.S. Air Force base at Wiesbaden, West Germany, for training. When this was completed in the fall of 1950, the Poles, along with Rudkowski, were set up in a CIA safe house in Athens, Greece.

The flight crew thus ready, on 11 October 1950 the initial group of sixteen Albanians was selected for further training. They were driven at night in a closed truck to a large, walled villa outside Heidelberg, West Germany. It was important that the Albanians not know where their training base was located, in the event of capture. For the same reason, their U.S. trainers used pseudonyms—Colonel Smith, Majors Emile and Wells, and Captains Raymond, Joseph, and Giovanni. The Albanians underwent night tactical exercises and physical training, and practiced guerrilla techniques.

The CIA was under pressure to get the first group of Albanians into action before winter would prevent the drop. As a result, the guerrillas underwent merely a brief, three-week training program. There were, for example, no actual parachute jumps from a plane. Rather, they jumped from a platform onto a sawdust-covered floor to learn how to land. Gaqi Gogo, a member of the Committee for Free Albania who met them at the villa, felt that the training was too brief, and that they were not up to the mission, either physically or mentally. But any delay in the drop date to allow for additional training meant the mission would be delayed until the following spring.

The sixteen Albanians were finally sent to a large safe house outside Athens. As they talked over their missions, they began to have doubts, and seven dropped out. The nine who remained were divided into two teams. In the first group were Adem Gjura, Sali Daliu, Iliaz Toptani, Selim Daci, and Xhetan Daci, who would be dropped in the Martanesh area. Gjura had fought against both the Germans and the Communists during World War II, whereas Toptani was a veteran of the French Foreign Legion. The second group was made up of Myftar Planeja, Halil Nerguti, Ramadan Cenaj, and Rexh Berisha, who would be parachuted farther north, near the town of Kukes. The CIA believed that there were still anti-Communist resistance units operating in these areas. The teams were to locate and make contact with them.

On the night of 10 November, the nine Albanians were driven in a rickety truck to a military airfield outside Athens, where they boarded the C-54. As the plane prepared to take off, Rudkowski asked permission to go aboard, to check that everything was ready, and to say good-bye to the crew. Once on the plane, however, he ordered it to take off.

The plane flew north across Greece. Around midnight, as the plane neared the Albanian border, the pilots reduced altitude until they were flying merely fifty feet above the ground, and followed a route through rivers and valleys, using mountain peaks as landmarks. The plane was equipped with a radar altimeter, which sounded a warning whenever the plane went too low. The copilot kept watch for any tree, chimney, or building that might be in the way. One of the Poles said later: "We went anywhere we wanted. We could have flown over Red Square if we felt like it. And you can do it in any old plane, so long as the pilot has quick enough reactions to stay no more than fifty feet from the ground."

The flight into Albania had been successful, but the Polish navigator could not find the Martanesh drop zone. The plane had climbed to the drop altitude of five to eight hundred feet, where it could be tracked on radar. The crew spent several minutes trying to locate the correct area in the dark landscape, but was still unsuccessful. If they lingered, the plane might be intercepted, so rather than having the Albanians make a jump at an unknown location, the Poles decided to return to Greece. The plane turned west, and was soon over the Adriatic Sea. Two hours later, the C-54 landed back at Athens, with the nine Albanians still aboard. (It is not clear whether there were any repercussions about Rudkowski's unauthorized ride on the airplane.)

The second attempt was made on 19 November, but again the crew could not find the drop zone. Neither the Albanians nor the Poles wanted to again return to Greece, so after a hurried conference, the first group jumped. Gjura, Daliu, Selim Daci, and Xhetan Daci landed in a wooded area about twenty-five miles northeast of Tirana, fairly close to the planned drop zone. There was no trace of Toptani, however, nor of the group's equipment, which should have been dropped after them.

The C-54 continued to the north, toward the second drop point. After flying fifty miles, the pilot climbed and began looking for the drop zone. Yet again, they could not find it. Nerguti asked the navigator whether they might actually be over Yugoslavia. He reassured them that they were over Albania, and not far from the planned drop zone. The second group decided to jump. All four made it to the ground safely, but, like the first group, without any of the supplies that were to have been dropped. The Poles were supposed to have circled back around, but instead they dropped the supplies farther on. The parachutes landed in a village, and had to be abandoned.

The C-54 crew dropped some leaflets; they then turned west and were soon over the Adriatic Sea. The few lights of Tirana visible to the plane's left proved too attractive, however. The crew turned back and flew at a low level straight down the main street of the Albanian capital. They then successfully returned to Athens. At the postflight debriefing, the Poles complained that there seemed to be just three lightbulbs working in all of Albania.

The four members of the first group spent the night in the woods. Early the following afternoon, the four Albanians were spotted and, within minutes, had been surrounded. They agreed to make a run for it. Gjura and Daliu ran to the right, while Selim Daci and Xhetan Daci went to the left. Gjura was hit in the leg, but he and Daliu kept running. Selim Daci was captured; Xhetan Daci was shot and killed. A similar fate also befell Iliaz Toptani, the fifth member of the first group, who had become separated from the others. Toptani had taken refuge in a house, but was denounced and captured.

Although they had escaped, Gjura had trouble walking, and neither he nor Daliu knew where they were. When hungry, they would stop at an isolated house and ask for food. They also asked for salt and sugar, which they used to treat Gjura's leg wound. In exchange, they paid with one gold napoleon coin. The villagers were too frightened to help them. They gave Gjura and Daliu what they asked for, and begged them to leave. From these encounters, the parachutists also learned that they had barely escaped a trap. Two days before the drop, several hundred security police had been moved into the Martanesh area. A man had been placed in every group of houses, and the entire force had been on alert during the night of 19–20 November. The police even knew their names: one villager remembered asking what the police were doing there, and he was told they had come to capture Adem Gjura. It was only because the

Polish navigator had been unable to find the drop zone that the group had not parachuted directly into the waiting arms of the police.

The pair finally found a family who hid them for two weeks. As Gjura's wound healed, he and Daliu discussed what to do next. At first they considered continuing with their mission. They soon realized that would be impossible, and they headed for Yugoslavia. Just before the end of December 1950, they found a local man who, for thirty gold napoleons, was willing to take them across the frontier. They had been on the run for six weeks.

The Albanian police were also waiting at the second drop zone. The agents escaped only because they landed some twelve miles away, a considerably larger navigation error than that for the first group. The Albanian police learned of their location only when their equipment landed in a village. By the time the police began searching the area, Planeja, Nerguti, Cenaj, and Berisha were all hidden in a forest. They hid for five days and nights, subsisting on the little food they had been carrying with them. When a local shepherd told them that the police patrols had left, they headed toward the border region of Has. Like their comrades in the first group, these four begged food and sought shelter from the snows in remote stables and huts. They were trying to reach Nerguti's home village of Gjegjen, where they hoped to find members of his family. By mid-December 1950, they realized that the snow was becoming too deep for them to attempt that long journey. Instead, the team made their way to the Yugoslav town of Prizren, ten miles from the Albanian border.

The CIA knew nothing of what had happened after the drops. Throughout late November and early December, the Poles flew over the Martanesh and Has areas, trying to make contact with the two groups using the special short-range radios that had been dropped with their supplies. Each time, nothing was heard. The CIA and OPC personnel began to believe that both groups had been wiped out. The first indication that there were survivors was when the Committee for Free Albania received a series of postcards from Nerguti. When Gjura and Daliu also escaped from Albania at the end of December, Yugoslavs held them for several months. When Gjura was finally released, he sent coded messages to the committee, warning, "Do not send any more packages to the original address, because they all get lost on the way."

The second group continued to operate, using Prizren as their base. The local Albanians, Cenaj recalled, were thrilled to hear that the Americans had sent them. The group began recruiting some of the locals as guerrillas, paying for weapons with their supply of gold napoleons. By February 1951, they had assembled fourteen additional volunteers. They reentered Albania in small groups at the end of the month. Initially, the Albanians welcomed the volunteers, but the villagers also wanted to see the massive drops of men and equipment like those made by the SOE during World War II. When the weeks passed, and there were no drops, the villagers began to ask Cenaj, "Where are your American and English friends? Still up in the sky?" Without proof of Western support, the villagers were unwilling to commit themselves to the resistance movement.

During the spring of 1951, the volunteers engaged in combat with Albanian security forces. As losses mounted, and the drops failed to materialize, disillusionment spread. Finally, the original four members of the second group realized they could not continue. They decided to surrender to the Yugoslav authorities. They sent intermediaries to explain their situation, and a deal was struck. The four crossed back into Yugoslavia and surrendered on 9 May 1951.

The Albanian police inflicted a terrible revenge against the families of the guerrillas. Unable to capture Adem Gjura, they shot his cousin and his uncle. Gjura's family, as well as forty brothers, nephews, and cousins, were also arrested. They were kept in such brutal conditions that most of them, including three of Gjura's children, soon died. Nerguti's family also suffered: his brother was shot, and his father died in a prison camp.

Despite the failure of the first drop, BGFiend continued. Additional Albanians were sent to the German villa for training during the spring and early summer of 1951. They received forty days of guerrilla training, twice that of the first groups. Twelve men—divided into three groups of four men each—were selected for the next drop. The drop was made on the night of 23–24 July 1951, and it ended in total disaster. The first group took refuge in a house. The police found them, set fire to the house, and all four burned to death. The four members of the second group were also killed, having been ambushed by the Albanian police as soon as the four landed in the drop zone. Of the third group, two were killed, and two others—Kasem Shehu and Muhamet Hoxha—were captured. (Muhamet Hoxha was not related to Enver Hoxha, the Albanians' Communist leader at the time.)

As with the first CIA airdrop, the mission had been "blown" before the plane ever took off. Efforts were made to discover the security breach, but without success. What was not yet realized was that the leaks were coming from within the heart of the operation itself.

2

The Soviet Counterintelligence State

I do not know what happened to the parties concerned. But I can make an informed guess.

— Harold A. R. "Kim" Philby, on the agents he betrayed

With the end of World War II, Stalin sought to isolate the Soviet people from any Western influences or contacts with the outside world. Harrison E. Salisbury, who had been a *New York Times* correspondent in the USSR during World War II, experienced this effort firsthand after his return to Russia in 1949. He wrote:

As I walked down the streets, not infrequently I would meet someone whom I had met during the war. At first I tried to speak to them, but they would look right through me and go straight ahead without speaking. I quickly understood it was too dangerous to talk with me. And for any Russian to have a contact with me was equivalent, almost certainly, to arrest.

Combined with these efforts to isolate the Soviet people, Stalin also sought to eliminate any perceived "enemies of the people." By early 1949, a massive purge was under way. Peer de Silva, a CIA officer who traveled to and from the Soviet Union with the cover of a diplomatic courier, likewise saw the results of Stalin's policy, on both an individual and a large scale. De Silva was walking in downtown Moscow, along a street called Kusnetzky Most, surrounded by large crowds of Muscovites bundled against the winter cold. He noticed a man standing in an apartment doorway, smoking a cigarette and looking out into the street. De Silva related what happened next:

> I heard the sound of a car. A large black limousine drew up to the curb abreast of me in front of the door where the man was standing. I was close enough to see his eyes open with fear; he dropped his cigarette. Two men in heavy coats got out of the limousine, crossed the sidewalk to the entryway, and propelled the man into the car.

De Silva watched as the door slammed shut and the car drove off. Then, he recalled:

> I looked around and found that the streets and sidewalks of Kusnetzky Most had emptied of every pedestrian; moments before there had been large crowds. They had scattered and disappeared like minnows before a feeding trout. . . . Terror, part of life in Moscow, on a bright sunlit day.

De Silva further learned how great this everyday terror was becoming during a train ride he took from Moscow to Leningrad that same winter. While his train was parked in a railyard, de Silva noticed a cattle train standing three tracks over. It had about fifteen to eighteen cattle cars, each with sides and floors made of wooden slats. He wrote:

> As I gazed at [the train] I was horrified to realize that there were no cattle; there were people, many of them very young. From the darkness within, their faces with large empty eyes simply stared across the tracks to the car in which I stood, as though in mute appeal. The entire train was a prisoner transport, carrying men, woman, and children to some undisclosed location.

It was in this climate of fear that the Western agents and guerrillas had to operate, to form anti-Soviet networks, and to collect military, economic, and political intelligence.

The Operational Game in the Baltic States

Maj. Janis Lukasevics of the MGB began the second stage in the operational game against the British SIS efforts in the Baltic states in mid-1948. He recruited a Latvian nationalist, Vidvuds Sveics, to penetrate the anti-Soviet underground. Sveics then "escaped" to the Swedish island of Gotland in October 1948 and made contact with the SIS. He was accepted as a genuine Latvian partisan and underwent training by the SIS and Swedish intelligence. The SIS effort within the Baltic states, now code-named "Jungle," was also undergoing a major expansion. The prospective agents were brought to England, and then trained in Morse code, tradecraft, intelligence requirements, and small arms at an old Victorian house in Chelsea. Outdoor training at Fort Monkton in Gosport, and guerrilla exercises on Dartmoor and the Scottish Highlands, followed. Once completed, the graduates were issued forged internal passports, work permits, identification cards, and L-pills.

The SIS preferred to use boats to return the agents to the Baltic states, believing that this was less likely to attract Soviet attention than an airdrop. Royal Navy Comdr. Anthony Courtney said, "I was struck by the potential capabilities of stripped-down ex-Kriegsmarine E-boat hulls, powered by the incomparable twin Mercedes-Benz 528 diesel engines." John Harvey-Jones of the Naval Intelligence Division was put in charge of the project. He found that the Royal Navy still had two E-boats, and had them sent to Portsmouth for modifications. He later reported: "We decided to strip one of them down and increase her power. With the combination of her low weight and enhanced power she would be able to show her heels to any other surface ship then afloat." The E-boat's top speed was about forty-five knots. It had also been fitted with underwater exhaust pipes, in order to reduce the noise from its engines.

To preserve plausible deniability, a German captain and crew would man the E-boat. Courtney and Harvey-Jones recruited an ex-E-boat captain named Hans Helmut Klose. He knew the Baltic and, more importantly, had dropped German sabotage agents behind Soviet lines in 1944 and early 1945. Harvey-Jones supervised the recruitment of the E-boat's crew from among Klose's wartime comrades. They operated under the cover of the British Control Commission's

Fishery Protection Service. This group was responsible for preventing interference with German fishing boats by the Soviet navy and for destroying mines in the Baltic. Training missions familiarized the crew with both the Baltic and Soviet coastal defenses. Harvey-Johns later said that the Baltic "was our oyster and we roamed it at will."

The first group of Jungle agents completed the training and were scheduled to be returned by E-boat in early May 1949. The six SIS agents, which included the double agent Sveics, were landed at Palange beach in Lithuania. The agents made it ashore without incident and headed for the woods. Sveics was able to separate himself from the group and betrayed them to the local militia. In the resulting firefight, two of the SIS agents were killed, but Kazimieras Piplys and Jonas Deksnys were able to escape. (Piplys was killed in a bunker later that year.) Sveics continued to act as a double agent against the partisans, and he passed information on their activities to the MGB. Some SIS officers were now beginning to have doubts about their agents in the Baltic states. Harry Carr, the SIS officer running the project, still believed they were not under Soviet control, and any doubts were not yet strong enough to have an impact.

British mistakes continued with the next landing in the fall. On the night of 31 October 1949, two more agents, Vitolds Berkis and Andrei Galins, were landed in Latvia by the E-boat. Their arrival was undetected, but they compromised themselves by immediately contacting Augusts Bergmanis, the original MGB double agent amidst the partisans. They told him (and the MGB) that they were the first of a series of agents who were to contact partisan leaders. Bergmanis put them up in an MGB safe house. The two agents continued to operate, but they were now unknowingly under the Soviets' control.

With the operational game now in its fourth year, Lukasevics created a fictional resistance movement. This was based on the "Syndicate" and "Trust" deceptions of the 1920s against Russian émigré groups. Representatives from those bogus anti-Soviet conspiracies had contacted émigré leaders, who were lured to the USSR for meetings with their leaders. Once inside Soviet territory, the anti-Soviet émigrés were arrested, interrogated, and shot.

The MGB finally gave its approval, and in the winter of 1949–50, a bogus partisan group, code-named "Maxis," began training in the Kurzeme Forest. Its commander was MGB Maj. Alberts Bundulis. In May 1950, Berkis and Galins went to live in the Maxis camp. During 1950, the MGB established a second fake resistance group, code-named "Roberts." To further extend the deception, SIS agent Jonas Deksnys (a survivor of the betrayed May 1949 team) was captured and forced to become a double agent, while MGB agent Janis Erglis, masquerading as a member of the anti-Soviet resistance, left for London to discuss plans for future operations in the Baltic states. The two fake resistance groups created the illusion that the anti-Soviet partisans were successful and expanding their activities.

The reality was that organized resistance in the Baltic states ended in 1950. The last battle in Latvia occurred in February, whereas resistance in Estonia was limited to isolated bands. Some five thousand guerrillas remained in Lithuania, but MGB mopping-up operations had effectively ended their resistance. In addition to combat sweeps, the establishment of collective farms had cut off the guerrillas' food supply, while mass deportations had ended the guerrillas' ability to operate among the population.

The MGB now controlled the SIS agents, had destroyed the resistance forces, and had created bogus resistance groups that could be used to deceive the SIS. The Soviets were in the position to undertake a double-cross operation. The intelligence requirements sent to the MGB-controlled agents indicated British future intentions. As each new team of agents landed, they would be captured. Control of the British agents also allowed the MGB to learn about the tradecraft of the SIS, as well as its code and cipher systems. Finally, the disinformation sent by the captured agents could manipulate British actions and change their intentions. The Soviets had a unique opportunity, but failed to take advantage of it.

The reason for this failure was basic to the Soviet system. All military, industrial, and social information was secret, and no one in the MGB or Soviet military was willing to release even the most trivial data, called "chicken feed," in order to support the larger deception. Even if the data had no value, the MGB was afraid they would later be denounced as having betrayed the USSR. The MGB was even forbidden to create fictional information, lest the SIS begin to ask for more. The results were soon apparent to SIS analysts, who judged that the intelligence was "bland and imprecise." When the SIS complained, the partisans justified their silence by saying they were freedom fighters, not spies.

The CIA was now involved in agent operations against the Baltic states. The OPC had agreed with the SIS to fund the E-boat operations, in exchange for access to the intelligence. An agreement was also reached to allow CIA-sponsored agents to be infiltrated into the Baltic states via both the E-boat and airdrops. By the summer of 1950, however, the CIA was also beginning to have doubts about the SIS agents. In June, George Belic, the CIA's chief of Soviet affairs in Munich, informed the SIS that the CIA suspected that Jonas Deksnys had been turned and was working for the MGB. Although the SIS knew that Deksnys had recently failed a security check, they still believed the operations in the Baltic states were secure, and they reassured the CIA that the suspicions were due to émigré politics.

In October 1950, the first CIA airdrop was made into the Baltic states. The unmarked C-47 took off from the airbase at Wiesbaden in West Germany. The airplane was flown by two Czechoslovakian ex-RAF pilots, and carried three agents: Benediktas Trumpys, Klemensas Sirvys, and the team leader, Juoas Luksa. The C-47 reached Lithuania and all three CIA agents success-fully parachuted into the drop zone without detection. The new team's arrival was marked by an increase in guerrilla activity.

In the spring of 1951, both the SIS and CIA mounted further missions into the Baltic states. A four-man SIS team was landed in April, which included SIS agent Lodis Upans, who was to investigate the Maxis partisan group, and the team's radio operator, MGB agent Janis Erglis. As with the earlier Syndicate and Trust deceptions, several of the SIS agents met with the bogus guerrilla groups, who were living in the woods. Upans was apparently fooled into believing that the Maxis group was real. The other SIS agents were captured, and then either became double agents or were shot.

A second CIA airdrop was carried out in April 1951, and it ended in total fail-ure. Most of the team was captured soon after landing, and they were then forced to send false intelligence. One of the radio operators was able to send a warning to the CIA station in Munich that he was under MGB control. Only Julijonas Butenas, a journalist who had been active in the wartime anti-Nazi resistance, was able to evade the trap. A month later, however, he was tracked down and surrounded by MGB troops. Butenas killed himself rather than be captured.

Continuing the pattern of sending in agents in the spring and fall of the year, a three-man SIS team was landed in Latvia by E-boat in late September 1951. The team was led by Bolislov Pitans, and was to contact the Estonian underground with the help of the Maxis group. The E-boat crew also picked up Arvits Gailitis, the "leader" of the Maxis group, who was actually working for the MGB. Once in London, Rudolph Silarajs of the SIS debriefed Gailitis. Gailitis was able to maintain his cover, but he was under such stress that by the time he returned to the Baltic states, he was reduced to a nervous wreck.

The losses among the partisans continued. In October 1951, Juoas Luksa, who was the team leader for the first CIA airdrop, was killed by MGB troops making a sweep.

In the spring of 1952, the next group of SIS agents was landed from the E-boat. Among them was a Latvian named Zigurd Kruminsh. According to his later account, he had joined the German SS in 1944, when the Soviet army threatened Latvia. The following months were a long retreat, as his unit was pushed back through Poland and into Nazi Germany. It was now apparent that the war was lost. Many of the foreign volunteers had joined the SS to fight the Soviets, but they had no intention of fighting the Western Allies. When ordered to do so, many, including Kruminsh, deserted and headed west. To hide that he had fought for the Germans, he burned off two tattoos on his shoulder, which had been applied when he enlisted. Kruminsh was captured by the British and was sent first to a POW camp, then to a displaced persons camp.

Kruminsh learned English and got a job as a guard at a British base. It was there that the SIS recruited him. Kruminsh was flown to Britain and underwent training in operating and repairing radios. After returning to Latvia, Kruminsh said that he spent the next eighteen months transmitting messages and helping smuggle people out of the country. His primary function was not sabotage, but rather to provide intelligence and to serve as the basis for an anti-Soviet underground movement should war break out with the West.

The group could live in the forests during the summer, but during the winter they had to take shelter on farms. One freezing cold winter evening, the group was warned that Soviet security troops were closing in on the transmitter. A guide arrived to take them to a spot on a road where a truck was to pick them up. After walking some distance, the guide left them by the side of the road. Kruminsh was carrying the radio on his back, and to avoid being seen, he moved about a hundred feet off the road. He then sat down on a log.

When Kruminsh opened his eyes again, he was not in the forest, but rather found himself looking at a wooden floor. He also had been cold, but now he was warm. Only then did Kruminsh realize he was bound to a chair in an MGB interrogation room. He did not know how long he had been unconscious, or how he had been captured, but he was sure that the group had been betrayed by an informant. He suspected the guide had led them into the trap. Because Kruminsh had been so far from the road, he thought that the MGB must have already been waiting for the group before they arrived. Kruminsh underwent what he called a "farce of a trial" and was sentenced to fifteen years.

In the fall of 1952, the E-boat picked up a senior leader of the Maxis group, Janis Klimkans. He, like Arvits Gailitis before him, was an MGB plant. Also like his predecessor, Klimkans was able to maintain his cover under intense questioning, and was fully accepted by the SIS as genuine. Based on this, Carr and other SIS officials who continued to believe that Jungle was a success could fend off the doubters. Klimkans subsequently underwent three months of training. During his stay in London, Klimkans had access to plans for future operations, which he passed on to members of the Soviet trade delegation. Klimkans was returned to the Baltic states in the fall of 1953 with weapons, supplies, and a million rubles, which the MGB used to continue its deception of the SIS.

The WiN Deception in Poland

The Soviet operational game in the Baltic states became the pattern for several similar efforts throughout Eastern Europe. The first of these was in Poland. After the Red Army forced the Nazis out of Poland, the Poles found themselves under Soviet domination. The pro-Western elements in Poland were systematically eliminated. The Home Army, the non-Communist resistance group, was officially disbanded. Over the following months, some fifty thousand former members of the Home Army were rounded up by the Soviets and deported to Siberia.

The Communist government in the first months of peace was still weak, while the Polish secret police, the "UB," was small and infiltrated by Home Army supporters. Many UB officers were also reluctant to kill their fellow Poles. Western leaders knew about Soviet actions in Poland, but they wanted to avoid any disputes with Stalin. They recognized the Polish Communist government, and made no protests over the wide-scale arrests.

Many former Home Army members who had escaped the Soviet arrests were unwilling to submit to Soviet rule and still wanted to continue the armed struggle. In the summer of 1945, Polish Col. Jan Rzepecki put together a unified underground movement, based on the old Home Army networks. In August, this effort was disbanded. The following month, however, Colonel Rzepecki formed another new group. Called "Freedom and Independence" (WiN), its primary activity was to keep alive opposition to Soviet control. Despite a Soviet offer of amnesty for the remaining Home Army members, by the second half of 1945 the Communist authorities estimated that there were some eighty thousand WiN supporters.

In November 1945, Colonel Rzepecki was arrested, and he subsequently called for a halt to underground activities. Few in WiN were willing to lay down their arms, however, and the struggle continued. The MGB and UB had little success against WiN for most of 1946. September and October saw the heaviest level of WiN activities, as well as of MGB and UB security operations. The WiN, MGB, and UB all suffered heavy losses during these battles. In October 1946, WiN President Franciszek Niepokolczychi and seventeen other members of its supreme command were arrested. A new leadership, under Wincenty Kwiecinski, was quickly organized, but in early January 1947, it too was arrested. Similar damage was done to WiN's regional and provincial networks, and underground activity declined.

The Soviets followed this with another amnesty during February and March 1947. Some fifty-five thousand WiN troops and supporters, the majority of its forces, surrendered to the Communist authorities. Many of these ex-WiN members, amnesty notwithstanding, were actually imprisoned or deported.

Ironically, although WiN itself had been destroyed, the Polish authorities could still exploit it as an excuse for continued repression.

Just before this final collapse, however, representatives of WiN were secretly sent to London, Washington, and Paris, where they reported that WiN was, yet again, being rebuilt. Their claims attracted the attention of Harry Carr of the SIS, who was also running the Baltic operation. By June 1947, the SIS began a two-pronged effort. The first was code-named "Broadway," and involved parachuting agents into Poland to make contact with WiN. The second took advantage of Soviet efforts to encourage Polish army exiles in the West to return home. The SIS recruited a number of agents before they left for Poland. Most of the returnees ended up in low-level jobs; a few gained senior posts and provided the SIS with valuable information.

Then, in 1949, Stefan Sienko, a senior WiN official, escaped to the West and contacted Polish general Wladyslaw Anders. A czarist cavalry officer before the revolution, General Anders had led the Polish army in Italy during World War II. With the end of the war, most of his forces remained in Western Europe rather than returning to Communist Poland. The Soviets believed that his Polish corps was being kept in existence in order to carry out guerrilla activities inside Poland. Sienko met with General Anders in London and told him that WiN still existed, and that with funding and equipment from the West, it would be able to carry out espionage and subversion within Poland. Sienko claimed that thirty thousand guerrillas could be mobilized. General Anders was impressed by Sienko and informed the SIS of his proposals. The SIS made indirect contact with WiN during the summer of 1950, using letters to "family" from "friends" outside Poland, along with occasional meetings arranged by a WiN courier to the West.

The support given to WiN reflected the fears of a Soviet attack on Western Europe. The Soviet lines of communication to East Germany ran through Poland. In the event of war, sabotage of rail, road, and communications links would disrupt a Soviet advance. WiN's ability to undermine a Soviet attack represented an "ace in the hole" for the West—except that the new WiN was a Soviet deception.

The UB had earlier captured and turned Sienko, who had agreed to become a double agent because he could see no chance to continue the struggle. The

WiN courier to the West was kept under tight control, while the meetings held in Poland were actually at UB safe houses. The goal of the WiN deception was to neutralize the anti-Soviet threat represented by General Anders and his remaining Polish forces in the West. After a slow start in the Baltic states, the MGB was now willing to embark on a much more ambitious operational game. Not only would the Soviets create a fake resistance, they apparently also "fought" against it. An 18 August 1950 intelligence report to President Truman stated, "There is fragmentary evidence of a recent relatively large scale police operation against Polish resistance groups south of Warsaw. There have been anti-resistance police operations for several years, but this is the first large scale operation reported since last fall."

As with Albania and the Baltic states, the OPC was soon involved with Broadway and WiN. CIA official George Muslin recalled that the support of WiN "got too expensive for the British and they passed it on to us." In November 1950, an agreement was reached among the OPC, the SIS, and representatives of the WiN Center Abroad. Two OPC officers, Walpole Davis and John Evalosky, were sent to London to work on the Polish operation.

The OPC began air-dropping agents, arms, radios, explosives, and gold coins (amounting to $1 million) to WiN. Frank Wisner, the head of OPC, believed that he had "the loyalty of 500 activists, 20,000 partially active members and 100,000 sympathizers who were ready for service in the advent of war." WiN's resistance activities were pure fiction, but the reports were sufficient to convince Wisner that WiN represented a serious threat to Soviet control. According to one account, Wisner said after one series of optimistic reports that WiN only needed antitank weapons "to drive the Red Army out of Warsaw." With both OPC and SIS support, WiN claimed during 1951 to be building toward a force capable of blunting a Soviet attack on Western Europe. As Wisner's belief in WiN's abilities grew, so did WiN's demands for U.S. support. This finally included a request that a U.S. Army general be parachuted into Poland to organize the resistance.

Not all shared Wisner's faith in WiN, however. Lt. Gen. Walter Bedell Smith replaced the ineffective Roscoe Hillenkoetter as DCI on 7 October 1950. Smith had served as U.S. ambassador to Moscow between 1946 and 1949, and then as commanding general of the First Army in 1949–50. Smith also had a fiery temper, once remarking, "I have a more even disposition than anyone else. Always terrible." Much of his anger was directed at covert operations, which as a regular army officer he saw as useless.

After Smith was sworn in as DCI, his first act was to bring the OPC fully under his control. The OPC, along with the CIA's own covert collections division, the OSO, was placed under the control of Allen Dulles, who was named deputy director for plans. The two groups subsequently were combined to form the Directorate of Plans. Smith also established an Office of National Estimates to produce assessments based on the input from all elements of the intelligence community.

Smith also picked Gen. Lucian Truscott as his "special representative" to examine CIA operations in Europe. General Truscott, who had commanded troops in the Anzio invasion and during the drive into Germany, shared DCI Smith's dislike of covert operations. When General Truscott left to examine CIA operations in West Germany in April 1951, he told DCI Smith, "I'm going to go out there to find out what those weirdoes are up to."

General Truscott was not impressed with either Davis or the WiN agents. After watching them being trained, he declared, "those agents won't survive . . . the émigré groups are sure to be penetrated." General Truscott was also not impressed with the intelligence WiN was providing, considering it useless. However, it was not General Truscott who was to shut down the operation, but rather the Polish government.

Unlike the still-ongoing deception in the Baltic states, the Polish WiN deception lasted just over two years. The clues were there, if only they could be seen. The UB knew in advance where and when agents were being parachuted into Poland. As a result, they were captured as soon as they landed. It was clear, as one participant recalled, "WiN was leaking like a sieve." According to Muslin, the CIA finally realized that WiN had been compromised "when one of the agents managed to get back out of Poland and told us we'd been had." Muslin further claimed, "we closed down the whole operation, abandoned it on the spot."

The Poles revealed the WiN deception in a mocking two-hour Radio Warsaw broadcast on 27 December 1952. UB officers, masquerading as WiN leaders, "confessed" that they had realized two years before that their support came solely from "people whose moral value was nil," whereas "the agents who were sent to us from abroad also were adventurers, cynical hirelings . . . interested above all in their own direct gain." Realizing that WiN could not fight "the people's power . . . without acting at the same time against the interests of the Polish nation," they decided that they could no longer "recruit depraved young people for the U.S. Secret Service," but rather "paralyze the attempts of the Americans and their émigré hirelings to develop espionage and subversive work in Poland."

The gold supplied by the OPC and SIS went directly to the UB, the broadcast said, to fund the deception. UB officers in charge of its day-to-day operations later said that the intelligence supplied by WiN "might just as well have been written in London or Paris on the basis of Warsaw newspapers. Gentlemen from the U.S. Secret Service did not get from us even such data concerning everyday life in our country as the prices of goods or the levels of supplies of consumer goods for particular centers, which they were so anxious to get."

The Radio Warsaw broadcast continued,

> There was no crime in Poland after the war . . . in which U.S. intelligence did not have its fingers and its dollars, whether it was the part of the U.S. ambassador in the anti-Polish scheming between the Vatican and the reactionary section of the clergy, or the systematic incitement by the dozens of radio yappers controlled by the U.S.A., and the recruitment of outcasts for mean and treacherous work. No chance of harming our country was neglected by the Wall Street monopolists.

Endgame in Albania

The failures of the early landings and airdrops into Albania had long indicated there were leaks of information. The Albanian police had been alerted to the time, place, and even the identity of the agents. The SIS and OPC both assumed the leaks were coming from within the émigrés themselves. In reality, the source was a Soviet "mole" in Washington, D.C.—Harold A. R. "Kim" Philby. He had joined the SIS during World War II, and was seen as a rising star. Since the 1930s, however, he had also been a Communist working for the Soviets. In the summer of 1949, Philby had been offered the post of the liaison officer to the OPC. He quickly accepted, and as part of his new duties, he was briefed on the Albanian operation. Philby quickly passed word to his Soviet controller, Yuri Modin. Thus, the Soviets knew about British plans to establish a guerrilla movement before the first landing was ever made.

For the next year and a half, Philby continued to provide information to the Soviets. He was ideally placed to betray the joint U.S./British secret war against the USSR. The agent drops and Albanian operations had to be coordinated, and it was through Philby that this was done. Based on his information, the Soviets were able to send false émigrés into the programs. These double agents were then able to identify those involved and develop sources inside the effort.

Yet even as Philby was betraying the agents, he could see the approach of his own downfall. He was also briefed on the "Venona" project, the decoding of Soviet cables sent during the war. These cables gave the names and details of Soviet spies in the United States and Britain, including the first leads on the spy ring led by Julius Rosenberg. The network provided the Soviets with design information on the U.S. A-bomb, and the Soviets had used the data to produce a clone. Philby had provided warnings that allowed several members of the network to escape.

It was also Venona that unmasked Philby's activities as a Soviet mole. In February 1949, a decoded message indicated that the Soviets had been given British foreign office telegrams sent to the Washington embassy. The list of possible suspects was long, and it was not until early May 1951 that the source was finally identified as Donald Maclean, a foreign office official who had been at the Washington embassy during the war. Philby was able to send a warning, and on 25 May 1951, Maclean and another Soviet spy in the foreign office, Guy Burgess, fled to the USSR.

A Joint Chiefs of Staff (JCS) damage assessment on their defections noted, "In the fields of U.S./U.K./Canadian planning on atomic energy, U.S./U.K. post-war planning and policy in Europe all information up to the date of defection undoubtedly reached Soviet hands." Soviet defectors later said that Burgess had supplied briefcases full of foreign office documents. Maclean also used his position as head of the American desk at the foreign office to pass to the Soviets briefing papers for the December 1950 meeting between President Truman and British Prime Minister Clement Attlee, as well as the subsequent cabinet report on the outcome.

In the wake of Maclean's and Burgess's defections, suspicion immediately fell on Philby. Burgess had spent the previous year living with Philby and his family in Washington, D.C. The same day Maclean's and Burgess's defections were discovered, Philby drove into the Virginia countryside and buried the photographic equipment he had used to copy documents. The MGB had worked out an escape plan for Philby, but he decided to bluff his way out. DCI Smith was not fooled and informed the British that Philby was not acceptable as liaison officer. Philby was sent back to England and dismissed from the SIS. Without a confession, however, he could not be successfully prosecuted. Philby continued to claim to be the innocent victim of a witch hunt. Only in 1963 did he finally defect to the USSR.

Yet even as Philby was under investigation, the Albanian operation BGFiend was collapsing. On 10 October 1951, Daci and Toptani, who had been captured in the first CIA airdrop in November 1950, as well as Shehu and Hoxha, the only survivors of the second airdrop that July, were brought before a show trial. They provided the names of almost all the CIA trainees, as well as dates and other details. Also on trial with them were ten other men accused of being British, Greek, Italian, or Yugoslavian agents. Two of them were sentenced to death, whereas Daci and Toptani were given life in prison, and Shehu and Hoxha received twenty years each. The other eight received lesser terms. None of them ever reappeared after the trial, and their relatives believed they were all killed.

On 15 October 1951, even as the show trial was under way in Tirana, the CIA made another airdrop into Albania of five guerrillas. The team leader, Hysen Salku, broke both legs on landing. (He had received no parachute training.) The other four—Hysen Bajrami, Ramazan Dalipi, Hajrulla Terpeza, and Hakik Abdullah—tried to collect their equipment, but most of it was caught in trees and had to be abandoned. Salku was carried a short distance away, but at dawn the team was attacked with machine guns and mortars. Salku and Bajrami were killed, while the other three escaped. Lost and without equipment, they had no choice but to head for Greece. They reached safety on 31 October, having dodged Communist patrols the whole time.

In assessing the first two years of the Albanian operation, the U.S. and British officials involved reached very different conclusions. Although the SIS made four more landings in the summer of 1952, by the end of the year they had abandoned the operation and closed down their bases or turned them over to the CIA. For its part, the CIA was optimistic, believing that the operation was at last showing prospects of success.

This was based on the achievements of Hamit Matjani. He had fought against the Italians and Germans in World War II, then against the Albanian Communists. Matjani was a Robin Hood figure, semiliterate, but able to operate at will inside Albania. He had made twelve successful missions inside the country, always traveling on foot with two or three others. Based on these forays, Matjani provided the CIA with rough maps showing police and military strongpoints and lists of sympathetic villages and of anti-Communists within the Albanian army. Matjani also indicated that the economic situation was very bad and the army lacked motivation.

Matjani's estimate fit in with the CIA's belief that the resistance movement was finally having an impact. OPC believed that one more big push would bring down the Albanian Communists. In August 1951, the exiled King Zog of Albania met with Gratian Yatsevich and other CIA officials. All agreed that Matjani was the only guerrilla who had shown any success. The CIA shifted its support to Matjani, and away from the earlier coalition resistance movement. Yatsevich told King Zog that Albanian officers Matjani had contacted wanted proof of both royal and U.S. backing. Only then would they move against the Communist government.

King Zog said that the only people who could give these assurances were members of his own royal guard. Yatsevich selected eight Albanians for training during 1951 and early 1952. Once the training was complete, Yatsevich and King Zog discussed whom to send on the mission; they selected three—Zenel Shehu, Halil Branica, and Haxhi Gjyle. On 28 April 1952, the three guardsmen, along with Matjani, a guide named Xhelo Tresova, and the group's radio operator, Tahir Prenci, crossed into Albania on foot. Branica soon became ill and returned to Greece. The others continued onto a base in northern Albania where they met the anti-Communist guerrillas that Matjani had recruited earlier. Shehu and Prenci remained with them, while Matjani, Gjyle, and Tresova made their way back to Greece.

The CIA was finally in radio contact with agents in the field. Prenci's messages indicated that they were recruiting more individuals. Regular drops of machine guns, ammunition, clothing, gold sovereigns, and even a can of beige paint were made at Prenci's request. The aircraft used had also been expanded. The Polish pilots were checked out in B-26 light bombers, which were used to drop agents and supplies. Branica had now recovered from his illness, and on 4 August 1952, he parachuted into Albania at the time and place given in one of Prenci's radio messages. Subsequent radio messages from Shehu and Branica were even more encouraging. The network of bases had expanded, the weapons had been distributed, and they had now recruited a small group of Albanian police and army officers who were ready to move against the Communist government. All that was needed now was for Matjani and a team to parachute into Albania.

There was one small doubt. Prenci had said in an early radio message that he had broken his right arm, and had to transmit using his left hand. As a result his "fist," the distinctive way each person taps a Morse code key, was different. As time passed, however, he did not revert to his normal fist. Despite this, each time Prenci was tested with prearranged signals, he gave the correct response. Yatsevich and King Zog discussed the proposed drop. Both believed there was a real chance that the Communist government might be overthrown. They approved the drop.

Matjani, Naum Sula, and Gani Malushi parachuted into Albania at the pre-arranged spot on May Day 1953. Radio messages continued to be sent after the drop, but none of the ambitious plans were carried out. In reality, it was all a Soviet operational game called "John." On New Year's Eve, Albanian radio announced that Matjani, Shehu, Branica, Sula, Malushi, and several locally re-cruited guerrillas had all been captured.

The show trial in April 1954 revealed that Shehu had been captured almost as soon as he had arrived at the base. The radio messages had been concocted by the Albanians. Prenci had either been killed or gone over to the Communists. Based on the fake messages, Matjani and the others had parachuted into a trap. On 12 April 1954, Shehu, Branica, Sula, and Malushi were all sentenced to be shot, whereas Matjani was to hang. They were not the only ones to lose their lives. All those contacted by the guerrillas were executed, whereas their families were sent to the camps, where most died. The total number to die is estimated to be several thousand.

Enver Hoxha, the dictator of Albania, later took all the credit for the failure of the SIS/CIA operation.

We forced the captured agents to make radio contact with their espionage centers in Italy and elsewhere, hence to play our game. . . . The bands of the criminals who were dropped in by parachute or infiltrated across the border at our request came like lambs to the slaughter, while the armaments and other materials which they dropped or brought with them went to our account. . . . Our famous radio game brought about the ignominious failure of the plans of the foreign enemy, not the merits of a certain Kim Philby, as some have claimed.

The Failure of Agent Operations in the USSR

Although the aircraft making the agent drops into the USSR were detected, the Soviets initially made no diplomatic or public protests. Then, in the summer of 1950, the East Germans and Czechs raised the issue for the first time. This was done, however, in an indirect manner. The East German and Czechoslovakian press claimed in June and July 1950 that U.S. aircraft had been dropping Colorado beetles, with the intention of damaging their potato crops.

Then, on 2 July 1950, Radio Moscow announced that a protest note had been sent to the U.S. government. The note, dated 30 June, referred to an East German government report "to the effect that between 22 May and 7 June of this year American planes, violating existing rules concerning aviation flights, dropped a large quantity of Colorado beetles" over East Germany "with the aim of inflicting damage to the food supplies of the German people and also of creating a threat that the Colorado beetle would spread to the potato-growing areas in countries bordering on the German Democratic Republic." The note continued that "the Soviet Government insists that the guilty persons be brought to book and expects the United States Government to adopt proper measures to guarantee that there is no repetition of similar acts in the future."

The U.S. State Department issued a press release on 6 July, ridiculing both the Soviet note and the Eastern European claims about the beetles. In response, the Czechoslovakian government made a formal protest on 10 July. The note claimed that there was "undeniable proof" that the United States had dropped the Colorado beetles, and added that the U.S. airplanes had recently "increased their illegal flights over Czechoslovak territory." Some eight instances of alleged violations were listed, along with demands for an investigation and an immediate explanation from U.S. officials.

A State Department report on the potato bug affair noted, "Numerous reasons have been advanced for these atrocity stories—alibi for poor crops, shortage of insecticides, build-up for subsequent interference with Western air access to Berlin, excuse for establishing an East German air 'police.'" The report also allowed the Soviets to protest the agent operations without actually mentioning them.

On 22 January 1951, the Czechoslovakian government made a further, more specific, protest about alleged U.S. air activities. The note charged that U.S. aircraft had made fifty-eight violations of Czech airspace between October 1950 and mid-January 1951. The breakdown given was eight flights in October 1950, eighteen in November, six in December, and another twenty-six between 1 and 15 January 1951. In the note, according to a Reuters dispatch, the Czech government accused the United States of dropping radio transmitters for subversive elements. Some of these radios were described as having accidentally come down in neighboring Austria. The note continued that the U.S. air violations were being deliberately made in support of what were described as "hostile reconnaissance espionage activities" and "individual and terrorist actions of hostile elements on the territory of the Czechoslovak Republic." The U.S. government was called upon to investigate the fifty-eight incidents and report the findings.

The day after the Czech note was delivered, an official Air Force spokesman in Frankfurt, West Germany, dismissed the charges of spying by U.S. airplanes as "completely ridiculous." This was followed on 7 February 1951 by a rejection of the Czech charges by U.S. officials, who said that the claims appeared "to have been fabricated solely for propaganda purposes."

The next protests were the first to refer directly to the agent drops. As previously, it was an Eastern European country, rather than the USSR itself, that acted as a diplomatic surrogate. On 15 December 1951, the Romanian government made a diplomatic protest over the parachuting of two spies into the region of Transylvania. The note said that the agents had been dropped on 18 October from a U.S. aircraft that had taken off from Athens. After the two spies were captured, they confessed to having been recruited in an Italian displaced persons camp, then being trained in an "American special spy school" in Italy. The note said that the two agents had admitted they were to organize guerrilla activities and to collect intelligence on the Romanian army.

Then, on 19 December 1951, the official Soviet news agency Tass announced that two U.S. spies, A. I. Osmanov and I. K. Sarancev, had been arrested and shot. The report said that they had parachuted into the Moldavian Socialist Republic, located in the southwestern USSR, during August 1951. The two agents were captured soon after the landing, and open parachutes were found nearby. The two men, the story continued, were carrying money, forged documents, weapons, and "other equipment for carrying out diversionist and terrorist activities."

Both Osmanov and Sarancev confessed to having been recruited by the United States in West Germany, where they had been living in a displaced persons camp. They had been trained in topography, the use of weapons, parachuting, and "organization of acts of diversion, terror, and carrying out of espionage." Once this was completed, they were flown to Greece and then parachuted into Moldavia. When their assignment was completed, the two agents said they were to have gone to Kars, Turkey, where U.S. intelligence officers were to have met them. The two pleaded guilty to charges of espionage and diversionistic activities, and were executed by a firing squad.

The Tass statement was followed up on 27 December 1951 by an announcement from the Romanian government that five men, rather than just two, had parachuted into the country. They had been captured, then tried and convicted as "terrorists, diversionists, and American tools." Four of the men had been executed; the fifth had committed suicide.

The U.S. State Department made official denials that such operations were being undertaken, but these hid a grim reality. Peer de Silva became Chief of Operations at the CIA's Soviet Russia Division at this time. His review of the files convinced him that the agent program was a failure. Soon after each agent was dropped, the control signals appeared in his radio messages, indicating he had been captured. Virtually every single parachuted agent was under Soviet control, and each one's messages contained only false or misleading information. As a result, the United States had *no* sources within the USSR. De Silva resolved to close down "these bankrupt efforts." The program, he later noted, had by then acquired a "mindless momentum," however, and continued for several more years.

Philby also had a major responsibility for the failure of agent operations inside the USSR. Between 1947 and 1949, he had been the SIS station commander in Turkey, where he had overseen efforts to infiltrate agents overland into the USSR. He betrayed them, as well as their contacts and their families. As SIS liaison in Washington, D.C., Philby had been involved in coordinating CIA and SIS airdrops of agents. In the spring of 1951, shortly before Maclean's and Burgess's defections, Philby was able to give his Soviet controller information on three groups of six SIS agents who were about to parachute into the Ukraine.

Philby was not the only source of leaks on the air-dropped agents, however. As in the 1920s and 1930s, the Soviets still viewed Russian exile groups as a major threat to their rule. The old fears of a counterrevolutionary conspiracy by the exiles and their Western supporters continued to affect Soviet actions. In the 1940s and 1950s, the OUN and the NTS were targeted for infiltration. These efforts resulted in the next Soviet announcement of captured Western agents.

The Soviets issued a communiqué on 27 May 1953 that four more spies had been shot. Their names were given as Alexander V. Lakhno, Alexander N. Makov, Sergei I. Gorbunov, and Dmitri N. Remigi. They were Ukrainians and members of the NTS. The four had taken off from Athens, Greece, in an unmarked DC-4 on the night of 26 April 1953. They had parachuted into drop zones between Kiev and Odessa. Lakhno and Makov were arrested the next day. They admitted under interrogation that another team of two agents, using the spy names of "John" and "Dick," had been dropped with them. Gorbunov and Remigi were soon captured.

The announcement said that the four agents had carried forged Soviet passports and military tickets, weapons, L-pills, four shortwave transmitters, Soviet currency and foreign gold coins, the means for preparing false Soviet documents, and mimeographic equipment for producing anti-Soviet leaflets. They were trained to carry out "terroristic, diversionist, and espionage acts" and were to make radio contact with U.S. intelligence. After confessing their role as spies, they were shot.

The State Department publicly dismissed the Soviet statement, saying it was "too fantastic to deserve comment." The Air Force spokesmen in Frankfurt, West Germany, said the USSR had spun another fairy tale. While the denials were being made, however, an investigation was launched. This resulted in the exposure of a Soviet mole within the NTS training school. He was a Soviet army officer who had defected to the West in November 1949. The officer had acted out of love, rather than ideology; he wanted to stay with his German mistress. The Soviets tracked him down in West Germany and used threats against his family, who were still in the USSR, to recruit him as an agent. Acting on Soviet instructions, the officer joined the NTS and soon became an instructor in the NTS's school for agents who were to be dropped into the Ukraine, as well as a consultant to U.S. military intelligence. His role as a double agent was not discovered, however, until the Soviet announcement.

A year later, another report of an executed spy was published. The Soviet army newspaper *Red Star* reported on 20 May 1954 that a military tribunal of the Kiev district had convicted Vasily O. Okhrimovich of spying and that he had been shot. The paper said he had "recently" parachuted into the Ukraine from a C-47, which had taken off from Frankfurt, West Germany. He had made radio contact with U.S. intelligence officers in West Germany before being captured. Okhrimovich was described as "one of the chiefs of the so-called Organization of Ukrainian Nationalists." He had been supplied with a radio, L-pill, weapons, blank false documents and stamps, and Soviet and foreign money.

As with the other agents whose executions had been announced, Okhrimovich was described as having been a Nazi collaborator during World War II who had fled to the West before being recruited by the CIA. He was said to have admitted his guilt and to have provided details of the OUN efforts to establish espionage and diversion centers in the Ukraine before being shot.

A month later, on 15 June 1954, two more agents were made public. Nikolai I. Yakuta and Mikhail P. Kudryavtsev had parachuted into the USSR in April 1953, but, the Soviet account said, "the loneliness of the Soviet land became unbearable," and they surrendered to the police in April 1954. For this reason, they were not shot, but rather received a twenty-five-year term in a labor camp. Both agents were members of the NTS.

The Soviets were also attempting to run some of the captured Western spies as double agents. Unlike the operational games in Eastern Europe, this deception was soon discovered. Nearly all of the captured agents transmitted their control signals, warning that they had been captured. The CIA controllers played along in order to keep the captured agent alive as long as possible. In one radio game, the Soviets tried for more than a year and a half to convince the CIA to contact the captured agent through another agent operating in the USSR. The double agent operations were often clumsy. In one example, an agent communicated with his controllers using invisible ink on letters mailed to cover addresses in Europe. When the handwriting was analyzed, the CIA found the messages had been written by *seven* different people.

The air-dropping of agents into the USSR finally stopped in 1954. Despite the lack of any significant success, many in the CIA were still thinking in terms of agents. The new DCI, Allen Dulles, commented during a review of the air-dropped agents, "At least we're getting the kind of experience we need for the next war."

The Baltic Deception Exposed

Even as the Western effort in Albania collapsed, the OPC was humiliated by the WiN deception, and the airdrops of agents into the USSR stopped, the first Soviet postwar deception—in the Baltic states—continued. This, despite growing suspicions by SIS young Turks, such as George Young and John Liudzius, that it was a deception. Young, who had experience during World War II in double agent and deception operations, studied the radio traffic and lack of useful intelligence from the Maxis and Roberts resistance groups. He soon realized that the whole effort was under Soviet control. Harry Carr, however, continued to have the backing of the head of the SIS, John Sinclair. Liudzius said later, "No one was willing to listen to me and they posted me to the Far East." It was an error on the Soviet's part that finally exposed the deception.

The SIS Scientific Section had asked that the Roberts group collect a sample of water from the river Tobol, in the Urals. A nuclear reactor was believed to have been built in the area. If a low level of radioactive contamination was detected in the water sample, it would confirm the existence of the reactor, and allow estimates of its capabilities to be made. The Roberts group finally "agreed," and they "collected" a liter of water, which was then "passed" to the Maxis resistance group. When the E-boat dropped off the next group of SIS agents in March 1954, the water sample was brought out. When analyzed, the water was found to be so radioactive that it could only have come from inside the reactor core itself. Clearly, the account of it being collected from the river Tobol was false. The SIS's initial reaction was to wonder whether the Soviets had really made so gross a blunder. Then they realized they had. The SIS officials who believed that the Baltic operation had been compromised finally had the proof they needed.

When the SIS radio messages began asking the agents pointed questions about the water sample, Major Lukasevics realized that the British had finally discovered that the operation was a deception. In hopes of keeping the operation going, Lukasevics sent Margers Vitolin (yet another double agent) to London in September 1954. His mission was to answer SIS questions about the radioactive water sample. Previous double agents had been able to pass SIS interrogations; not so Vitolin. After Vitolin arrived in Kiel, he underwent two weeks of questioning by George Young and SIS lawyer Helmus Milmo. Vitolin confessed to being a Communist, and Young finally had the proof that the Baltic operation was blown. Carr and a number of other SIS officers were quietly retired. The British also soon realized that not only the Baltic operations, but all the other SIS operations inside the USSR, had fallen victim to similar deceptions.

Vitolin was sent back to Latvia, where he underwent another round of interrogations, this time by the Soviets. His answers led the Soviets to believe that the SIS knew about the deception. The sudden halt in landings in the Baltic of both SIS and CIA agents further indicated this. In June 1955, the SIS sent a final radio message to their remaining eleven agents in the Baltic states. It said: "We can no longer help you. Will be sending you no physical or material help. All safe houses are blown. . . . Destroy or keep the radios and codes. This is our last message until better times. We will listen to you until 30 June. Thereafter, God help you."

Major Lukasevics continued his attempts to salvage the now-collapsing deception. In July, he sent another double agent, Janis Klimkans, to Sweden in an attempt to renew contacts with the SIS. Klimkans was brought to London in September and underwent four weeks of interrogation. Worn out by the daily questioning, he made a full confession. Klimkans was returned to Sweden and delivered by the SIS to the Soviet embassy. He was given a message for Major Lukasevics: "Tell your masters that we're grateful for the lessons but we're not complete fools. And finally tell them to treat our people as well as we've treated you."

That proved to be a vain hope. The agents were arrested, while the few remaining anti-Soviet guerrillas melted back into society, still hunted by the Soviets. The last survivor, August Sabe, was found in 1978. Two agents posing as fishermen tracked him down in Estonia. When they tried to arrest him, Sabe wrestled one of the agents into the river. More agents closed in, and Sabe jumped into the river, hooked himself to a submerged log, and drowned.

Although the West had now discovered their deceptions, the Soviets continued to exploit their success for propaganda. In February 1957, the Soviets held a press conference where two more captured agents were unveiled. Konstantin I. Khmelnitsky had parachuted into the USSR, according to the Soviet statement, on 29 April 1953 and was arrested three days later. The statement continued that he had been sending false information to the CIA as late as December 1956. Aleksandr G. Novikov surrendered in November 1953, soon after he was dropped. Both agents were reported to have belonged to the NTS. Also at the press conference were Yakuta and Kudryavtsev, whose capture had been made public three years earlier. On display were radios, guns, identification papers, money, codebooks, and L-pills.

The secret war by the CIA and the SIS against the USSR and Eastern Europe reflected fears of an attack against Western Europe and the United States. The agents and resistance groups were to provide early warning of a Soviet attack, and to blunt an invasion should it be launched. At the same time, however, the operations were influenced and, indeed, driven by outside events. The fears of an attack by the USSR were based not only on their actions in Western Europe, but also by events on the other side of the Soviet empire. While war threatened in Europe, it was actually being fought in Korea. The outbreak of the Korean War in June 1950 transformed the Cold War into a worldwide struggle, and expanded covert operations to new battlefields.

II
Asia

3

Covert Action in the Korean War

To the American people it was a truly and completely unprovoked attack. The reaction was not (as it had been to Pearl Harbor) one of massive unity in defense and retaliation; it was one, rather, of bewilderment. Nothing quite like this had ever happened to us before.

— Walter Millis, *Arms and Men: A Study in American Military History*

At the end of World War II, the Korean peninsula, then a colony of Japan, was divided. In the north, the Democratic People's Republic of Korea was established under Kim Il Sung. In the south, Syngman Rhee ruled the Republic of Korea. The dividing line was the 38th parallel. Kim made plans for an attack on South Korea, to unify the country under Communist rule. Stalin had little interest in Korea until early 1949, when a number of border incidents with South Korean police and military units occurred. He feared these would lead to an attack on North Korea and wanted to avoid provoking the United States and South Korea. Stalin met with Kim Il Sung in Moscow on 5 March 1949 and turned down Kim's request for permission to attack the South. Stalin told him emphatically: "The 38th parallel must be peaceful. It is very important."

The Road to Inchon

Nevertheless, Kim continued to seek Stalin's permission for a limited attack on South Korea. On 11 September 1949, Stalin ordered the Soviet embassy to prepare an "evaluation of the situation and of how real and advisable is the proposal of our friend." Three days later, the embassy cabled back a highly negative assessment. On 24 September, the Soviet ambassador to North Korea, T. F. Shtykov, received a message that he was to give to Kim. It stated, in part: "From the military side it is impossible to consider that the [North Korean] People's Army is prepared for such an attack."

The message complained that "until now very little has been done to raise the broad masses of South Korea to an active struggle.... only in conditions of a people's uprising... could a military attack on the south play a decisive role in the... task of the unification of all Korea into a single democratic state." The potential U.S. response continued to influence Soviet thinking. The message further noted, "Moreover, it is necessary to consider that if military actions begin at the initiative of the North and acquire a prolonged character, then this can give to the Americans cause for any kind of interference in Korean affairs."

Events now caused a fateful change in plans. Mao Tse-tung proclaimed the founding of the People's Republic of China on 1 October 1949. With the victory of the Communists in China and the successful test of a Soviet A-bomb, Stalin was now more confident of the Communist bloc's strength, and less fearful of capabilities of the United States and its will to intervene in Korea. Stalin decided to approve the war that Kim had so long sought. On 30 January 1950, Stalin sent a ciphered telegram to Shtykov. It read:

> I received your report. I understand the dissatisfaction of Comrade Kim Il Sung, but he must understand that such a large matter in regard to South Korea such as he wants to undertake needs large preparation. The matter must be organized so that there would not be too great a risk. If he wants to discuss this matter with me, then I will always be ready to receive him and discuss with him. Transmit all this to Kim Il Sung and tell him that I am ready to help him in this matter.
>
> I have a request for Comrade Kim Il Sung. The Soviet Union is experiencing a great insufficiency in lead. We would like to receive from Korea a yearly minimum of 25,000 tons of lead. Korea would render us a great assistance if it could yearly send to the Soviet Union the indicated amount of lead. I hope that Kim Il Sung will not refuse us in this. It is possible that Kim Il Sung needs our technical assistance and

some number of Soviet specialists. We are ready to render this assistance. Transmit this request of mine to Comrade Kim Il Sung and ask him for me, to communicate to me his consideration on this matter.

Kim and a North Korean delegation spent April 1950 in Moscow, planning the attack. Rather than the limited attack Kim originally planned, a massive tank assault against the whole of South Korea would be made to ensure that the war was won quickly. Not until *after* the plan was completed were the Chinese told. Mao was put in the position of approving the plan that Stalin and Kim had already worked out. At a meeting with Kim, Mao stressed his support of a military reunification of Korea and was confident of victory over the South. Mao said that he did not exclude the possibility of U.S. intervention. If this happened, China would help.

The North Korean attack was launched at 4:00 A.M. local time on 25 June 1950. The Communists' armored drive scattered the lightly armed South Korean army before it. However, both Stalin and Kim had miscalculated the U.S. response. When Secretary of State Dean Acheson told President Truman that a full-scale invasion was under way, Truman replied, "Dean, we've got to stop the sons of bitches no matter what." Truman saw the North Korean attack as the first step in a general Communist plot to "pass from subversion" to "armed invasion and war." This plot was, in Truman's view, directed from Moscow, and was the action of a monolithic Communist bloc. Despite U.S. air and naval support, the North Koreans continued their advance against the South Korean army and the initial U.S. Army units now being sent into action. By early September, the survivors had been forced back into the "Pusan pocket," on the southeast coast of South Korea.

Amid the chaos of the North Korean advance, the Far East Command Liaison Group was hurriedly organized by the U.S. Army to conduct both short-range tactical and deep-penetration intelligence missions. The Tactical Liaison Office (TLO) conducted short-range missions. By September 1950, each U.S. infantry division had a TLO team assigned to it. These were "line-crossers" who operated within twenty miles of the front line. The normal procedure was for a Korean to accompany an Army or Marine patrol into no-man's land. The U.S. troops would then return to friendly lines, while the Korean agent continued on. After completing his mission, the Korean would recross the lines and report his observations to a case officer.

By this time, the Pusan pocket was holding, but the U.S. and South Korean troops were still bottled up. Gen. Douglas MacArthur, head of the Far East Command (FEC), planned to undertake a daring, but very risky, end run around the North Koreans. This was a landing at the port of Inchon, located on the west coast of South Korea, near the capital of Seoul. His plan was approved, and Marine units came ashore at Inchon on the morning of 15 September 1950. The following day, the breakout from the Pusan pocket began. Air-dropping agents deep behind enemy lines would support this advance.

Aviary

The air-dropped agent effort was given the designation "Aviary." The first group of South Korean agents began training in August 1950, even as the North Korean attacks continued. For security reasons, the case officers called their agents "rabbits." A simple jump school was established in the Pusan pocket. It lacked the time and resources available to give the potential South Korean agents a complete paratroop course. One of those involved in the jump school, 1st Lt. Bob Brewer, had to ask that standard troop-type chutes be supplied, rather than the cargo parachutes initially issued. He argued that "disregarding all humanitarian reasons for the moment, an agent who lands and breaks a leg . . . compromises the whole mission and alerts hostile forces to this type of entry by our agents."

Ironically, the actual jump training was intentionally de-emphasized. This was done primarily for psychological reasons—it was discovered that the inexperienced agents were more worried about the night parachute jump than they were about operating behind North Korean lines. The rabbits were given an initial two-hour orientation by a Korean instructor, after which Brewer gave the group another six hours of instruction. In this period, he covered "proper door habit, body position, parachute manipulation during descent, how to land, water landing, tree landing, and how to ball and chain a parachute for burial." Also included were such field activities as assembly techniques and night compass navigation.

The agents were to report on the routes the North Koreans were taking, whether they had tanks and artillery, where the reserve units were located, and whether the North Koreans were making a fighting retreat or being routed. The agents were not equipped with radios, however. Rather, they were to collect the intelligence on the North Korean units, then, like the TLO agents, make their way back to the front lines and allow themselves to be captured. They were provided with a code word with which to identify themselves once they were brought to the POW camps for interrogation.

With their hurried training completed and the northward drive under way, the first two groups of nine agents were readied for their missions. On the night of 26 September 1950, they boarded two C-47s from the 21st Troop Carrier Squadron, flown by regular U.S. Air Force crews. (Because the United States was in combat against North Korea, plausible deniability was not an issue.) The airdrops were carried out by a special detachment designated "Unit 4." The two aircraft took off from Taegu South Airfield and flew toward the two drop zones, which were in the path of the retreating North Korean Army. Five of the agents were dropped in one zone, and four agents in the other. The C-47 crews observed that all nine landed safely.

Of the nine agents, eight eventually recrossed the front lines and reported to their case officers. This was a remarkable success, especially given the limited training they had received. The first drops did reveal some problems. Because the agents had to walk out, their information was delayed, and some was out of date.

With the success of the first drops, Aviary went into high gear to support MacArthur's drive north across the 38th parallel. The agents were dropped as soon as they could be recruited and trained. Brewer later complained about the lack of training and preparation given to the rabbits. He wrote, "My explanation of the failure of previous parachute operations would be that the men were completely lost after a landing and psychologically incapable of rectifying the situation." He added, "I would ask for 48 hours notice in order to prepare my notes, construct an improvised sand table, and find out . . . about enemy forces likely to be encountered. I would then brief the agents 12 to 24 hours before takeoff time." Despite these problems, the survival rate of the agents was around 70 percent, better than average for such high-risk missions.

The backgrounds of the agents varied. Many were refugees from the North. They were familiar with the areas they were to cover and had the right accents to blend in. Lt. Col. H. F. Walterhouse, a Liaison Group staff member, later observed that Koreans were susceptible to a number of inducements. These were "profit, patriotism, revenge, excitement, and coercion," along with an "inherent element of brigandage" he believed existed in a large part of the Korean population.

For others, the reasons were religious. Early in the recruitment effort, Lieutenant Brewer learned of an obscure religious sect called the "Ch'ondogyo." One consequence of the centuries of foreign domination had been the persecution of the indigenous Korean religions. They were outlawed and driven underground. As a result, they were forced to learn covert survival and communications skills. Brewer later marveled at how the sect's members were able to bring back vital intelligence from situations that no one else could have survived. Similarly, the Christian minority in Korea, suppressed by both the Japanese colonizers and later the Communists, was also a source of reliable agents.

By the end of October 1950, the front line stretched across the northernmost part of the Korean peninsula. One section overlooked the Yalu River, which formed the border between North Korea and China. Victory seemed near. However, just as U.S. intelligence had failed to anticipate the North Korean attack, it also did not foresee the disaster that was about to occur.

China Enters the Korean War

On 30 September 1950, with his army cut in half and in a headlong rout, Kim sent a letter to Stalin that literally begged for either direct Soviet military assistance or "volunteer units of China and other countries of people's democracy." The Chinese had made promises of military aid during August and September, saying that if U.S. troops crossed the 38th parallel, Chinese troops, disguised as Koreans, would be sent to enter the war. The reality was that the Chinese were worried that the Korean War could drag on, and that China would pay a considerable price if it became involved.

Stalin concluded that only Chinese troops could now save North Korea. He sent a message on 1 October to Mao asking the Chinese "to move to the 38th parallel at least 5–6 divisions in order to give our Korean comrades a chance to organize under the protection of your troops' military reserves to the north of the 38th parallel." Mao refused, telling Stalin that Chinese troops were too weak to take on the Americans, that a war with the United States would ruin China's plans for reconstruction, and that the USSR would be dragged into the war.

Stalin was stunned by the Chinese refusal. He tried to argue with them, reminding the Chinese of their earlier promises of support. Stalin also said that the United States would not dare to start a major war and would be forced to accept a Korean settlement on Communist terms. This, he continued, would mean that China would reclaim Taiwan, the offshore island where the remnants of the Nationalist Chinese forces had taken refuge. Stalin continued that if a war should break out, it would be better now than later, when Japan was rearmed and all of Korea was under Rhee's control. Still the Chinese refused to send troops, and on 12 October, Stalin recommended to Kim that the North Koreans should evacuate. The following day, however, the Chinese told Stalin that they would intervene after all. Mao was finally convinced by the arguments of pro-Soviet Chinese officials that if North Korea should fall, it would pose a mortal danger to the Chinese revolution.

Brewer saw the first indications of Chinese involvement in agent reports in mid-October 1950. By this point, he had dozens of Aviary agents all along the border between China and North Korea. By late October, Brewer was sure that large numbers of Chinese troops had entered North Korea. The agent reports indicated a force of more than 60,000 Chinese. When the Chinese finally struck, it was against the South Koreans. On 25 and 26 October, they attacked South Korean units near the Yalu River. This was followed on 29 October by reports from South Korean troops that they had encountered Chinese troops along the east coast.

Maj. Gen. Charles A. Willoughby, the FEC's senior intelligence officer, ordered Brewer on 31 October to send him the principal agent from the Kangge-Mampojin border area for an in-depth interview. Brewer recalled, "The agent gave a rather complete picture of the Chinese units that had crossed the Mampojin Bridge into Korea during the month of October, including heavy weapons and hospital units, indicating that Chinese intentions were something more than mere border protection." During the evening of 1 November, Chinese troops struck several U.S. and South Korean units, inflicting heavy casualties. Then, just as suddenly, the Chinese troops vanished.

Despite the agent reports, neither General MacArthur nor the U.S. government realized (or perhaps were willing to accept) the scale of the Chinese involvement. MacArthur's staff initially estimated that about 17,000 Chinese troops were in North Korea; the actual number was close to *180,000*. After regrouping, General MacArthur launched an offensive on 24 November. He estimated that his 200,000 troops, half of whom were South Korean, now faced about 70,000 Chinese troops, and a slightly larger number of North Korean soldiers. The reality was that some 300,000 Chinese "volunteers" were then inside North Korea.

The Chinese counterattacked on 25 November, and within days the U.S. Army units on the west coast of Korea collapsed and were driven back, while the U.S. Marines around the Chosin Reservoir were surrounded and had to fight their way back to the coast. As the Army units retreated, they broke contact with the Chinese. U.S. commanders had no way to tell where the Chinese forces were massing for their next attacks.

Lt. Gen. Walton Walker, the Eighth Army commander, ordered that Aviary agents "blanket the waist of Korea." Brewer said later, "Walker explained he could stop the Chinese attack only if he knew in advance where the main blow was coming." This put Brewer in a difficult position: he did not want to send in radio teams on such short notice, and it would take too long to get the agents into position by sending them in on foot or landing them from ships. To meet the chaotic situation, Brewer improvised with "smoke jumps."

Unit 4's C-47s dropped twenty groups of two-man agent teams about ten to twenty miles north of the U.S. lines. The agents then hid and watched for enemy troops. They were not equipped with radios, but rather with a supply of smoke grenades. The undersides of the C-47s used to support the smoke jumps were painted with black and white stripes, similar to the markings put on Allied planes for D-Day. Each day at noon, the specially marked C-47s would fly low over the areas where the teams had been dropped. When the agents saw the plane, they would set off a smoke grenade to signal the number of enemy troops in the vicinity. A red smoke grenade meant they had seen Chinese troops in over-battalion strength, yellow smoke meant North Korean troops were in the area, and green smoke signaled little or no enemy activity.

Despite the winter weather that soon became a low, solid overcast, the Unit 4 crews observed about 25 percent of the total possible number of smoke signals. As with earlier drops, the agents would have to walk back to friendly areas. Despite the ever-present risks, all but two of the rabbits made it back.

The smoke jumps provided basic intelligence when it was desperately needed, but the technique was too dependent on good weather. To correct this, the first radio-equipped agent team was trained. The team, designated "Hotel Victor One," was given an AN/GRC-9 radio. They were dropped on the night of 9 December 1950 in an area that placed the team in the path of the advancing Chinese army. To pick up their transmissions, C-47s from Unit 4 flew night missions over the areas where the agents operated.

Between December 1950 and February 1951, a total of four teams were dropped in the area around the North Korean capital of Pyongyang. The "Angry 9" radio was bulky and difficult for the hastily trained agents to operate. Eventually, it was replaced with the lighter and simpler SCR-300 infantry radio, and the Unit 4 aircraft were fitted with SCR-300 radios and recorders. A long coaxial cable trailing behind the plane acted as a giant radio antenna.

The demands faced by radio agents were illustrated in this Army report: "One man, in late middle age ... lived in a trench ten feet long and four feet deep for three months without seeing the light of day. He broadcast information collected by local partisans to a plane flying overhead every third night. He stayed at his post ... although almost prostrate from fever and shaken repeatedly by friendly aerial and artillery bombardment."

The courage demanded from a small group of young female agents, however, was far greater than that required of any of their male counterparts. Before the war, Madam Rhee, the wife of South Korean President Syngman Rhee, had been a matron of the arts and knew a circle of theater actresses. She recruited some of these women for the missions. Harry C. Aderholt, then a captain and commander of Unit 4, said of these rabbits:

> They had all the movie stars and everybody, the best-looking girls. We put them out over enemy territory during the winter of '50–'51 when the outside air temperature was forty to fifty degrees below zero. They would go out in cotton padded shoes and suits. They wouldn't weigh enough to get to the ground, you would think.

Once they had landed, they sought out senior Chinese or North Korean officers and provided them with sex. The rabbits would learn from the officers the details of their units, locations, and planned offensives. The success of the mission and their personal survival depended entirely on the agent's own skill at deceiving the officers, and their ability to endure their degrading assignment. Once the rabbits had the information, they would slip away in the confusion, cross the front lines, and contact their case officers. Aderholt recalled that one of the rabbits was able to warn of an impending attack. He described the incident as follows:

> Everyone was frantic. Where have they [the Chinese] gone We were retreating then . . . the 2nd (U.S. Army) Division had been beaten up and was paper thin. One of them [a female agent] came out. She had slept with a lieutenant colonel, Chinese Army, and had their whole order of battle . . . three or four Chinese divisions had side-slipped about 80 miles and were poised head-on against the 2nd Division. That report saved the day . . . the Marines moved up behind the 2nd Division . . . and kicked the shit out of them [the Chinese].

In early January 1951, Seoul again fell, and the Chinese drive continued. Not until 15 January 1951 did the U.S. and Allied troops finally establish a defensive line about forty miles south of Seoul and begin to consolidate their positions. The following day, Mao suggested to Kim that Chinese forces rest in preparation for a final offensive in April or May 1951. Mao was so confident that he even suggested that once the Americans learned of the preparations, they would simply cease resisting and leave Korea.

The Communist euphoria proved short-lived. On 28 January 1951, Mao informed Stalin that U.S. troops had launched an unexpected offensive. Stalin's mood became one of fear and confusion as the U.S. troops continued a slow advance. Mao told Stalin on 1 March that a general offensive by Chinese forces was no longer possible. Two weeks later, Allied forces recaptured Seoul for the second and final time. U.S. troops crossed the 38th parallel and advanced a limited distance into North Korea. Mao and Kim both realized they had no choice but to seek truce talks. The first meetings were held in early July. The Korean War now settled into a violent stalemate.

Stalemate

The outbreak of the Korean War, and the subsequent Chinese intervention, brought significant changes in the U.S. conduct of the Cold War. President Truman declared a national emergency on 16 December 1950, saying, "The increasing menace of the forces of Communist aggression requires that the national defense of the United States be strengthened as quickly as possible." The CIA warned that they did not know whether the USSR intended to start a global war, but direct or indirect Soviet aggression against Europe and Asia was considered likely. Intelligence reports submitted to President Truman in December 1950 noted that Soviet propaganda was drawing parallels between the situation in Western Europe and that existing in Korea before the start of the Korean War. At the same time, Western European Communist parties seemed to be preparing for action.

Once the military situation stabilized in early 1951, airdrop sabotage missions similar to U.S. Army Ranger and British commando operations in World War II were begun. The first of these was code-named "Virginia." Four U.S. Army Rangers and nineteen South Koreans were dropped behind Chinese lines on 15 March 1951 to sabotage rail traffic. The mission failed, with all but five of the South Koreans killed and one of the Rangers captured. "Spitfire" followed three months later, which was to establish a partisan base behind enemy lines. The first drop was made on the night of 18 June, when two Americans, one Briton, and two South Korean partisans parachuted into North Korea. (During the Korean War, "partisans" referred to South Koreans fighting behind enemy lines; "guerrillas" was the term used for North Koreans in the south.) Two more United Nations (UN) personnel and nine South Koreans followed on 25 June.

The inexperience of the aircrew ruined the Spitfire mission. Ten days after the second drop, a resupply mission was scheduled. The crew could not find the base at night, so they returned after dawn and made the drop. The sight of the descending parachutes alerted the enemy, and the partisans had to flee. The team was ambushed the next morning. U.S. Army SFC William T. Miles and a South Korean scout held off the enemy troops long enough for the rest to escape. Eventually, most of the partisans reached friendly lines. Specialist First Class Miles was not among them, however. As a result of the failures of the Virginia and Spitfire operations, subsequent deep penetration sabotage missions used only Korean personnel.

As the Korean War continued, intelligence and covert operations run by the different services proliferated. In addition to the short-range TLO missions and the Aviary and sabotage team airdrops, the Army also ran a seaborne agent program called Salamander and supported raids by South Korean partisans against coastal targets. U.S. Navy Underwater Demolition Teams, U.S. Marine reconnaissance units, and Royal Marine commandos undertook similar seaborne raids.

Running in parallel with the Army's Aviary airdrops was a similar program by the U.S. Air Force. Maj. Donald Nichols put together a small jump school to train the agents. (This was different from the jump school set up for the agents at Pusan.) When a planeload of trainees refused to jump, Major Nichols donned a parachute and, once over the drop zone, jumped. The trainees followed him out the door. During the early months of the war, Nichols directed the airdrop of forty-eight South Koreans on thirteen different missions. The agents were to collect target data for the Air Force. By the end of 1952, thirty-two sub-detachments run by Major Nichols were sending radio reports from behind enemy lines. Although on a much smaller scale than the Army missions, the Air Force also dropped saboteur teams behind enemy lines.

In late 1950, Nichols also started an Air Force program to establish partisan units on islands off the North Korean coast and behind the lines to aid downed airmen. To support both the agent and the rescue activities, the Air Force also operated a small fleet of crash rescue boats. These vessels moved supplies to the islands, dropped off agents in both North Korea and mainland China, rescued downed airmen, and picked up partisan units under attack.

As these airdrop programs expanded, the Air Force unit underwent changes. The Special Air Mission (SAM) Detachment of the 21st Troop Carrier Squadron was activated on 21 February 1951. SAM provided transport for South Korean President Rhee, U.S. Ambassador John J. Muccio, and senior Army commanders. At night, however, SAM dropped agents into North Korea and picked up their radio transmissions, dropped leaflets, and operated two C-47s modified with loudspeakers for propaganda missions against enemy troops.

JACK—The CIA in Korea

The CIA had also finally entered the Korean War. For the first three years of its existence, General MacArthur had prevented the CIA from operating in Japan and Korea. Not until May 1950, after pressure from the JCS and the NCS, did General MacArthur finally permit the CIA to operate in Japan. In July 1950, the relationship between MacArthur and the CIA underwent further strain when the OPC arrived in Japan. Hans Tofte, who was an OSS veteran, ran the OPC unit. General Willoughby, the FEC's senior intelligence officer, soon ordered Japanese counterintelligence agents to follow Tofte's agents around. Tofte later commented, "MacArthur has three enemies: the Russians, the Chinese, and the North Koreans. I have four, those three plus MacArthur!"

The first CIA airdrops were made in September 1950, following the Inchon landings. The first OSO teams were dropped into areas along the northern borders with China and the USSR. They were to establish observation posts to watch roads used to bring in supplies. Although the initial results were considered disappointing, a number of the teams were able to reach friendly lines. CIA airdrops continued as U.S. forces moved north, and then were driven back down the peninsula by the Chinese. As in other areas, the OSO/OPC efforts overlapped. It was not unusual for both OSO and OPC agents to be on the same aircraft, scheduled for drops in different areas for completely different missions.

Although the drop zones were in remote areas to avoid detection, they had to be within a three-day march of the target area. In addition, at least one member of the team had friends or relatives in the target area, which could provide support. The teams often carried a pair of homing pigeons. These would be used to carry coded messages to report the team's safe arrival. Unlike a radio, these messages could not be intercepted or triangulated, giving away the teams' locations. Each member of the team wore civilian clothing and used a T-10 parachute, but no reserve chute; the drop altitude of five hundred feet was too low for it to open in time.

Each team member was given a cover story and false documents. The CIA later noted that keeping up with changes in North Korean documents was a "major problem." Despite this, the still-chaotic internal security situation within North Korea meant that the agent survival rate remained above average. Each team also brought with them various bribery items. These included gold rings, medical supplies, and other hard-to-find items that could be exchanged for help or silence.

By the early months of 1951, the CIA had the nucleus of a partisan movement in the northeast corner of North Korea. It was also now apparent that the different special operations by the different groups were resulting in both overlaps and gaps in intelligence coverage. The initial attempt to sort out the problems was to establish territorial boundaries. The Army was given responsibility for partisan activities in the western half of North Korea and around the east coast port of Wonsan. The OPC partisans operated from Wonsan north to the Soviet border. Despite the boundaries, the Air Force and Navy continued to conduct their own operations. Sometimes these were in support of the Army or CIA, other times with the British or South Korean navy, and still other times independently.

Just as DCI Smith had forced the OSO and OPC to be combined into the Directorate of Plans, so too were the separate OSO and OPC efforts in Korea unified. On 2 July 1951, the "Joint Advisory Commission—Korea" (JACK) was established. Much of the CIA's efforts in Korea focused on meeting the Eighth

Army's tactical needs. The OSO reports distributed between 1 November 1950 and 31 October 1951 broke down as 50 percent military/tactical intelligence, 30 percent North Korean political information, 15 percent economic data, and 5 percent biographical. The CIA had agents within the North Korean military, party, and government.

These agents could be used for more than the passive collection of intelligence. The CIA's graphics shop was able to produce reams of forged Communist Chinese army field orders. Korean agents inserted these into the Communist command structure to disrupt operations. The deployment of CIA-sponsored resistance groups into North Korea was called "Blossom." As with the French resistance and similar World War II groups, it was assumed that the Blossom teams would receive support from the local civilian population. Starting in the winter of 1950, Blossom teams were sent by air and sea into central and northeastern North Korea. Some of the teams were lost immediately after the drop, whereas others established themselves and conducted sabotage and intelligence operations.

One of the CIA partisan functions was to collect targeting data. Although General MacArthur was relieved of duty on 11 April 1951 by President Truman, relations between the CIA and the Army remained poor. Perhaps in the spirit of interservice rivalry, relations between the CIA and the Navy, on the other hand, were good. JACK established a procedure by which intelligence from the Blossom teams was supplied to the Task Force 77 commander, who directed the Navy's fast carriers operating in Korean waters. The commander could then use the data to attack targets in North Korea. In some cases, the target data were "perishable" and had to be acted upon immediately or the opportunity would be lost. One of JACK's greatest successes was the result of such CIA/Navy cooperation.

JACK informed Adm. John Perry, the Task Force 77 commander, on 29 October 1951 that partisans had discovered that a meeting of senior Chinese and North Korean political, security, and military officials would be held at 9:00 A.M. the next day at Kapsan, a town in the rugged mountains of northeast Korea. Admiral Perry saw this as a chance to destroy the enemy command structure in a single blow. He immediately ordered an F9F Panther photoreconnaissance aircraft to cover the area. The photos showed a cluster of twelve buildings at the compound, including a records archive, security center, and guard barracks.

At 7:30 A.M. on 30 October, a strike force of eight AD Skyraiders took off from the USS *Essex*. Each plane carried two 1,000-pound bombs, a napalm tank, eight 250-pound bombs, and a full load of 20-millimeter ammunition. The mission was timed so that the strike force and its escorts arrived about fifteen minutes after the meeting began. The Skyraiders climbed over the ridgeline behind Kapsan at 9:13 A.M., then rolled in on the target. Each plane dropped its 1,000-pound bombs, and then made strafing runs, napalm drops, and, finally, attacks with the 250-pound bombs. When the final run was finished, the compound was smoking rubble. Two days later, the JACK partisans reported that more than five hundred North Koreans and Chinese had been killed in the attack, and the archive of the North Korean Communist Party was destroyed.

The Korean War was now well into its second year, but there still remained the problem of coordinating the various U.S. Army, Air Force, Navy, CIA, and South Korean agent and partisan operations. The CIA believed that it should take the lead in these efforts, and in discussions held during November 1951, this principle seemed to have been accepted by Gen. Matthew B. Ridgway (FEC commander), Gen. James A. Van Fleet (Eighth Army commander), Gen. Frank Everest (Fifth Air Force commander), and Vice Adm. Harold M. Martin (Seventh Fleet commander). Disagreeing were intelligence officers of the Eighth Army and FEC headquarters.

In December 1951, FEC Intelligence issued orders establishing the Covert, Clandestine, and Related Activities—Korea (CCRAK). Contrary to CIA expectations, and without consulting the Air Force or Navy, this was a U.S. Army–controlled organization that had responsibility for all agent and partisan efforts. CCRAK reported to FEC Intelligence, which had long battled with the CIA. The later CIA assessment was that FEC Intelligence seemed to be intent on gaining control over the CIA efforts, and then present a fait accompli to the Air Force and the Navy. The reality was that CCRAK did little to bring order to covert operations in North Korea. The CIA deeply resented what it perceived as FEC Intelligence's high-handed actions, and both the CIA and the Air Force felt that the Army lacked the experience and ability to extend its operations into China. CCRAK itself had responsibility for covert operations, but it lacked direct command authority. As a result, the headquarters rivalries continued.

There were also changes at lower levels. A reorganization in the Fifth Air Force resulted in the establishment on April Fools Day 1952 of B Flight, 6167th Operations Squadron. B Flight, which operated out of Seoul City Air Base, performed the special missions that Unit 4/SAM had flown in the early part of the war. In July 1952 alone, B Flight undertook sixty-four clandestine missions. For agent drops, B Flight initially used C-47s and C-46 transports, but eventually settled on black-painted B-26C bombers. These fast twin-engine light bombers proved ideal for such hazardous missions.

Some of B Flight's missions crossed the Yalu River into China. The maps used on these missions left much to be desired—they were dated 1912 and were stamped "Japanese General Staff." According to one account, three B-26 pilots made six agent-drop missions into Manchuria in a period of ten days. One of the pilots wrote later, "I can say I was not scared one bit, just terrified." He never met the agents because they boarded his B-26 in the arm/dearm area just short of the runway. The agents rode inside the B-26's bomb bay on wooden benches attached to the bomb racks, which could seat up to six agents. After crossing into enemy territory, the B-26 crew would look for the drop zone, which was a large sandbar on the Han River. The bomb bay doors opened, and when the green jump light came on, the agents simply had to slide off the benches, into the night. Maj. P. G. Moore, a B Flight navigator, remembered another feature. "In the event they hesitated, we had a toggle switch in the cockpit that dropped the whole lot . . . bomb racks, benches, and parachutists from the aircraft." The agents had reason to hesitate: fewer and fewer of them were returning from their missions.

North Korean Internal Security and the Fate of Agent Operations

During the first year of operations, the agent missions had about a 70 percent success rate. These early missions took advantage of the confusion of the continuing advances and retreats. By mid-1951, with the war settled into a stalemate, the Communist authorities turned their attention to countering the agent operations. The North Korean army, which had been destroyed in 1950, was rebuilt, with most of the units deployed for internal security duties.

The impact of this step-up in North Korean internal security was not immediately apparent. The Kapsan raid had been a major success, and between October 1951 and January 1952, JACK's penetration of the North Korean military, party, and government expanded. As before, much of the effort—some 40 percent—was in direct support of military operations. The remaining 60 percent dealt with political, social, economic, and counterintelligence reports of a longer-term nature.

At the same time as the networks were being expanded, however, their loss rates began to build. In November 1951, a month after the Kapsan raid, the CIA had steady radio contact with barely half of agent teams that had been infiltrated over the previous few months. With the onset of the severe Korean winter, the remaining teams were instructed to break up into smaller groups and go into hiding until the following spring. Even this proved ineffective, as by January 1952, merely a handful of the teams were still in contact.

The losses were not restricted to the teams themselves. During the night of 18–19 February 1952, a C-46 took off from Seoul City Air Base to make several drops. On board were the U.S. Air Force crew and several Chinese agents. The first drops were successful, and the C-46 then headed toward a drop zone near the Yalu River. As the plane reached the area, it slowed to drop speed. The first Chinese agent went out the door, but the second agent hesitated, threw a grenade into the forward section of the plane, and then jumped. The grenade exploded, killing or wounding the remaining four Chinese agents and one of the two American loadmasters. With the C-46 on fire and breaking up, the Americans bailed out. The Chinese quickly captured everyone. The reason for the loss of the plane was unknown until the surviving crew members were released at the end of the war.

In March 1952, the CIA concluded that their agent networks within North Korea had been "rolled up." JACK started to rebuild the Blossom networks the following month, and expanded its efforts to include air-and-seaborne raids. These were to acquire North Korean documents and local-area intelligence, kidnap local Communist officials, conduct sabotage, build supply caches, and establish cells to organize resistance units. By the summer of 1952, JACK was slowly becoming aware that these new teams being sent in were actually controlled by the North Koreans. Not only were the North Koreans successful in hunting down the teams, they were also penetrating the efforts with their own agents. The double agents would be recruited by JACK, undergo training, and, in the process, learn the names of the other teams and their missions. Once they were dropped into North Korea, they would immediately betray the team.

In some cases, the captured team would continue to send low-quality intelligence to JACK. If the deception was not recognized, JACK would resupply the team and drop additional agents as reinforcements, who would either be killed or forced to become double agents. In other cases, North Korean mistakes revealed the deception. In the spring of 1952, two small teams reported to JACK that they had joined forces. They explained that one team had lost its radio but not its codes and communications plan, whereas the other had a radio but no codes. Fortunately, the two groups had stumbled into each other.

JACK personnel were suspicious, but they agreed to the plan, as no other groups were operating in their area. JACK's doubts continued to grow over the next several months. When the now-combined team was asked test questions to prove their identity, they gave wrong answers. The team also requested the drop of luxury items and women's clothing. The CIA knew these were highly prized by Communist officials. A defector from the area finally confirmed that the Communists controlled the team. JACK officials decided to close down the team with a flourish.

The team was told that a special airdrop would be made on the night of 3 August 1952, which would include a bundle with the requested clothing and other items. This bundle had been rigged so that when these were removed, a bomb concealed inside would explode. A second bundle contained a note to the local Communist provincial chief, whom the CIA knew by name. The note stated that his "southern neighbors" had known for some time that the team was under Communist control, and had profited from what had been learned. The airdrop was successful, and, the CIA noted, the team "was never heard from again." By November 1952, JACK concluded that its operations "had been too thoroughly penetrated by Communists, and would have to be abandoned."

The U.S. Army program of partisan airdrops inside North Korea had accelerated during 1952 and met the same fate. Gen. Mark Clark replaced Ridgway as FEC commander on 12 May 1952. Soon after, General Clark ordered a major expansion of the partisan effort. The focus also shifted, from intelligence collection to combat against the North Koreans and Chinese. During the summer of 1952, as the partisan effort was expanded, the Army and Navy coastal raids began to drop off. It was the partisans who would have to carry the burden of these operations.

Mustang involved a series of sabotage missions in January, March, May, and October that engaged a total of sixty-six personnel. Three of the teams were lost immediately, whereas the Mustang IV team operated for about six days before its members were caught or killed. In "Jesse James," three drops totaling thirty partisans were made in December, also for attacks on supply routes. The result was the same—the partisans were killed either in the drop zone or within days of landing. By late 1952, North Korean internal security was so effective that the drops were suicide missions.

The year 1953 began with Green Dragon, which was an attempt to establish a base for operations. The drop was made on 25 January and involved ninety-seven personnel. Boxer—another sabotage mission—followed in February. The Hurricane drop was made on 31 March, consisting of five partisans who were to attempt to set up a base. The team had apparently been compromised and was lost soon after the drop. The following day (1 April), forty partisans parachuted into North Korea on a sabotage mission code-named "Rabbit." On 6 April, another six saboteurs reinforced them. The final partisan drop made by the Fifth Air Force was, like the year's first mission, code-named "Green Dragon" and was also to establish a partisan base. Fifty-seven partisans made the jump on 19 May 1953. Within a few weeks, all had been captured or killed.

On 27 July, just over two months after the final Green Dragon mission was launched, a truce ended the Korean War. The dividing line between the two nations had changed only slightly after three years of war. The secret war against the Soviet bloc, however, had greatly expanded.

4

Civil Air Transport and the Secret War against Mainland China

The world's most shot-at airline.

— Claire Lee Chennault, on CAT

With the Chinese entry into the Korean War, agent and partisan operations were extended to the mainland. The effort began in February 1951 when the Joint Strategic Plans Committee suggested to the JCS the possibility of supporting guerrilla activities inside China. The Nationalist Chinese government claimed to control a resistance force of some 1 million on the mainland. A study by the Joint Intelligence Group gave a lower estimate of 600,000 anti-Communists, only half of whom were loyal to Chiang Kai-shek, the exiled Nationalist leader. Despite this, the study concluded that "external logistic support would probably accelerate the tempo, increase the combat effectiveness, and widen the area of guerrilla activity."

Ambitious plans were quickly developed for agent drops and resistance movements. The Nationalists still controlled some fifty offshore islands. Guerrillas from these islands would be infiltrated onto the mainland. They would establish bases in the mountains and link up with guerrillas in the countryside and the new recruits that were expected to flock to them. Supplies would be delivered by airdrops. Once "liberated areas" had been established, American advisers would parachute in to assist with intelligence, logistics, and training. The goal of the operations was to draw off Chinese troops from Korea, while maintaining plausible deniability of direct U.S. involvement.

CAT

The guerrilla activities inside mainland China would rely on one of the most unusual airlines ever to operate—Civil Air Transport (CAT). Its founder was Maj. Gen. Claire Lee Chennault, the leader of the Flying Tigers. After the end of World War II, Chennault returned to China to start an airline to move relief supplies within the war-ravaged country. After CAT was formally established on 26 October 1946, Chennault bought twenty C-46 and four C-47 aircraft, which had been declared war surplus and were in storage in Hawaii. The engines had been removed and the fuselages coated with Cosmoline preservative. The CAT ground crew worked for several months to reassemble and test all the aircraft. They also added Chinese registrations and CAT markings. The first CAT C-46s arrived in Shanghai on 2 March 1947.

CAT attracted a unique breed of pilots—adventurers and individualists who had fallen in love with the Orient. A number of CAT pilots were ex-Flying Tigers who, like Chennault, had returned to China after the war. CAT operated out of dirt strips and abandoned airfields. It was a kind of aviation not seen in the United States since the romantic days of barnstorming and flying the mail two decades earlier. Although CAT started out as a cargo airline, its pilots were soon handling passengers and even live animals. Stuart Dew, one of CAT's first pilots, recalled: "Passengers and animals often found themselves side by side in the aircraft without either being too bothered. The movement of the cows in the cabin was continually modifying the plane's stability, but you soon got used to it." Dew added: "One day a curious cow even put her head into the cockpit. [Her] nostrils were only a foot away from my nose. She was chewing her hay as if everything was quite normal. She looked around and then returned to the back, apparently quite satisfied. My co-pilot was killing himself laughing and I was flabbergasted."

CAT was soon caught up in the civil war in China. Following the end of World War II, the United States had encouraged the Nationalists (also called the Kuomintang) and the Communists to establish a coalition government. This failed, and in June 1946 fighting resumed. The Nationalist forces had to rely on aircraft to move troops, supplies, and food to cities threatened by Communist forces. As a result, CAT and the Chinese-owned domestic airlines became paramilitary adjuncts of the Nationalist Chinese Air Force. When the Communist forces laid siege to the city of Mukden in May 1948, CAT made twenty-two flights each day to bring food into the city and take out refugees. By the time Mukden fell to the Communists in October 1948, CAT had airlifted 17,208 tons of supplies into the city.

The defeats inflicted on the Nationalists in late 1948 convinced Mao that final victory was drawing near. The Communists began propaganda attacks on "U.S. imperialists and their accomplices," with CAT singled out as a target. On 26 November 1948, the Communist radio announced that "during period (existence) Chennault's air transport force [has] already joined Kuomintang air force and, moreover, already gave effect to plan of slaughtering the people. This makes clear American imperialistic government is just tolerating these actions of slaughtering Chinese people. The Chinese people and Chinese People's Liberation Army resolutely [propose] to end such actions."

As the Nationalist Army collapsed before the Communist onslaught, CAT pilots found themselves amid scenes of panic and desperation. Ed Morton, a CAT C-47 pilot, said later: "We were overloaded with refugees, others were still arriving, hanging on the doors of the aircraft, frantically trying to get on board. We had to hit them to make them let go so that we could take off." The CAT pilots were offered dollars, jewelry, or gold for a seat. In the final days, panicked soldiers also tried to force their way aboard CAT aircraft. The CAT pilots were flying 18 hours or more in a single day. Randall Richardson held the record: on 3 March 1949, he logged 21 hours and 45 minutes of flight time in a 24-hour period.

In the fall of 1949, Nationalist resistance collapsed, and Mao took over all of China. The CAT aircraft escaped to Taiwan and Hong Kong, but the company was nearly broke. CAT personnel were put on leave of absence without pay, except for a small staff and ten flight crews. Chennault was also lobbying Washington officials to authorize a new Flying Tigers to assist Chiang Kai-shek in regaining the mainland. The U.S. government had earlier rejected the proposal, as it would represent a direct U.S. involvement in the civil war. Secretary of State Dean Acheson wanted nothing to do with Chennault. It was Frank Wisner, the head of OPC, who saw the possibilities in CAT.

Owning an airline, one that operated under the flag of Taiwan and with a Nationalist Chinese charter, would be useful to the CIA in conducting covert activities. Its personnel could travel freely throughout Asia with few questions asked. Although the pilots and CIA agents aboard the planes were Americans, Chennault's close ties with the Nationalists and Chiang Kai-shek, along with CAT's headquarters in Taiwan, created plausible deniability.

A deal was soon struck. The U.S. government secretly paid $950,000 to buy CAT, and a new company, Civil Air Transport Inc., was incorporated on 10 July 1950 as a Delaware corporation that was, in turn, operated by a holding company, American Airdale Corporation. Chennault was named chairman of the board. In reality, CAT was a "proprietary," a seemingly independent company that was actually CIA owned.

The first indication of the new management was the appearance of high-ranking strangers at CAT's Hong Kong headquarters. Alfred Cox was the new "chief executive officer," whereas John Mason was the "special assistant to the president." There was also a new "director of traffic," and another new-comer without a title, an ex-FBI special agent whom CAT pilot Felix Smith described as "six-foot-two and corpulent; he had a poker face that spelled *cop.*"

At an informal "hangar flying" session soon afterward, some of the CAT pilots groused about the newcomers. One pilot commented, "For an airline that's broke, we're sure hiring a lot of wheels." Another, noting Cox's background as a former paratrooper, complained, "A guy who'd jump out of 'em can't be expected to run 'em." Finally, James B. McGovern, know as "Earthquake Magoon," said, "It doesn't take a gypsy fortune-teller with a piss pot full of tea leaves to tell it's the CIA." Robert E. Rousselot, CAT's chief pilot, became angry and warned them: "I don't want to hear you guys say 'CIA.' Not ever again. Not even to each other. If you have to refer to the organization, just call them our customers. You'll have me to reckon with."

By all public appearances, however, CAT continued to operate as a normal airline, carrying passengers and cargo on a regular schedule to Japan, Okinawa, Iwo Jima, Guam, and other points in the Far East. However, CAT was also now flying other, "nonscheduled" routes.

Paper

CAT's first covert action after becoming a CIA proprietary was code-named "Paper." Although most of the Nationalist forces to escape the mainland had gone to Taiwan, several thousand troops under Gen. Li Mi had crossed into Burma. Alfred Cox, who, in addition to his position at CAT, was also OPC's Hong Kong station chief, suggested that they be armed and equipped to serve as a diversionary force on China's southern flank in order to draw troops away from Korea. DCI Smith was dubious about the effort, noting that the Communist Chinese had several million men under arms, and harassment by a few thousand poorly trained and equipped troops some two thousand miles away was unlikely to have any effect in Korea. Despite DCI Smith's doubts, President Truman gave his approval. The Chinese were inflicting heavy losses on U.S. forces, and Korea was still threatening to trigger World War III.

Desmond FitzGerald, the executive officer for OPC's Far East Division, was selected to head Paper. His outlook was very different from that of DCI Smith's. FitzGerald saw covert action as a more effective way of fighting the Cold War than using huge armies. FitzGerald had been a U.S. Army captain serving as a liaison officer with a regiment of Nationalist Chinese troops. With a romantic view of the individual, he was also wary of mass movements and was appalled by the Communist efforts at brainwashing the Chinese population.

Airdrops of equipment and American advisers to Li Mi's troops began in March 1951. A camp for the Nationalist guerrillas was soon established on the Chinese border. Operating out of Thailand, the Overseas Southeast Asia Supply Company (Sea Supply) directed the operation. Like CAT, Sea Supply was a proprietary. The Burmese were soon aware of unmarked aircraft flying missions in the north of the country, but a protracted civil war with the Karen tribe and Communist guerrillas meant the government was in no position to interfere.

Li Mi's troops went into action in April of 1951. Two groups of some two thousand men each crossed the border into Yunnan Province, with CAT dropping supplies. The advance proved short-lived; the Chinese Peoples Liberation Army (PLA) inflicted heavy losses on the Nationalist troops and pushed them back in less than a week. FitzGerald tried to put the best face on the attempt. In a 10 August memo, he wrote, "Anti-Communist Chinese spirit throughout the Far East has been given a shot of adrenalin." FitzGerald was not ready to give up on Li Mi, saying that he should create "small, mobile hard-hitting groups." DCI Smith remained doubtful about the grandly renamed "Yunnan Province Anti-Communist National Salvation Army," complaining, "All those guys do is skate up and down the wrong side of the border."

The CIA expanded its support of Li Mi's troops. An abandoned World War II airfield in Burma was secretly restored to service. This allowed direct CAT flights from Taiwan to Burma, and eliminated the need for parachute drops of supplies. An airlift brought Nationalist soldiers and supplies to the base. The weapons included mortars and heavy machine guns. The amount of supplies was such that Li Mi was able to equip an army of some eight thousand Burmese peasants who lived in the surrounding hills. Within a year, the force had grown to some twelve thousand troops.

Such levels of activities did not go unnoticed, however. The *New York Times* carried an article on 11 February 1952 quoting witnesses in Burma as saying that Li Mi's troops were carrying brand-new U.S. weapons. The Burmese government said that CAT was flying a twice-weekly shuttle service from Taiwan to the secret airbase. Li Mi's troops were becoming a state within a state. They were collecting taxes within the areas they occupied and were beginning to control the local opium markets. In response to the reports, Secretary of State Dean Acheson denied any U.S. involvement with Li Mi's troops. When the U.S. ambassador repeated these denials at a diplomatic reception in Rangoon, the Burmese Army Chief of Staff bluntly told him: "Mr. Ambassador, you bore me. If I were you, I would shut up."

In the summer of 1952, the Yunnan Province Anti-Communist National Salvation Army launched a second attack into mainland China. The twelve thousand troops were able to advance some sixty miles before being turned back by the PLA. There was no mass uprising, nor did the local population rally to Li Mi's forces. The CIA subsequently discovered that Li Mi's radio operator at Sea Supply in Bangkok was actually a double agent who provided information on troop locations and strengths to Communist Chinese intelligence.

The CIA ended Paper after the failure of the second offensive. Li Mi became a local warlord and opium producer in the border areas of Burma, Northern Thailand, and Laos. He continued to receive supplies from the Nationalist Chinese government and to fight the local Communist rebels and PLA.

As Paper was starting, "Western Enterprises Incorporated" (WEI) was being established to run the covert operations conducted from the island of Quemoy, as well as the agent drop operations out of Taiwan. Its cover was as an import-export firm, but like CAT and Sea Supply, WEI was actually owned by the CIA. WEI personnel began arriving in Taiwan in March 1951. They were a colorful, larger-than-life group. Ed Hamilton, the WEI commander on the island of Quemoy, had lost an eye while serving in the U.S. Army in France, and he became known as the "One-Eyed Dragon." Jim Creacy, the communications officer on Quemoy, was a Texan who wore a ten-gallon hat and cowboy boots, while packing a pair of revolvers with dragon carvings and ivory handles. He was dubbed "Two-Gun, Scourge of the Communists and Other Outlaws." Many WEI employees were college football players that had tried out with the pros but had been cut. The "import-export" business proved attractive to a number of these individuals.

Chinese court politics had for centuries proven difficult for Westerners to fathom, and so it remained when WEI set up shop in Taiwan. Nationalist Chinese intelligence operations were under the control of Gen. Mao Jen-feng of the Secrets Preservation Bureau. Inside the Ministry of National Defense, however, was the newly formed Continental Operations Department, which also claimed control of irregular forces on the mainland. To further confuse the picture, the Kuomintang Party's Sixth Department had responsibility for propaganda against the mainland, which meant it was involved with leaflet drops. The real power behind the throne was Madame Chiang Kai-shek, who became known to WEI personnel as "the mother of the guerrillas."

By mid-September 1951, the first groups were ready to return to the mainland. Ernest J. Tsikerdanos had trained the unit of 175 guerrillas picked to establish the first base. The original plan was for Tsikerdanos to go ashore with the guerrillas, but the day before they sailed, he was ordered to wait until the base was established.

The guerrillas landed and started moving inland. Their initial radio reports indicated only light resistance from local militia units. As the guerrillas continued toward the planned base area, they reported being shadowed by increasing numbers of militiamen. After about forty miles the trap closed, and regular PLA units attached the guerrillas. Only four of the guerrillas made it back from the Battle of the Lonesome Tree, named for the outnumbered guerrillas' final position, where the PLA's mortars zeroed in on them.

A second attempt, made just a short time later, ended the same way. A force of two hundred guerrillas was landed from Quemoy. To avoid being trapped by larger PLA units like the first group, their orders were to move inland as fast as possible, to set up the resistance base, and to await aerial resupply of machine guns and bazookas. PLA reinforcements were quickly moved in by truck, then surrounded the guerrillas, and within a few days, had wiped them out.

The twin disasters forced the large-scale operations to be abandoned. As a replacement, hit-and-run raids were planned against weakly defended coastal areas. These would be made on short notice and tightly held to avoid leaks. The raids were to gain recruits and capture Communist Party officials, militiamen, and documents, as well as blow up party headquarters and other installations.

A total of eighteen coastal raids and eleven marginal acts of sabotage were conducted. In the most ambitious action—against the Communist-held island of Tung-shan—paratroopers were dropped in advance of the landings. Some one thousand Communist troops were killed in this raid, and a similar number were taken prisoner. Nationalist losses during the raid, however, were comparatively high, making the results mixed.

Agent Drops into Mainland China

Agent operations from Taiwan began concurrent with the raids against coastal targets. Unlike the raids, which were controlled by OPC, OSO personnel directed the agents' activities. An intelligence mission against coastal targets was done either by a single agent or by a two- or three-man team. Once a target area had been selected, the Nationalist Chinese reconnaissance platoons were searched for individuals who were native to the area, and that still had friends or relatives who could hide them. If none of the reconnaissance platoon members was suitable, volunteers were sought from the crews of the motorized junks or members of the raiding battalions.

Once selected, the agent or the intelligence team would be dressed in appropriate and authentic clothing, complete with "pocket litter" such as Chinese-made matches. They would also carry forged or altered documents. Chinese security controls and documents proved to be much more subtle than those seen in the USSR and Eastern Europe. A Chinese travel document might be stamped with a number of hand-carved official "chops." The lower the official's status, the larger and bolder his chop. The critical party cadre's chop and initials might appear to be an afterthought. A CIA specialist was usually on call to prepare the needed documents.

The agents were taken to the drop site in a motorized junk and then were taken ashore in a sampan. The place and time for the pickup several days later was prearranged and used the same procedure. There were also backup sites and dates if bad weather prevented a pickup as originally planned. The small agent teams proved very successful, despite occasional run-ins with Communist gunboats, bad weather, or, in the case of agent V-69, faulty flashlight batteries that almost prevented a pickup.

Agent operations deep inside mainland China, which started in the spring of 1952, were a far more difficult proposition than these coastal missions. The Nationalist agents would have to make "blind" drops into unprepared locations, where they were to organize intelligence networks or resistance movements from scratch. They could not count on any help from friends or relatives, nor was there any possibility of returning to Taiwan.

Rousselot did the operational planning for these agent drops, as well as selecting the CAT crew members. He had been a U.S. Marine Corps fighter pilot in the Pacific during World War II. After the war ended, Rousselot volunteered for a fifteen-month tour in China. In late 1946, he asked Chennault for a job with CAT. Rousselot had only limited multiengine time, but Chennault was impressed with the young lieutenant and gave him a job. By 1948, Rousselot was CAT's chief pilot. Rousselot led by example. When the planning was completed, Rousselot scheduled himself as pilot on the first agent drop flights.

These were to be daylight missions, flown on 15 and 17 March 1952, to areas in western China. Flying with Rousselot was navigator Cyril M. Pinkava. Clouds over 75 percent of the route plagued the second flight, and the plane missed the drop zone by sixty-five miles. Although Madame Chiang personally thanked Rousselot and the rest of the crew, the four Nationalist Chinese agents they had dropped were lost.

Soon after, Rousselot and Pinkava were sent to Kadena Air Base on Okinawa to be checked out in an Air Force B-17. The plane was subsequently turned over to CAT, stripped of any markings, and used for long-range missions. Rousselot, William J. Welk, and Merrill D. Johnson took turns flying the B-17 on the agent drops. Such agent or supply drops required careful planning. The crews had to follow an exact time schedule involving coastline penetration points, ground speed, approach corridors to the drop zone, checkpoints for sending radio messages, and the plane's return route.

The pilots' briefings had a touch of the surreal. Rousselot would send the pilots to the Miramar Hotel in Hong Kong, where CAT had a room. This offered more privacy than the frantic head office. Cox would meet them and take them into the bathroom. Cox sat on the toilet seat and gave the briefing, while the pilot sat on the edge of the tub. McGovern said, "CAT is the only airline with a hotel room for a head office and a toilet for a conference room."

Although about 75 percent of the CAT pilots flew covert missions at one time or another, a select group flew the most hazardous ones. In addition to Rousselot, Welk, Johnson, and Pinkava, this included Robert C. Snoddy, Norman A. Schwartz, Eddie F. Sims, Paul R. Holden, and Roy F. Watts. They were all individuals who would complete a mission if possible, but who had the maturity to abort if the situation required it. Patriotism and adventure, rather than money, motivated these pilots. Hazard pay amounted to merely $10 per hour overtime, and this was not always available. One pilot later explained, "I believed in the purpose of the operations."

In the fall of 1952, CAT put into operation for the agent drops a DC-4 that the airline had bought in 1947. The DC-4 carried the Chinese registration B-1002. For most of each month, it was used for passenger flights throughout the Far East. However, when the moon was full, the DC-4 was transformed.

The passenger seats were removed and replaced with drop tracks, static line, and signal lights. The crew for the agent drop missions consisted of pilot, copilot, radio operator, and two or three CIA parachute dispatch officers (PDOs). They gave the agents the signal to jump or pushed the cargo out the plane's door. The PDOs were informally known by the CAT crew members as "cruise directors."

The flights were made on nights around the time of a full moon so rivers, lakes, mountains, or other ground landmarks would be visible. The route was planned in segments, going from one landmark to the next. The crew relied on dead reckoning, flying a specific airspeed and direction for a precalculated elapsed time until the next landmark came into sight. CAT's meteorologist, the aptly named John Fogg, made the weather forecasts. He used historical data and decoded transmissions from mainland Chinese weather stations. Fogg's forecasts were critical to the missions, as the wind speed aloft had to be factored into the flight plan.

Watts said that the DC-4 flights, particularly those to the inner and outer Mongolia areas, "were hair raisers whose distance and duration were impressive." The aircraft had been stripped of everything not needed for the drop, and had a range far beyond that of a normal airliner. Watts and Holden later claimed the duration record for a mission—14 hours and 21 minutes in the air.

Eric Shilling flew several of the CAT agent drop missions in the DC-4. He had been one of the Flying Tigers and had designed the shark-mouth insignia carried on their P-40 fighters. He had returned to China after the war and begun flying for China National Aviation Corporation (CNAC). Shilling joined CAT in 1947, after he and twelve other former Flying Tigers were let go by CNAC.

Shilling recalled that most of his airdrop missions took off from Clark AFB in the Philippines and sometimes penetrated as deep as Szechwan Province in central China before landing back at Taiwan. On several of his missions, the agents had been ambushed as soon as they landed in the drop zone, and Shilling suspected leaks within Nationalist intelligence. He decided to take a different approach on one mission from Okinawa, and told the agent that he would fly past the planned drop zone and select a nearby site where no one would be waiting. Shilling would then continue on another hundred miles, turn around, and then drop the agent over the alternative location. The agent agreed with his idea.

Shilling took off from Okinawa and flew the DC-4 merely five hundred feet above the ocean. Reaching a point about forty miles from the coastline, the large airliner descended to only thirty feet. The DC-4 crossed the coast south of Shanghai and then continued deeper into China. As the airplane passed the city of Hankow, Shilling saw its lights go out. He said later: "This told us that they knew we were there. I remained calm and unperturbed, partly because this fellow told me that if we had to go down, to stick with him and he would get me out. I believed him."

The DC-4 finally reached the drop zone outside Chungking, some nine hundred miles inside the mainland. Shilling flew past the planned drop zone, and then turned back toward the new site he had picked on the way in. The DC-4 climbed to jump altitude, and on the jump-bell signal, the agent parachuted into the darkness. The flight back was as uneventful as flying a DC-4 at treetop altitude at night could be. Shilling cleared the Chinese coastline without being intercepted and landed in Taiwan.

The following night, Shilling attended a dinner hosted by Madame Chiang. When he entered the presidential palace, Madame Chiang said to him, "Congratulations." Later, he asked her, "Congratulations for what?" Madame Chiang replied, "Congratulations for a good flight." A surprised Shilling responded, "I was not aware that you knew we were making these flights." Madame Chiang's reply was an even bigger surprise to Shilling—"I did not go to bed until I knew that you had landed safely."

The mainland Chinese lacked night fighters, and their radar coverage was spotty. The major risk to an airplane on an agent drop mission was mechanical failure. The CAT crews spent the long hours flying over China listening for any irregularity in the engines. If they were forced down, they knew that there was no return. The CAT crews were offered L-pills, but Watts recalled that they "were usually politely turned down." On one of Watts and Holden's flights, the number three engine failed about four hours after the DC-4 crossed the Chinese coast. Watts noted, "The engine quit with such a jolt that we thought we had taken a hit." Watts feathered the propeller, and the mission was completed on three engines.

When the moon began to wane, and the agent drops were finished for the month, the DC-4 was again transformed. The drop equipment was removed, the passenger seats were reinstalled, and the plane was returned to airline service. The DC-4's passengers had no reason to suspect what the airplane had been doing and the places it had been to. After all, CAT was just an airline.

With the agent drops under way, CAT also began making flights in support of Nationalist guerrilla activities in western China. These vast and harsh regions represented 60 percent of the Chinese landmass, but were inhabited by just 7 percent of its total population. These were primarily ethnic minorities, such as Tibetans, and religious minorities, such as Muslims, who had historically acted independently during times of dynastic change. In the confusion after the fall of the Nationalist government, resistance activities had sprung up in western China.

The Muslim Hui clans were among these groups. In the final months of the civil war, Hui troops had fought against the Communists. After the Nationalist defeat, some of these troops had remained to continue the fight. Hui horsemen, under the command of Ma Pu-fang, had been involved in heavy fighting against the Communists during 1951. The Hui were spread throughout China, and information about Ma Pu-fang's resistance activities reached the CIA and Nationalist intelligence. By the end of 1951, OPC, WEI, and Gen. Mao Jen-fang had sufficient contacts to begin planning the start of supply missions by CAT.

A four-man radio team was selected and began training, which involved not only radio procedures and coding and decoding messages, but also how to make weather observations. CAT meteorologist John Fogg was their instructor. He taught the agents how to use simple instruments to measure temperature, humidity, and wind speed and direction and how to identify cloud types, heights, movements, and the degree of coverage. Also critical to the airdrops were the team's reports of surface visibility, dust, and precipitation.

Robert Rousselot scheduled himself to be the DC-4's pilot on the first airdrop because of the flight's importance and because this would be CAT's first mission into western China. With Rousselot were Paul Holden as the copilot and Cyril Pinkava as navigator. Henry Lee was the radio operator, and two PDOs completed the crew. The DC-4 was to take off from Tao-yuan Air Base on Taiwan, and the flight would last some fourteen hours before returning. Also aboard the airliner were some 5,600 pounds of supplies, weapons, and ammunition to be dropped with the radio team. To preserve plausible deniability, the weapons were surplus and could not be traced back to the United States. The CIA bought weapons from around the world, with the newly independent European colonies being a primary source.

As dusk fell, Pan Chin-wu, the deputy at the Secrets Preservation Bureau, brought the team members to the air base. During their training, he developed close bonds with the team and imbued them with a patriotic fervor for the tasks ahead. Pan was also a realist about the odds that the team faced. As he watched the DC-4 take off, according to one account, there were tears in his eyes as he said, "I'll probably never see these lads again."

The DC-4 crossed the Chinese coastline between Amoy and Chuan-chou, and then passed above the Min River and over the Wuyi Mountains. It then swung north to avoid the city of Nanchang. Pinkava followed a series of landmarks; first Poyang Lake, then along the Yangtze River until the DC-4 reached the edge of Tung-ting Lake. Rousselot then turned the airliner north until they were clear of the city of Wuhan. The crew followed the Han River to the west, and then headed northwest toward the Great Wall, their final landmark before the turn to the southwest and the drop zone.

Below was the vast expanse of northwestern China. The crew began looking for the small bonfire that would pinpoint the drop site. Rousselot and his crew could see the smoldering remnants of a few isolated campfires on the ground below, but nothing that resembled a signal fire. For a full ten minutes, Rousselot circled the rendezvous point. With a long flight back to Taiwan and a diminishing fuel supply, Rousselot decided to fly another fifty miles to the southwest, turn around, and start making the drop. He talked with the radio team, explaining the situation. After landing, they were to find a hiding place and radio that they were safe.

The radio team was first out the door, followed by the weapons and supplies. The boxes formed a straight line across the barren desert, which almost reached the original rendezvous point. With the drop completed, but the success of the mission still unknown, the DC-4 began the trip back. The airliner headed back along the Great Wall, reaching a point north of Yenan, the Communists' wartime capital. Then the crew followed the Yellow River to the Huai River and onto the Yangtze River, to a point near Po-yang Lake. From there, the DC-4 made a straight flight to Tao-yuan Air Base.

Upon their return, Rousselot and his crew were greeted with the news that the radio team had reported making contact with the guerrillas. They were collecting the supplies, and then would be heading for a safe area. A few days later, Rousselot, Holden, and Pinkava made a second supply flight to western China. Rousselot then turned the flights over to regular CAT crews. Initially, the DC-4 was used, but it was subsequently replaced by the B-17, which had been turned over to CAT by the U.S. Air Force. The B-17 had better altitude performance, but the agents and supplies had to be dropped through a hole in the floor where the belly turret had been, rather than out a large side cargo door as in the DC-4.

CAT continued to fly missions in support of Ma Pu-fang's resistance activities for more than a year. In time, however, the PLA finally brought sufficient troops to bear against them. The Communist Chinese claimed that organized resistance had ended in 1954, but the area was not fully pacified until 1955.

Tropic

Although these agent and resistance activities were a joint effort between the CIA and the Nationalist Chinese, CAT was also involved with a separate CIA airdrop program code-named "Tropic." The Joint Intelligence Group study had noted that at least half the guerrillas on the mainland had no ties with the Nationalists. These non-Nationalist guerrillas were known as the "Third Force."

The Third Force also grew out of U.S. disillusionment with the Nationalists. During the civil war, CAT pilots had seen Nationalist Chinese air force commanders rent their cargo airplanes to local merchants and pocket the cash. In the meantime, B-25 bombers sat on the ground, rather than be used to support Nationalist troops against the Communists. After reaching Taiwan, the Nationalists were militarily and psychologically beaten. Frank Holober, an early WEI recruit, wrote later, "the scent of decay pervaded the air."

Support to the Third Force guerrillas was to be an important part of the covert actions against China, but it posed a dilemma. CAT owed its existence to the special relationship between Chennault and Chiang, and its use as the CIA's covert airline was built upon this. The CIA had to both keep the Third Force guerrillas secret from the Nationalists while simultaneously limiting knowledge of Tropic within CAT.

Recruitment of the Third Force guerrillas began in Hong Kong in 1951, under the guise of employment with the Far East Development Company on Guam. Those selected were sent to the Navy Technical Training Unit on Saipan, or to another CIA facility at Chigasaki, Japan. The would-be agents sent to Saipan were blindfolded during the flight to and from the base so they would not know its location. Their initial training was in parachuting, use of explosives and small arms, radio operations, and similar skills. Then teams were organized and instructed on setting up bases, preparing drop zones, and establishing networks. The target areas for the Third Force teams were in Manchuria, just north of the Korean border. Once the teams had parachuted in, they would recruit local guerrillas, collect intelligence and weather data, and help downed U.S. aircrews.

Schwartz and Snoddy were selected as the primary crew for Tropic in December 1951. Schwartz was a former Marine fighter pilot who had no multiengine time before joining CAT in 1948. He was single, was a good golfer, and had been the pitcher on the CAT softball team in Shanghai. Snoddy had flown Navy PB4Y patrol bombers during World War II, and then he worked for Hawaiian Airlines and Trans-Pacific Airlines before joining CAT in 1948. He had a reputation for being a little wild on the ground, but was all business in the air. His wife, Charlotte, became pregnant while Snoddy was working on Tropic.

Schwartz and Snoddy initially went to South Korea to fly indoctrination missions with the Air Force. CAT also brought three C-47s from Trans-Asiatic Airways for use in Tropic. Unlike the DC-4, there would be no pretense that these were airliners. They were painted olive green and were fitted with static lines, drop signals, and flame suppressors on the engine exhaust pipes to make the planes harder to see at night. The three C-47s were given Chinese registration numbers of B-813, B-815, and B-817. They, along with the unmarked B-17, were the planes used on Tropic.

In March 1952, final preparations began for CAT's role in Tropic and the Third Force. Chennault was called to Washington, D.C., for "consultations" with the CIA, and so was out of the way. CAT's operations director, Camille J. Rosbert, flew to Japan for a briefing on Tropic. Rosbert had been a Flying Tigers ace, was intensely loyal to Chennault, and was close friends with Chiang and his family. His initial reaction to first learning about Tropic was one of anger. Rosbert confided to his private journal:

> We'll never learn that you can't win the faith of a people by stupidly dividing the house. Why not get the third force elements into the first force Because we were divided before, the second force (communism) has all the mainland. I'm really burned on this type of thinking. . . . I'm disgusted with the so-called thinkers in Washington who work out these utterly stupid plans.

Given such reactions, as well as the political sensitivities of the Third Force program, Tropic was based in Japan. The CAT crews assigned to the project lived in Tachikawa. When a mission was scheduled, they ferried a C-47 from Tachikawa to nearby Naval Air Station (NAS) Atsugi, which was home to the CIA's cover organization for the Third Force, the Joint Technical Advisory Group (JTAG). The CAT crew was briefed and then flew to South Korea. At dusk, they took off from Seoul City Air Base, or an airfield at Pusan, and headed east until they were out of range of Air Force radar. The C-47 then turned north and crossed into China. Once the drop zone was located, the C-47 came in at low altitude, and the PDOs sent the agents or supplies out the cargo door. With the drop completed, the C-47 flew back to its home base, and the crew was debriefed.

Schwartz and Snoddy made most of the Tropic flights flown in the spring and summer of 1952. John T. Downey was a PDO on many of their flights. He was a student at Yale, planning to go to law school, when a CIA recruiter visited the campus. Downey was enthralled by his talk, later recalling, "Hey, that was as glamorous as anything we could hope for." Downey applied to join the CIA and was accepted in June 1951. He underwent three months of training and was successful, despite a low grade in survival training. He was then assigned to the Third Force project at NAS Atsugi.

One of Downey's early assignments was to select a four-man team to be sent into Jilin Province in Manchuria. Chang Tsai-wen, a twenty-eight-year-old native of the area, led the team. "Team Wen" parachuted into Manchuria in July 1952 by CAT. In October, another agent, Li Chun-ying, was dropped to observe Team Wen in action. Team Wen subsequently sent a radio message saying that Li Chun-ying was ready to be brought out, using a ground-to-air pickup technique.

This technique had been developed by All America Aviation in the late 1930s to pick up airmail from small towns in the Appalachian Mountains that lacked airports. During World War II, it had been tested as a possible means to recover agents in occupied Europe. The pickup system used two poles placed in the ground, with a rope suspended between them. This rope was attached by a line to a harness worn by the agent. A C-47 made a low pass, trailing a long cable with a grappling hook that snagged the rope. A special winch reduced the initial shock at the moment of pickup, and then reeled the agent aboard. To ensure the agent was not dragged on the ground, the plane made a sharp pull-up after the hook caught the rope.

Schwartz and Snoddy made a number of successful practice pickups in preparation for the return of Li Chun-ying. During the training, Snoddy was showing the stress from flying the secret missions and having a pregnant wife. Fellow CAT pilot Felix Smith had long been friends with Schwartz and Snoddy. One day in November 1952, they were in the "menagerie," a remote tarmac for aircraft assigned to CAT's special missions. Smith noticed the camouflaged C-47 had been fitted with flame suppressors, and realized that it was used for covert missions.

Smith did not ask about the missions, but after a long silence, Snoddy said in a very matter-of-fact way to Smith, "I've seen the lights of Vladivostok." Smith then asked, "How about my going with you sometime?" Snoddy replied: "Jeez, don't volunteer. Once you get on these you never get off. The customer figures the fewer that go, the tighter the security."

The CIA was concerned over the pickup; the "fist" of Team Wen's radio operator sending the messages was different. He had sent the correct code word, indicating he was not under Chinese control. However, his individual style of tapping the radio key had changed from that which he had shown during training. The CIA finally judged the flight to be a high-priority but minimal-risk mission, and the first operational pickup was scheduled for the night of 29 November 1952. Aboard B-813 were Schwartz, Snoddy, Downey, and Richard G. Fecteau, a PDO who had been with the CIA only five months. Downey later described the events of that night.

> The aircraft was a C-47 . . . that carried no markings, was "sterilized" as a security precaution to prevent tracing its origin. The purpose of retrieving the agent was to debrief him on the results of his mission. The aircraft took off from Seoul shortly after 9 p.m. Weather during the flight was clear and cold, visibility good. We followed a route that was generally used for . . . flights into China, that is, from Seoul roughly east to the coast, then north over water. [We] crossed the Korean-Chinese border at 12 midnight and reached the pickup area fifteen minutes later.

The pickup site was in the rugged foothills of Manchuria, near the town of Antuin in Jilin Province. The crew made radio contact with the team's radio operator and dropped the package with the recovery equipment. When the people on the ground signaled they were ready, the C-47 slowed to just above stall speed and flew toward the pickup point. Only about sixty feet above the ground, the C-47 and its crew never had a chance. Team Wen had been captured, and the airplane had flown into an ambush. A squad of PLA troops threw back the tarpaulins they had used as camouflage and opened fire with machine guns. The C-47 was hit and pancaked into the ground. Schwartz and Snoddy were killed in the crash, and their burned bodies were buried at the snow-covered site. Downey and Fecteau survived and were captured. They spent the next two years in solitary confinement. Much of that time they were under interrogation and kept in chains.

When the C-47 failed to return, CAT put out the cover story that the plane had disappeared during a flight between Korea and Japan on 3 December 1952. John Mason, the "special assistant to the president," flew to Korea. He had the tower communication log at Taegu Airfield falsified to indicate that the missing C-47 had reported in en route to Japan. Charlotte Shoddy's father came to Japan to return her to the United States. Many of the CAT pilots saw her off. Before she left, Charlotte gave Smith a gift—Shoddy's navigation chronometer. She subsequently gave birth to a daughter, named Roberta. Several years later, a stranger knocked on Charlotte's door, talked about an insurance policy, and handed her a check that put Roberta through college.

The Chinese did not announce they had shot down the C-47, and all four crewmen were listed by the CIA as being missing and presumed dead. There was no information about their actual fate until 22 November 1954, when Downey and Fecteau were subjected to a show trial. Fecteau was brought into the courtroom, while Downey was already in the dock, wearing a black padded suit, shoes, and a beanie hat, and looking dejected. Fecteau, whom the CIA evaluators had thought during his training should "be more serious," whispered to Downey, "Who's your tailor?" Downey was sentenced to life in prison for espionage, while Fecteau received twenty years. The U.S. government denounced their sentences, and denied they were CIA agents.

The Chinese responded by claiming that of the 212 Chinese agents who had parachuted into the mainland between 1951 and 1953, 101 had been killed, whereas the other 111 had surrendered on landing or been captured. They also claimed to have captured a total of 6 mortars, 998 rifles, 179,000 rounds of ammunition, and 96 radios, as well as codes, invisible ink, forged documents, and gold bars.

During their imprisonment after the show trial, Fecteau and Downey were listed on CIA records as serving on "Special Detail Foreign" at "Official Station Undetermined." During the endless years, they had to get through each day subjected to Communist propaganda without losing hope. At home, their parents struggled for their release, assembled care packages filled with cookies, warm socks, and issues of *Sports Illustrated*, not knowing whether they would ever be delivered.

Fecteau spent nineteen years in Chinese prisons, and was finally released on 12 December 1971. He became an assistant director of athletics at Boston University until his retirement in 1989. Downey was released on 12 March 1973, after the United States officially acknowledged he had been with the CIA. He went to Harvard Law School, entered private practice, and was named a judge on the Connecticut Superior Court. DCI George J. Tenet awarded

Fecteau and Downey the Director's Medal on 25 June 1998, which is inscribed with the words "Extraordinary Fidelity and Essential Service."

In December 1998, a closed ceremony was held for the next of kin of Schwartz and Snoddy. The two lost pilots were posthumously awarded the Distinguished Intelligence Cross. Two unmarked stars for them are carved in the north wall of the entrance to CIA headquarters, beside other stars that represent CIA personnel who met anonymous deaths in the line of duty.

Cold War Case 00012 (C-47 Aircraft, Two Unaccounted For)

The downing of Schwartz and Snoddy's C-47 was not the only such incident during the Cold War. The Soviets, Chinese, and North Koreans also shot down U.S. Air Force and Navy intelligence aircraft. The CAT aircraft was designated Cold War Case 00012 (C-47 Aircraft, Two Unaccounted For). In July 2002, the Chinese gave permission for a team from the U.S. Army's Central Identification Laboratory to visit the crash site. This was the first time the Chinese government permitted a search for remains linked to a Cold War incident. Chinese Foreign Ministry spokesman Liu Jianchao said in a news briefing that the government had approved the search as a humanitarian gesture.

The search team reached the rugged, remote site that same month, and their excavation revealed aircraft fragments. Small bits of debris are often all that remains at an aircraft crash site after the main wreckage is removed or scavenged. No human remains were found during the search, however, and the U.S. requested Chinese permission to make another search. This was granted, and the second visit to the C-47 crash site was scheduled for the following year. It was not until the late spring of 2004, however, that the trip to the site finally took place.

The recovery team arrived at the site on 11 June 2004 and began the excavation. The search recovered possible human remains, personal effects, and aircraft wreckage. The remains were then taken to Hawaii for examination. They were identified in late March 2005 as those of Robert C. Snoddy. His sister, Ruth Boss, commented, "It's nice to finally bring him home." She intends to have her brother buried in the cemetery where their parents have been laid to rest.

5

ARCWs and SAFE Areas

Fifth Air Force radar plots had shown twenty of the "day-only" fighters rising up to intercept Stardust 40. At approximately the same time, radar-controlled searchlights lit up the B-29, making it an easy target for the cannon-firing MiGs.

— Lt. Col. George Pittman, 581st Air Resupply Squadron commander, on the loss of one of the unit's B-29s

During World War II, specialized U.S. Army Air Forces squadrons dropped agents and supplies into occupied Europe. The squadrons were called "carpetbaggers," and operated black-painted B-24s on solo missions over Nazi Germany. With the end of the war, these units were demobilized. In the late 1940s, with World War III looming over Berlin, there was again a need for similar units. Should hostilities break out, special forces troops would have to be dropped into Soviet-occupied Europe and the USSR on intelligence and sabotage missions. The CIA, or, as the later official history put it, "an agency outside the Department of Defense," requested in 1949 that the secretary of defense "provide support services similar to the type that provided covert airlift operations during World War II." The request gained the support of the National Security Council and the Joint Chiefs of Staff.

The Air Resupply and Communications Service

On 5 January 1951, the Air Force's Military Air Transport Service (MATS) was assigned responsibility for organizing, training, and equipping the special operations wings. For security purposes, these were given the bland title of "Air Resupply and Communications Wing" (ARCW). The Air Resupply and Communications Service (ARCS) was established on 23 February 1951, at Andrews Air Force Base outside Washington, D.C., to serve as the headquarters.

The 580th ARCW, the first special operations wing, was activated on 15 March 1951 at Mountain Home AFB, Idaho. When the advance party arrived at the base, they discovered that the abandoned maintenance buildings and barracks were filled to their ceilings with tumbleweeds. There were also shortages of tools, printing machines for leaflets, and radios. Despite the squalid conditions at the base, the wartime pressure meant that the second special operations wing, the 581st ARCW, was activated at Mountain Home AFB three months later.

The B-29 was the only aircraft able to drop rangers and their supplies into the USSR. The aircraft had a range of four thousand nautical miles, a minimum payload of four thousand pounds, and the ability to fly low-level, long-range missions. A number of B-29s in storage at Robins AFB in Georgia were modified. This included removing all of the guns except those in the tail turret. A hole in the fuselage was added where the aft belly turret had been, to allow the rangers to be dropped. The racks in the two bomb bays were modified to carry supply bundles. The B-29s were also fitted with obstruction warning radar. This would warn the pilot to pull up to avoid hitting the ground.

Even with these modifications, the B-29 was not an ideal aircraft for the ARCW missions. Designed as a high-speed, high-altitude day bomber, the B-29 would now have to make low-level flights at night. The B-29 had limited maneuverability at low speeds, while at parachute drop speeds it would be close to stalling.

Each ARCW had twelve of the reconditioned B-29s. There were also four C-119 cargo aircraft and four SA-16 amphibians attached to each unit. These lacked the range and payload of the B-29s, but the C-119s could land on rough forward airstrips, while the SA-16s could operate from the open ocean. The 581st ARCW was also equipped with four H-19 helicopters, for agent infiltrations and recovery.

Each ARCW also had a self-contained psychological warfare unit whose personnel underwent extensive training. The first stage was four months at

Georgetown University's Institute of Language and Linguistics near Washington, D.C. A second stage, at Mountain Home AFB, covered practical applications of the theoretical concepts taught at Georgetown. Stage three involved advanced language, intelligence, or guerrilla training, depending on the individual's final duty assignment. In all, the training covered international relations, local cultures, psychology, geography, languages, communications, and propaganda techniques. (One of the 555 officers who completed this demanding course was William Peter Blatty, later known for his novel *The Exorcist*—and the movie adaptation of it.)

Supporting the psychological warfare unit were several other groups. The air material assembly squadron packaged weapons and food for drops by the B-29s. A holding and briefing squadron prepared personnel being dropped behind enemy lines, while a communications squadron maintained radio contact with these units in the field. Finally, the reproduction squadron could print four million leaflets per day.

The ARCWs were intended to be the Cold War counterparts of the carpetbaggers, and they faced many of the same problems. Even after the first two wings had been established, Headquarters Air Force was still unable to define their mission. A more pressing problem was that of getting experienced aircrews. Following the outbreak of the Korean War, B-29 pilots were in demand, which the B-29 Combat Crew Training Squadron (CCTS) at Randolph AFB was hard-pressed to meet.

The commander of the 580th Air Resupply Squadron noted: "Without exception all aircraft commanders received by us were recalled officers with low total time and very little experience within the last five years. The total time within this period, including the B-29 training, ran from 90 to 130 hours." Following an inspection of aircrew proficiency at Mountain Home AFB in July 1951, the ARCS commander was informed that the director of training at Randolph AFB had said that the poorest students at the B-29 CCTS were being assigned to the unit. Two months later, a flight examiner from the Chief Pilot's Division of MATS completed a similar inspection of proficiency and recommended that "the C-119 and B-29 schools be investigated to determine whether the least qualified crews are being assigned to ARCS."

To correct the lack of proficiency, ARCS asked that an aircrew training squadron be assigned to Mountain Home AFB. As an interim step, MATS headquarters assigned a single instructor pilot, 1st Lt. Robert S. Ross, to Mountain Home AFB pending a more complete evaluation. Less than two months later, however, Lieutenant Ross and six others aboard his B-29 were killed when it crashed during a night training mission. The ARCS commander later noted, "The investigation reveals that a probable cause factor was the practicing of engine failure procedures at low altitudes before the student pilot's operational ability had progressed to the point where he could cope with such practice."

Headquarters Air Force eventually decided that ARCS's request for instructors was "unfeasible," and rejected the idea that the crewmen sent to ARCS were unqualified. The reality was that Headquarters Air Force did not understand the demands placed on the new aircrews. In addition to learning to fly the large bomber below three hundred feet at night, the inexperienced aircrews also had to determine the limits of both themselves and their aircraft. Test missions lasting as long as twenty hours were flown, with the B-29 remaining below three hundred feet throughout the flight.

Even routine flying carried risks, as an SA-16 crew from the 580th ARCW discovered. The flight was a long-range night navigation mission from Mountain Home AFB to San Diego and back. This round-trip distance of about fifteen hundred miles would take about ten hours to complete. The aircraft and its six-man crew took off late on the afternoon of 24 January 1952. Darkness soon fell, and the amphibian continued toward San Diego at an altitude of eleven thousand feet. Above the desert southwest, the weather was clear and cold, with the stars shining brightly overhead.

The SA-16 was about an hour out of Barstow, California, when the tachometer for the left engine started to fluctuate and then stabilized. The pilot could find no indications of mechanical problems. Then the tachometer needle began to swing wildly and erratically. The pilot moved the mixture control to auto-rich, to burn off any lead deposits that might be fouling the spark plugs. In response, the needle vibrated violently, and the left engine's revolutions per minute began to decrease. A loud blast then shook the airplane and sent glowing carbon particles out the left engine's exhaust pipes. A second blast was followed by numerous popping sounds. The tachometer needle began to unwind, and the SA-16's speed and altitude dropped.

The pilot shut down the left engine, feathered its propellers, and increased the power on the right engine, to maintain altitude. Despite full throttle, the SA-16 began to descend at five hundred feet per minute. Ahead in the darkness waited several mountain peaks. The navigator and three other crewmen opened the airplane's rear door in preparation for a bailout. The copilot radioed a Mayday message, saying they were about to bail out north of Barstow. Before he finished, the pilot pushed the bailout bell switch, and the four crewmen in back jumped. Within moments the pilot and copilot followed them.

The six crewmen all landed safely in the desert. They had come down close together and could see the faint glow of lights in the distance. They decided to head south toward them, and after many hours of walking, during which they covered about fourteen miles, they finally arrived at the small resort of Furnace Creek in Death Valley. They reported the crash to the local authorities, but not their unit, for security reasons.

Their SA-16 met a different fate. It had flown on another twenty miles and crash-landed on the side of a mountain ridge near Towne Summit, at an elevation of 6,500 feet. The forward fuselage was destroyed, but the wings and aft fuselage were largely intact. A recovery team salvaged some of the equipment, and the wreckage was left on the rugged mountainside.

The 581st ARCW in Korea

With the Korean War about to enter its second year, the 581st ARCW received orders to report to Clark AFB in the Philippines by July 1952. The aircraft were flown across the Pacific, while the personnel arrived on the U.S. Naval Service (USNS) troop ship *General William Weigle.* The 581st ARCW commander, Col. John K. Arnold Jr., flew to Tokyo to brief Far East Air Force (FEAF) staff on the unit. From these meetings, an operational plan emerged. Four of the twelve B-29s would be sent on a sixty-day rotation with the 91st Strategic

Reconnaissance Wing, based at Yokoto Air Base, Japan. Each crew would fly every four days, dropping leaflets over North Korea and China, and complete fifteen tactical missions before rotating back to Clark AFB.

The unit's SA-16 amphibians and H-19 helicopters were to conduct agent operations. Two of the four SA-16s and their crews were sent on extended temporary duty to Seoul City Airport to support B Flight. These aircraft were painted black, like B Flight's B-26s. All four of the 581st ARCW's H-19 helicopters were stationed with the 2157th Air Rescue Squadron (ARS), also at the Seoul City Airport. The amphibians and helicopters also had the secondary mission of providing search and rescue for downed U.S. pilots.

Attaching the B-29s, SA-16s, and H-19s to existing operational units gave the 581st ARCW cover for its secret activities. For the 3rd Air Rescue Group (ARG), however, the presence of the newcomers took some adjustment. The 3rd ARG commander objected to the night missions planned for the 581st H-19s. He told Lt. Col. George Pittman, the 581st Air Resupply Squadron commander, "helicopter flying at night is too dangerous." Colonel Pittman was equally blunt, reminding him that the 3rd ARG was responsible for providing maintenance and living arrangements for the 581st crews. As for the rest of their activities, "It's none of your business, don't worry about what we're doing." The 2157th ARS commander ordered the "rescue" markings removed from the 581st's H-19s. The 581st helicopter crews thought that the rescue pilots did not want the North Koreans mistaking their aircraft for those of the covert unit. Eventually, the 581st H-19s would, like their SA-16s, be painted black overall.

The 581st helicopter pilots had to be adaptive too. When they arrived in Korea, they did not have any helicopters or any idea of their mission. When the pilots asked Fifth Air Force staff officers for both their helicopters and mission, they were told that the 581st did not exist. By October 1952, the Helicopter Flight had four new H-19s, six pilots, one NCO, and twelve airmen. They also now learned that their mission was to infiltrate agents into North Korea, at night and at low altitude to escape radar detection. Their initial experimental agent insertion sorties into North Korea were made between 27 and 29 December 1952.

The Helicopter Flight usually operated from Cho-do Island, ten miles off the North Korean coast, but some sixty miles north of the front lines. The H-19s would fly to Cho-do in daylight, and the crew would receive the final mission briefing, then get a few hours' sleep until nightfall. The tradition of confused lines of authority for covert actions in Korea continued with the 581st. Although the 581st was assigned to the 3rd ARG, the helicopter crews took their orders from B Flight, except when Fifth Air Force Intelligence directly assigned them a mission.

With darkness to hide their approach, the H-19 took off and flew just above the waves to the drop-off point on the North Korean coast, under total radio silence. The North Koreans tried to down the H-19s. 2nd Lt. Robert Sullivan recalled one particular night-insertion mission. His helicopter, call sign Treefrog 33, was heading north along the coast. The crew heard "Kodak," which was the U.S. radar station on Cho-do ask, "Treefrog 33, how many treefrogs are out there?" The crew maintained radio silence, and Kodak then called, "Treefrog 33, I am painting five, repeat five, slow-moving targets near your vicinity." The H-19 avoided the North Korean interception attempt, turned out to sea, and returned to Cho-do.

The 581st Helicopter Flight logged nearly a thousand hours in Korea. This included both the agent missions and air rescue flights to pick up downed pilots, all without a single accident, combat loss, or fatality. They had survived low-level night flying, North Korean ground fire, air-to-air interception, and ambush attempts on the ground. One of the unit's B-29 crews, however, would not be so lucky.

The Loss of Stardust 40

On the night of 12 February 1953, a 581st ARCW B-29, call sign Stardust 40, was to make leaflet drops over target areas in northwestern Korea. In addition to the regular twelve-man crew, the 581st ARCW commander, Colonel Arnold, and the operations officer of the 91st Strategic Reconnaissance Squadron, Maj. William H. Baumer, were aboard the B-29. The mission was routine until Stardust 40 neared its final target area, about fifteen miles south of the Yalu

River, at 11:30 P.M. The aircraft was flying at twenty-two thousand feet when it was intercepted by twelve MiG-15 jet fighters and simultaneously illuminated with radar-controlled searchlights. Within seconds, three of the B-29's four engines were on fire, and the crew had to bail out.

Lt. Wallace L. Brown, the aircraft's pilot, later remarked, "We landed safely in North Korean territory... [but] we were scattered all over the countryside." The B-29 crewmen were rounded up by the local militia the following day and turned over to Chinese troops. The unusual circumstances of Stardust 40's loss—the coordinated use of massed MiG-15s and searchlights, a technique not used before or after, and the presence of both Colonel Arnold and Major Baumer aboard the B-29—suggested this was a deliberate ambush. Nine days after the B-29 was reported missing, Peking Radio announced that eleven crewmen from the aircraft had been captured.

Both the Chinese and the Soviets were quick to realize the importance of their prisoners. Semyon D. Ignatyev, the head of the MGB, sent a report to senior Soviet officials on 29 January 1953 about their capture. It read:

I am reporting that, according to the report from the MGB USSR adviser in China, 9 crewmembers [sic] of an aircraft from the 91st Reconnaissance Detachment, American Strategic Aviation, which was shot down in the area of Andun on 12 Jan 53, were taken prisoner. The chief of the communication services and supply, Colonel Arnold, and the staff officer of operational reconnaissance service, 91st Detachment, Major Baumer (last names were given in Chinese transcription), were also on the aircraft. On the instructions of the TsK Communist Party of China, they will be sent to Peking and subjected to interrogation.

The Minister of Public Security of China, having reported on 27 Jan 53 to our advisor on this decision of the TsK KPK, requested that our advisor help the Chinese investigators organize the interrogation of the prisoners of war and check their work.

The MGB USSR advisor was ordered by us to render such help.

The interrogations of the ARCW B-29 crewmen were described as involving "more brutality, tricks, and contrivances" than those of any other U.S. prisoners during the Korean War. Colonel Arnold confessed, "I was in a state that I would classify as a complete nervous breakdown." The interrogations and brutal treatment of the B-29 crewmen continued even after the 27 July 1953 armistice ending the Korean War.

The eleven airmen, along with John T. Downey and Richard Fecteau, were taken before a Chinese military tribunal on 22 November 1954 to face charges of spying. Colonel Arnold received ten years; Major Baumer received eight years; Capt. Eugene J. Vaadi received six years; and Capt. Elmer F. Llewellyn and Lt. Wallace L. Brown were each sentenced to five years. The rest of the crew—Lt. John W. Buck, Sgt. Howard W. Brown, and Airmen Harry M. Benjamin Jr., John W. Thompson, Steve E. Kiba Jr., and Daniel C. Schmidt— each received four-year sentences. At the same show trial, Downey was sentenced to life, Fecteau got twenty years, and nine Nationalist Chinese accused of working for the United States were sentenced to penalties ranging up to death. A Peking Radio broadcast the following day said that the Americans had been working for the CIA, and that all had "admitted the crimes committed by them."

The State Department issued "the strongest possible protest" over the sentences, while the Department of Defense said the charges were "utterly false." President Dwight D. Eisenhower, in a telephone call to the mother of Major Baumer, said that the United States would do everything "humanly possible within peaceful means" to gain their release. The B-29 crew's situation was not unique. Despite the truce in Korea, the Chinese continued to hold U.S. airmen who had been shot down over China, as well as U.S. civilians captured during the civil war. At the same time, about one hundred Chinese scientists and students who wanted to return to the mainland were being kept in the United States, as they had technical training of military value. The United States and Communist China held talks in Geneva on the issue of prisoner reparations in June 1954, but these broke down after only four meetings.

The Chinese continued to link the B-29 crew to the espionage activities of Downey and Fecteau. Chinese Premier Chou En-lai told the U.N. secretary general on 8 February 1955:

According to material in our possession, the 581st air wing is a special operations wing with the exclusive task of carrying out operations for the Central Intelligence Agency. The wing works under cover of psychological warfare, such as leaflet operations [but] . . . its special task is to send agents and supplies to agents. . . .

On Arnold's aircraft, one person [Airman 2nd Class Harry M. Benjamin Jr.] was in charge of parachutes. The presence of this man in the crew is unusual. Benjamin had received special training at Fort Benning, Georgia, which was the same special kind of training as that given Downey and Fecteau. This fact proves that the persons involved in the two cases received the same training from the same institution.

Despite Chou's hard-line attitude, there was movement on the issue of detained Chinese nationals. The Chinese released four captured U.S. airmen on 30 May 1955. (None was from the ARCW B-29 crew.) In June, Eisenhower said he was willing to send the Chinese back. The restraining orders on all but a few dozen of the Chinese nationals were soon dropped. On 11 July, the U.S. government told the Chinese that it wanted to resume the talks in Geneva.

On 4 August 1955, the Chinese released the eleven crew members of Stardust 40 in Hong Kong. They showed the effects of their long imprisonment and torture. Major Baumer had to walk on crutches when he and the others arrived in Hawaii. The U.S. Air Force and the CIA subsequently debriefed these eleven, the last prisoners of the Korean War. The Chinese also got what they wanted: ninety-four scientists who had been educated in the United States. These repatriated scientists made up nearly half of the key personnel who turned China into a nuclear power.

ARCWs in the Middle East and Europe

While the 581st ARCW was seeing action in Korea, the other two special operations wings were deployed to their overseas bases. Originally, the 580th ARCW was scheduled to be the first unit to go overseas. In November 1951, the 580th ARCW received its deployment orders to Wheelus Air Base in Libya, and Col. John R. Kane was named the new wing commander. "Killer" Kane, as he was known, had been awarded the Medal of Honor for his actions during the low-level bombing raid on the Ploesti oil refineries in Rumania.

By early December the move was under way. Then, abruptly, the deployment was canceled. The wing was ordered back to Mountain Home AFB; the single reason given was "political unrest in North Africa." The unit history noted, "the morale of the troops took a sharp drop at the word of the return, because—in the minds of most of the personnel—Mountain Home in the winter was not the most desirable place to be." It has been suggested that the exposure of Kim Philby as a Soviet spy was the real reason for the change in plan. He had been briefed on the ARCWs and their involvement with the CIA. There is also the belief that Philby's information was used in the ambush of Stardust 40.

It was the following summer before the 580th ARCW finally deployed to Libya. The ground personnel went by troopship, sailing in July and September 1952 aboard the USNS *General R. E. Callen* and the USNS *General Hodges*. The B-29s left Westover AFB, made a refueling stop in the Azores, and then flew on to Wheelus Air Base. The shorter range C-119s and SA-19s had to make additional stops, flying from Westover to Iceland, England, and Italy before the final leg over the Mediterranean Sea to Libya.

The quarters that awaited them in the North African desert were not an improvement over those left behind at Mountain Home. The first indication was the entrance to the unit's section at Wheelus, which was marked by a crudely painted sign saying "Main Gate 580 ARC Wing" nailed to a palm tree. The early living quarters, dubbed "Garden City," consisted of makeshift huts with wooden walls, wire mesh windows, and tent roofs. It took several more months before better accommodations were ready.

While the unit's personnel were settling into their new home, Colonel Kane began an intensive training program. During the Ploesti raid in 1943, formations of B-24 bombers had flown to and from the targets at only five hundred feet. Kane was determined to go this one better. On training flights over the Mediterranean Sea, the B-29 crews learned the true meaning of "low level." Pilots later described flying so low that the aircraft actually raised rooster tails of sea spray behind them. On night training flights over the Libyan Desert, the B-29s flew at five hundred feet, their crews relying on the obstruction warning radar. Such training took a toll. On 15 January 1954, one of the 580th ARCW's B-29s flew into the desert floor.

The 580th ARCW was to provide support for the soldiers of the 10th Special Forces Group (Airborne), who were to undertake a wide range of unconventional warfare behind enemy lines, including conducting raids and sabotage, organizing resistance groups, collecting intelligence, and assisting with the escape and evasion of downed U.S. pilots. These activities were more akin to those of the OSS rather than traditional Army ranger units. Not surprisingly, their training, organization, and concepts were based on those of the OSS.

The establishment of the Special Forces faced resistance within the regular Army and from the Air Force and CIA. On 15 January 1951, Brig. Gen. Robert A. McClure succeeded in establishing the Office of the Chief of Psychological Warfare as a special staff within the Department of the Army. In doing so, he had overcome Army officers who viewed guerrilla and psychological warfare as having little importance and were also suspicious of elite units, seeing them as drawing off skilled manpower needed in regular units. The Army's future, as they saw it, was in push button warfare and battlefield nuclear weapons.

In May 1951, General McClure asked the Air Force director of operations to reassign "the special air wings being organized to support CIA activities in Korea . . . for use by [Army] psychological warfare." He soon discovered that the Air Force had their own plans to take a leading role in guerrilla operations, while the CIA was already undertaking such operations within the Soviet bloc.

The Army, Air Force, and CIA proposals were submitted to the JCS in early 1952. The JCS decided that the Department of Defense, rather than the CIA, should have wartime responsibility for organizing guerrilla operations. (The CIA retained peacetime covert activities.) Because the Army was responsible for ground combat activities, it was given the job of organizing the units. Army Chief of Staff J. Lawton Collins was able to convince President Eisenhower to give his approval to establish the Special Forces.

In November 1953, the 10th Special Forces Group was shipped to the Bavarian alpine town of Bad Tolz. In addition to field training in West Germany, using local civilians, police, and U.S. Army units, the "Green Berets," as they were called for their distinctive (and, as yet, unauthorized headgear), also were deployed to Libya for exercises with the 580th. These involved low-level parachute drops and desert survival, weapons, and demolitions training. For drop exercises, the Green Berets would ride in the B-29's bomb bay. Over the drop zone, the B-29 would climb to a thousand feet, and the Green Berets would make static line jumps.

The 10th Special Forces Group also worked with the third special operations unit. The 582nd ARCW was activated on 24 September 1952, at Mountain Home AFB, under the command of Col. Robert W. Fish. (He had been a member of the carpetbaggers during World War II.) As their training began, the special operations units underwent major cutbacks. The original plan was for seven ARCWs. This was soon cut to four wings, and then to three. On 8 September 1953, all three units were reduced from wings and renamed Air Resupply Groups. The units lost their reproduction, holding and briefing, and communications squadrons, reducing their personnel by half, from twelve hundred to merely six hundred officers and airmen. The ARCS headquarters was also shut down.

This cutback came even as the units' support of Green Beret training was being increased. During the same time that the 582nd was reduced to a group, it was supporting "Operation Cleo," a massive unconventional warfare exercise carried out in the Chattahoochee National Forest in Georgia. The Green Berets played the role of the guerrillas, while civilians living in the area acted as their support organization, providing live and dead letter drops, safe houses, an escape and evasion network, and intelligence on the "aggressor forces." Local police and a Georgia Army National Guard military police unit played the role of the aggressors. The 582nd ARG's B-29s, SA-16s, and C-119s dropped more than six hundred parachutists and some three hundred supply containers.

In February 1954, the 582nd ARG made its deployment to Royal Air Force (RAF) Molesworth in England. The group provided the bulk of the air support for the 10th Special Forces Group. Night missions were the norm, with amphibious exercises carried out using the SA-16s. Despite the need for support by the Green Berets, it was clear that the ARGs' days were numbered.

The first to go was the 581st. In October 1954, it had left Clark AFB and moved to Okinawa. Four months later, the 581st ARG lost a B-29 on a low-level flight when it struck a hill on the south end of the island. In September 1955, a second B-29 was lost on an over-water training mission. Some debris was found, but no cause could be determined. The number of qualified aircrews dwindled, and during the summer of 1956, most of the unit's aircraft were ordered transferred to other units. In September 1956, the 581st was officially deactivated.

The other two ARGs were soon to follow. Headquarters Seventeenth Air Force issued an order on 12 October 1956 to deactivate the 580th ARG. The aircraft and most of its personnel were reassigned to other units. Six days later, the Third Air Force issued a similar order deactivating the 582nd ARG. There still remained the question of who would provide support to the 10th Special Forces Group in Europe and 1st Special Forces Group, which was to be established in Okinawa the following year.

Shortly before the 581st ARG was phased out, its remaining C-119s and SA-16s were transferred to the 322nd Troop Carrier Squadron (Medium) (Special), based on Okinawa. The same story occurred at RAF Molesworth. A month before the 582nd ARG was deactivated, a new unit, the 42nd Troop Carrier Squadron (Medium) (Special), was activated at the base. It also took over the 582nd's aircraft.

In 1955, the year before the Air Force ARGs were deactivated, the Air National Guard in California, West Virginia, Maryland, and Rhode Island had each established ARG units. They initially used C-46s, but these were replaced with black-painted SA-16s. Publicly, the Rhode Island Air National Guard explained that the ARG's mission was to provide "air transportation for airborne forces" and "long-range movement of personnel." A briefing for Rhode Island's adjutant general was more direct, if no more informative: "The mission of this unit is classified and will be explained in detail at a later date."

The Air National Guard ARG pilots performed the same missions as those of their active duty counterparts—low-level, single-aircraft missions, both day and night, into remote airfields. Active duty ARG personnel and the CIA initially conducted the training of the Air National Guard personnel. Ironically, from the mid-1950s to the mid-1960s, the bulk of Air Force expertise in special operations was with these Air National Guard units.

The rise and fall of the Air Force special operations wings in the 1950s was a reflection of the changes in military strategy. President Eisenhower relied on "Massive Retaliation" to deter a Soviet attack. In one attack plan, nuclear weapons with a total yield of one hundred megatons were to be launched against targets in and around Moscow. Of this, the Strategic Air Command (SAC) estimated that some sixty-six megatons would actually reach their targets. Moscow would be hit, in order, by intermediate range ballistic missiles launched from Western Europe, submarine-launched missiles, air-to-surface missiles, intercontinental ballistic missiles launched from the United States, and, finally, SAC bombers. Similar destruction would be inflicted on other Soviet, Eastern Europe, and Chinese targets.

Given this, it seemed pointless to maintain Air Force units to support guerrilla warfare when large areas of the Soviet landmass would be reduced to a radioactive wasteland within days of the outbreak of a war. However, although this focus on nuclear weapons meant the ARGs were downgraded, it also resulted in the formation of another covert Air Force unit.

Escape and Evasion in World War II, Korea, and the USSR

During World War II, only a small percentage of downed aircrews was ever able to reach friendly lines. Between August 1943 and March 1944, RAF Bomber Command made nineteen raids on Berlin. As a result, 2,690 crewmen were killed and 987 were captured, but only 34 men were able to return to England. The techniques used by evaders varied widely. RAF crewmen were told to seek help at large houses in France owned by the professional classes, as they were less likely to be collaborators. The French resistance was another possibility. Other downed crewmen avoided all human contact, moving only at night and hiding by day.

The war in Korea proved a very different situation. A downed pilot could not blend into the local Asian population. Bailing out over the North Korean interior meant near-certain capture. The only hope for a downed crewman was rescue by a partisan unit, and there was still the problem of getting back to friendly lines.

For pilot pickups deep inside North Korea, the All America recovery system was introduced in late 1952. C-47s (and possibly B-26s) operated by B Flight were fitted with the winch. The poles, ropes, and harnesses were packed in a fifty-pound container that could be dropped by either the recovery airplane or a fighter. The equipment was officially referred to as "Personnel Pick-up Ground Station" (and unofficially as the "snatch system"). It was demonstrated to the pilots at a number of fighter bases in South Korea. Soon after, in November 1952, Fifth Air Force Headquarters requested that all aircrews that operated north of the bomb line be instructed in its use.

B Flight used the All America system twice during early 1953. The first attempt failed when the downed crewman was captured before the pickup aircraft could reach the crash site. The second was made on 24 May and involved five B-29 crewmen shot down the previous January. The airmen were believed to have been found by a partisan group, who had protected them for four months. The C-47 reached the area at dawn, and its crew made radio contact with the B-29's pilot, 1st Lt. Gilbert L. Ashley, who assured them that the area was clear of enemy troops. The C-47's pilot, Maj. David M. Taylor, ordered the recovery package dropped. When Ashley radioed that the polls were rigged, Major Taylor began the first pickup pass.

Taylor remembered thinking as he made his approach: "It just didn't look right to me. . . . I called Ashley on the final seconds of the approach and told him, 'If there's anything wrong, now's your chance to tell me.'" Lieutenant Ashley replied, "Everything is fine." As the C-47 reached the pickup point, its underside was riddled by ground fire. The poles were actually .50-caliber machine guns. The C-47 was able to land back at its base despite the damage.

The partisans and B-29 crewmen had all been captured, and Lieutenant Ashley had been forced by his Communist captors to say it was safe to make the pickup. There was an unusual postscript to the incident. Several days later, Major Taylor was flying in the same area when he again established radio contact with the B-29 crewmen. He was able to determine their identities using the information provided by U.S. intelligence. More surprising, they acted as if nothing unusual had happened during the previous pickup attempt. The

Communists were apparently still trying to use them as bait to lure another C-47 rescue plane into an ambush. This radio message was the last that anyone ever heard from the five men. They were not among the prisoners returned after the end of the Korean War in July 1953.

As difficult as escape and evasion had been during the Korean War, aircrew rescue from inside the USSR was a near-impossible task. The issue was critical because many targets inside the USSR would be at the bomber's extreme range. Even with mid-air refueling and forward bases, the aircraft might not have enough fuel to reach neutral airspace. The issue of such one-way missions was first discussed at the August 1947 meeting of the Aircraft and Weapons Board. Because of the lack of range in existing and proposed bombers, and the cost and limited number of A-bombs available, Maj. Gen. Earl Partridge thought that one-way missions would be acceptable. He said that the best thing would be to "expend the crew, expend the bomb, expend the airplane all at once. Kiss them goodbye and let them go." The only possible solution offered was by the representative of the Air University, who noted that the USSR had large remote areas where crew pickups might be made.

The problem of escape and evasion from the USSR was very much on the mind of SAC's new commander, Gen. Curtis E. LeMay. Despite his stern exterior, LeMay cared about the well-being of SAC's personnel. The most valuable of these were the combat aircrews, and he wanted both to keep them out of enemy hands and to return them to duty if they were downed. OPC official Frank Lindsay was summoned to SAC headquarters at Offutt AFB in Omaha. General LeMay pounded on his desk and demanded to know how Lindsay planned to rescue SAC crewmen behind the Iron Curtain. Although Lindsay participated in setting up "stay-behind" groups in Western Europe to assist downed pilots, it was SAC that took the lead.

The 8th Air Rescue Group

SAC headquarters issued General Order Number 55 on 23 August 1950. It directed that the 8th ARS be reactivated and assigned to the 3902nd Air Base Wing at Camp Carson in Colorado, where SAC then had its survival school. The

8th ARS was to rescue downed U.S. bomber crews by landing at improvised airstrips deep inside the Soviet Union.

Initially, the 8th ARS had but a few C-47 transports, but it was soon caught up in a struggle between the Air Rescue Service and SAC. The Air Rescue Service argued that the mission of the 8th ARS should be part of its responsibility. Finally, the inspector general of the Air Force held an operational readiness test to decide the issue. The Air Rescue Service matched the 14th ARG versus SAC's 8th ARS. When the test was complete, the Air Rescue Service had shown it could handle the SAC aircrew recovery mission.

As a result, the squadron was transferred from SAC to the Air Rescue Service and was expanded, becoming the 8th ARG on 1 September 1954. The group headquarters was at the survival school at Stead AFB, located about ten miles north of Reno, Nevada, which was also home base for the unit's 61st and 62nd ARSs. Two other squadrons, the 63rd and 64th, were at Norton AFB, in San Bernardino, California. The group's first commander was Col. Stanley I. Hand.

The first step in the Strategic Aircrew Recovery Program (SARP) was the selection of "SAFE" areas, which stood for "Selected Areas for Evasion." These were locations within the USSR that had no roads or towns, were located away from any targets, and were outside the projected fallout from nuclear strikes. If a bomber was low on fuel, or had been damaged and could not reach friendly airspace, the crew was to head for the nearest SAFE area and bail out.

Each crewman carried an E-1 escape and evasion kit, which weighed forty-one pounds. It was packed with food, a .22-caliber survival rifle, and other supplies. Each bomber also carried an RS-6 radio along with several URC-4 VHF/UHF handheld transceivers. The RS-6 was the state-of-the-art in mid-1950s' electronic technology. Developed by Motorola, it used "peanut" vacuum tubes for compactness. It was packaged in four small metal boxes and had a range in excess of three thousand miles. The URC-4 transceivers could send and receive voice communications, as well as a homing signal. Both were powered by special batteries that could operate continuously for ten hours. These radios would be the downed crew's link with the 8th ARG.

Once the crew had found a relatively secure hiding place, they would determine their approximate location using survival maps and ground navigation techniques. They would then encode this using a "one-time-pad," which was sheets of random numbers added to the basic code. If each sheet was used only once, the message was unbreakable. The crew would then transmit their special call sign and the coded message, using the RS-6's telegraph key. If the message was successfully picked up and decoded, a reply would be sent, in which the crew would be asked security checks to ensure they were not under enemy control. When the crew had responded to this message, they would be told to stand by for another message within twenty-four hours. Once the 8th ARG was certain the messages were valid, the crew would be told when to expect a pickup.

The 8th ARG's four squadrons operated about sixty-six SC-47 transports. (The "S" stood for "search.") The SC-47s had been extensively modified. On the nose of the aircraft was the antenna for the ARA-25 receiver. This picked up the homing beacon signals from the URC-4. Internally, the SC-47s had been fitted with two large fuel tanks, placed on either side of a narrow central aisle. The passenger seats had been stripped out to make room and to save weight. To withstand the shock of the full-stall landing, pins that had been especially hardened replaced the standard landing gear link pins. The tires were also underinflated to give better traction. Once the rescued crewmen were aboard, a short-field takeoff would be made using two JATO rockets. The flight to and from the improvised landing strip would be made at below-treetop altitude, to avoid Soviet air defenses.

From the exterior, there was little to distinguish the 8th ARG's aircraft from other C-47s. To protect the classified SARP efforts, the group's personnel were told simply to say that they were assigned to an air rescue squadron, which conducted normal search activities. Their mission, however, required extensive training in low-level flight, night flying, and mountain flying, as well as landing and taking off from crude, improvised strips. The two squadrons at Stead AFB flew their missions in the mountains near the base. Their SC-47s also made low-level flights in the vicinity of Truckee and other towns in the Sierra foothills. The Norton AFB squadrons had the advantage that nearby were the San Jacinto and San Gabriel mountain ranges, which rose to elevations of nearly twelve thousand feet. Low-level flights were conducted in the Mojave Desert to the east. The squadrons would also occasionally make airdrops to Boy Scout troops.

The demanding training took a toll. During an early morning mission in August 1955, Maj. Charles F. Dunn and his six-man crew were killed when their SC-47 hit a mountain outside Hawthorne, Nevada. About a month later, on 24 September, Lt. Thomas Kelly and his crew died in a crash near Cheyenne, Wyoming.

Just as the SC-47 crews had to train to undertake the SARP missions, so too did the SAC crews in order to correctly carry out all the tasks required for a successful recovery. Even holding the URC-4 the wrong way could prevent the signal from being received by the SC-47s. The 1875th Aircraft Airways and Communications Service squadron conducted training in the proper use of the different radios and the one-time pads. Attached to the 8th ARG, this unit's wartime role was to pick up the messages sent by the downed aircrews. The unit could deploy anywhere in the world on six hours' notice should war seem imminent.

The SAC crews were also trained in the selection of the improvised landing strips the SC-47s would use. To judge whether the ground was hard enough to bear the airplane's weight, the aircrews were told to "carry a man on your back, piggy-back fashion, and walk up and down the desired runway area and if you don't sink in the dirt any deeper than your ankles the SC-47 can land and take off from the strip." The length of the runway had to be determined based on the altitude of the area. The SC-47 crew would be guided to the general area by the URC-4's homing signal. Once the SAC crewmen saw the airplane, they would switch to voice transmissions and direct the SC-47 to the landing strip. At this point, about one minute before touchdown, the crew would hurriedly mark the landing strip, using cloth torn from their parachutes. This was not done beforehand to prevent the airstrip from being detected. The SC-47 pilot would make the final judgment as to whether the strip was suitable.

Armageddon Airlines

In addition to their normal training flights, one of the 8th ARG's squadrons would undertake extensive simulated rescue missions with SAC combat crews every month. The first such exercise was Operation Meadowlark, which was conducted between 9 and 16 December 1954. Among the SAC crews involved in the exercise was an RB-36 crew based at Ellsworth AFB. This first exercise was not a full dress rehearsal of the SARP mission. The "bailout" location for the crew was an old emergency dirt landing strip near the small town of Shamrock, Texas. There was an old lean-to structure at the strip, but the crew made use of a National Guard Armory a short distance down the road.

An intelligence officer had traveled with the RB-36 crew, and he gave them a daily class. The crew also conducted escape and evasion hikes and even some target practice. The critical activities were the radio sessions. The crew rigged the antenna on the armory roof, and took turns cranking a generator to power the radio. (Apparently, the RS-6 radio was not yet available.) Once everyone had taken a turn on the generator and, in the process, gained an appreciation of the effort needed to produce electricity, they plugged the radio into a wall socket. The radio procedures were carried out correctly, and the pickup was scheduled. At least one crew did not follow the proper procedures; they were left out in a remote area for three extra days.

Two SC-47s were sent at different times to pick up the RB-36 crew. Several minutes before the scheduled pickup time, the crew positioned itself at the takeoff end of the strip and waited. Then, as one of them recalled, "We could hear the distant unmistakable sweet sound of two Pratt and Whitney R-1830 engines." The SC-47 appeared low overhead, and the crew completed the final authentication checks. The SC-47 pilot dropped the airplane's wheels and flaps and made a short-field landing. As the airplane slowed, the pilot stood on the right brake and advanced the left engine's throttle, turning it around for a fast taxi back to the takeoff end, where the crew waited.

The SC-47 turned around and came to a full stop. The cargo doors immediately opened, and the crew tossed out the JATO bottles and then jumped down. While they were attaching the JATO bottles to the SC-47's underside, the RB-36 crew threw their gear aboard and climbed in as fast as they could. To minimize the chance of being caught on the ground, the SC-47 had to be ready to take off in three minutes. The briefing put it more simply: "If you aren't on board when the ground crew climbs into the aircraft, the doors will be closed behind them and you're out of luck." The RB-36 crew sat on the floor and found something to hang on to.

The cargo doors were slammed shut and locked, and the two engines were run up to full power. The pilot then released the brakes, and the SC-47 began its takeoff roll. As it bounced down the dirt strip, the JATO bottles were fired, and the airplane leaped into the air. The brief acceleration ended as the rockets burned out.

The SC-47 leveled out at low altitude and began a simulated flight back to a friendly base. The SC-47 flew northwest across the Texas panhandle, then into New Mexico. The aircraft penetrated the Albuquerque Air Defense Identification Zone (ADIZ) in a test of the SC-47's ability to evade detection, which was done by flying at very low altitude along a zigzag course, using hills and valleys to hide the aircraft from radar.

The flight lasted several hours, so to fill the time, the RB-36 crew began playing Hearts soon after the takeoff. As he sat on the floor, one of the crewmen being dealt the cards glanced out a window. He was rather surprised to see a windmill pass by, higher than the airplane. He folded his hand and went to the cockpit to watch the rest of the flight. The SC-47 stampeded several herd of horses and cattle, and successfully evaded detection in the ADIZ. After passing Truth or Consequences, New Mexico, the SC-47 climbed to a normal altitude and set course for Biggs AFB. After landing, the RB-36 crew underwent an intelligence debriefing, and then had a shower, a meal, and finally a good night's sleep.

Operation Meadowlark was the first in a series of such exercises conducted over the next several years. These included Round Up, Meadowlark II, and Chuckwagon. A pilot might go through several SARP exercises during his time with SAC. As for SARP itself, one of the participants in Operation Meadowlark wrote later, "I'm sure that if we had ever gone to war in the [RB-36] and gone down in enemy territory, our confidence would have been fairly high that a couple of round P[ratt] & W[hitney]'s would come, pulling a C-47 to our rescue."

Although the SC-47 crews of the 8th ARG continued to fly their monthly rotation exercises, by the late 1950s the Air Rescue Service was in the process of reorganization. Under an Air Rescue Service directive published on 25 September 1958, its units were to support peacetime air operations. Wartime rescue operations were to be dictated by the capabilities of these peacetime efforts. The directive also noted, "No special units or specially designed aircraft will be provided for the sole purpose of wartime search and rescue."

In line with the new directive, the 8th ARG was deactivated, and its aircraft and personnel were reassigned. This also brought an end to a wartime role for the Air Rescue Service. Because of this, when combat rescue was again required, many downed U.S. pilots would have to rely on a covert effort run by "an agency outside the Department of Defense."

III
After Stalin

6

Tinker, Tailor, Tourist, Spy

I thought I was absolutely the male version of Mata Hari.

—John Le Carre, British spy and spy novelist

In late 1952 and early 1953, the postwar purge inside the Soviet Union and Eastern Europe grew. This had now taken on an anti-Semitic tone, and Jews were purged from the government and universities, while "vigilance" against "imperialist spies" was demanded of the population. Then, on 13 January 1953, the Soviets announced the "Doctor's Plot." A group of senior physicians, many of whom were Jewish, had been arrested and charged with murdering senior Soviet officials. They had acted, the Soviets claimed, under the orders of the United States, Britain, and a "corrupt Jewish bourgeois nationalist organization." This was to be the start of a new Great Purge. For the next six weeks, the atmosphere in the Soviet bloc was of impending doom.

Then, on 4 March 1953, Radio Moscow announced that Stalin had suffered a stroke during the night of 1–2 March. Subsequent medical bulletins indicated his condition had become worse. Finally, at 6:00 A.M. on 6 March, the Soviets announced that Stalin had died the night before. The new Soviet leadership began a struggle for power and survival. Secret police chief Lavrenty P. Beria moved to consolidate his power by combining the MGB with the Ministry of the Interior (MVD) to form an enlarged MVD. He now controlled the domestic police, internal counterintelligence, foreign intelligence activities, the labor camp system, and the Soviet nuclear program.

The other members of the new Soviet leadership were threatened by Beria's growing power, and he was arrested and shot. This removed the threat of a coup by Beria, and allowed the new Soviet leaders to use him as a scapegoat for the decades of terror under Stalin. Beria's secret police empire was also soon broken up. In March 1954, the MGB was split from the MVD, downgraded from a ministry to a committee, and lost its control of the USSR's nuclear program. Now renamed the Committee of State Security, it would be known as "KGB" (the initials of the official Russian name).

The end of the Stalinist era was marked by reduced tensions. The panicky, near-wartime atmosphere of the late 1940s and early 1950s began to ease. A truce brought an end to the Korean War on 27 July 1953. There seemed to be the possibility of better relations between the East and the West. A measure of freedom began to appear within the Soviet bloc. The pressure that had set the agent and paramilitary operations in motion now faded. U.S. intelligence activities began to focus on technical collection and overhead reconnaissance. Yet, spies were still valuable sources. In the wake of Stalin's death, part of the U.S. human intelligence collection effort would rely on an improbable group of agents.

The CIA Domestic Contact Service

The roots of this activity go back to World War II, when Allied intelligence services realized that road maps, holiday snapshots, postcards, reports of travelers, and similar "open" sources could provide valuable intelligence data. When the CIA was established, it was given responsibility for overt collection of foreign intelligence within the United States. The CIA's Domestic Contact Service (DCS) conducted these activities. The DCS was established in 1948 as a non-covert section of the CIA's Office of Special Operations. The DCS approached Americans who had knowledge of potential intelligence value because of such activities as their travels, their attendance at international conferences, their work as missionaries, or their business contacts. To do this, the DCS opened offices in several major cities throughout the United States.

One early result of the DCS's work was reports on the involvement of the Soviet commercial mission, called Amtorg, with the USSR's A-bomb program.

Domestic reports provided the names of Soviet officials assigned to Amtorg who later appeared in mail intercepts as those who were directing the German atomic scientists. Some $3 million in orders from Amtorg's New York office were also later identified as being for the nuclear program. This included machinery for a complete factory to extract radium from uranium ore wastes. By the time the reports were collected, however, the Soviets had changed their procedures, and the reports were useful only as background information on the Soviet A-bomb program.

Much of the intelligence data collected focused on more routine commercial activities and political trends. Among those who provided intelligence to the DCS in its early years of operation was New Orleans businessman Clay L. Shaw. He made his first report to the DCS in December 1948 regarding efforts by the new Communist government of Czechoslovakia to lease exhibition space at the New Orleans Trade Mart. Shaw was an astute observer and businessman who spoke Spanish fluently and traveled widely in Central and South America, as well as in Europe. Over the next eight years, Shaw made thirty-three reports to the DCS, covering such subjects as currency devaluation in Peru, a proposed highway in Nicaragua, and the desire of Western European countries to trade with the Soviet bloc. His reports were invariably graded "of value" and "reliable." Like other DCS sources, Shaw was never paid, nor did he have any other involvement with the CIA beyond his reports to the DCS.

The new atmosphere following Stalin's death in 1953 resulted in expanded opportunities for the DCS. An increased number of travelers, ranging from government officials to businessmen, students, and even ordinary tourists, were visiting the USSR and other Soviet bloc countries. Many of the travel restrictions imposed on foreigners during Stalin's time were eased, although sensitive areas remained out-of-bounds. The total ban on personal contacts between Soviet citizens and Westerners was also eased. Simply speaking to a foreigner was no longer grounds for arrest. Another result of the changes in the USSR was exchanges of official delegations, which toured power stations, scientific institutions, or cultural sites and met with senior Soviet officials, scientists, and engineers.

The DCS's recruiting effort of a new source would begin with a lead from trade journals, established sources, CIA headquarters, or other government agencies. Before any action was taken, the "contact officer" would first have to match the lead against the current intelligence requirements and then familiarize himself with the organization, and, if possible, the person he would be contacting.

The contact officer made his initial approach to the president of the company if the source was commercial, or, in an academic situation, the president of the university, to ensure cooperation at the highest levels. Here the contact officer ran into his first hurtle. To make an appointment with the boss, the contact officer had to go through the boss's secretary. Her job was to keep away unwanted visitors and to screen phone calls. The contact officer gave his name, stated he was a representative of "the government," and asked to speak with her boss on a confidential matter. If she should ask questions, the contact officer said that he would explain his purpose more fully to the boss. Once the contact officer was put through, he told the boss that he was connected with "U.S. intelligence." The contact officer then briefly outlined his reasons for seeking a personal interview and asked for an appointment as early as possible.

As in more conventional situations, first impressions were important. The contact officer showed up promptly at the appointed time and dressed conservatively. Once the contact officer was ushered into the source's office, he immediately presented his CIA credentials. This was to make it clear to the source that he did not represent the IRS, the FBI, or some other law enforcement agency. If the source was a businessman, for example, his initial reaction to the DCS's approach was often fear that he was about to undergo a tax audit or antitrust suit.

The contact officer's goal was to establish an ongoing intelligence relationship with the prospective source. To do this, he had to quickly accomplish three goals—explain the intelligence mission, show the source how he or his organization could be of assistance, and assess the usefulness of the source to CIA intelligence requirements. The sequence of an interview followed an almost set pattern. First the contact officer oriented the possible source, who generally had only a meager understanding of how intelligence worked. The contact officer stressed how important it was that policy makers be fully informed about conditions around the world. The contact officer then told the source that he could make a contribution to the national security of the United States by providing information on foreign factories, research activities, or similar matters.

Having heard the contact officer's "pitch," the usual response of a potential source was to express a willingness to cooperate, but also to indicate that he failed to see how any information his organization might have was of intelligence value. The contact officer then asked questions about the company's foreign branches and affiliates, and the degree to which the home office was informed about foreign economic and financial conditions. The source soon realized his organization did have information with intelligence value.

With this realization, however, a source often became fearful that providing the CIA with this information might backfire on him. This could take the form of legal action by other government agencies, the loss of information to a competing company, or problems with a foreign government should they learn of his cooperation with the CIA. The contact officer reassured him that the source's name would never be connected with the information, it would never be turned over to another federal agency for legal action, and the information would be circulated strictly within intelligence channels and would be classified. The source was told not to be apprehensive regarding his assistance to the CIA. The contact officer also pointed out that the need for security was mutual; the source must never discuss the visit with anyone.

While all this was going on, the contact officer was assessing the source's intelligence potential. With experience, this was done quickly. If the assessment was negative, then the contact officer made a polite exit. If the assessment was positive, the contact officer explored the possibilities as completely as the source's attitude and appointment book allowed. An occupational hazard for contact officers was a source that started talking about what was "wrong with Washington." In such cases, the contact officer politely steered the conversation back to the subject at hand, creating an impression that he also was a busy man.

The initial interview was concluded with an understanding that the contact officer would probably return to further explore the company's information. If a return was actually being considered, the contact officer gave the source his calling card, which listed his name, the field office's post office box, and his unlisted office telephone number. The card did not mention the CIA. A week or ten days later, the contact officer sent a letter to the source thanking him for his assistance and mentioning that he looked forward to meeting the source again.

If the source was thought to be capable of providing valuable intelligence, a report on the interview was submitted to CIA headquarters, as was a request for a security check. The contact officer subsequently made several visits a year to a source, both to collect information and to keep the source active. An ideal source was "trained" to call the contact officer whenever he had information of interest. The scale of the DCS operations was huge. Between 1948 and 1959, more than 40,000 individuals and companies provided intelligence to the CIA on every possible field, and from every part of the world. By the mid-1970s, DCS files contained the names of some 150,000 individuals who had provided intelligence data or were considered promising sources.

Tourists in Denied Areas

The most valuable sources for the DCS were travelers who went to "denied areas," particularly to the Soviet bloc. A contact officer tried to arrange advance notification when a cleared source was going overseas. Contact officers also approached tourists and other individuals traveling to the USSR. Harry Rositzke, a CIA officer who had worked on the air-dropped agent program, wrote: "The new tourists were a global assortment. . . . There were Americans, Western Europeans, and third-world nationals. There were government officials, visiting diplomats, East-West traders, chess players, church leaders, athletes, ordinary tourists. There were port-callers, both Americans and foreign. . . . they were all volunteers."

The contact officer dealing with these tourist spies had to make a decision about their ability to handle a mission. They were inexperienced and untrained. Most of all, they had to be discreet while in denied areas. Not all met this requirement, as some business travelers were unable to resist the temptation to boast that they were getting "inside dope for the CIA." If the contact officer's judgment was favorable, the normal procedure was to remind the traveler of the general interests of the CIA, and to suggest that whatever was of interest in his specific line of work would be of intelligence interest as well.

Once the source returned from the Soviet bloc, the contact officer would arrange an interview as soon as it was mutually convenient. This posed a final difficulty. The contact officer attempted to get as much detail as possible on items of interest, including a source's verbal account, trip report, maps, photographs, and floor plans. The source, however, had to deal with the personal and business matters that had piled up in his absence. His extracurricular intelligence activities were purely voluntary, carried out without reward and at his personal risk. The contact officer's "flag waving" might not be enough for the source to neglect what he saw as more pressing requirements.

In the end, all of these efforts yielded an "information report" from the source. One such report, from a tourist who had been to Czechoslovakia in August 1956, indicated both the methods used and the range of intelligence that a tourist could provide. The text read:

During my two weeks' trip to Czechoslovakia . . . I hired a car and guide to go from Prague to Karlsbad [Karlovy Vary]. My guide, who said he was a former manager of Skoda in New York, offered to show me the U.S. balloons which had been captured in Czechoslovakia. He warned me to say I was English if anyone asked. I don't know what building we went to, but we went up some stairs and there were five balloons with all sorts of photographic equipment. No other visitors were there at the time.

From what I could tell in my two weeks, Czech popular morale is good; the standard of living seems adequate. I saw no poor-looking people. If I hadn't known, I wouldn't have thought it was a Communist country, except for the Red Star flags everywhere. A woman guide pointed out the huge Stalin monument, saying, "We hope to take it down someday, but it will cost much money." It was a little surprising to me to find the Czechs so happy, because I had been in Berlin when the Soviets were there and hostility seemed the prevailing mood.

Touring in Czechoslovakia is very pleasant. Service is excellent, food is delicious, the cities [Prague, Bratislava, and Karlovy Vary] are lovely, and everything is very clean. The hotel and restaurant personnel and the guides were most gracious and helpful.

This particular source's report was based on observations made during normal tourist sightseeing, rather than on any covert activities. The captured U.S. reconnaissance balloons he saw were in a public display similar to those organized in other Eastern European countries, the USSR, and China. The guide was showing him interesting sights and keeping him out of trouble. The source's impressions of the Czech popular mood and the economic situation were subjective, but were nonetheless those of a person who had traveled in Europe previously. The comments of the woman guide provided an insight into Czech opinion about both the USSR and its control. CIA analysts evaluated information reports from travelers, assessed the information and the sources' reliability, and combined the data to make an estimate of conditions within the Soviet bloc.

Giving a tourist agent a specific assignment, rather than simply asking for general observations, posed both security and psychological hazards and was rarely done. In effect, the tourist was being told what the United States *did not know* about the USSR. To reveal such information to an untrained individual, who faced possible capture and interrogation, was not done lightly. There was also the risk that a business traveler might become outraged at being recruited as a "spy." In addition, the contact officer had to be completely sure that the source could successfully undertake the mission, was reliable, and would not interpret the briefing as a license to embark on a cloak-and-dagger adventure.

The tourists were sometimes asked to sightsee, but not in the way normally associated with a vacation. Once the route the traveler would take within the Soviet Union was known, the CIA would assemble a list of targets for the traveler. Because the tourists' technical knowledge about nuclear energy, biological warfare, or missile technology was limited, any visual observations by the tourists were kept simple. They were asked to remember the color of the smoke coming out of a factory chimney or that of a sand pile outside a plant, for example.

If a tourist was being asked to photograph a target, he had to do much more than just avoid detection. Specific details had to be remembered. These included: the geographic location where the photo was taken, such as "300 yards SSE of the intersection of highways N30 and N12"; the date and the time taken [within five minutes]; the type of camera and focal length of lens used; the distance to the object, as well as how this was estimated; and any unusual sounds, smells, colors, smoke, or anything else that might help identify an unknown activity. In addition, complete and uncropped negatives should be provided to the analysts. These details allowed the analysts to calculate the actual size of an object.

In addition to a briefing on their mission and what observation techniques to use, the tourist agents were also warned about the physical surveillance and bugging they would be subjected to and what provocations they might encounter. Then they set off for the Soviet Union, to match wits with the KGB.

Although many of the Stalin-era controls on Westerners in the USSR had been eased, tourists in the USSR continued to be viewed as security and ideological threats to Communist control. In the 1950s, an ordinary tourist could not travel freely inside the USSR. Rather, a visa and the purchase of a preset package tour from Intourist, the Soviet tourist agency, were required. Intourist provided the guides for each group, as well as the hotels at which they stayed. Intourist hotels had a clerk, called a *dezhuranya*, on each floor. When a tourist went out, he was required to leave his room key with the clerk for safekeeping. The *dezhuranyas*, the Intourist guides, and other staff members were actually informants of the Tourist Division of the KGB's Second Chief Directorate, which was responsible for internal counterintelligence activities. Throughout the tourist's stay, he was shepherded and watched over by the KGB.

For its part, the KGB seemed to have viewed the tourists' activities with benign indifference. The KGB knew perfectly well what they were doing, but turned a half-blind eye as long as the tourists did not go too far. One professor who was found by the police photographing an off-limits military installation was handled most politely, while during 1958 and 1959, a few tourists were quietly arrested and expelled.

The tourist operations produced thousands of photos and contributed to the CIA's understanding of Soviet military and industrial activities. One example occurred in the summer of 1955. For several years, Western intelligence services had been trying to identify a number of unusual facilities outside Moscow. Each had an oddly shaped "herringbone" road network with a long, grass-covered bunker nearby. At one end of the bunker was a strange structure, variously described as a large ventilator that was rocking violently, or two large wheels at right angles that were spinning rapidly. Because of the object's shape, it was dubbed the "Yo-Yo."

Although it was suspected that the Yo-Yo was a surface-to-air missile (SAM) guidance antenna, and the road network, dubbed the "herringbone" after its shape, was the SAM launch site, this had yet to be proven. There was no solid evidence that the bunker and the herringbone were actually related; that the herringbone was a SAM site, rather than a housing area, or for crop or ammunition storage; or that the Yo-Yo was even an electronic device, as opposed to a rock crusher, as suggested by some British experts. Even the Yo-Yo's true shape and appearance were not clear from the few observations that had been made.

Then, in early August 1955, a CIA electronic analyst received a package of photos of a Yo-Yo bunker southeast of Moscow. These had been taken from several different angles, which finally revealed its true shape. Unfortunately, the make of the camera used to take the photos, the focal length of its lens, and a distance estimate were not provided. Even the negative size was not known, as there was no black edge to show whether the photos had been cropped. Without these data, no size measurements could be made.

Finally, an indicator of scale was discovered. In one of the photos, several cows were visible beyond the bunker. These were identified as Angus cows, and the CIA asked the Department of Agriculture for the average hip-to-ground height of this breed. (One is hard-pressed to think of a more unlikely item of intelligence interest.) With the measurement in hand, the process of triangulation began, and the resulting measurements were later found to be within 10 percent of the correct size. The photos, subsequent analysis, and information from a captured German scientist confirmed that the Yo-Yo was guidance radar used by the SA-1 SAM.

Mounted Operations

Although the tourist operations were able to provide "instant intelligence" about major cities and transport routes inside the USSR, the limitations were also clear. The capabilities and knowledge of the individuals meant that the missions had to be kept simple. The package tours closed off many areas of interest. This problem of access went even further, however. An ordinary tourist visited Red Square, museums, war memorials, and similar cultural sites. He had no opportunity to tour an electrical power plant or to meet a Soviet nuclear scientist, an aircraft designer, or a senior Communist Party official.

To collect such intelligence required "mounted operations," which took advantage of the official visitors and delegations making trips to the USSR. These groups or individual travelers were involved with educational, professional, business, or cultural exchanges. Although the travelers were still escorted by Intourist guides, they had access to people and places off-limits to ordinary tourists, and had a greater opportunity to ask questions of intelligence interest.

The first step was to screen possible candidates. Many were graduate students or professors specializing in the USSR. They usually could speak Russian and were knowledgeable about the USSR, and were thus more qualified than the ordinary tourist. Those who passed the screening were offered an all-expense-paid trip, courtesy of the CIA. Many of those approached were young and adventurous. Older, established academics were more cautious, but often just as willing to serve as agents. In other cases, the person approached was an engineer or a scientist who could provide a firsthand technical assessment.

One such mission was undertaken by William P. Lear, a designer of such electronic equipment for aircraft as automatic direction finders, autopilots, and radios. Lear's experience allowed him to answer the CIA's questions about Soviet aviation technology. In the spring of 1956, a CIA officer visited Lear's Santa Monica headquarters with photos of the Soviet's new jet airliner, the Tu-104. On the sides of the aircraft were what looked like handrails, and the CIA officer asked what they might be. Lear heard the questions, and asked the CIA officer into his office. The CIA officer asked whether Lear would be willing to find out their purpose. The flamboyant and attention-loving Lear agreed to undertake the mission.

Lear and his wife, Moya, arranged to attend the 1956 Soviet Aviation Day Air Show. Rather than traveling on an airliner, however, Lear would pilot his own Cessna 310 twin-engine light airplane into the USSR. Permission was granted, although a Soviet navigator would have to ride with them. On 26 June 1956, the Lears and their Soviet escort took off from East Berlin. After two and a half hours, the Cessna arrived at Vilna Airport in the USSR. Lear took mental notes about the facility and later reported: "[It] was just a little strip twenty-nine hundred feet long. . . . And this was one of the major airports in Russia! It had an administration building that was a rather dilapidated structure outside, but in a pretty good state of repair inside. The control tower (they let me into it) was really antiquated. . . . It had radio equipment that might have come out about 1935 or 1940 at the latest."

The Lears then flew on to the Vnukovo Airport in Moscow, where reporters covering the official visit of the U.S. Air Force Chief of Staff, Gen. Nathan Twining, met them. The general and his party had complained about the limited access they were given to Soviet aircraft. In contrast, Lear was hosted by the Soviet minister of foreign trade, Alexander Vladimlov, who put the couple up in a suite at the National Hotel. Lear took Vladimlov and three other officials for a ride over Moscow to demonstrate the Cessna's autopilot. The Soviets officials were very impressed by the device. While Lear was showing it off, his airplane drifted off its assigned altitude. The tower immediately radioed him for his position. Given the poor quality of the communications equipment he had seen, Lear was surprised that Soviet radar was so accurate.

During the socializing, the Soviets had asked Lear whether there was anything he wanted to see while in Moscow. Lear replied quite casually that he would like to see the Tu-104 airliner. While General Twining had only been allowed to poke his head inside the airplane, Andrei N. Tupolov, its designer, gave Lear a personal tour. A *Life* magazine photographer had been asking Lear and his wife whether they would pose with their Cessna. Lear asked Vladimlov whether it would be all right if the photographer could film them with the Tu-104. The trade minister agreed. As the photographer followed Lear and Tupolov around the airliner, Lear pointed to the handrail-shaped object on the side of the airliner. There followed a brief exchange between Lear and one of the Soviets:

"What's that?"
"That's an antenna."
"Transmitting or receiving?"
"Both."
"That's a very interesting design."

In addition to learning the function of the handrail antenna, Lear also studied the Tu-104's electronics. He noted that the Tu-104 used a World War II-era C-1 autopilot, which could be bought as surplus for $6.00. The airliner's altimeter was also of World War II vintage, but it was adequate for high-altitude use. The radios were old and operated on medium and high frequencies. Lear was more impressed by the airliner's radar, which looked like an advanced U.S. prototype. The same was true of its runway altimeter, which showed the airliner's height near to the ground. Lear's assessment was that although much of the Soviet's equipment was behind that of the West, they were able to produce advanced systems where they were needed.

Lear and his wife left Moscow on 29 June 1956 and flew the Cessna to West Berlin, where U.S. intelligence officials debriefed him. The *Life* magazine photos of the Tu-104 tour were smuggled out of Moscow by a Pan American pilot who passed them to an intelligence contact. Many of the photos were removed before the film was returned to the Lears and *Life*. The CIA had its answers, while William Lear had had fun.

In other cases, the CIA and military had their own personnel accompany the official party. One such example occurred in the fall of 1955, with a visit by Sen. Richard B. Russell (D-Georgia) to the USSR. Russell was the chairman of the Armed Services Committee, and one of the Senate's most senior and influential members. He was a Southern Democrat—conservative, strongly pro-defense, anti–civil rights, and one of the few congressmen briefed on CIA activities.

In mid-August 1955, he set out on a junket to Europe to visit U.S. and NATO military bases. Accompanying him on the trip was Army Lt. Col. Edward N. Hathaway, who was assigned to the congressional liaison staff. They spent the next month visiting London, Madrid, Paris, Frankfurt, Amsterdam, Copenhagen, and Oslo. Their next stop was Helsinki, Finland, where Reuben Efron joined them. He was a Russian-born American citizen who would serve as translator during the two weeks they would spend in the Soviet Union. Efron may also have been a CIA clandestine service officer.

Russell, Hathaway, and Efron arrived in Leningrad on 23 September 1955 and spent the next three days sightseeing. Once in the USSR, Efron began compiling a long classified journal with observations on Soviet food, living quarters, and economic conditions. Hathaway was also making notes on military activities, aircraft, and transport facilities. By accompanying Russell, they had access to areas in the USSR and Eastern Europe that had not been seen by Westerners in some time. The party then went by train to Moscow. Although they had an Intourist guide, Russell's status gave him the ability to go where he wished. To the annoyance of the Soviets, Russell insisted on visiting Borodino, the site of a Russian defeat during Napoleon's invasion in 1812. Colonel Hathaway also did some "sightseeing" of his own. A report about his activities noted:

> On the way [to Borodino], exactly at the 42 kilometer signpost from Moscow on the Moscow to Minsk highway, on the right side of the road, there was a radar site (size unknown) with two radars. From the sketches of Col. Hathaway, they have been tentatively identified as one Woodgage or Gage and one square type Pole Freya. . . . (Approx. 200–250 yards off side of road.)

While in Moscow, the party was joined by a fourth American, Robert R. Gros, the vice president for public relations at Pacific Gas and Electric Company. He was in the middle of a five-week trip through the USSR. Gros had managed a special tenth anniversary commemorative session of the United Nations in San Francisco earlier in 1955. There he met Soviet Foreign Minister Vyacheslav Molotov. Gros remarked: "Every time I saw Molotov he gave me a platitudinous rhetorical sort of invitation, 'You must come visit the USSR some day.' . . . I had no illusions about his sincerity but the day before he left I decided to take him up. To my utter amazement he called over his ambassador . . . and told him to visa me whenever I wished." When Gros crossed paths with the Russell group, he insisted on joining them.

The four men left Moscow and headed to Stalingrad, then flew to Baku, which was the capital of Azerbaijan and a major Soviet oil-producing area. Colonel Hathaway continued his note taking. A subsequent report stated: "The party landed at Baku by aircraft, the civilian field being located an hour from the city. A military airfield was passed on the outskirts of Baku on the way from the commercial field. The Intourist guide stated that this was a military training airfield and Col. Hathaway recognized some dark green transports parked there."

Throughout their journey, the group had been watched over by a succession of Intourist guides, and Russell was growing weary of them. Their guide in Baku was a short woman with steel teeth whom Russell dubbed "Snappin' Annie." After seeing the approved tourist sites, the four decided that they wanted to have a better view of the Caspian Sea, and pressured Snappin' Annie into taking them to a war memorial overlooking the Baku waterfront. Russell and Hathaway both had 35-mm cameras, while Gros had both a 16-mm movie camera and a Leica still camera. Over Snappin' Annie's protests, they photographed possible intelligence targets along the waterfront. Gros recalled seeing what he thought were Soviet submarines.

On the evening of 4 October 1955, the party left Baku by train.

A long RR [railroad] train composed of flat cars was seen outside of Baku. Each flatcar had one landing craft which was described by Col. Hathaway as being platoon size, with a slot at the rear for an outboard engine and the tops of the boats covered with canvas. Men were seen in the vicinity wearing a unique uniform which he could not recognize.

The train had left Baku at about 6:00 P.M. and had gone south along the Caspian Sea before turning west at Alyat (spelled "Atjaty" in the report). The train stopped briefly at the Alyat station at about 7:00 P.M. The car that the Russell party was riding was "sealed"—the doors at both ends were locked, so they would be isolated until reaching Tbilisi, in Soviet Georgia, the next morning. Russell was not feeling well, so he was resting on the bunk in his darkened sleeper compartment, watching the scenery roll by in the twilight. About ten minutes after the train left the Alyat station, Russell noticed a light that he initially thought was a reflection on the window. He quickly realized that it was actually in the sky and some distance from the train. The senator thought the small yellow-green light was spinning as it rose rapidly on a near-vertical path.

The other three men were talking in the other compartment when Russell burst in and shouted, "I just saw a flying saucer!" Someone turned out the compartment lights, and all four were able to see the light as it climbed in the sky, high and to their right. Gros grabbed his cameras and began filming. A few moments later, the four men saw a second, similar light at a distance they estimated to be a mile or two from the train, which spiraled rapidly into the dark sky. To Hathaway and Efron, it appeared to be circular, about the size of a fighter, and spinning rather slowly as it seemed to emit a hint of fire or sparks. There was no smoke trail, and none of the group could hear any sound over the noise of the train. Gros recalled that "it *shhhhot* into the sky!" The second light followed a path similar to that of the first. One or two searchlights were visible near where the two lights had appeared, so the group assumed that the area was a military base, although no runways or buildings could be seen.

The four men were still excited and continued to watch for several minutes after the second light disappeared. Russell said: "We saw a flying saucer. I wanted you boys to see it so that I would have witnesses." Efron later wrote: "Everyone in the compartment was convinced that we had seen something real and unusual. I asked if it could have been some kind of airplane and the others replied, 'No, there was no resemblance.'" However, they saw no more lights, and the train conductors soon came into their compartments, pulled down the window shades, and indicated that further sightseeing was not allowed.

The group arrived at Tbilisi the following day, and Hathaway spotted "a large helicopter resembling a banana with two large, main rotors at each end and having many more windows than a banana type I had seen in the USA." Gros left the group at this point and returned to Moscow, while Russell and the two others continued on to Sochi by train. About twenty minutes outside Sochi, Hathaway reported seeing "a T-34 tank which had a muzzle brake on the gun, but looked very different from any he had seen during a combat tour in Korea. The tank was on a flatcar."

During this period, Russell and his party encountered a middle-age Russian named Egorov. He was accompanied by a young engineer whose "job was to keep Egorov supplied with spirits. Egorov was feeling pretty good when he met the Americans and proceeded to continue the party with them." Egorov told them that he had been one of the Soviet pilots who had made a transpolar flight to Washington State in 1935 or 1936. Egorov said he was now retired, was a hero of the Soviet Union, and had shot down seventeen German airplanes during World War II. Egorov spoke "fairly freely about the internal situation in the USSR." Senator Russell invited Egorov to visit his office if he ever came to the United States.

The senator's Soviet journey continued, with the group arriving at Dnepropetrovsk Airfield on 9 October by a DC-3-type aircraft. Colonel Hathaway noted: "The airfield is grass-sod. The parking ramp is of octagonal brick or cement. . . . One jet bomber was parked at the airfield. . . . Col. Hathaway counted 42 very stubby jet fighters parked at the field. The jet fighters were described as 'short, stubby, smaller and higher horizontal tailplane, wings more forward, canopy more forward.'"

The group finally left the USSR on the morning of 12 October, going by train from Kiev and crossing into Czechoslovakia. Colonel Hathaway made extensive observations of the Soviet railroads, which used a different width of tracks from those in Eastern Europe. Hathaway gave an extensive description of a building used to switch the train from one gage to the other. After entering Czechoslovakia, he observed a factory that he thought produced "long, aluminum RR cars," as well as "very large RR marshaling yards with tracks stretching as far as [I] could see on both sides of [the] track. Guard towers were manned and located in the huge RR yards. There were 5 tracks at the border branching into many in the yards." As Hathaway went through the yards, he observed that on his left side were loaded or full freight cars, while on his right were all the empty freight cars for quite a distance. Hathaway also described the use of prefabricated track sections with "rails already hooked to the sleepers."

Meanwhile, the Russell party arrived in Prague, Czechoslovakia, at 9:45 P.M. on 12 October and was taken to the U.S. residency. After dinner, Colonel Hathaway took Lt. Col. Thomas S. Ryan, the air attaché, aside and said that he had something of the utmost importance to tell him, "something you may not believe, but something that we've been told by your people [USAF] doesn't exist." Colonel Ryan said that they should not talk at the residency, as it lacked security precautions. He suggested that they discuss the matter at the embassy the next morning.

Hathaway and Efron met with both Colonel Ryan and the Army attaché, Col. Thomas Dooley, at 9:00 A.M. the next day. Senator Russell was with the embassy's chief of mission, and so was not present. Hathaway began to describe the sighting by saying, "I doubt if you're going to believe this, but we all saw it." Ryan replied, "I don't disbelieve anything after having been in Czechoslovakia for 17 months." As Hathaway and Efron gave their descriptions of the two lights, Colonel Ryan was impressed.

Ryan's attitude seems to have been shaped by two events. The first was the behavior of the Soviets after the sighting. Hathaway recalled, "After we saw the two discs, the Soviet trainmen became excited, closing curtains and telling us that we were not allowed to look out of the windows." Ryan commented in his notes that "the behavior of the trainmen was such as to indicate that the U.S. passengers had seen something that they were not supposed to see." The other was the meeting with Egorov. Colonel Ryan noted, "It is difficult for me to believe that this experienced pilot in polar navigation would be retired and doing nothing but traveling around the Trans Caucasus region with a young engineer." The implication seemed to be that Egorov was connected with the sighting. Colonel Ryan sent a "Top Secret" cable to U.S. Air Force Headquarters, followed by a nine-page Air Intelligence Information Report. It was also classified "Top Secret" and included Hathaway and Efron's descriptions of the objects. Colonel Ryan suggested that they "lend credence to many 'saucer' reports."

Wilton E. Lexow, head of the CIA's Applied Science Division, made an initial analysis of the Russell sighting. His memo, dated 19 October 1955, noted its contradictory implications.

> Since two objects were reportedly seen in operation at one time in an area where it is most unlikely that experimental flying would be conducted, it is likely that these objects were in service. This would indicate very rapid progress in this development for the Soviets. It does, however, seem inconsistent that the Soviets, if they have such an object in service, would continue their large development and production program on conventional type aircraft.

It was clear that further information was required, and so Herbert "Pete" Scoville, the assistant director of the CIA's Office of Scientific Intelligence (OSI), arranged to have Russell questioned because he was considered the primary witness. Senator Russell arrived back in Washington, D.C., on 26 October, and Scoville met with him the next day.

The agitated train conductors had been a major piece of evidence in support of a Soviet flying saucer. When Scoville asked Russell about this, he was told that the conductors had closed the window blinds at least ten minutes after the sighting. This was after Russell had returned to his own compartment. Russell did not feel that they were trying to hide anything. There were also discrepancies in the witnesses' accounts about the shape of the saucers, the number of lights on each, and their flight path. Three of the four said that it had followed a fairly continuous, although wobbly course. Colonel Hathaway, in contrast, insisted that the light made a sharp transition from vertical to horizontal flight. The clear evidence for a Soviet flying saucer indicated by Colonel Ryan's report was becoming fuzzier.

Scoville's assessment of the Russell sighting was detailed in a 27 October 1955 memorandum.

> The testimony . . . does not in my opinion support the theory that the Russians have developed saucer-like or unconventional aircraft. It is quite possible that the objects seen were the exhausts of normal jet aircraft in a steep climb. The fact that none were seen on the ground might indicate that the aircraft were in a dive followed by a sharp pull-up in such a way that nothing was seen until the exhausts were visible to the observers on the train.

Tourist Support of U-2 Overflights

As the Russell sighting was being analyzed, a revolution in technological intelligence collection was taking shape. In August 1955, the U-2 made its initial test flights at Groom Lake, Nevada. Within two months, the aircraft had proven it could remain at altitudes of seventy thousand feet for hours at a time. In early July 1956, the first series of U-2 overflights of the USSR was made. For the next four years, U-2 overflights provided 90 percent of the intelligence the United States had on Soviet capabilities. Far from ending the tourist operations, however, the U-2 resulted in their expansion.

The peak of the tourist operations was 1958 to 1960, with much of the effort focused on support of the overflights. The tourist reports, along with information from attachés, returning German ex-POWs and scientists, refugees, defectors, and published accounts, collected over nearly a decade, were used to target the U-2 overflights and analyze their photos.

Soviet nuclear production facilities scattered across the Urals, Siberia, and Central Asia were among the primary targets of the U-2 overflights. The amount of enriched uranium or plutonium that a facility could produce was directly proportional to the amount of electrical power that it consumed. The CIA began assembling data on electrical generating stations, transmission lines, and power consumption in areas where nuclear facilities were known or suspected to exist. The goal was to determine the electrical capacity going to the nuclear production facilities.

Tourists and other travelers were part of this effort. In 1956, a general requirement to photograph transmission lines was issued. Over the next two years, this produced about twenty-five ground photos from the Sverdlovsk area alone. The following year, a British power delegation made an official visit to the Mid-Urals *gres* (Russian for regional power plant) north of Sverdlovsk and the South Urals *gres* outside Chelyabinsk. In all, 103 Soviet press reports, 11 ex-POW reports, 4 delegation visits, some 25 ground photos of power lines, and photos from two reconnaissance balloons were assembled to give the CIA a fairly complete understanding of the Urals power grid. From these, the power consumption of the nuclear plants could also be estimated.

This analysis was put to the test by a U-2 overflight on 9 July 1959. Mission 4125, given the code name "Touchdown," was to cover the Ural nuclear facilities. Marty Knutson, the U-2's pilot, successfully covered most of the targets. When the photos were interpreted, they indicated that the estimated power consumption was nearly correct.

The photo interpreters used "collateral" intelligence on the facilities, such as the tourist reports and other information, to make sense of the U-2 images. An example of this was U-2 Mission 4045, flown by Sammy Snyder on 20 August 1957. The mission's primary target was a suspected nuclear facility at Tomsk.

When Snyder reached the area, he photographed a nuclear complex covering some forty square miles.

In September 1958, more than a year after Mission 4045 was flown, the Second Conference on the Peaceful Uses of Atomic Energy was held in Geneva, Switzerland. The CIA, the Atomic Energy Commission (AEC), and the Air Force all had official representatives at the conference. In addition, the DCS had given questions to a number of non-AEC American delegates before they had left the United States. These individuals were judged reliable enough to act on their own initiative with the Soviets.

Halfway through the meeting, the Soviet delegation announced that they had put into operation an atomic power station "somewhere in Siberia." They also began showing a film on the power station. The images in the film and the description of the power station seemed very much like the reactor complex at Tomsk photographed by the U-2 overflight. Here was an opportunity to gain insights that could aid with the interpretation of the Mission 4045 photos and the state of Soviet reactor technology.

To exploit the opportunity, the CIA representatives suggested that the AEC power plant experts in the U.S. delegation should discuss technical details with the Soviet reactor designers and the personnel manning the booths in the exhibition hall. The individuals briefed by the DCS and those working for the Air Force would also seek out information.

One source, a chemical engineer specializing in nuclear reactors, was told by a friend that S. M. Feinberg had said, "the reactor has two steam circuits, one operating at 180 degrees C, the other at 30 lbs. per square inch [sic]. The fuel elements are cylindrical tubes holding graphite moderator and the fuel elements themselves. The latter were cylindrical, 10-mm internal diameter. Through them flows water. The fuel consists of uranium-magnesium, 0.7-mm thick (presumably cladding thickness) and clad on both sides with aluminum." The source added that his friend had language difficulties in understanding the fuel element description. He thought that the fuel was "compressed powder." The source was surprised by this design, which he said was "quite different from our design."

Another source reported: "the reactor has 20 control rods . . . which were identified by green squares on the 'map.' The control room has an illuminated panel for fuel channel temperature, and there is 'automatic replacement' of fuel by a key at the control panel. . . . Under the reactor is a shielded two-man carriage or gondola for the servicing of mechanical difficulties at the discharge face."

A third source reported that a U.S. scientist had taken the direct approach and asked a Soviet scientist where the reactor was located. He noted that "the question was completely ignored 'due to translation difficulties.'" The source did provide very specific design information, however, saying: "This reactor operates on natural uranium fuel elements clad in aluminum silicon (AlSi) alloy of 1–2 percent silicon content. . . . Since the AlSi alloy is good only to 200–250 degrees C, I asked the Soviets why they had selected this alloy and not an aluminum nickel alloy (which the Soviets had tested and found to be good to about 300 degrees C). They replied the aluminum nickel alloy absorbed too many neutrons."

Another source of information was the film the Soviets were showing. It was soon apparent that the Soviets would not allow the United States to have a copy. To gain information from the film, the help of a group of U.S. reactor engineers was needed. An American engineering firm working under contract to the OSI employed these engineers to provide an evaluation of Soviet reactor engineering practices. John R. Craig, an OSI staff employee, produced a detailed plan. Each of the engineers was told to watch and listen for specific information. Among the members of the group, all facets of the atomic power station were covered. In addition, still photos of the screen were covertly taken during the showings using a pair of very fine Leica cameras and extremely high-speed film. The plan was successful, and the engineers' notes and photos were the most complete of any provided on the film.

Henry S. Lowenhaupt, a CIA analyst on nuclear energy who had participated in the planning of the U-2 overflights, also attended the final showing of the film. He had spent five months interpreting the Tomsk photos and had memorized the photos before coming to Geneva. His initial reaction was one of confusion. The U-2 photos taken in 1957 had shown a "construction shambles," as he recalled. The main housing area, with six-story apartment buildings, the statue of Lenin on horseback, and the children's playground, was unfamiliar to him. However, within seconds of seeing the initial view of the reactor complex,

Lowenhaupt knew the reactor was at Tomsk. He was even able to figure out where the movie camera had been positioned to take the shot.

The published Soviet papers, reports from U.S. sources, the covert photos of the movie, and the U-2 photos of Tomsk were all combined as part of a detailed analysis. The Tomsk reactor core was determined to be a vertical cylinder 37 feet in diameter and 24.5 feet tall. Based on the fact the reactor had 2,100 fuel rods, and assuming the Soviets were being truthful when they said the reactor was loaded with 200 metric tons of uranium metal, the conclusion was made that the fuel rods were between 1.18 and 1.25 inches in diameter.

To estimate the reactor's power levels, the CIA used a report from a U.S. source and the published Soviet papers; each source indicated that the maximum operating temperature was 220 degrees Celsius. Analysis of the photos of the plant's steam turbines, cooling towers, and transformers showed that the reactor had an efficiency of 14 percent. The final bit of evidence was the U-2 photos of the reactor's effluent channel, which indicated a flow of forty-two thousand gallons of primary circuit cooling water. If this hot water was pumped over and over through the reactor (called a closed cycle), it would then produce 700 megawatts of power—100 megawatts in the form of electrical power and the remaining 600 megawatts released through the cooling towers. If the hot water was discharged into the effluent channel, then the reactor's maximum power output was 1,700 megawatts. As in the closed-cycle operation, 100 megawatts of electrical power would be produced, while 600 megawatts was discharged through the cooling towers.

The result of the detailed analysis showed that the reactor was actually designed for the production of plutonium for nuclear weapons. The amount of plutonium produced would depend on the reactor's power level. The electrical power generated was only a minor by-product. Lowenhaupt later observed that the U-2 photos, the Soviet information, and the intelligence collected by the DCS and other sources had allowed the CIA to deduce "with very great precision indeed the technical characteristics of Russian plutonium production reactors—one of the great 'military' secrets of the USSR."

The peak of the tourist operations in 1958–60 also coincided with the "Missile Gap" controversy. On 4 October 1957 the Soviets had launched Sputnik I, the first artificial satellite. Following the launch, the CIA estimated that the USSR would deploy a large force of intercontinental ballistic missiles (ICBMs). Soviet Premier Nikita Khrushchev exploited the perception—created by Sputnik—of Soviet missile leadership to pressure the West. The Soviets demanded a German peace treaty and that West Berlin be turned into a "free city," with access in the hands of the USSR and East Germany. Because of the unsettled international situation over Berlin and other East/West issues, U-2 overflights were halted between March 1958 and July 1959. As a result, observations by tourists and other Western travelers were one of the few sources available on Soviet missile deployment.

Visual observations from trains were particularly important, as the United States believed the Soviet ICBMs were being deployed near rail lines. Such observations faced limitations on coverage. A particular problem with trains was their speed of travel, which meant that an observer had a limited time to recognize features. More general problems included such factors as weather, terrain, vegetation, and buildings, and the fact that the view was limited to one side of the vehicle. While an airline passenger could see a band about ten miles wide (compared to five miles for ground transportation), altitude, cloud cover, and seat location were all problems. Not surprisingly, no Soviet ICBM sites were observed. When U-2 overflights resumed in July 1959, they were also unsuccessful in spotting any ICBMs.

In early 1960, however, two possible ICBM sites had been identified. These were at Yuri, located in the central USSR, and at Plesetsk in northwestern Russia. To cover the two sites, a U-2 overflight was planned. The mission would take off from a base in Pakistan, fly across the width of the USSR, and land in Norway. Frances Gary Powers made the overflight, code-named "Grand Slam," on 1 May 1960. As he neared the city of Sverdlovsk, a SAM exploded near his U-2 and brought it down. Powers survived, but he was captured upon landing.

Spy Scare

Following the downing of the U-2, Khrushchev asked KGB Chairman Alexander Shelepin for a plan to exploit the incident. Khrushchev received the report on 7 June. The plan's main intent was to use forgeries and other "measures" to slander DCI Allen Dulles. The KGB also wanted to use its successes against Western covert operations of nearly a decade earlier as propaganda. Shelepin suggested that the Soviets "discuss with our Polish and Albanians friends the advisability of bringing to the attention of government circles and of the public of the United States the fact that the security agencies of Poland and Albania for a number of years had been deluding American intelligence in the operational games 'WiN' and 'John' and had obtained millions of dollars, weapons, equipment, etc. from it."

The KGB also considered using a fake operational game. Shelepin's report proposed "to fabricate the failure of an American agent 'Fyodorov,' dropped into the Soviet Union by plane in 1952 and used by organs of the KGB in an operational game with the adversary," and "to publish in the Soviet press an announcement about the arrest of 'Fyodorov' as an American agent and, if necessary, to arrange a press-conference about this affair."

A virtual "open season" on alleged tourist agents soon began. As the August 1960 show trial of Powers approached, the Soviets began a daily press campaign publicizing a series of expulsions of Westerners. An American student on a YMCA-sponsored tour of the Soviet Union was expelled for giving a Russian a Bible. Another American student was also expelled after being told that he had been "convicted of spying." He had been accused of photographing railroad stations, radio transmission towers, harbor facilities, and "other military objects." Powers was sentenced to ten years on 19 August 1960. His cellmate at Vladimir prison was the Latvian SIS agent Zigurd Kruminsh.

Khrushchev continued his threats against Berlin in the New Year. At a summit meeting with President John F. Kennedy in Vienna in June 1961, Khrushchev set a 31 December 1961 deadline for a German peace treaty. After this, he said, "all rights of access to Berlin will expire because the state of war will cease to exist." Khrushchev continued that the "USSR considered that all of Berlin to be GDR [German Democratic Republic, or East German] territory," and that all Allied troops would have to leave West Berlin.

Coinciding with Khrushchev's renewed threats, the Soviet spy scare campaign against tourists was again stepped up. During 1960, the tourists who had been arrested were simply kicked out of the country. During the latter half of 1961, seven individuals were arrested and put on trial as U.S. spies. Only one was actually an American. He was Marvin W. Makinen, a twenty-two-year-old student at the University of Pennsylvania. He was also a soccer player who knew nine languages, including Russian. After being awarded a second one-year Fulbright scholarship at the Free University in West Berlin, he had spent the summer of 1961 touring Czechoslovakia and Hungary in his Volkswagen before going to Kiev in the USSR. There he was arrested for spying.

The Soviet account said that two CIA agents, named "Jim" and "Dyer," had recruited Makinen in Berlin. He was then given an intensive six-week course in photography, codes, and map reading, assigned a car, and given a list of military facilities to photograph. At Makinen's closed trial, Victor Daniluk, a Kiev taxi driver, said that Makinen had hired his cab on 27 July, giving him an address on the outskirts of town. Daniluk continued: "When I brought the tourist to that street, he was uneasy. He squirmed in his seat, turning his head in all directions and scrutinizing every building. He was interested in military installations on the street but pretended he was interested in street repairs." Daniluk told the police, who were waiting when Makinen returned in his Volkswagen. The Soviets said Makinen was taking photos when two policemen arrested him.

Confronted with the films, Makinen reportedly confessed, saying, "Yes, those are not tourist photographs." The published confession described how Makinen had kept a coded diary: "When I saw soldiers, I wrote that I saw peasants and when I saw a military barracks I wrote that it was raining. When I came across military cars I used the expression 'big traffic.'" Makinen was sentenced to eight years in prison.

By early December 1961, six Western Europeans traveling in the USSR had been tried and convicted of spying for the United States. Ewert Reidon and Lou de Yaher, two junior officers in the Dutch merchant marine, were the first arrested for espionage. One of the officers confessed that he had spied on Soviet ports for five years. Both were sentenced to thirteen years and sent to Vladimir prison, where Powers was being held.

The next two arrested were an unlikely pair of spies. Adolf Werner was a shoe salesman in a department store in Karlsruhe, West Germany, and Hermine

Werner was his wife and a cashier in the same store. They had been arrested while traveling in the Ukraine. They told the military court in Kiev that two CIA agents, named "Johnson" and "Dan," had recruited them to photograph Soviet military installations during their Soviet vacation. Adolf Werner said that he had dictated notes to his wife, which she then wrote in a notebook using invisible ink.

Newsweek observed that much of their testimony "had a self-degrading Kafkaesque ring about it." Hermine Werner sobbed as she said, "Yes, I am a spy—but I did not know at the time I was one." Adolf Werner said, "The capitalists found one more fool to pull chestnuts out of the fire for them." Adolf Werner received a term of fifteen years, while his wife was given seven years.

Two other West Germans also underwent a similar show trial. Peter Sonntag and Walter Naumann were sentenced to twelve years in jail by a Moscow court. They said two American agents named "Mark" and "Olsen" had recruited them at the Red Ox Tavern in Heidelberg. Their sentences, like those given Ewert Reidon, Lou de Yaher, and Adolf Werner, were considerably harsher than that given to Powers (ten years). Indeed, only the sentences of Makinen (eight years) and Hermine Werner (seven years) were lighter than that given the U-2 pilot.

The downing of the U-2 and the campaign against the alleged tourist agents provided propaganda victories over the West, but they ultimately proved hollow. During this time, the Corona photoreconnaissance satellites became operational. Each satellite could photograph a greater area of the USSR than that covered by all twenty-three U-2 overflights combined.

As Khrushchev continued his threats, a revised CIA estimate on Soviet missile forces was issued on 21 September 1961, based on the Corona photos. In the CIA report's conclusions was the statement: "We now estimate that the present Soviet ICBM strength is in the range of 10–25 launchers from which missiles can be fired against the U.S., and that this force level will not increase markedly during the months immediately ahead." With that one sentence, the Missile Gap ended. The Soviets did not really have the massive ICBM force they claimed to have, and which had set the whole Missile Gap controversy in motion. More important, the United States no longer had to estimate how many ICBMs the Soviets had, or guess where they might be located. The United States *knew*.

The spy scare, which began with show trials and propaganda, ended with a spy exchange. Powers was subsequently exchanged for a convicted Soviet spy named Rudolf Able on 10 February 1962. As part of the trade, Frederick L. Pryor, a Yale student arrested in East Germany six months earlier, was also released. Later, Marvin Makinen was also set free.

By the time of the Powers/Able exchange, satellite reconnaissance had become fully operational. Such technical means of espionage had also come to be seen as superior to human agents. At the same time, however, covert operations were still an important element of U.S. foreign policy, particularly on the fringes of the Soviet bloc.

7

Tibet—The Covert War for Shangri-la

We arrived safely. Next time, please drop us fifty yards downstream because there was a house nearby with dogs who barked at us when we landed last night. We are well. We have cached our parachutes and are off to buy a horse to go to Lhasa tomorrow.

— First radio message from the Tibetan resistance, October 1957

Soon after Dwight D. Eisenhower became president in January 1953, U.S. covert operations against the Soviet bloc underwent a reassessment. It was now clear to the CIA that no popular uprising could hope to succeed against Soviet tanks. However, this did not mean the end of U.S. covert actions. Now leftist governments in third world countries would be the primary targets of such operations. These governments lacked the absolute control of society that existed in the Soviet bloc. Factions still existed that opposed their policies, and which could be used as a means to overthrow what were seen as pro-Soviet governments.

Such covert action was a key part of President Eisenhower's foreign policy. Behind the ready smile and grandfatherly manner, Eisenhower was a ruthless secret warrior. In his view, covert action represented an alternative between doing nothing when U.S. interests were threatened and sending in U.S. troops. Covert actions were among Eisenhower's first foreign policy efforts. In August 1953, the CIA and the SIS organized a coup in Iran, code-named "TPAjax," aimed at overthrowing left-wing Prime Minister Mohammad Mossadeq. First, the CIA organized a bogus pro-Communist street demonstration to spread fear of a Soviet-backed coup and to provoke a royalist backlash. Then, a small pro-Shah protest followed, which quickly turned into a full-fledged riot. Mossadeq fled, and the exiled Shah returned to power.

Soon after the Iran operation was completed, planning began for "PBSuccess" to overthrow President Jacobo Arbenz Guzman of Guatemala. Arbenz was seen as pro-Soviet, running a government dominated by Communists. PBSuccess would use a small band of rebel troops and a makeshift air force of three P-51s, six P-47s, a Cessna 180, a P-38, and a PBY amphibian. The "Voice of Liberation" radio would create the illusion that this tiny force was actually the vanguard of a massive army. The coup was launched on 18 June 1954 and immediately went awry. The 150-man rebel "army" moved six miles and then halted, far from their targets. The rebel "air force" was summarily ineffective. The Cessna 180 pilot dropped grenades and gasoline-filled bottles, which did no real damage. An attack on the government radio station actually destroyed a transmitter belonging to a group of Christian missionaries. Two of the rebel aircraft were damaged by ground fire, and another ran out of gas and crash-landed in Mexico.

Although the coup seemed on the verge of collapse, the Voice of Liberation radio breathlessly reported pitched battles and heavy government casualties. These claims gained credibility when a hospital train arrived in Guatemala City with several dozen wounded government soldiers. This incident, the result of a small firefight with the rebels, became a turning point in the coup. Another was the change in fortune of the rebel air force. Eisenhower authorized the supply of two replacement P-51s. These launched a seventy-two-hour bombing campaign. A large smoke bomb dropped on the Fort Matamoros parade ground made it appear that the government was under siege. The Guatemalan population referred to the bombs as "laxatives," for their effects on the government and army. Stories circulated of whole towns being destroyed, of bodies in the streets, and of the populations fleeing. Upon hearing reports of two massive columns heading for Guatemala City, Arbenz panicked and fled.

Against the background of the twin successes in Iran and Guatemala, the CIA's most ambitious, and romantic, covert action was undertaken, amid the towering snowcapped peaks of Tibet.

STCircus

A nineteenth-century traveler called Tibet "the most frightening desert in the world." Tibet covers an area about the same size as Western Europe. Its "lowlands" were at thirteen thousand feet, whereas some peaks reached beyond twenty-five thousand feet. The few inhabitants of this harsh land belonged to the Khampa and Amdo tribes. A supreme Buddhist priest called the Dalai Lama, who succeeded to the position through reincarnation, held both religious and temporal powers. Throughout their history, the Tibetans had fiercely defended their society from foreigners, rival sects, or even fellow sect members. The monasteries, which were the centers of Tibetan society, also had arsenals.

Since the fall of the last Chinese emperor in 1911, Tibet had enjoyed independence from outside control. Soon after the fall of the Nationalist government to the Chinese Communists under Mao Tse-tung, this independence ended. Troops of the PLA attacked in October 1950, and within two weeks they had crushed the small Tibetan army. The Chinese then began a "socialist reconstruction" to rid Tibet of its "antiquated religious beliefs."

The Dalai Lama attempted to avoid direct confrontations with the Chinese, to protect Tibetan society and to avoid a war with the Chinese. It was his older brother, Gyalo Thondup, who sought covert Western support to start a unified resistance movement. He met with little initial success because the U.S. government believed that the resistance was too weak for aid to be effective. Only moral support and help should the Dalai Lama decide to leave Tibet were offered.

The Tibetan revolt was triggered in the summer of 1956 when the Chinese began a punitive campaign that leveled the monastery at Litang, built in 1580 and home to some five thousand monks. Its arsenal of ancient rifles was no match for Chinese airpower. The destruction of the Litang monastery finally convinced the common people, the monks, and the bitterly feuding clans to unite against the Chinese.

When Gyalo Thondup went to the U.S. consulate in Calcutta to seek aid, he found that U.S. attitudes had now changed. The U.S. support for the Tibetans had little to do with Tibet, but everything to do with China. Secretary of State

John Foster Dulles (DCI Allen Dulles's brother) and Undersecretary Herbert Hoover Jr. wanted to use the resistance to keep the Chinese off balance, to prevent them from extending their influence. At this time, the Domino Theory held that third world countries would fall victim, one-by-one, to Communist subversion directed by the USSR and aided by the Chinese.

During the summer of 1956, Gyalo Thondup and his brother Takster met with CIA officials, who agreed to train an initial group of six Tibetans who would parachute back into Tibet. The CIA would use their reports to determine what support to provide the resistance. This initial group was also to serve as instructors for resistance groups who would fight as guerrillas rather than take on the massed Chinese troops in pitched battles. The CIA support for the Tibetan resistance was given the code name "STCircus."

The initial group of six Tibetans was from the Litang area. Gompo Tashi, an emerging leader of the resistance, recommended them. The six were then approved by Gyalo Thondup, Takster, and other exiled Tibetan leaders. The six trainees were brought out of Tibet, which required several days to cross the harsh winter landscape. They were then flown to a CIA facility on Saipan in December 1956 to begin their training. Takster and a monk named Geshe Wangyal aided the CIA officers by serving as advisers and translators.

Once on Saipan, the six Tibetans were taught how to use the RS-1 radio and Morse code, and to encrypt and decrypt messages using one-time pads. This required the development of a special vocabulary to describe things not in the Tibetan language. In this way, both the Tibetans and the CIA could understand the messages. Takster and Geshe Wangyal assisted in the development of this vocabulary. The Tibetans also learned intelligence collection and reporting techniques. To support future air resupply missions, they were taught to make weather reports, as well as how to identify and prepare drop zones. Other areas of instruction included such guerrilla tactics as how to prepare ambushes and how to blow up bridges.

Once the six Tibetans had completed their four-and-a-half-months training period on Saipan, two radio teams were formed. The first team consisted of two Tibetans, named Lhotse and Athar Norbu, known to the CIA personnel as "Tom" and "Lou." Roger McCarthy, the CIA officer in charge of STCircus, recalled that Lhotse was a "big fellow" who was "extremely friendly, warm, and incredibly strong." Athar Norbu was "built more like a fireplug, but extremely strong." McCarthy added, "It was easy for all of us to look at them, to treat them, to think of them as brothers."

Lhotse and Athar Norbu were then sent to Okinawa for parachute training. CIA personnel modified standard T-10 parachutes with slots and tails to improve their maneuverability. The two Tibetans wore padded jumpsuits and helmets with face protectors used by American smoke jumpers. They each made three parachute jumps from a B-17. The four other Tibetans who comprised the second radio team also underwent parachute training. But, whereas Lhotse and Athar Norbu successfully completed their jumps, one of the four others washed out and had to return to Tibet on foot.

CAT and STBarnum

As with earlier agent drops into China during the Korean War, CAT would fly the missions. The drops of the two teams into Tibet were to be made from an unmarked CAT B-17 flown by Polish and Czech crewmen. This was done for plausible deniability; B-17s were available as war surplus, and the pilots were non-Americans. Should the aircraft and crew be lost over Tibet, both could be disowned by the United States. The first radio team was to be dropped onto sandbanks formed by the receding floodwaters of the Brahmaputra River, sixty miles south of the Tibetan capital of Lhasa. The second, three-man team, led by Gyato Wangdu, was to be dropped into an area near Litang. The airdrop operations were given a separate code name. As the overall code name for the support of the Tibetan resistance was STCircus, the CIA decided to call the airdrops of personnel and weapons "STBarnum."

The planning of the drops was difficult primarily because the CIA's chief cartographer had to use old British maps dating from a 1904 military expedition into Tibet led by Col. Francis Younghusband. A more recent source was photographs from the first U-2 overflight of Tibet that had occurred on 21 August 1957. CIA pilot Bill Hall's overflight had been a success and covered most of Tibet.

With their training complete and the moon nearly full, Lhotse, Athar Norbu, and the three other Tibetans were sent in October 1957 to a Strategic Air Command emergency recovery field at Kermitola, near Dacca in East Pakistan (now Bangladesh). Lhotse and Athar Norbu would be dropped first, followed by the second team the next night. The drops had to be made within five nights before or after a full moon to allow visual navigation. The weather forecast was good, and the two Tibetans boarded the B-17. The aircraft took off and began the long flight. As the B-17 headed toward the drop zone inside Tibet, the snow-covered mountains were brightly illuminated by the full moon.

Nearing the drop zone, Lhotse and Athar Norbu prepared to make the jump. The radio and other supplies were attached to one end of a three-hundred-foot line. The line's other end was attached to Athar Norbu's waist. Once on the ground, Athar Norbu had only to follow the line to recover the supplies. The B-17 then descended to a mere thousand feet above the ground. When the sandbank came into sight, the pilot turned on the jump signal. A parachute dispatch officer tossed the equipment bag from the airplane. Athar Norbu jumped, and Lhotse followed.

Both men successfully landed on the sandbank, right on target. Athar Norbu recovered the radio undamaged. The only mishap was that the two landed close to a house and disturbed several dogs. They hid their parachutes and reported their safe arrival. The radio and other equipment were then hidden, and Lhotse and Athar Norbu bought a horse for the journey to Lhasa. This accomplished, they retrieved the gear, loaded it on the horse, and set out on their mission.

The two Tibetans were able to contact Gompo Tashi and pass on a message for Phala Dronyer Chenmo, the head of the Dalai Lama's personal staff. The U.S. government, he was told, would give aid to the resistance if the Dalai Lama asked. The Dalai Lama responded that he could not approve of violence. Despite his refusal, the State Department agreed to continue STCircus, as the Tibetans were undertaking resistance activities on their own.

The original plan was for the second radio team to be dropped the following night. However, the weather took a turn for the worse. Heavy cloud cover prevented the drop, and the October full moon period passed. The drop had to be delayed a month. The three-man team was to contact resistance groups in

Gyato Wangdu's home area around Litang. Gyato Wangdu was the brother of a Khampa monk named Gyatotsang, who had met with Gyalo Thondup a year before, whereas Gompo Tashi was his uncle. Their training had been marked by friction due to differences in social status and clan memberships. Despite the differences, the three were able to work together as a team.

The weather was favorable for the drop in the November full moon period, and the B-17 took off from the East Pakistan airfield. The aircraft reached the drop zone, located nine miles from the team members' hometown. When the three men landed, a resistance group was nearby. They had not been alerted to the drop, however, and thought the three were Chinese paratroopers. A brief firefight started, but the team was able to identify themselves before either side suffered casualties.

When Gyato Wangdu's team reached their hometown, they discovered it was occupied by Chinese troops. They slipped away and made contact with one of Gyato Wangdu's brothers, who led a local resistance unit. Unfortunately, Chinese troops attacked, and among those killed were Gyato Wangdu's two teammates. With the radio operator dead, contact with the CIA was lost. Gyato Wangdu made his way to the resistance headquarters five hundred miles away in central Tibet. It would be the late summer of 1958 before he was able to reach the new headquarters.

Gompo Tashi began mobilizing his forces in late April 1958 when he called some three hundred followers together in Lhasa for a planning session. Their decision on how to proceed used an ancient Tibetan divination ritual. The two possibilities, to protect the Dalai Lama or to attack the Chinese army, were written on two pieces of paper, which were then wrapped in two balls of barley flour dough. These were then placed inside a cup that was spun clockwise in front of a statue of the Buddha. The ball with the second choice fell out. The divination having spoken, all that remained was to pick the time and place to begin the attack.

Gompo Tashi set up headquarters at Triguthang, a few days' travel south of Lhasa, where the formation of the Volunteer Freedom Fighters for Religious and Political Resistance (VFF) was proclaimed. This was done at a cavalry parade with burning incenses, a photograph of the Dalai Lama, and the unfurling of the VFF flag, which incorporated crossed swords and the traditional Tibetan thunderbolt and Buddhist lotus. The VFF filmed the parade, and the footage was smuggled out of the country and provided to both the CIA and the television producers.

The first airdrop of arms and supplies to the VFF was being prepared at this time. Athar Norbu made his way back to India to coordinate the initial drop. Lhotse remained behind to receive the supplies. Making the supply drops proved difficult. The flights would have to cover several thousand miles, and CAT's C-46s and C-47s lacked the range needed.

The CIA finally went to the 322nd Troop Carrier Squadron based on Okinawa, which had a C-118 aircraft (the Air Force version of the DC-6). This aircraft had just enough range to fly the airdrop missions over Tibet, although with a reduced payload of nine thousand pounds. The squadron also had a small cell that flew support missions for the CIA. The Air Force loaned the C-118 to the CIA, while CAT provided the pilots, navigators, radio operators, and PDOs.

The first drop was conducted in July 1958. The C-118 took off from Okinawa and then flew to Clark Air Base in the Philippines, where it was refueled and took aboard communications specialists. The C-118 then proceeded to the airfield at Kermitola, and from there, into Tibet. The drop was successful, and Lhotse arranged for the arms to be delivered to the VFF headquarters for distribution.

The VFF Takes the Offensive

The start of action by the VFF took place soon after the first C-118 drop. Gompo Tashi and 750 men headed toward the government armory hidden at the monastery Shang Gaden Choekhor, to capture weapons. The Chinese ambushed the force at about the midway point, which resulted in a three-day battle in late August 1958. The Chinese lost some two hundred dead; forty Tibetans were killed. When the force reached the armory, a surrender of the weapons was arranged, which netted mortars, machine guns, rifles, and ammunition.

In late October, the VFF engaged in a series of running battles with Chinese troops. The VFF claimed lopsided victories, inflicting thousands of casualties on the Chinese while saying their own losses were in the hundreds. Gompo

Tashi, who had been wounded in one of the battles, turned his forces east, reaching a relatively secure area at Chagra Pembar in early December 1958. Gompo Tashi's forces regrouped, recruited new troops, and prepared for their next attack.

Gompo Tashi's group then cut the Sichuan-Lhasa highway in a two-week-long battle. Again, heavy losses were inflicted on the Chinese, while the Tibetans reported only light casualties. With additional recruits and captured arms, in early January 1959 three of Gompo Tashi's commanders and their troops overran Tengchen, a Chinese fortress about two hundred miles east of Lhasa. Gompo Tashi's forces then fought a series of battles north of the Sichuan-Lhasa highway against PLA troops. These continued until the end of February 1959, when the campaign received a major setback.

The Chinese brought in aircraft, which flew ground-attack missions against the guerrillas. The resistance forces had only small arms, and Gompo Tashi said later that they "were simply not equipped to resist this type of warfare." Gompo Tashi changed the VFF's tactics; rather than fighting as large units, the resistance would operate as small guerrilla bands and concentrate on cutting roads and other communications.

At the same time, the VFF forces in the Lhoka area were also expanding. They controlled much of the countryside, operating on the PLA's doorstep. In January 1959, the VFF besieged and destroyed the Chinese garrison at Tsetang. This was both a symbolic and a military victory, as Tsetang was the legendary birthplace of the Tibetan race and was located just a two-day-march from the capital of Lhasa.

The preparations for the second C-118 airdrop were also under way. Athar Norbu had made his way back into Tibet and rejoined Lhotse. The drop was made on 22 February 1959. These two drops had mixed results, however. Because of the payload restrictions on the aircraft, the two drops totaled merely 403 Lee-Enfield rifles, 60 hand grenades, 20 machine guns, and 26,000 rounds of ammunition. This amounted to only a small percentage of the weapons needed to arm the volunteers in the Lhoka area. However, Lhotse and Athar Norbu were unable to distribute the supplies before the resistance was overtaken by the final break between the Dalai Lama and the Chinese.

As the rebellion against Chinese occupation grew, the Dalai Lama had been undertaking his final studies of Buddhist logic, philosophy, and metaphysics. On 5 March 1959, he completed his final examinations and was accredited as the reincarnated Dalai Lama. Gen. Tan Guansen, the Chinese political commissar, invited him to attend a theatrical performance in the PLA camp outside Lhasa. General Tan insisted that the Dalai Lama leave behind his twenty-five armed bodyguards. The Dalai Lama accepted the Chinese demands, but rumors spread that the Chinese would attempt to kidnap him. On the day of the performance, the Dalai Lama found his summer palace was surrounded by an estimated thirty thousand Tibetans intent on preventing him from meeting with the Chinese. The weeklong standoff continued until the afternoon of 17 March, when two mortar shells hit in the marshes outside the north gate of the palace. The Dalai Lama realized that he would have to leave Lhasa.

That evening, Phala Dronyer Chenmo helped put together the small escape party. The Dalai Lama, his brother-in-law, Phala Dronyer Chenmo, a senior abbot, and two soldiers slipped through the crowds and crossed a river a quarter of a mile away. They were then reunited with family members and the rest of the escape group, along with being met by thirty Khampa soldiers and the CIA radio team.

Once the party had reached resistance-controlled territory, they split up into smaller groups that were protected by resistance bands on their flanks as they made their way across the mountains. The CIA radio operator, who also sent progress reports to Washington, D.C., filmed the escape in color. When the groups reached an area about a hundred miles south of Lhasa, a courier brought word to the Dalai Lama that the Chinese had shelled the palace forty-eight hours after he had escaped. The Chinese then attacked the crowds surrounding the palace.

The Dalai Lama still faced the moral dilemma over the use of violence to preserve a Buddhist society. He wrote later that he "very much admired their courage and their determination to carry on the grim battle they had started for our freedom, culture, and religion." The Dalai Lama added that he "could not in honesty advise them to avoid violence. In order to fight, they had sacrificed their homes and all the comforts and benefits of a peaceful life. Now they could see no alternative but to go on fighting, and I had none to offer."

The Dalai Lama's hopes of negotiating a settlement ended on 28 March 1959, when the Chinese dissolved the Tibetan government and ordered that "democratic reforms" be imposed. The Dalai Lama realized that he had to establish a Tibetan government, lest the people believe he had accepted the Chinese statement. The ceremony was held at a rebel stronghold about sixty miles from the Indian border, with full religious rites and more than a thousand people in attendance. The event was filmed by one of the CIA radio operators. The color film was later provided to the CIA and the media.

The Dalai Lama and his advisers quickly concluded that they would have to escape to India. President Eisenhower and a small group of CIA officials had been following the Dalai Lama's escape through radio messages from the CIA radio team. These reported that the Dalai Lama had crossed the Indian border on 31 March and would be arriving at Tawang in India's North-East Frontier Agency within three days. The reports also described the continuing shelling of Lhasa's population and asked the United States to "help us as soon as possible and send us weapons for 30,000 men by airplane."

The Struggle for Tibet

DCI Allen Dulles informed President Eisenhower on 1 April 1959 that plans were being made by the CIA, "within existing policy authorization . . . in light of the recent upsurge of Tibetan resistance and the flight of the Dalai Lama," to increase CIA backing. Plans were already being made to make additional airdrops of weapons during the spring to VFF headquarters. These plans were soon abandoned, however, when PLA troops launched a series of anti-guerrilla sweeps that lasted two weeks. The Chinese overran the VFF base at Tsetang and several other strongholds, and then they took the Tibetan resistance's main base at Tsona near the Indian border on 14 April.

On 20 April, Allen Dulles briefed the chairman of the JCS, Air Force Gen. Nathan Twining, regarding the situation in Tibet. The DCI told General Twining that the Chinese were waging an effective anti-guerrilla campaign, which used more airpower than either the United States or the Tibetans had expected. As a result, Dulles said, "the resistance boys had been badly trapped." When General Twining asked whether there was anything the military could do to help, Dulles replied that they had already provided a great deal of help, but there was nothing at the moment that they could do. The Tibetans had asked that the planned airdrops be postponed, as they had lost control of the areas to the PLA.

Dulles provided an equally gloomy briefing to the NSC three days later. He informed them that the latest messages indicated that the VFF "had been severely beaten by the Chinese Communists." Dulles added that the VFF forces in the Khan area "had been pretty well knocked into pieces," while the same was also probably true for the resistance forces in the Lhasa area. Under Chinese air and ground attack, the Tibetans had run out of both food and ammunition. Dulles reported a week later that Gompo Tashi's resistance forces had been effectively crushed by the Chinese sweeps. He continued that the Tibetans had made the mistake of fighting in large groups, but he believed that in the future they would "probably discover that the essence of guerrilla warfare consists of fighting in small bands."

The changing situation in Tibet took place against the background of a major reorganization within the CIA, its U-2 operations, and the agency's covert air activities. Frank Wisner, the CIA's deputy director for plans (DDP), was no longer in charge of covert actions. His fall began with the Hungarian revolution in October 1956 when he had been forced to stand by and do nothing as the Soviets crushed the popular uprising against Communist rule. As many as thirty thousand Hungarians had been killed, and large numbers of refugees escaped into Austria. They told reporters and relief workers that Radio Free Europe broadcasts had encouraged them to believe that the United States would come to their aid. Earlier, Wisner had shown signs of manic depression, but the failure of the Hungarian revolution, the accusations against the CIA-sponsored Radio Free Europe, and an attack of hepatitis in December 1956 accelerated his mental collapse.

Wisner returned to work in the spring of 1957, but mental and physical breakdown continued, forcing his resignation as DDP. In the fall of 1958, he underwent several months of psychological treatment. On 1 January 1959, Richard M. Bissell Jr. replaced Wisner as DDP. Bissell was the head of the Development Projects Staff, which oversaw the U-2. He had previously opposed the idea of bringing control of the CIA's air assets under a single office. When he became DDP, however, Bissell's opinion changed. The Development Projects Staff was renamed on 16 February the Development Projects Division and became part of Bissell's Directorate of Plans.

The CIA's air assets had undergone a series of reorganizations during this period. The American Airdale Corporation, the CIA-owned holding company that controlled CAT, changed its name on 7 October 1957 to the Pacific Corporation. To further hide CIA control, there was another change in early 1959. The commercial airline for Taiwan remained in its existing form and was still called CAT. The covert elements underwent a name change to give the appearance of an airline owned by another airline. On 31 March 1959, the same day that the Dalai Lama crossed into India, these covert elements became "Air America."

The VFF would have to be rebuilt after the setbacks inflicted by the PLA. This required more Tibetans trained in guerrilla warfare and more arms drops. In early May 1959, President Eisenhower authorized an increase in support. In preparation, a pair of U-2 overflights of Tibet were made. These were to identify potential drop zones and sabotage targets, as well as to produce maps for the airdrops, which would begin in late summer.

Following President Eisenhower's approval, personnel from Detachment C, based in Japan, were deployed to NAS Cubi Point in the Philippines, and preparations began to make the overflights. The two overflights would be long and demand the most of their pilots. The first overflight was made on 12 May with Tom Crull as pilot. The route took the airplane across North Vietnam and Laos, then into China. Crull then turned south and covered Tibet. The mission, which lasted nine hours and ten minutes, finally landed at Kermitola, in East Pakistan.

The second overflight occurred two days later on 14 May. Lyle Rudd was the pilot, and the difficulties facing him were even greater. The route went farther north, across China to Mongolia, then south across the endless plains of western

China to Tibet. As Rudd flew above Lhasa, he could see the Potala Palace, the former residence of the Dalai Lama. Like Crull before him, Rudd landed at Kermitola. The long flight had stretched the U-2's capability to its limit. Before he found the airfield, the low-fuel light had already come on. When he finally landed, Rudd had been in the air for nine hours and forty minutes, covering some 4,200 nautical miles. The photos from both missions were good.

The most important result of these overflights was the improved mapping. Before the U-2 missions, the B-17 and C-118 pilots had been forced to make do with inadequate World Aeronautical Charts. Lawrence Ropka, an Air Force navigator assigned to STBarnum, recalled: "Many of them had white sploshes in them, rather than colors, and that denoted that there was no accurate data available. As you would marry one chart with another, as was the custom at the time . . . it was always intriguing because the mountain ridges and rivers on one chart wouldn't match the mountain ridges and rivers on another, which didn't instill a lot of confidence in the charts."

Additional Tibetan guerrillas were also now undergoing training. This was not done on Saipan, like the first group, but in the United States at what was described as an "eastern seacoast site" (presumably, the CIA's Camp Peary, located near Williamsburg, Virginia). The Tibetans were becoming ill, however, and by early 1958, the CIA instructors realized this was due to the low altitude. The Department of Defense offered the use of Camp Hale outside Leadville, Colorado. Originally built to train the U.S. Army's Tenth Mountain Division in World War II, it was now deactivated. The base was located at an elevation of ten thousand feet in the Rocky Mountains, and the terrain was similar to eastern Tibet. On Memorial Day 1958, the second group of Tibetan guerrillas was relocated to the new site to continue their training.

Some seven hundred Tibetans underwent a six-month period of guerrilla training at the site over several years. When each group of Tibetans arrived at Camp Hale, they were issued green Army fatigues and black boots. After breakfast, they were shown around the camp, which consisted of ten buildings near the bank of a small river. The Tibetans were restricted to their barracks, mess hall, classrooms, and the recreation room. They named the site "Dhumra" after the Tibetan word for garden. The instructors were CIA/OPC veterans of earlier covert operations in Asia, whom the Tibetans called *ghegen* (Tibetan for teacher). At the end of the first lecture, the Tibetans were asked, "Will you jump from an airplane? If so, raise your hand." After the hands were raised, the *ghegen* then asked, "Who wants to fight the Chinese?"

The Tibetans organized themselves into teams rather than having individuals be assigned tasks. This was based on regional ties, personal compatibility, and useful skills. The result was a lack of visible friction between the team members despite the hard training and close quarters they endured. Reveille each morning at Camp Hale was sounded not by bugle, but with tapes of popular Japanese songs. Breakfast of eggs, toast, and oatmeal was served at 5:30 A.M., as the Tibetans said their morning prayers. Classroom and field training followed.

A full half of the six-month course was spent in learning radio communications. Radio operators were expected to send and receive Morse code at fifteen to twenty words per minute, and to use the codebooks and one-time pads. Others would crank the hand generators, which provided power. This was familiar to the Tibetans, as their religious rituals included endlessly turning prayer wheels. The Tibetans were also trained to make weather observations. Other classroom instruction included map reading, land navigation using compass and stars (which many of the Tibetans could already do better than their instructors), and intelligence techniques such as running networks. It was not unusual for the guerrilla trainees to chant Buddhist mantras on breaks or even during classes.

The initial rifles supplied to the Tibetans were British-made Lee-Enfields. These were common in Tibet, and not easily traceable to the United States. With Eisenhower's decision to step up support, M-1 Garand rifles were selected as the standard weapon. Although made in the United States, the increased firepower they provided was judged to outweigh any considerations of plausible deniability. The Tibetans were also trained in the use of 60-mm and 81-mm mortars, 57-mm and 75-mm recoilless rifles, and pistols.

The classroom and firing range training was put to practical use in field exercises. These included setting up ambushes, securing drop zones, and marking them with an illuminated "T," and receiving the air-dropped supplies. Camp Hale had several hundred acres of mountainous terrain for the field exercises, which were run day and night and in all kinds of weather. These activities, despite Camp Hale's isolation, attracted the attention of the local population. This resulted in a local legend that the area was actually a nuclear test site. This rumor was deliberately reinforced by strenuous official denials and the occasional loud explosion, all of which discouraged the curious hiker.

The long hours, hard training, and cramped quarters created a bond between the *ghegens* and the Tibetans. The CIA instructors saw the Tibetans as self-reliant "straight shooters" who found their way of life under brutal attack by outsiders, and who sought only to defend themselves. Despite the differences in culture and religion, the *ghegens* had the utmost respect for the Tibetans. This was an opinion shared by the Tibetans. Thinlay Paljor fondly reminisced years later, "We, the Tibetans and the American instructors, all lived together as one large family." The relationship worked because the Tibetans believed in their cause, and the CIA instructors found it was a cause that they could embrace wholeheartedly.

Before the Tibetans' training was complete, they had to be parachute qualified. The initial jump training was done from a platform made from felled trees. The only time that the Tibetans left Camp Hale was when they made their three qualifying parachute jumps at a nearby airfield. Reflecting the close bonds between the Americans and Tibetans, some of the instructors accompanied the Tibetans on their jumps. The Tibetans called the airplane a *namdu,* which literally means "sky boat." With the three jumps successfully accomplished, the Tibetans were ready to return to their homeland and to continue the secret war.

CIA Airdrops Resume

By the late summer of 1959, the situation inside Tibet was clearer. Despite the Chinese sweeps, some pockets of resistance still existed. The CIA decided to parachute Tibetans teams into the areas where resistance activities had been reported. If the situation warranted it, they would call in airdrops. The first series of drops would be made during the September 1959 full moon period. Rather than an individual mission, several C-118 flights into Tibet would be made during this period. This meant that additional Air America crewmen, both pilots and PDOs, would be needed. The PDOs came from an unusual source—the U.S. Forest Service.

During the early 1950s, the CIA had recruited a former smoke jumper named Gar Thorsrud for drops into northwestern China. Thorsrud left the CIA with the end of the Korean War, joining the Montana Air National Guard as a fighter pilot. In 1957, he accepted a senior position with the CIA's air branch. Thorsrud's first job was to oversee the supply drops for Operation Haik. This was an effort in Indonesia by the CIA to assist rebellious army officers who were trying to overthrow President Sukarno. The effort collapsed in May 1958 when a CAT B-26 pilot named Allen L. Pope was shot down and captured by the Indonesians.

As STBarnum resumed, Thorsrud used his forest service contacts to recruit additional smoke jumpers as PDOs. One of those recruited, Andy Anderson, recalled that, like smoke jumping, his work for the CIA was "seasonal." He noted, "I stayed with the forest service in the summertime and fought fires, and then most of the stuff [in Tibet] was done in the wintertime. So when fire season was over, I'd just go back to Tibet." Another PDO, Miles Johnson, knew twelve other smoke jumpers who became involved with the missions to Tibet—six from McCall, Idaho, and six from Missoula, Montana. They called themselves the "Missoula Mafia."

Before the C-118 could fly its dangerous missions over Tibet, the U-2 would provide photographic coverage. The CIA had made arrangements to use an airfield at Takhli, Thailand, for U-2 missions by Detachment C pilots. These overflights not only covered Tibet and China, but also Communist North Vietnam and the neighboring country of Laos, where a Communist-led guerrilla war was beginning. Of the six U-2 overflights out of Takhli, three were of Tibet and China. The initial missions were flown on 3 and 4 September 1959. The moon grew brighter over the next several nights, and the airdrop window was about to open. The final coverage of Tibet before the drops began was an overflight on 9 September.

A team of nine Tibetans parachuted from the C-118 on 19 September into a drop zone near Ringtso, where some four thousand guerrillas were reportedly active. The nine Tibetans carried a heavy load of equipment—two radios, codebooks, signal plans, radio spare parts, maps, compasses, and binoculars. As the CIA did not know what reception they might meet on this "blind drop," the team was armed with M-1s and Sten submachine guns. Their orders were to locate Natsang Phurpo, the leader of the guerrillas, and convince him to attack the Chinese trucks carrying borax from local mines.

The team landed successfully and made its way to the location where the group was last reported to be operating. The team discovered that the guerrillas had been betrayed, and the Chinese had moved in and dispersed the force. The team had no option but to bury their radios and head to India. This was a hard eight-week march, covering some 350 miles before the team finally returned to the Mustang area of Nepal. They contacted the resistance leaders, who debriefed them on the mission and the escape. Within a few weeks, the CIA secretly brought them out of India and flew them a second time to Dhumra for further debriefings and to begin preparations for more missions into Tibet.

Three other teams, totaling eighteen men, were also dropped into the Pembar area during the September 1959 full moon period. This area was where Gompo Tashi had recruited a small guerrilla force the previous spring. It had become a refuge for guerrillas who had been forced out of areas farther east by the Chinese. The Pembar area also had strategic importance, as it was between the northern and southern branches of the Sichuan-Lhasa highway. The three teams were to confirm the presence of resistance forces and to encourage them to attack Chinese supply and troop convoys. Their position between the two major supply routes put the Tibetans in a position to disrupt the Chinese efforts to suppress the revolt.

The first team had seven members, who were to train the Pembar resistance groups in guerrilla tactics and to prepare to receive arms drops. The second team, of six men, was initially ordered to move overland to Zayul, near the border with Burma, but this was changed and they were told to stay at Pembar and assist with the airdrops. All thirteen members of the first and second teams were Khampas from the Yangtze River area. The third team was of a mixed ethnic makeup. Of its five members, three were from the Amdo plateau and two were from central Tibet. These five went to the southern part of Amdo and reported sizable resistance groups. The guerrillas agreed to stage attacks on the Qinghai-Lhasa highway, once arms had been supplied, and they accepted the team's radio operator, Nasar Tashi Tsering, as their leader.

During the next two full moon periods, two supply drops were made in the Pembar area. The first drop included 370 M-1 rifles and 71,040 rounds of ammunition; 4 machine guns and 1,000 rounds; and 2 radio sets. The second drop carried a similar load, with the addition of 3 recoilless rifles and 150 rounds. Although the resumption of U.S. support for the Tibetan resistance was now under way, the seven airdrop missions flown using the C-118 were exposing the shortcomings of the aircraft.

None of the CAT/Air America crews liked the aircraft. CAT navigator Jim Keck recalled, "For one thing, it didn't have the power." Even with the nine-thousand-pound payload limit, the C-118 could not fly above the mountains; rather, it would have to weave its way through them. The crew had to rely not only on good weather and bright moonlight, but also on celestial navigation, dead-reckoning, and spotting landmarks. Keck also recalled that the C-118 "had a radar set that was mainly for weather avoidance; it wasn't a navigator's radar. The antenna wasn't stabilized so when you went into a turn, you lost all your picture. So a lot of times in the [C-118] I'd tell them, 'You have to roll out. I can't see anything.'"

A far more serious threat was the loss of an engine in flight. Ropka calculated that the C-118 could just barely make it back to East Pakistan if an engine failed over Tibet. An Air Force team arrived on Okinawa in late 1958 to run tests on the C-118. Based on the results, they cut Ropka's three-engine performance estimates by 7 to 8 percent. He observed later, "If this was correct, the airplane could never have gotten back on three engines."

There were also operational shortcomings with the C-118. The aircraft was basically an obsolete DC-6 civilian airliner. Its side door could not be opened in flight and consequently was removed before takeoff. As a result, the crew members and passengers were exposed to the numbing cold at high altitudes. Because the door was too small to allow the cargo to be dropped in a single pass, each C-118 had to make several passes, increasing the airplane's exposure time. Despite this, only two near misses occurred. On one flight, a PDO was knocked unconscious by a loose static line. The same crewman was almost forced out of the airplane during a later drop over Tibet.

C-130s over Tibet—The Airlift Expands

Air Force Lt. Gen. Charles P. Cabell, the deputy director of central intelligence, oversaw the airdrops and was well aware of the C-118's shortcomings. He called Gen. Curtis LeMay, the vice chief of staff of the Air Force, to ask for use of C-130A transports. General Cabell believed that the larger, more powerful, and higher-flying C-130s would be safer than the C-118. Although the airplanes would be stripped of their U.S. Air Force markings, using the C-130s meant the end of plausible deniability for the Tibetan missions; only the U.S. military used C-130s. General LeMay quickly agreed to Cabell's request. The C-130s would come from the 315th Troop Carrier Wing at Naha Air Base on Okinawa. Air America crews were checked out in the C-130s, and then began operations over Tibet in November 1959.

The preparations for the C-130 missions actually began in Tibet. The radio operators with the resistance forces requested supplies, providing a primary drop zone as well as a backup site. When their requests reached Washington, D.C., specialists with the CIA's Far East Division air branch would then plot routes to and from the drop sites using the U-2 photos. Factored into the plan were estimates of the Chinese air threat, the payload, and the weather forecast. When the flight plan was completed, the chief of the air branch would take it to Richard Helms, who was Bissell's deputy at the Directorate of Plans. When he approved the mission, it was sent to Cabell for the final go-ahead. The radio operators were then told the drop zones, the number of bundles, and how many pack animals they would need to carry the load.

A minimum of three days before the start of the full moon cycle, Air Force pilots from the 315th Troop Carrier Wing flew the C-130s from Naha to Kadena Air Base on Okinawa, where CIA personnel loaded the aircraft. The arms and ammunition were prepackaged in eighty- to eighty-five-pound bundles, which could be quickly placed on the backs of pack animals. After loading was completed, Air America crews flew the C-130s to the CIA's airfield at Takhli, Thailand, accompanied by Air Force pilots who checked their proficiency during the flight. After the C-130s landed at Takhli, all military markings were removed from them.

One or two days before the scheduled mission, the air branch headquarters would send an alert message to Takhli. This would be followed by messages with the word "affirm" twelve hours, six hours, two hours, and one hour before the takeoff time. Final approval, based primarily on the weather forecast for the drop zones, would be sent at launch time. This, in turn, was based on weather reports sent by the radio teams. They had cards that showed cloud types and coverage, and their observations were transmitted in Morse code. CIA officer Roger McCarthy recalled, "We soon found that the weather reports from the teams were usually more accurate than those reported by all the 'modern' weather reporting services, including the military."

The Air America crewmen were also making their final preparations. The pilots, navigators, and radio operators were briefed on the route and weather, while the three PDOs aboard each airplane made a final check that the cargo was securely tied down and that there were at least three walk-around oxygen bottles for each of them. Each bottle lasted about thirty minutes; they were used when the C-130 was depressurized for the drop. One to three aircraft operated each night. When the final approval came, the C-130s took off at fifteen-minute intervals.

The C-130s headed to the northwest, crossing the border between Thailand and Burma at dusk. The aircraft climbed to the optimum altitude, which was as high as thirty-five thousand feet. The C-130s crossed into Indian airspace, then over the Himalayas and into Tibet. One navigator watched the APN-59 mapping radar for landmarks, while the other navigator made star sightings to cross-check the route. The radio operator would send a brief Morse code signal, "QQQ," when each checkpoint was reached. The flight to the drop zones might take as long as six or seven hours on some missions. The C-130 pilots would sometimes pass the time by giving the PDOs a guided tour, pointing out Mount Everest, K-2, and other towering peaks. PDO Miles Johnson recalled, "All the flights were moonlit flights, and it was just crystal clear and it looked like in some cases you could just reach out and touch [the mountains]."

As the C-130 approached the drop zone, the airplane descended until it was flying a thousand feet above the ground. The C-130 was depressurized and the rear cargo ramp was lowered. The combined noise of the four turboprop engines and the airflow over the ramp was deafening. Johnson recalled that it sounded "like a roaring freight train." Bonfires that formed a T marked the drop zone. As the C-130 passed over it, the pilot would turn on a green light, ring a bell, and pull up. The PDOs would release the restraints, and cargo would slide out of the airplane. The whole procedure took only a few seconds. Johnson recalled, "You could look out the rear as we made the drop and see all the little Tibetans running around and their pack horses and their little food fires, and all that kind of stuff."

As the Tibetans gathered up the bundles, the PDOs aboard the C-130s closed the ramps and repressurized the aircraft. The pilots climbed and turned south, back toward Takhli. They landed after spending as long as twelve to fourteen hours in the air. Despite the dangers and difficulties, Air America crews were eager to make the flights. There was never a shortage of volunteers, and those not selected for the covert missions were upset at being passed over.

In December 1959, the resistance forces around Pembar received 226 pallets, which contained 800 M-1 rifles, 113 carbines, 20 cases of hand grenades, and 200 cases of ammunition, totaling 2 million rounds. On 13 December, during the same full moon period, the forces in southern Amdo received the first of eight supply drops. Two C-130s delivered 290 pallets to their encampment at Nira Tsogeng. Included were 1,680 rifles and 368,800 rounds of ammunition.

Despite these apparent successes, there were still major problems with the airlift. During November and December 1959, less than half of the nine to twelve flights planned for each full moon period were completed. The main problem was the APN-59 radar used for navigation. The equipment had a high failure rate, forcing several aborts. Additionally, despite the larger payload of the C-130s, the long missions required forty thousand pounds of fuel, which meant only twenty-six thousand pounds of cargo could be carried on each flight.

To correct the problems, the CIA arranged for the Air Force to assign a new commander to the airlift in January 1960. He was Maj. Harry C. Aderholt, who had overseen similar agent drops during the Korean War. On his first morning, Major Aderholt met with the personnel and made clear the new situation. He told them that they would be expanding operations and said, "It is going to be exciting." He continued, "If you are not ready to be part of it, now is the time to raise your hand and get out."

Part of the problems affecting both morale and efficiency was the secrecy of the missions. Only the commander and one other officer had been briefed about the airlift. The rest of the unit had no idea what was going on. Aderholt thought this made no sense, saying later, "How in the hell could you expect troops to take pride in their work if they didn't know why they were doing it?" He arranged for the whole unit to be briefed on the project. Although the Air America crews made the actual drops, Aderholt wanted his Air Force personnel to understand how critical their support role was to the missions.

Aderholt also improved the unit's living conditions. He had the supply Quonset hut at Kadena Air Base converted into a recreation room, outfitted with a pool table, a ping-pong table, and a snack bar. The situation at Takhli was worse. There was no transportation, personnel lived and worked in a small, run-down hangar, and there was no regular mess hall or bathing facilities. Aderholt arranged for fifty bicycles and a VW van to serve as the unit's transport, got new buildings authorized, and had a cook brought in. The turnaround in morale was quickly apparent.

Aderholt also dealt with the C-130s' technical and payload shortcomings. He brought in CIA communication specialists, whom he called "the best in the business," to check the APN-59 radar sets. They found that the radars were fine, but the C-130's electrical system was shorting them out when the airplanes' wheels retracted. The CIA personnel quickly fixed the aircraft. Recalled Aderholt, "We never had to abort another mission because a radar set went out."

Aderholt also had all unneeded equipment removed from the C-130s to increase their payload. The main increase in payload, however, resulted from a change in procedures. The C-130's normal maximum gross takeoff weight was 124,000 pounds, but the airplane's Emergency Wartime Planning maximum weight was 135,000 pounds. Aderholt talked with Lockheed personnel and learned that the difference was due to limitations on the landing gear. When the C-130 taxied, any turns put side loads on the landing gear. To overcome this, Aderholt had the C-130s taxied out to the end of the runway prior to the airplane's fuel tanks being topped off. Thus, the side loads were avoided, and the C-130s could then be loaded to the wartime weight, raising the payload from 26,000 pounds to 37,000 pounds.

The affect of the changes that Aderholt brought about became apparent during the January 1960 full moon period. On 6 January, three C-130s dropped 657 pallets of arms and supplies to the resistance forces at Pembar. The supplies included thirty cases of medicine, twelve cases of food, a mimeograph machine, and a box of propaganda booklets. The Air America pilots reported that the drop zones were exactly at the map coordinates the Tibetans had reported and were clearly marked by T-shaped bonfires. They also said that the Tibetans had gathered some two hundred mules in the drop zones to pick up the supplies, forming a huge encampment.

Two C-130s were also sent to the encampment at Nira Tsogeng on 10 January, but only one of the aircraft was able to make a drop. Five days later, four C-130s parachuted arms and other supplies to the site. In all, some four thousand resistance fighters had been armed. Also dropped were three teams, totaling fourteen men, who were led by Ngawang Phuljung, who was Gompo Tashi's nephew. Among them were six of the nine Tibetans who had parachuted into Ringtso the previous year. The teams' assignment was to convince the Tibetans to disperse into small guerrilla bands rather than continue to use the huge encampment at Nira Tsogeng, and to begin attacks to close the northern road to Lhasa.

Although the risk of a Chinese ambush of the crews was great, greater still was the danger of bad weather. The closest call started one night when two separate C-130 navigators corrected for nonexistent jet stream winds. This error was soon compounded by poor visibility in rain and fog. As a result, the two airplanes were soon lost. Unable to find the drop zone, the two C-130s turned back, taking separate routes. Baker flight, piloted by William Welk and A. L. Judkins, headed to Kermitola, which now served as an emergency field. (Welk had flown many of the early CAT covert missions over China.) With fuel running low, they arrived over the field, only to find rain and a thirty-knot crosswind. The field had no lights, and its only navigation aid was a nondirectional radio beacon. After passing over the beacon, the crew began a descent. Suddenly, lightning illuminated the runway, and Welk and Judkins landed without incident.

The pilots of Able flight, Jack Stiles and M. D. "Doc" Johnson, decided to try to reach Takhli. By the time they reached the field, the low-fuel warning light had come on. Takhli was shrouded in fog, and they had only enough time for one landing attempt. Aderholt and Ropka went to the end of the runway and began shooting flares into the sky. As two of the C-130's four engines shut down from fuel exhaustion, Johnson spotted one of the flares. He told Stiles that he would take over the controls, and he put the C-130 into a tight descent to avoid the hills near the runway. Entering the fog, the crew searched for the runway. Johnson spotted it when the C-130 was merely two hundred feet above the ground. He had barely enough time to line up on the runway and touch down before the C-130's tanks ran dry.

As with the CAT covert flights, the Air America C-130 crews were paid bonus money. And as with the earlier missions, the amount was actually minimal. Aderholt pointed out later that the crews actually lost money flying into Tibet. Consequently, Aderholt established a sliding scale based on the level of difficulty. For a routine "A" mission, each crew member received $300. The pay for "B" missions was slightly higher, at $500. (This amounted to about $25 to $40 per hour.) Aderholt thought Stiles, Johnson, and their crew each deserved the $1,000 paid for a "C" mission. Robert E. Rousselot, Air America's vice president for operations, turned down Aderholt's recommendation. Rousselot was just as demanding as he had been when CAT flew China missions. He refused to approve any C mission payments, as he felt that "it would spoil the pilots."

Most mishaps were far less serious. PDO Andy Andersen recalled one mission to a drop zone near the Mongolian border. Unlike most of the drops, this one involved just one Tibetan, named "Dennis." As the C-130 crossed over the drop zone, it pulled up and the cargo was released. As the C-130 pitched up, Dennis made an instinctive grab for Andersen, who recalled: "We were standing there hugging each other, and then I finally pushed him out [of the C-130], and somehow he got kind of tangled up. I had about a hundred feet of intercom cord on my harness with an alligator clip and he took the whole thing with him. He pulled it right out of the box where it goes into the airplane."

The night's adventures were not yet over, however. When Andersen tried to close the ramp, he found the system had malfunctioned. Andersen, Miles Johnson, and the other PDO had to close it by hand. Johnson said: "This consequently used up more oxygen than normal and we were trying to monitor each other's oxygen in the meantime. Andy was getting pretty weak so we got another bottle and plugged him in. By the time we had gotten the static lines in and had hand-pumped the door closed, all the portable walk-around bottles had been used up."

Sometimes the mishaps were simply embarrassing. Major Aderholt was dissatisfied with the briefings given the Air America crews for the January 1960 missions and believed their survival equipment and training was inadequate. To correct the situation, Aderholt signed for a large supply of gold coins, which would be used by a downed crew to buy or bribe their way out of trouble. He broke these down into individual packages for each crewman.

"Doc" Johnson was the first to be issued the coins. He signed for the entire crew's packages as he was going out to the runway. Boarding the C-130, he set the coins on top of the bundles, then went to the cockpit and took his seat. The flight was routine, until he returned to Takhli and Aderholt asked for the gold coins. Johnson suddenly realized he had left the coins on top of the cargo, and they had been dropped with it. Aderholt was philosophical about the incident, observing later, "It's amusing now, but I sure wasn't amused at the time."

The early months of 1960 were the peak of the CIA's airdrop program in support of the Tibetan resistance. The resistance had been rebuilt, and the airlift was in high gear. In addition, although the picture was still incomplete, the United States had indications that the Chinese were hard-pressed in early 1960. The failure of Mao's "Great Leap Forward," a program of forced industrialization, was becoming apparent. This would soon lead to twenty million deaths from famine. Within the Communist government, there was instability. However, just as with the earlier paramilitary operations in Eastern Europe and the USSR, defeat of the Tibetan resistance movement was waiting around the corner.

The Defeat of the Tibetan Resistance

DCI Dulles briefed President Eisenhower on 4 February 1960 and asked for his approval to continue the operation. Eisenhower expressed concern over the cost the Tibetans were paying for the revolt, and he wondered whether continuing the aid might result in even more brutal reprisals by the Chinese. Desmond FitzGerald, the head of the CIA's Far East Division, replied that "there could be no greater brutality than had been experienced in Tibet in the past." According to documents later captured, the Chinese had killed about eighty-seven thousand Tibetans in 1959 alone. Eisenhower then asked Secretary of State Christian Herter whether he supported continuing the operation. Herter replied that "not only would continued successful resistance by the Tibetans prove to be a serious harassment to the Chinese Communists but it would serve to keep the spark alive in the entire area." The results could "mean much to the free world apart from humanitarian considerations for the Tibetans." Eisenhower gave his approval.

Yet despite repeated urging by the CIA radio teams, the Tibetans had still not dispersed into small guerrilla bands. The Tibetan resistance fought with their families and livestock. Much of Tibet was too barren for the guerrillas to live off the land. It was not possible for them to abandon their families and herds and take to the mountains. As a result, the Tibetan resistance had lost the key advantage of the guerrilla: the ability to strike and then disappear before conventional forces could be mustered.

The Chinese were determined to crush the revolt. An entire air division was moved into western China to provide support for mass ground sweeps. A month after the January 1960 airdrops, PLA ground forces backed by aircraft launched an attack on the Pembar camp area. By late spring of 1960, they had destroyed or dispersed the resistance forces and their families and animals. With only rifles and small arms, the Tibetans could not counter the massed Chinese airpower. Of the thirteen men of the two teams dropped into Pembar during September 1959, just five made their way back to India several months later.

The same story unfolded at the encampment at Nira Tsogeng. By early 1960, it had grown to include herds of some thirty thousand animals. The area surrounding the encampment lacked both cover and supplies of food necessary for guerrilla bands. On 22 February 1960 the PLA launched air and ground attacks against the resistance forces. As the guerrillas attempted to flee across the desolate landscape, PLA cavalry and tanks pursued them. Again, the Tibetans were decimated as a fighting force. As the Chinese continued their attacks in the months that followed, the Tibetan resistance suffered another blow. After the loss of Powers's U-2 on 1 May, Eisenhower ordered a halt to the C-130 resupply missions. He was unwilling to risk the loss of another aircraft over a denied area. This cut off any chance of resupplying the remaining forces.

Within six months, the guerrillas were destroyed. Many tried to escape, but most died along the way because of a lack of fresh water. Among them were the four radio teams that had been dropped in September 1959 and January 1960. One CIA radio operator was able to reach India, whereas another, named Yeshe, surrendered to the Chinese. He was imprisoned for the next nineteen years. The resistance fighters who survived the Chinese attacks fled to India and Nepal. Soon, significant numbers of refugees had gathered in these border areas.

In November 1960, John F. Kennedy was elected president in a narrow victory. The following month, he met with DCI Dulles and was briefed on the Tibetan operation. Kennedy indicated he would continue backing the Tibetans. He had read Mao's writings on guerrilla warfare and saw covert action and counterinsurgency as necessary to counter wars of national liberation.

In early 1960, as the resistance effort was collapsing, Gyalo Thondup had proposed a new approach for the resistance. A base would be established inside the kingdom of Mustang. Small groups would then cross into Tibet and find areas where they could disperse and operate as guerrillas rather than as large conventional units. The CIA would drop arms, supplies, and leaders to the areas. Soon after Kennedy's inauguration, the Mustang operation began in earnest. The Tibetans were organized into sixteen companies, composed of one hundred men each from different tribes, areas, and cities to break up the hometown units that perpetuated local feuds and rivalries. They were put through hard daily training, and their morale soared. By early spring of 1961, Kennedy had given the CIA approval to resume airdrops into Tibet.

The airdrops were made on 15 March 1961, with the C-130s delivering enough arms and radio operators to equip four of the companies. The drop site was inside Tibet, south of the Brahmaputra River and opposite the border with Mustang. The arms and personnel were recovered without incident and taken back across the border. Gyen Yeshe, the de facto commander of the Mustang force, decided to divide the weapons between eight companies.

Also during the March 1961 full moon period, a final team of seven men was dropped into the Markam area on the western side of the Yangtze River. The leader of the team was Yeshe Wangyal, the twenty-year-old son of a Khampa chieftain in the area who led a small resistance group. Known to the instructors as "Tim," he was regarded as the most intelligent of the Tibetans, with a natural gift for guerrilla warfare. He had been on the ill-fated 19 September 1959 drop into Ringtso. After his escape to Nepal, he had returned to Dhumra. Tim was then assigned to a second mission, this time in the Kham area of Tibet. A few hours before he and the team were to board the C-130, they calmly, but firmly, refused to go on the mission. They objected to making a blind drop into an area they did not know, and where they had no contacts. The *ghegens* tried to convince Tim and the others to go, as they feared that the cancellation of the mission represented both a personal failure and a threat to the future of the operation. Nonetheless, Tim and the others refused, and the drop was scrubbed.

Soon after, the C-130 drops were halted, and Tim spent several months in a Pacific holding area. Tim and the other team members volunteered to be dropped into the Markam area, which he knew. On the flight to the drop zone, the team was euphoric at finally setting out. They also were impressed by the fact that several of the C-130 crewmen were not wearing parachutes, meaning they shared the risk of death if the airplane crashed. The CIA briefers instructed them to contact Tim's father and two other local resistance leaders, Mepa Pon and Dakpa Lama. They were also told to head for India if the Chinese forces were too strong. The team asked that L-pills be included in their packs, so they could kill themselves rather than be captured.

The seven men were dropped near the small village of Gojo. It was a late winter night, and the ground had a light dusting of snow. One of the team was injured in the drop, but it was otherwise successful. The team hid its parachutes and supplies in small stone huts. After two nights' travel, they encountered three herdsmen, one of whom turned out to have been a servant to Tim's father. They told the guerrillas that Tim's father had been killed several months before, and the two other resistance leaders were hiding out. The herdsmen refused to sell the team any food, and ordered them to leave or risk being reported to the Chinese.

Tim continued his mission, and several days later was able to contact a nephew, who arranged a meeting between Tim and his team member nicknamed "Ken" and Mepa Pon and Dakpa Lama. At the meeting Mepa Pon confirmed that Tim's father was dead and that he had taken command of his group, which consisted of about eighty people, including women, children, and elders. Tim offered to supply weapons, ammunition, and money, and Mepa Pon expressed his interest. Ken, three other team members, and six of Mepa Pon's men returned to the drop zone to recover the equipment.

The team successfully recovered the equipment, but they also discovered that the Chinese controlled the local villages. Their concern grew when Tim and the two other team members failed to make the rendezvous on the agreed-upon date. It was not until four days later that Tim and the others finally arrived. After a joyful reunion, they explained that Chinese patrols had forced them to miss the rendezvous. The team then assessed their situation.

They wanted to fight, but the Chinese had sufficient forces and control to make guerrilla operations impossible. The team decided it would have to flee to India. To avoid the Chinese patrols sealing off the Indian border, the team decided to go north and follow the same route Tim had used in his earlier escape. Tim and Ken told Mepa Pon and Dakpa Lama of their plan, and offered to take their guerrillas and dependents with them. The group would move slowly and live off the wild animals. The guerrilla leaders agreed, and the group began their trek north.

They were attacked by the Chinese almost immediately and were forced into a series of running battles. During the second fight, a team member nicknamed "Colin" was killed. Over nearly three months, the group fought a total of nine battles. By the early summer of 1961, they had traveled less than a hundred miles from the drop zone. Only Tim, five team members, and about forty of the guerrillas remained. All were exhausted and starving. Ken recalled feeling no fear, as "human beings lose fear when they are desperate."

The group hid for the night in a small mountain forest, hoping this would shield them from the Chinese patrols. At 6:00 A.M. the next morning, however, the Chinese appeared in large numbers. Tim and the others realized there would be no escape. Ken crushed into powder small clay charms that had been blessed by the Dalai Lama. He then gave the powder to the team members as a lucky charm. The six men took up positions and began firing on the Chinese. Ken lost all fear, and began to enjoy shooting, even feeling "intoxicated," as the Chinese bullets whizzed by without striking him.

In mid-morning, Ken crawled over to "Aaron" and "Luke." He found they were both dead; they had used the L-pills rather than be taken captive. At noon, the Chinese overran the team's position. Ken had the L-pill in his mouth when he was knocked unconscious by a rifle butt; the captors removed his cyanide capsule. When Ken awoke, the rest of the team was dead, and he and fifteen to twenty of the guerrillas were prisoners of the Chinese.

Ken was denounced as an American spy and taken to a military prison near Lhasa. He was tortured for a week. He initially told the Chinese he had come from India, but finally he admitted this was a lie. After further torture, he told the Chinese everything—how he was picked for training, how he traveled from India to Colorado, the names of his instructors and of the other students, how many Tibetans were being trained, what they were taught, and the goals of the United States in supporting the Tibetan resistance. The Chinese never released the information they had extracted from Ken.

The loss of Tim and his fellow team members marked the end of the air-dropped teams. Of the forty-nine men who had parachuted into Tibet between October 1957 and March 1961, only twelve survived. Ten were able to escape to India, while Ken and Yeshe (the CIA operator who surrendered to the Chinese) were held until 1979. The other thirty-seven men were killed in battles with the Chinese or died in their attempts to cross the barren mountains. In the course of the STBarnum missions, more than 500,000 pounds of arms, ammunition, radios, medical supplies, printing presses, and other equipment were dropped to the resistance. The bulk of these drops, both in the amount of supplies and the number of missions, was done following the introduction of the C-130s in November 1959. About forty missions were flown without the loss of an aircraft or crew member, under the harshest conditions of weather and terrain.

Doubts and Divisions

Despite President Kennedy's approval of the March 1961 airdrops into Tibet, his administration had deep policy divisions between "hawks" and "doves" over covert operations such as the Tibetan resistance. The Harvard economist and social critic John Kenneth Galbraith was one of the doves. He was named as the U.S. ambassador to India in early 1961 and was briefed on CIA activities in the region. Galbraith opposed covert action in general and the Tibetan operation in particular. He called it a "particularly insane enterprise" in which "planes dropped weapons, ammunition and other supplies for dissident and deeply unhygienic tribesmen who had once roamed over the neighboring Tibetan countryside and who now relieve their boredom with raids back into the territory from which they had been extruded." When Galbraith returned to Washington, D.C., for consultations in May 1961, he was determined to end CIA covert actions within India itself and to stop the CIA airdrops into Tibet. Kennedy eventually agreed to Galbraith's demands.

Although the president had agreed to halt the airdrops, the Mustang-based guerrilla operations were allowed to continue. Their first series of operations were made in August 1961. Their major success came in October when a group lead by a Dhumra graduate named Ragra ambushed a Chinese convoy, wiping it out. Among those killed was a PLA assistant regimental commander who was carrying a pouch with more than sixteen hundred classified documents. The guerrillas were able to recover the Chinese officer's bloodstained pouch and its documents intact, providing an intelligence windfall. Included in the haul were twenty-nine issues of the *Bulletin of Activities of the General Political Department of the People's Liberation Army.*

The captured documents gave a window into the situation facing China. They made clear the suffering caused by the Great Leap Forward and its effect on PLA morale. They also showed that the People's Militia was of no military value and had even been involved in local uprisings against the Communist authorities. The captured papers made clear that China was in no position to retake Taiwan. The most valuable intelligence from the captured documents, however, was about the relationship between the USSR and China. The conventional wisdom since 1949 was that the two Communist countries were close allies in a monolithic Communist bloc. The documents showed that, in reality, relations were badly strained. They made it clear that the Sino-Soviet split was real and not a Communist ploy.

The intelligence from the captured pouch neutralized Galbraith's efforts to end the Mustang operation. During November 1961, DCI Dulles made a dramatic appearance before the NSC's Special Group, bearing the documents and pouch. The intelligence the operation had provided, and the unwillingness of the U.S. government to abandon a potentially useful weapon against the Chinese, caused President Kennedy to approve a resumption of the airdrops. The drops were made on 10 December 1961 in an area inside Tibet. The arms were recovered and taken to Mustang.

Despite this, the debate over the utility of the Mustang guerrillas versus the political risks they posed to the administration continued, resulting in a policy stalemate. The arms from the March and December 1961 drops were sufficient to supply merely half the guerrillas in Mustang. So armed, the resistance fighters mounted periodic raids against Chinese convoys and camps south of the Brahmaputra River. However, the divided Kennedy administration was unwilling to supply sufficient weapons to arm the entire guerrilla force, to authorize a full-scale effort against the Chinese, or to shut down the effort.

In early 1964, a change in the focus of the Tibetan operation was made. The Special Group approved a revised program, with the focus on intelligence gathering and political action. In May 1965 a final airdrop was made to a drop zone inside Mustang. A total of 250 rifles, 1,000 grenades, 6 mortars, 36 Bren machine guns, 42 Sten submachine guns, 6 recoilless rifles, 75 handguns, and 72,000 rounds of ammunition were successfully delivered. This was still only a small proportion of the weapons needed to fully arm the guerrillas based in Mustang.

Over the next three years, a total of twenty-five small teams attempted to operate inside Tibet. The most successful team was able to send radio messages for more than two years from their location north of Mount Everest. Two other teams operated for seven and two months, respectively. Most of the teams were forced to return within a few weeks, having been unable to find a secure base or even sources of food. They found little support among the local population, who feared Chinese retribution and wanted nothing to do with them. Five team members were captured. The Chinese forced one of the prisoners to transmit false messages, but the CIA immediately realized this when he used his real name in the radio transmissions, rather than his prearranged code name. By 1967, the CIA concluded that the effort was not producing significant results and ordered the remaining teams still in the field back to India.

Raiding parties continued to enter Tibet from August through April, but Chinese border forces took an increased toll. In the spring of 1968, Chinese control was so firm that guerrilla operations were deemed futile, and the Mustang force was directed to undertake intelligence activities. Small groups were sent into Tibet to collect intelligence on Chinese activities. Five radio teams located just over the border in Nepal forwarded the data. In addition, two road watch teams operated on the Lhasa-Xinjiang highway. They monitored military convoys and radioed their reports. Plans were also under way to send in teams to wiretap landlines inside Tibet, to pick up military communications.

None of these efforts required the eighteen hundred men still in Mustang, and in early 1969 the CIA notified Gyalo Thondup that the agency was ending its support for Gyen Yeshe's forces. Gyalo Thondup was asked to prepare a resettlement plan for those who remained. It was not until 1974, however, that the last of the Mustang force surrendered their weapons to Nepal's government, and the Tibetan paramilitary resistance passed into history.

8

Thunderball

In the early 1960s, the spy entered Cold War popular culture in the form of British secret agent 007. James Bond was the creation of *London Times* foreign editor and wartime British naval intelligence officer Ian Fleming. The public's fascination with Bond's adventures was also shared by senior CIA officials, among them DCI Allen Dulles. As an experienced case officer, however, Dulles knew that Bond was fantasy. He noted, "I feel that James Bond in real life would have had a thick dossier in the Kremlin after his first exploit and would not have survived the second."

With the release of the first three James Bond films—*Dr. No*, *From Russia with Love*, and *Goldfinger*—the British secret agent became an international phenomenon. The Soviets even referred to Bond as the "opiate of the oppressed and working classes." Bond was no longer simply a fictional character. Like Sherlock Holmes before him and Capt. James T. Kirk afterward, the name "James

Bond" was immediately recognizable across language, national, and cultural boundaries.

The fourth Bond film was *Thunderball,* in which Bond foils SPECTRE's attempt to blackmail the West with two stolen A-bombs. Filming began in France on 16 February 1965. The production then descended on Nassau in the Bahamas on 22 March. Not only did this involve the film crew and actors, but also a mockup Vulcan bomber, the hydrofoil yacht *Disco Volante,* mini-submarines, diving equipment, and live sharks. The movie also required official assistance from both the British and the U.S. militaries.

Russhon. Charles Russhon.

Lt. Col. Charles Russhon, U.S. Air Force (Ret.), arranged the military support for *Thunderball.* Desmond Llewelyn, who played the weapons expert "Q" in the series, called Russhon, "A remarkable man . . . who used to get lots of gadgets for us from the American Army and Navy." Peter Lamont, the head draftsman on the film's production design staff, added, "He did amazing things. . . . I've seen things done in high places." Russhon first became involved with the Bond movies during the filming of *From Russia with Love,* when he arranged limited U.S. military support in Turkey. For *Goldfinger,* he arranged permission to film at the Army base at Fort Knox. In gratitude for his work on *Thunderball,* he appeared in several scenes as a U.S. Air Force general. His most important role in the film, however, was to change its ending.

In the original shooting script, Bond and CIA agent Felix Leiter chase the *Disco Volante* in a hovercraft. Bond then boards the yacht, kills SPECTRE agent Emilio Largo, and rescues the heroine, Domino. Kutze—an Eastern European nuclear scientist who assisted SPECTRE—destroys the *Disco Volante* and the remaining A-bomb by igniting the ship's fuel tanks. Leiter picks up Bond after the explosion.

This ending was changed when Russhon helped arrange the use of a modified B-17G, operated by Intermountain Aviation, Inc. Based at Marana Air Park outside Tucson, Arizona, the company undertook, among certain other things, drops of smoke jumpers during fire season, and supplied food and hay to snowbound Indian reservations in winter. The B-17 had been fitted with a special air-to-ground pickup device called the "Skyhook." A large yoke was mounted on the airplane's nose. This caught a 500-foot braided nylon line carried aloft by a dirigible-shaped balloon. The other end of the line was attached to a harness, which was worn by the person being picked up. The balloon, line, harness, and helium tanks fit into a package that was dropped to a person on the ground.

A pickup could be made from a relatively small clearing. Once the balloon was inflated, the B-17 would fly toward the line. The pilot aimed for a bright orange nylon marker at the 425-foot level on the line. The yoke would guide the line into a "sky anchor" on the nose of the airplane, which both caught the line and released the balloon. The person being picked up was first lifted off the ground vertically, and then was accelerated to the speed of the airplane. The jolt and acceleration were not severe. As the person was towed behind the B-17, the line trained along the underside of the aircraft. A crewman would catch the line with a J-hook. The line was then attached to a winch, and the person was reeled aboard. The process took about six minutes and seemed ideal for a Bond film.

The *Thunderball* script was rewritten to include Intermountain Aviation's B-17. The hovercraft was dropped and, in the new ending, Bond simply swims to the *Disco Volante* and climbs aboard via one of the hydrofoils. After the onboard battle, the yacht is heading for destruction on a reef, and Bond, Domino, and Kutze jump overboard. Kutze, who cannot swim, fares no better in the rewrite, and disappears. The *Disco Volante* hits the reef, and it and the bomb are destroyed. As Bond and Domino float in the ocean, the B-17 flies over and drops a life raft. They climb aboard, and Bond inflates the balloon, connects the line, and wraps his arms around Domino. As the music builds, the B-17 begins its run and snags the line. Bond and Domino are lifted out of the raft, and as the airplane flies off with them in tow, the credits begin.

The Intermountain Aviation pilot for the *Thunderball* filming was Robert Zimmer. He had participated in the B-17's first operational mission three years earlier, under more demanding conditions, and for higher stakes. Although the B-17's appearance in the movie was brief, this involved a number of shots. The aircraft was filmed from the water as it dropped the raft and then made the pickup. The B-17 was also filmed from the air as it headed toward the balloon and caught it. Finally, a camera was mounted inside the cockpit, shooting out through the windshield to film the moment when the line was caught. For the pickup, two dummies were placed in the life raft. The pickup went smoothly, but after the cameras stopped rolling, a problem occurred. The two dummies were too large to be brought aboard. When the B-17 landed, they bounced down the runway behind the airplane.

Thunderball was released on 21 December 1965 and proved an immediate success. More people saw it in its first release than any previous Bond movie. In the decades since then, millions of people have seen the B-17 make the pickup; yet, very few know what they have actually seen. Books and articles on *Thunderball* mention the B-17 only in passing, and Intermountain Aviation was not listed in the credits. This is ironic, as the B-17's appearance in *Thunderball* was emblematic of the 1960s. The decade was a time when the line between fantasy and reality was often blurred. *Thunderball* represented a fantasy covert action, while in reality the B-17 belonged to the CIA.

Development of the Fulton Skyhook System

The CIA's B-17 was the result of an inventive genius named Robert Edison Fulton Jr. Born on 15 April 1909, Fulton came from a family of transport pioneers. His maternal grandfather had founded the Pacific Coast Stage Coach Company; his father had been the president of the Mack Truck Company. After World War II, Fulton bought fifteen acres at the airport at Danbury, Connecticut, where he built a workshop and home. He then began work on a flying car called the "Airphibian." Only eight were built before the project was abandoned.

While flying the Airphibian, Fulton wondered what would happen if he was forced down in rough terrain. He had seen a demonstration of the All America system in London after World War II, but felt a superior method was needed. With the collapse of the Airphibian project, Fulton's attention shifted to the Skyhook recovery system. By 1953, he had worked out the concept and begun pickup tests with a Stinson Reliant light aircraft. Fulton mounted a V-shaped yoke on the Stinson's left wing. The first tests were done with a five-pound sandbag connected to a weather balloon with a nylon line. As the tests progressed, Fulton gradually increased the load until it reached thirty-five pounds. By May 1953, Fulton had made thirty-nine pickups. He then made additional tests at higher speeds and with heavier weights using a Twin Beechcraft.

Fulton then took his films of the tests to Adm. Louis de Florez, who had become the first director of technical research at the CIA. Despite the CIA's need to recover agents from denied areas, de Florez thought that Fulton's system would best be developed by the military. He put Fulton in contact with the Navy's Office of Naval Research (ONR), who awarded him a contract.

In October 1954, Fulton flew the Stinson to NAS El Centro, where the Joint Air Force–Navy Parachute Test Facility was located. A Navy P2V-2 had been modified with a larger yoke and heavier slot-type anchor. Over the next several years, the Skyhook system was modified, and the related equipment—the lines, harness, balloon, helium tanks, and the package—was developed. Fulton also worked on cables that would prevent the line from snagging the propellers, a bolt-on yoke, and a winch to bring the rescued person on board the aircraft.

By December 1957, both the Skyhook and related equipment were ready for operational testing. These were done at the U.S. Marine Corps base at Quantico, Virginia, using a P2V-5 flown by a Marine crew. Initial tests used a two-hundred-pound dummy, and then monkeys were used to test the response of a living creature to the shock and G-forces of the pickup. Finally, a pig was selected as the test specimen. The pickup was successful, but as the pig was towed behind the airplane at 125 knots, the pig spun around. When the pig was brought aboard the P2V, it was disoriented. The pig recovered and then attacked several crewmen. Later pigs were restrained and sedated.

Fulton believed that the system was ready for a human recovery. He was willing to be the test subject, but the Navy wanted him around to blame if anything went wrong. S/Sgt. Levi W. Woods volunteered to be the first live pickup. He was an experienced Marine parachutist. During the early evening of 12 August 1958, Sergeant Woods sat on the ground as a P2V piloted by Marine Capt. Stanley Osserman flew toward the line. The airplane's yoke caught the line and Sergeant Woods was lifted off the ground. He recalled afterward, "I felt like I was being eased into the air. There was no jerk or jolt. I sort of sat in a high chair and looked around at the people below me. Then I began to move up faster. It seemed like I went almost straight up." As Sergeant Woods was towed behind the P2V, he extended his arms and legs to control the tendency to oscillate. After six minutes, he was aboard the airplane. Sergeant Woods enjoyed the experience, commenting in his report, "As far as I am concerned, it really was a good ride and I'm ready to do it again as many times as you like."

The Bay of Pigs

The Bay of Pigs disaster led to the CIA's use of the Fulton Skyhook. In the summer of 1960, President Dwight D. Eisenhower approved the start of covert operations against the Communist government of Fidel Castro in Cuba. DCI Dulles and Richard Bissell, the CIA's deputy director for plans, informed the president on 18 August 1960 that "a unified Cuban opposition" had been created. Dulles added, however, that as yet "there is no real leader and all the individuals are prima donnas." Cuban exiles would be infiltrated to stiffen the resistance groups, who would be supplied by air. A landing force of some two hundred men would also be put ashore to assist the guerrillas. Plans were also made to have Castro assassinated using Mafia help.

The new Cuban operation involved a major expansion of the CIA's air proprietary companies. The CIA bought Southern Air Transport, a nearly bankrupt company with a single C-46, for $307,506 to serve as the nucleus of the logistics effort. The Cuban exile pilots for the airdrops were recruited by the Caribbean Marine Aero Corporation, while Double Check Corporation employed the American pilots who would train them in Guatemala. Gar Thorsrud, who helped recruit smoke jumpers as PDOs for STBarnum in Tibet, directed the training and air operations.

The first airdrop into Cuba was made on 28 September 1960 and was a parody of the Tibetan missions. The Cuban C-54 crew was to drop arms for a hundred men to an agent on the ground. They missed the drop zone by seven miles, and the weapons were recovered by Cuban troops. The agent was arrested and shot. Connie M. Seigrist, an instructor for the exile pilots, recalled that after the drop, the crew had turned on the autopilot for the long flight back to Guatemala, and then had fallen asleep. When the crew awoke, the C-54 had drifted off course, and they were lost. They ran out of fuel before reaching Guatemala and were forced to land in Mexico, where the C-54 was confiscated.

The airdrops resumed on 6 November, but faired poorly. A total of sixty-seven airdrops were made between November 1960 and March 1961. All were during the full moon period of each month. Of these sixty-seven missions, only seven were judged successful. Most of the missions did not spot any ground signals and dropped the supplies "blind" into the mountains. The Cuban farmers who made up the anti-Castro resistance were unable to reach the drop sites. The messages from the remaining guerrillas were increasingly desperate: "Impossible to fight. . . . Either the drops increase or we die . . . men without arms and equipment. God help us."

Castro had strengthened his control of both society and the military. The possibility of a popular uprising was fading. Additionally, Castro's agents were infiltrating the exile community in Miami. Just as significant, the covert operations were becoming public. There had already been a number of press articles about U.S. involvement with Cuban exiles being trained to overthrow Castro. Despite the failures, the operation was further expanded. By the spring of 1961, the small landing of a limited number of guerrillas had become a covert D-Day, complete with air support from Cuban-flown B-26 light bombers.

President John F. Kennedy had inherited the Cuban operation from Eisenhower, and was now getting conflicting advice about how to proceed. The CIA assured him the plan was feasible, while the JCS expressed some doubts. The State Department was opposed to this "major covert adventure." Secretary of State Dean Rusk warned that the invasion would have detrimental effects on the U.S. position at the United Nations and in Latin America. Any U.S. overt military involvement would be seen as aggression. Undersecretary of State

Chester Bowles warned, "The fresh, favorable image of the Kennedy Administration will be correspondingly dimmed."

Kennedy himself was no less conflicted. Cuba had been a major campaign issue in the 1960 presidential election, and he had promised vigorous action. Kennedy saw Cuba as posing the threat of Communist subversion throughout Latin America, but he also wanted to avoid even the appearance of U.S. backing for the invasion. He asked for more limited alternatives that did not involve U.S. ships, aircraft, and supplies. Evan Thomas best summed up the results in his book *The Very Best Men.* "In his own mind, the president made a calculus: the less the military risk, the greater the political risk, and vice versa. It was a foolish calculus because it invited the president to take half measures in an all-or-nothing situation."

Bissell briefed President Kennedy on 11 March 1961 about the invasion plan, code-named "Zapata." An exile force of more than fifteen hundred Cubans would make an amphibious/airborne landing near the city of Trinidad on Cuba's southern coast. Exile political leaders would then follow and proclaim a provisional government. This was to trigger an uprising that would overthrow the Communist government. Bissell based the Zapata plan on that of PBSuccess. For it to work, however, the tiny exile force would have to gain air superiority over the beach. The day before the landing, Cuban airfields would be struck twice by sixteen B-26s. The goal was to destroy the Cuban Air Force on the ground before it could attack the ships or beachhead.

Kennedy interrupted the briefing after several minutes and told Bissell that the plan was "too spectacular." The president continued, "You have to reduce the noise level of this thing." He told Bissell to find a more remote landing site and to create a plan with less "noise." Kennedy made clear that he wanted there to be no overt U.S. military involvement.

Over the next four days, Bissell and his staff prepared a revised plan to meet Kennedy's concerns. Kennedy was shown the new plan on 15 March, and the president gave his approval the following day. The new plan had a major consequence—the original landing site at Trinidad allowed a fallback position. Should the invasion fail, the Cuban exiles could make their way to the nearby Escambray Mountains and continue to fight as guerrillas. The new landing site was some eighty miles from the Escambray Mountains and was cut off by a large swamp. There was no guerrilla option. The new invasion site was at the Bay of Pigs.

Despite the less "spectacular" plan, President Kennedy continued to put pressure on Bissell. When told that sixteen B-26s would be used in the initial strikes, Kennedy replied, "I don't want it on that scale. I want it minimal." Bissell responded by changing the air strike plan. Only eight B-26s would make a single strike against the Cuban airfields two days before the invasion. If needed, a second strike could be flown the morning of the landing.

Zapata began on 15 April, when the eight exile B-26s flying from Nicaragua struck three Cuban airfields. Although the strikes achieved complete surprise, two Cuban B-26s, two or three Sea Fury propeller fighters, and two armed T-33 jet trainers survived. One exile B-26 and its two-man crew were lost to ground fire. There was the need for a second attack on the Cuban airfields, but Secretary of State Rusk and National Security Adviser McGeorge Bundy convinced President Kennedy to cancel the attack, as it would make U.S. involvement clear. The exile B-26s could provide air cover over the invasion beaches, but the airfields were off limits. When Thorsrud received the message canceling the follow-up strike, he found it "totally unbelievable" and concluded that any hope of success was over.

When the Cuban exiles hit the beach on 17 April, the Cuban Air Force launched its attacks. The Sea Furies sank two ships and drove the others off. The T-33s shot down three exile B-26s, while Sea Furies destroyed two more B-26s. This was half of the ten exile aircraft sent to cover the landing. Of the ten exile crewmen downed, eight were killed. The small invasion force was held on the beach by superior numbers of loyal Cuban troops, backed up by T-34 tanks and heavy artillery. With the ships gone, the exile force was left with little ammunition to fight them off.

A night attack on the Cuban airfields was then attempted with two flights. Of the three exile B-26s in the first flight, two turned back because of mechanical problems and the third could not find the target. A second flight of two B-26s was also unable to find the target. Manuel Villafana, the exile air commander, then canceled the B-26 strikes planned for 18 April because of the losses. As the day passed, reports indicated that the situation on the beach was becoming worse.

Connie M. Seigrist and another CIA instructor pilot, Douglas R. Price, volunteered to fly a mission. Thorsrud received approval, provided exile crews accompanied the Americans. Four such crews agreed to go with them. Seigrist and Price led separate flights, each with a pair of exile B-26s as wingmen. The six aircraft arrived at the Bay of Pigs an hour before sunset. Seigrist spotted a Cuban convoy approaching the beachhead on a road through the swamp. The tanks and trucks were without air cover, and the B-26s attacked. The convoy was hit with machine-gun fire, rockets, bombs, and napalm, leaving a two-mile stretch of road in flames. Some thirty vehicles were destroyed, and about nine hundred Cuban troops killed or wounded. It was the only successful air strike at the Bay of Pigs. The six exile B-26s had all been hit by ground fire, but none was seriously damaged. The aircraft then made a timely escape, as the T-33s arrived over the beachhead scarcely a minute after the B-26s had left the area.

Despite their success, the situation remained desperate for the Cubans on the beach. Bissell told Kennedy on the evening of 18 April that the only chance to save the operation was for U.S. planes to provide air cover. Having refused to approve any actions that might even hint at U.S. involvement, Kennedy now relented. He approved a flight of six A4D Skyhawks from the USS *Essex.* The jets were to provide cover for the B-26s while they attacked the Cuban ground forces surrounding the beachhead. Yet Kennedy still imposed limitations. The A4Ds were to have their U.S. markings painted out, they would be over the beach strictly between 6:30 and 7:30 A.M. as the exile B-26s attacked, and they could not actually attack any Cuban aircraft engaging the B-26s.

The B-26 crews took off on April 19 knowing there would be Navy aircraft to provide cover. However, when the five exile aircraft reached the beachhead, an error in timing meant that the A4Ds had not yet arrived. The Cuban T-33s were on time and quickly downed two more B-26s. The four crewmen were not Cuban exiles, however, but rather Alabama Air National Guard members. The pilot, Maj. Riley Shamburger, and the navigator, Wade Gray, were aboard the lead B-26, call sign "Mad Dog," while Capt. Thomas W. Ray and Leo Baker were in Mad Dog 4. The Americans were killed either in the crashes or when resisting capture.

When the A4D pilots finally reached the beachhead, the Cuban planes were still engaging the three remaining B-26s. A Navy pilot spotted a T-33 and got on its tail. As soon as he did, a controller on the *Essex* ordered him not to fire. A second A4D pilot spotted a Sea Fury attacking a B-26. The light bomber's right engine was already smoking. He requested permission to fire on the Cuban aircraft, but again, this was refused. The A4D pilot closed in and flew off the Sea Fury's wing. The two pilots looked at each other, for as long as a minute, and the Cuban pilot headed home. The B-26 pilot gave the Navy pilot a thumbs-up and headed back to Nicaragua. The Cuban exiles were overrun late that afternoon.

President Kennedy took responsibility for the failure, but Dulles and Bissell were forced to resign. The administration glossed over any role its last-minute changes and second-guessing had on the failure. Many within the CIA blamed Kennedy's actions for the failure, overlooking the flaws and faulty assumptions that had doomed their plan from the start. Zapata was intended to spark a military coup, but Castro had already purged the Cuban military of any who might try to overthrow him. During TPAjax in Iran and PBSuccess in Guatemala, the CIA efforts had forced the army to take action, and it was the army, not the CIA-sponsored rebels, who actually overthrew the government.

The failure of the Bay of Pigs invasion did not end the Kennedy administration's efforts against Castro. In November 1961, President Kennedy approved a further effort, code-named "Mongoose." It was under the effective command of Robert F. Kennedy, the president's brother and U.S. attorney general. Small teams were landed in Cuba by boat to recruit guerrillas for sabotage and economic disruption. Attempts to assassinate Castro continued to be planned. Various pretexts for a U.S. invasion of Cuba were also studied as part of Mongoose. Despite the efforts of large numbers of CIA officers and Cuban exiles, as well as the constant pressure from Robert Kennedy for results, Mongoose faired little better than the earlier efforts for all the same reasons. Mongoose ended in early 1963, but small-scale covert operations continued against Cuba until after Kennedy's death in November 1963.

Intermountain Aviation, Inc.

Following the Bay of Pigs, Seigrist and Price acted as caretakers for the equipment in Nicaragua. In late July 1961 both were ordered back to Washington, D.C. Thorsrud met Seigrist and Price when they arrived, and he told them they were now employees of Intermountain Aviation, Inc. This was officially a private company specializing in aerial resupply techniques, under contract to the Forest Service. The reality was that, following the Bay of Pigs, CIA officials decided they could not rely on U.S. Air Force support for covert operations in the future. Should Mongoose be successful in establishing a guerrilla force, airdrop missions using Cuban personnel were being considered. Intermountain Aviation would provide support and instructors for such activities.

Thorsrud was the president of Intermountain Aviation, while John D. Wall was the company's vice president and chief PDO. Seigrist was named the chief pilot, while Price was one of the pilots. Other employees included PDO Miles L. Johnson and his brother Shep, both ex-smoke jumpers. Many of them had known each other since the early days of CAT, Western Enterprises Incorporated, and the airdrops into mainland China and Tibet. For the moment, however, Intermountain Aviation still awaited its first airplane.

The aircraft that would later become famous in *Thunderball* began as a B-17G-95-DL, built at the Douglas Aircraft Company factory at Long Beach, California. The aircraft carried U.S. Army Air Forces serial number 44-83785 and was among the last B-17Gs built. After being delivered in June 1945, it was converted to a TB-17G trainer. Subsequently, the aircraft was again modified, this time into an SB-17G rescue airplane. Its gun turrets were removed, and a large lifeboat was attached to the airplane's underside. The lifeboat could be dropped by parachute to survivors in the water. The aircraft was then reconverted to a TB-17G trainer. Finally, the aircraft was transferred to CAT and flew covert missions for nearly a decade.

When Intermountain Aviation was established, the B-17 was returned to the United States and then underwent modifications at Lockheed Aircraft's Skunk Works in Burbank, California. The B-17 was fitted with electronic equipment from Collins, Bendix, Narco, and Pioneer. The airplane's electrical system was modified, and its cockpit was soundproofed and upholstered. Long-range fuel tanks could be carried in the bomb bay. Agents and cargo could be dropped through a hole in the airplane's belly. A person picked up with the Skyhook equipment would be brought aboard the airplane through the same hole.

On 18 August 1961, Intermountain Aviation took delivery of the B-17, which had the U.S. civil registration N809Z. After the airplane's arrival in Phoenix, Thorsrud told Seigrist that the B-17 was to be modified for tests of the Skyhook system at Intermountain Aviation's new facility at Marana Air Park. The B-17 might then be sent on its first operational mission. This would be to rescue Allen Pope from an Indonesian prison, where he was under a death sentence for his participation in the CIA-sponsored Operation Haik. (Ironically, fellow CAT pilot Seigrist had also been flying a B-26 mission the same day Pope was captured.) If the rescue were approved, a balloon, line, and hydrogen pellets would be smuggled into the prison. Pope would be picked up from a confined area inside the prison, next to a fourteen-foot-high wall.

A large fork, made of small-gage tubing, was fitted onto the nose of the B-17. At the same time, Intermountain Vice President Wall oversaw the construction of a wooden replica of the prison in a remote corner of the Marana facility. The major difficulty was that Pope would have to be picked up from *inside* the prison, without striking the wall on his way up. The Navy supplied four dummies for the training flights. Seigrist and Price began practice flights in October 1961, which showed that the rescue plan still had problems. During the first try, the dummy was slammed into the mock prison wall so hard that its arms were ripped off. On a later flight, the pickup was successful, but when the dummy was pulled within fifty feet of the B-17, it began whipping around and its head struck the fuselage so hard a real human would have been killed. The most dangerous incident occurred when the dummy began to oscillate severely and the line wrapped itself around the horizontal stabilizer. Seigrist and Price were barely able to maintain control and land the B-17.

Obviously, a new method of bringing a person aboard the B-17 was needed. The solution was to modify the tail gunner's position. A hole was cut where the turret had been, and to make boarding easier, a small slide was added to the aft fuselage. This mitigated the turbulence beneath the aircraft that had caused the dummy to whip around. This learning process took a toll on the four dummies. Two were destroyed, while the other two ended up being held together with tape and parachute shroud lines. The wooden prison walls also had to be rebuilt each time a dummy slammed into them. Despite all the problems, by early 1962 Seigrist felt sure that Pope could be rescued "without a scratch."

This proved unnecessary, as in February 1962 the United States received private assurances from the Indonesian government that Pope would be released. Five months later, he was returned to the United States, and later flew for the CIA's Southern Air Transport in South America. Although no rescue attempt was ever made, the training had formed the B-17's crew into a closely knit team. They now had the skills to pull off a successful covert pickup.

Coldfeet

At the same time that Fulton was involved with the CIA's Intermountain Aviation training for Pope's rescue, he was also working with the Navy's ONR for a covert examination of a Soviet ice station. Lt. Leonard A. LeSchack, a Naval Reserve geophysicist with the ONR, had conceived of the project in May 1961. The crew of a Navy aircraft on an aeromagnetic survey over the Arctic Ocean spotted the abandoned Soviet ice station, North Pole 9 (NP9). LeSchack realized that an examination of NP9 could indicate whether the Soviets were using ice stations to track U.S. submarines operating under the ice pack. This could also provide technical intelligence on Soviet equipment and allow the ONR to compare Soviet research activities on its ice stations to those of the United States. The problem was NP9's location. It was too far away to be reached by an icebreaker or a helicopter. A Skyhook-equipped P2V would be able both to reach NP9 and to recover the team after the base had been examined.

LeSchack gained the backing of Dr. Max Britton, head of the geophysical branch of the ONR. Together, they convinced Rear Adm. Leonidas D. Coates, the chief of ONR, to approve initial planning. The two men selected to parachute into the Soviet ice station were LeSchack and Air Force Maj. James Smith, who was an intelligence officer, parachutist, and Russian linguist. Smith had also been commander of the U.S. drift ice stations Alpha and Charlie. The operation was given the code name "Coldfeet."

There were doubts at high levels of the Navy that Coldfeet would be valuable, or that the team would survive. LeSchack, Dr. Britton, and the mission commander, Capt. John Cadwalader, worked to keep it alive. LeSchack dryly observed later that they had difficulty convincing the Navy that this was not some sort of James Bond stunt. As the spring of 1962 neared, there was no progress toward launching the mission. In the meantime, NP9 continued to drift farther and farther from Thule, Greenland, which was to be the base of operations.

Then, in March 1962, the Soviet press announced that another ice station, NP8, had been abandoned after 1,055 days of operation. The reports also gave the station's location, which was much more accessible than NP9. As NP8 had also been in operation for a year longer than the other station, LeSchack, Cadwalader, and Britton thought NP8 would be more likely to show evidence of recent submarine monitoring activity. The target for Coldfeet was changed to NP8.

After nearly a year of preparations, Coldfeet was finally about to get under way. The only change in plan to accommodate the new target was the mission's launch site. Rather than the Air Force base at Thule, the P2V recovery aircraft and a C-130 drop plane would use the Royal Canadian Air Force base at Resolute Bay, an estimated six hundred miles from NP8. The Canadian government soon gave diplomatic clearance to use the base.

Despite the go-ahead and the new target, Coldfeet remained jinxed. The C-130 took off from Resolute Bay on 20 April to search for NP8. The weather was perfect, with clear skies, no fog, and light winds. After several hours, there was no sign of NP8, and they turned back. The C-130 took off again on 21 April, and about midway through the search, the crew spotted buildings on the ice below. Smith recognized them as his old command, Ice Station Charlie. The same story was repeated on the next three flights. Charlie was spotted two more times, but there was still no sign of NP8. Given the ease with which Charlie had been spotted, there seemed no chance that NP8 could have been missed. Cadwalader called off the mission, and on 27 April, the two airplanes headed back to NAS Patuxent River.

It seemed that Coldfeet was over. The ONR was out of money, NP8's position was still unknown, and the P2V had other commitments. Then, on 10 May, LeSchack was informed that the monthly ice reconnaissance flight had spotted NP8. The station had been well to the east of the estimated position. Although the ONR was broke, the newly formed Defense Intelligence Agency (DIA) had become interested in Coldfeet. The DIA agreed to provide $30,000 for another attempt to find NP8.

Fulton suggested that the ONR charter Intermountain Aviation's B-17 and a C-46 support aircraft, rather than use the P2V. From his work with the Intermountain Aviation pilots during the training for the Pope rescue, Fulton believed they were capable of making the pickup. Negotiating a contract for the mission, LeSchack recalled, was "a wonderful farce." Despite Intermountain Aviation's public front, LeSchack was well aware it really belonged to the CIA. LeSchack also knew the $30,000 provided by the DIA would not cover Intermountain's costs, but Thorsrud was as interested in doing the mission as LeSchack was. An agreement was quickly reached.

Thorsrud told Seigrist on 15 May 1962 that he was to make the first operational mission. Time was limited; the B-17 and its support C-46 had to be at Point Barrow no later than 26 May. Using an airfield in Alaska removed the need for the Canadians to be involved. Seigrist made a practice pickup, and then the yokes were removed from the B-17 and loaded aboard the C-46. A large fuel tank was added to the B-17's bomb bay, and a Kearfoot directional gyro system for navigation in the far north was fitted to the aircraft.

After a mere eight days, everything was in readiness on 23 May. The two airplanes flew to Fairbanks along separate routes. The C-46 flew from Fulton's factory in Connecticut to Washington, D.C., for LeSchack, Smith, and the rest of the team, and then headed for Marana, arriving at the CIA base late at night. The C-46 took off again and headed north, via Great Falls, Montana, and Alberta, Canada. The B-17 headed up the West Coast with Price and Robert Zimmer as pilots. They made a stop in San Francisco to pick up Fulton and William R. Jordan, a Pan American navigator. Jordan had been told the mission was going to Thule, Greenland, to test Navy survival equipment. As the B-17 continued north, Fulton told Jordan that they were actually going to Point Barrow to search for a Soviet ice station. Jordan replied that he would not have missed the trip for the world. Both airplanes arrived at Point Barrow without incident.

After arriving at Point Barrow on 26 May, Cadwalader boarded a Navy P2V search plane, which took off for NP8's estimated position. On its last search pattern, the crew spotted NP8 and then headed south. When the B-17 flew out to the position the next day, however, there was no trace of the ice station. A long search revealed only a pile of fuel drums from NP8, and, yet again, Ice Station Charlie. Cadwalader decided that both airplanes would search the next day.

Ice Station NP8

On the morning of 28 May, the Navy P2V search plane took off at 9:00 A.M., while the B-17 followed at 10:50 A.M. The B-17 took some five hours to reach the search area. Aboard were Seigrist and Price, Jordan, LeSchack and Smith, Cadwalader, Fulton, and Thorsrud, as well as PDOs Wall and Johnson. Accompanying them was winch operator Jerrold B. Daniels, nose-trigger operator Randolph Scott, tail-position operator Robert H. Nicol, and Army doctor Daniel L. Walter. They faced a long and difficult flight. The four piston engines were loud and the airplane vibrated. There were few areas in the B-17 where the crew could stand upright or stretch out. The crowding was aggravated by the parkas they had to wear against the cold, and by the presence of six fifty-five-gallon fuel drums the airplane carried to extend its range. As the bomb bay tank was drained, these were hand-pumped into it. When each drum was empty, it was jettisoned.

The B-17 finally arrived over the search area at about 4:00 P.M. and began a search pattern. After an hour, the B-17 received a radio message from the P2V—"The magnetic survey has been completed." This was the code phrase indicating that they had found NP8. The P2V crew took a radio bearing on the B-17 and gave them a heading to the Soviet station. They were about forty-two miles away. As they headed toward NP8, LeSchack, Smith, and Dr. Walter checked their parachutes. If LeSchack or Smith were injured in the jump, Dr. Walter would be parachuted in to provide medical assistance. Fulton filmed the activities.

When the B-17 arrived over NP8, Seigrist began to circle at three hundred feet to look over the ice station. There were a number of buildings, a tractor, and a runway with a pressure ridge across its middle. Smith was also studying the base to ensure it was not Ice Station Charlie. He also wanted to make sure there were no polar bears. Satisfied on both counts, Smith told the others it was the long-sought NP8. Seigrist climbed to twelve hundred feet, while Johnson removed the cover on the hole in the airplane's belly.

Smith pointed out a drop zone, and Seigrist began his run. Seigrist, who was a former Army Air Forces pilot, would fly the B-17 for Smith's drop, while former Navy pilot Price would do the same when LeSchack jumped. Smith sat on a step by the edge of the hole, and as the airplane passed over the drop zone, he jumped. The parachute opened normally, but Smith had to steer his parachute away from the station's radio mast. He touched down in a foot and a half of snow. Smith popped a green smoke flare and then radioed the B-17 that he had landed safely, and he told them to make the next pass fifty yards to the right.

The B-17 came back around, and LeSchack pushed himself out the hole. The parachute opened with a jerk, and he saw NP8 below him. His earlier apprehension and elation were transformed into near euphoria. After all the difficulties he had faced, he was finally at NP8. He saw the smoke, and guided the parachute to a smooth landing.

With both men unharmed, Seigrist began dropping supplies for the planned seventy-two-hour stay. These included a Sterno stove, food, medical supplies, two Leica-M3 cameras, rolls of film, sleeping bags and air mattresses, radios, a map, and even a toboggan supplied by Fulton. It took eight passes before the last packages were on the ice. Smith activated a short-range Forest Service radio beacon. This would serve as a final guide to the B-17 during the pickup. At 6:45 P.M, Seigrist turned the B-17 south for the long flight to Point Barrow. The whole operation had taken just under an hour.

As the B-17 grew smaller and then finally vanished, LeSchack and Smith realized how isolated they were. They stood in the center of the ice station for what later seemed to be a long time. Finally, they set about exploring the camp. After an hour, they picked the senior scientist's hut as the best one in which to set up their equipment. It held two double-deck bunks, two tables, and a coal-burning stove. Smith lit their Sterno stove and began cooking cans of stew. Smith also pulled a pint of Canadian Club whiskey from his jump kit and prepared the traditional drink of polar explorers: C.C. and snow.

Both men quickly fell into a deep sleep. Waking up the following morning, 29 May, they made coffee and worked out the plan of action. Using the photo map of NP8, they divided the station into four sections. They would each check their individual areas and then discuss the findings that evening. LeSchack set up the radio in the base transmitter shack. He hooked up the radio to one of the Soviet antennas, connected the batteries, and turned it on. The radio worked perfectly. Both NP8 and Point Barrow would monitor the assigned frequency twice a day, but neither would transmit unless there was an emergency.

As LeSchack was setting up the radio, Smith explored NP8. He judged the huts to be "crude," made as they were of double-walled plywood and outfitted with "haphazard" electrical systems. Several had no electrical power at all. Neither Smith nor LeSchack was impressed by the mess hall, where they met later in the day. LeSchack later noted, "Food was still on the stove, frozen in greasy skillets," while animal carcasses were lying on the floor of an adjoining shed.

The squalid mess hall also gave insights into the Soviets' life on the ice. In a corner, LeSchack and Smith found twenty-one 16-mm movies. Most were newsreels dealing with Soviet economic, scientific, or transport activities. One was a "socialist realism" movie about a girl and her tractor. Tacked to the walls were several political posters. On one of the posters was a handwritten note, dated 19 March 1962, asking anyone who visited NP8 after that date to report their visit to the Arctic Institute in Leningrad. It was signed "Chief of Station Romanov." Smith took the poster down and put it into the pocket of his overalls.

After some twelve hours of work, both LeSchack and Smith returned to the chief scientist's hut to compare their findings. They then had a dinner of

C-rations and climbed into their sleeping bags. This brought their first full day at NP8 to a close.

The following day, 30 May, LeSchack and Smith undertook a systematic search of each hut. LeSchack's main activity was to collect data on the Soviet oceanographic research and any evidence that the Soviets had monitored U.S. submarines from NP8. He found that the station's diesel generator had been mounted on rubber tires to reduce sound and vibration. A large number of batteries were scattered on the ice; NP8 was capable of "silent running." LeSchack also found lengths of armored heavy-duty cable that could be used for acoustic equipment. They also found a "brass device" which they thought to be a geophone. Four notebooks contained information and diagrams dealing with acoustic measurements.

Much of the materials recovered were notebooks, manuals, charts, logbooks, instructions, and similar documents used to record scientific observations. These included cloud types, wind speed, water temperatures, magnetic observations, radiosonde balloon data, and ocean currents. LeSchack and Smith also found several copies of the KN-01, KN-03, and KN-04 codebooks for meteorological telegrams.

LeSchack and Smith similarly collected technical intelligence on Soviet electronics. Some of this was in the form of manuals, such as that for a "Radio Station Type 1-RSB-70," which was used aboard aircraft for long-range commutations and navigation. Other information came from recovered electronic equipment: two Type 8L029 cathode ray tubes, GMI-83 and OTK-15 vacuum tubes, a large transformer can, a motor generator Type U-600, and several resistors of different values. Also collected were two 15-amp fuses marked "Made in St. Louis, MO, USA."

Other information was on a more personal level. There were instructions to the duty galley man to clean and wash the tables, serve meals, haul water, and notify the doctor, who was to check all meals; a large ledger book marked "Receipt and Distribution of Supplies and Cigarettes"; a brochure titled "Techniques of Safety When Working on the Ice"; "Watch Instructions for the Camp Guard," which covered keeping the stoves lit and warnings of polar bears; and "Order No. 4 from the Chief of the Drift Station," which was a list of transgressions by base personnel such as improper watch standing, log entries, eating hours, and the like.

After completing their detailed search of NP8, LeSchack and Smith met back at their quarters. Reviewing their progress, both men were satisfied. They would complete their search of the station, pack the items they had recovered, and be ready when the B-17 returned the next afternoon. They turned in for the night.

The following morning, 31 May, LeSchack awoke and turned on the radio. At the scheduled time, LeSchack made a weather report to Point Barrow, using his own call sign of W4RVN and standard radio jargon. LeSchack heard no reply and assumed that Point Barrow had not received the transmission. In reality, Cadwalader had received part of it, which indicated conditions were favorable for the pickup that afternoon.

LeSchack and Smith packed their collection into a duffle bag. Its weight was limited to about 150 pounds, so they had to be selective about what they brought back. The pickup zone was away from the camp, located near the tractor. They also collected debris, including old tires, which would serve as a bonfire to guide the airplane. At 3:00 P.M., they lit the bonfire, turned on the Forest Service homing beacon, and then waited for the B-17.

LeSchack and Smith waited for several hours, but the B-17 did not arrive. They finally returned to their hut and began to clean house. They discarded furniture and debris, sweeping the hut out with a broom and rearranging the tapestries on the walls. They also lit the coal stove and took sponge baths. Their situation was not as perilous as it might have seemed. They had a month's supply of C-rations. Should these run out, there was the food in the lockers, which could supply them for a year or more. There was also an ample supply of coal for heat.

The next day, 1 June, LeSchack and Smith again awaited the arrival of the B-17. When it became apparent that again it was not coming, they resumed their examination of the camp. At the scheduled time for radio contact, they listened on the assigned frequency but did not transmit, for fear of alerting the Soviets to their presence on NP8. LeSchack and Smith then returned to their hut, had dinner, and discussed the day's activities before going to sleep.

With their extended stay at NP8 now in its third day, LeSchack and Smith spent 2 June taking additional notes and photos and collecting more artifacts. They added these new items and discarded former ones they now felt were not as important. LeSchack was hauling the toboggan from one of the huts when he heard an aircraft engine, then saw a P2V. He called out to Smith, who was inside another building. Smith contacted the P2V with a small survival radio and was told that the B-17 was still two hours away. LeSchack and Smith had a quick meal and then moved to the pickup location.

The two previous recovery attempts by the B-17 had been foiled by weather and equipment problems. Cadwalader decided to use a P2V as the lead search plane and have it fly ahead of the B-17. The Navy crew found the weather to be poorer than expected. They reached NP8's estimated position and then let down through the clouds. On their first search leg, they detected the Forest Service radio beacon and located the base. While the two men prepared, the P2V crew tried to contact the B-17. The patrol plane was low on fuel and would soon have to head for Point Barrow. Finally, the P2V crew established radio contact with the B-17 and gave them the location.

At the same time, the wind was picking up and blowing snow, reducing visibility. After a half hour, the B-17 appeared over NP8, and the P2V, now very low on fuel, flew off. Smith established radio contact with Seigrist aboard the B-17, asking him to drop the spare balloon and an extra tank of helium. LeSchack and Smith inflated three balloons and tethered them to the tractor. By this time, the wind had increased to fifteen knots, and both men had to struggle with the duffel bag to prevent it from being dragged across the ice.

Aboard the B-17, Seigrist also faced difficulties as he began the run toward the balloon. The gray overcast merged with the ice, providing little in the way of a visible horizon. As soon as NP8's huts disappeared below the right wing, Seigrist felt as if he was flying into a void. Although the line and the red Mylar marker gave a visual reference for him to keep the wings level, he was on the edge of vertigo. Seigrist flew into the line, made a good contact, and immediately went over to instruments.

In the nose, Randolph Scott triggered the sky anchor, which caught the line. The duffel bag was lifted off the ice and began trailing behind the B-17.

Winch operator Jerrold B. Daniels snagged the line and began reeling it in. With the bag hanging just behind the B-17, tail position operator Robert H. Nicol realized its contents had shifted during the pickup, and the bag could no longer fit through the opening in the tail. Nicol was in cramped quarters, just behind the retracted tail wheel in the narrow aft fuselage. Calling for assistance, he reached out through the opening and began removing several pieces of equipment. Finally, enough was removed so that the bag could be brought aboard.

It was now LeSchack's turn. As with the drop five days before, Price would fly the B-17 during LeSchack's pickup. The strong winds battered LeSchack, who was being dragged across the ice by the balloon toward the pressure ridge. Frantically, LeSchack tried to stop himself. To make matters worse, the ski mask on his face had been twisted around, and he could not see. Finally, he was able to dig small handholds in the ice, where he lay prone and held on. In the final moments before the B-17 made contact, he thought about how his unorthodox position might affect the pickup.

Like Seigrist, Price also felt vertigo as the B-17 neared the line. The yoke contacted the line below the Mylar marker, and Scott watched as it slid down the yoke and was caught by the sky anchor. LeSchack felt himself jerked into the air and then pulled face forward into the 125-knot airstream, which made it nearly impossible for him to breathe. He extended his arms, and made a 180-degree roll. He was flying with his back to the wind, and could now breathe. Holding this position, however, required all his strength as he was reeled in. The recovery took six and a half minutes before LeSchack clambered through the tail gunner's position and was aboard the B-17. Although LeSchack was disoriented, out of breath, and looked exhausted as a result of the ordeal, a quick examination by Dr. Walter showed no ill effects.

It was now time to recover Smith. Seigrist traded seats with Price and made ready for the final pickup. The weather continued to deteriorate. Seigrist made a tight approach over NP8, attempting to catch the line before being hit with vertigo. Despite this, as soon as he lost sight of the station, he had the illusion that he had to turn right to catch the line. Seigrist had to force himself not to. On the ice, Smith was also having problems. He had hoped to hold onto the tractor, but he was soon being dragged by the wind toward the pressure ridge. After skidding some seventy-five yards, Smith snagged a depression in the ice with his feet. To make matters worse, the hood of Smith's pickup overalls had been pulled down over his eyes, and he could see nothing.

Seigrist spotted the red Mylar marker at a range of two hundred yards. The B-17 was a little too far to the right, but Seigrist did not have time to correct his position. The line made contact near the tip of the left yoke, and Seigrist recalled that it just seemed to hang there for an eternity. Then, as if in slow motion, the line slid down the yoke and into the sky anchor. Smith suddenly found himself weightless and flying through the air. Seigrist could hear Smith singing over the radio as he was reeled in. The pickup went smoothly, and at 8:18 P.M., Smith was aboard the B-17, and the aircraft turned south. As it did, Thorsrud opened his briefcase and removed a bottle of Vat 69 scotch. The Coldfeet team toasted their success by drinking scotch from paper cups.

The B-17 returned to Point Barrow at 2:15 A.M. on 3 June 1962. The crews of the B-17 and P2V posed in front of the B-17 for a group photo, and then went to a party to celebrate the mission. In addition to the equipment, documents, photos, and notes brought back from NP8, LeSchack and Smith also had two packages of White Sea Canal cigarettes. These were passed around the group and sampled. The Navy intelligence assessment: "poorly made and taste ghastly." Cadwalader was presented with the poster Smith had taken from the NP8 mess hall.

Following the completion of Coldfeet, an ONI report on the operation noted that it had provided "firsthand observations of the nature, extent, and sophistication of the Soviet Arctic research program." The ONI analysts were particularly impressed with the Soviet's oceanographic and meteorological research, which were judged to be "well developed and apparently conducted with a high degree of efficiency." The analysts found their equipment was, in many cases, "superior in quality to comparable U.S. equipment." The weather observations seemed "extremely complete" and were in most respects "superior to U.S. drift station meteorological programs." Less conclusive was the evidence about Soviet monitoring of U.S. submarine activities. NP8 was capable of acoustic research, while the cable and the recovered notebooks indicated such research had been conducted.

The ONI was far less impressed by the living conditions at NP8. Sanitation seemed "non-existent," while all the books and films were "typical propaganda." They noted that "in spite of the austere, unsanitary, and politically pressured conditions under which the Soviet scientists lived, all evidence indicates that they were engaged in a highly developed, successful, and extremely useful program of science."

The ONI noted, "The U.S. intelligence community now has a tremendously more accurate and positive mass of data upon which to base its evaluation of Soviet activities on Arctic drift stations. Much speculation has been confirmed as fact; and some has been shown to have been unfounded. Only from first-hand observation by qualified observers could such an unusual and concrete intelligence result have been obtained." Both LeSchack and Smith received the Legion of Merit in November 1962.

The possibilities of the Fulton Skyhook for special operations and SAFE rescue missions were obvious. During the early 1960s, the sole Air Force special operations squadrons, now called Air Commando Groups, were part of the California, West Virginia, Maryland, and Rhode Island Air National Guards (ANGs). These four ANG units participated in Operation Sidewinder in the spring of 1964. This training exercise was conducted out of the Marana Air Park. The ANG crews were shown Intermountain Aviation's B-17, and a simulated pickup was made. A year later, the B-17 made its appearance in *Thunderball*. According to some accounts, the airplane's role in the film caused problems between the CIA and Intermountain Aviation.

Some CIA officials were displeased at having this special B-17 so publicly displayed. Intermountain Aviation officials were summoned to a meeting at CIA headquarters and were chewed out for allowing the airplane to be used in the movie. The reprimand proved to be perfunctory, however. The B-17 had been demonstrated before the Forest Service and the Air Force, and its existence was not secret.

At the same time, Intermountain Aviation was at war.

Intermountain Aviation in the Congo

During the 1950s and into the 1960s, the old European colonial empires in Africa broke up. Among these was the Congo, which Belgium granted independence on 30 June 1960. Little had been done to prepare the country, however, and the new nation was beset by tribal rivalries. Five days after independence, a civil war broke out. After three years, the United Nations restored a measure of stability, a pro-Western government was established, and Soviet influence was eliminated.

That state was soon upset by a new rebellion, however, that had begun during mid-1963 in Kwilu province. Pierre Mulele, the ex-minister of education in the Congolese government, led the revolt. Each rebel soldier was given a small phial containing a potion called "Mulele water," which allegedly protected him from bullets and gave him the strength of a lion. For this reason the rebels were known as "Simbas," after the word for lion. This magic did not work at night, or in the rain, the rebels believed, so they were inactive at those times. Although better armed, the Congolese army either fled before the Simbas' magic or joined their ranks.

The situation resembled that of the colonial wars of the nineteenth century, rather than the ideologically driven nuclear standoff of the Cold War (and was light years away from Bond's shaken-not-stirred martinis). The Simbas were a ragtag group of illiterate tribesmen, given to bloody massacres. They were not Communists, but they did pose a threat to the pro-Western government. For this reason, the USSR, China, and their client states provided arms and ammunition to the Simbas. This, in turn, led to the CIA being ordered to provide air support to the Congolese government. Richard L. Holm, a CIA officer who fought against the Simbas, later noted, "It was just that simple, and it was a scenario played out elsewhere in the world repeatedly during the first decades of the Cold War."

In late 1963, Intermountain Aviation was training exile Cuban pilots for combat missions over the Congo. As stateless persons, they had no visible links with the U.S. government and could be labeled white mercenaries employed by the Congolese army. Some of them—Jack Varela, Rene Garcia, and Gus

Ponzoa, for instance—were veterans of the Bay of Pigs. Others, such as Juan Peron, an exile crop-duster who had fled Cuba in March 1960, had no military experience. The Cubans initially flew T-28 trainers, which had been fitted with .50-caliber machine gun pods under the wings. They were easy to fly and maintain, and were effective light attack aircraft against guerrillas who lacked heavy antiaircraft guns.

Intermountain Aviation pilot John Merriman trained many of the Cuban pilots on the T-28s. On Ponzoa's first flight with Merriman, the Cuban was to perform a series of acrobatic rolls. Ponzoa had trouble flying the aircraft, allowing the G-forces to build up. As a result, he became airsick. By the following day, Merriman had him flying the T-28 proficiently. Ponzoa left Marana on 29 May 1964, arriving a month later in the Congo to head up a group of fifteen Cuban pilots.

Merriman soon followed. He had volunteered for duty in the Congo as head of the CIA's air operations. Merriman arrived in Leopoldville, the capital of the Congo, on 17 July. Three days later, he and three of the Cuban pilots—Varela, Garcia, and Ponzoa—flew three T-28s to a base at Kamina in Katanga province. With the Simbas continuing their advance, Merriman wrote to his wife, "The situation here is a real bucket of worms."

At the same time, the U.S. ambassador to the Congo, McMurtrie Godley, was fretting over the CIA's air operations. He sent a telegram to Secretary of State Rusk on 25 July saying, "We should indulge in no, repeat no, covert operations here that do not have [premier Moise] Tshombe's and/or [president Joseph] Kasavubu's blessing."

To preserve plausible deniability, neither Merriman nor any other American was to fly combat missions in the T-28s. He was eager to see action, however, and on 26 July, he received a Belgian intelligence report that indicated a Simba convoy was on the road from Kabalo. Merriman asked Ponzoa to fly with him to attack the convoy. Both Ponzoa and Garcia tried to talk him out of it, arguing it was too late in the day to attack so distant a target. Merriman would not be dissuaded, and Garcia and Varela agreed to go with him.

The three T-28 pilots found the Simba convoy of four jeeps and six trucks, and Merriman began the attack. The three pilots made one pass each, hitting the vehicles with machine-gun rounds. As Merriman pulled up, his T-28 was hit by ground fire and the engine began to leak oil. He was able to reach an abandoned airstrip, but the engine gave out on final approach. The shattered wreckage of his T-28 came to a stop in a cloud of dust. Garcia and Varela both thought Merriman had died in the crash.

The next morning, an old truck arrived at the Kamina air base. Two friendly Congolese had found Merriman still alive in the airplane's cockpit. They had pried the severely injured pilot out of the T-28 and brought him to the base. Merriman was taken to the base clinic, which lacked any medical supplies. Ambassador Godley's primary concern was not Merriman's condition, but that his crash did not disclose the U.S. involvement in the Congo. He expressed relief in a 30 July telegram that a news report had said that the pilot was Cuban.

Merriman remained at the Kamina air base clinic until 31 July, when he was flown on a DC-4 to Leopoldville and placed in a rundown hospital. Because of political sensitivity, he was checked in under the name "Mario Carlos" to maintain the cover story that he was a Cuban pilot. Over the following days, Ponzoa visited Merriman; the former was distressed by the lack of medical attention. Merriman was able to write a letter to his wife, saying only that he had been in an accident. It was not until 20 August, some three weeks after the crash, that Merriman was finally stable enough to move. He was put aboard an Air Force transport and flown out of the Congo. To maintain security, he was listed under the name of an Air Force officer. Merriman did not make it home; he died during the flight from a lung embolism.

Val Merriman was told her husband had died peacefully in his sleep at a hospital in Puerto Rico. The secrecy that had surrounded the final days of his life continued after his death. The widow was instructed to say that her husband had gone to Puerto Rico to finalize a contract. After his arrival, he rented a car and was driving into town from the airport. Merriman was tired and ran off the road. He was taken to Ramey AFB, where he later died. This distanced Merriman and Intermountain Aviation from both the CIA and the Congo. Val Merriman found that telling the cover story was hard. She recalled that it was "pretty tough to lie to your children and mother-in-law."

The CIA made arrangements for Merriman's family. A local attorney handled tax, insurance, and Social Security problems. Val Merriman received workmen's compensation insurance payments for her three children. What was unusual about the checks was that they were drawn on an offshore bank and were mailed to a Tucson post office box. John Merriman was posthumously awarded the Intelligence Star medal. Only his widow and parents were invited to the ceremony at CIA headquarters. Thereafter, President Lyndon B. Johnson met briefly with them in the White House.

On 21 August 1964, the day after John Merriman died, the B-26K was introduced to combat over the Congo. The On Mark Engineering Corporation had modified the aircraft; they now had more powerful engines, strengthened wings, and wing tip and bomb bay fuel tanks. The B-26Ks were armed with eight .50-caliber machine guns in the nose and hard points under the wings for 2.75-inch rocket pods. Under the pressure of the Simba advance, the first three B-26Ks were hurriedly flown to the Congo. The Cuban pilots, who included Ponzoa and Garcia, were quickly trained in the new aircraft.

A week after their introduction, a pair of B-26Ks was supporting a Congolese army attempt to recapture Albertville. The B-26Ks devastated the Simba troops and then landed at the Albertville airport, which had been retaken by ground troops. The new B-26Ks' firepower and performance so impressed the local Congolese commander that he prevented them from returning to Leopoldville. Ponzoa recalled: "He simply wanted to keep us for his personal use, to have his own little air force. We therefore had to use cunning and after one or two days of waiting, we were able to leave quietly with our planes."

The two types of aircraft were used in different roles. The T-28s were dispersed to airfields throughout the Congo to provide local air support for troops. The twin-engine B-26Ks, with their longer range and higher speed, made attacks against targets deep inside Simba-controlled territory. These included strikes on convoys, munitions depots, and troops. The Cuban pilots flew a demanding schedule of two missions per day, each lasting six to eight hours. The arrival of the B-26Ks also caused a change in the organization of the CIA's air force. The Western International Ground Maintenance Organization (WIGMO) was registered in Liechtenstein on 21 September 1964. WIGMO was "officially" under contract to the Congolese army to service the aircraft. In reality, it managed the CIA personnel in the Congo.

Soon after the B-26Ks were introduced, a pair spotted a Simba convoy advancing on the government-controlled town of Boende. As they flew over the cars and trucks, some 250 men were climbing out. Garcia, who was flying one of the B-26Ks, recalled: "Our arrival didn't change anything. They continued to disembark as if nothing had happened. They did not try to seek cover or disperse." The two aircraft began strafing the vehicles, and then attacked the Simba troops. Garcia was astonished when they did not take cover, but remained in the center of the road, firing at the two airplanes. They clearly thought the Mulele water would protect them. Garcia said later, "I felt like shouting 'Go and hide, Get out of the way!' but all they did was to pile up their dead on the side of the road." After running low on ammunition, the B-26Ks landed back at their base. The postflight examination showed only a few bullet holes.

Although this Simba convoy was wiped out by the B-26Ks, other Simba columns later took Boende. The Congolese army also believed in the magic power of the Mulele water, and usually broke and ran before the "indestructible" Simbas. More important, the Simbas had taken the regional capital of Stanleyville and were holding some two thousand Westerners hostage, including five Americans from the U.S. consulate. (Among the hostages were the senior CIA officer in Stanleyville and his two communications officers.) To prevent the killing of the hostages, a combined ground/airborne operation was planned.

On 1 November 1964 two motorized columns, Lima I and Lima II, set out for Stanleyville. The T-28s and B-26Ks provided air cover and scouted ahead of the columns. As they continued the drive toward Stanleyville, Operation Red Dragon was launched on 24 November. Belgian paratroopers were dropped into Stanleyville from a dozen U.S. Air Force C-130s. The Simbas killed some forty hostages following the drop, but the paratroopers and the Lima I and II columns rescued another twelve hundred captives, who were then flown out. Two B-26Ks provided weather reconnaissance for the drop, then provided air support. Two days later, a second drop was made on the town of Paulis. Operation Black Dragon saved the lives of another four hundred hostages. They were hurriedly assembled, taken to the airport, and flown out aboard the C-130s. Again, two B-26Ks provided support.

By the end of 1964, most of the towns in the far northeastern Congo were in government hands, but Simbas still roamed the countryside. The CIA agent networks were in shambles, and there was no information on the Simbas' locations or strengths. The Congolese army continued to be ineffective against the rebels, and the white mercenaries hired by the government lacked the numbers to quickly chase down the remaining Simbas. The Belgian paratroopers had been sent home after the airdrops because of international pressure and accusations of "neocolonialism."

In addition to John Merriman, others fighting the secret air war also suffered. The most serious incident took place on 17 February 1965. A pair of T-28s was flying a reconnaissance mission along the Sudanese border and was forced off course by a storm. Both aircraft ran low on fuel and made crash landings. One of the T-28s, flown by Juan Peron, with CIA officer Richard L. Holm in the backseat, caught fire on impact. Both survived, but Holm was badly burned. Peron hid him and then found help in a friendly village. The villagers cared for Holm, removing worms from his skin and covering his burns with a tribal remedy that included boiled snakes.

Peron, the village chief, and two other tribesmen set off to get help for Holm. They rode bicycles until they reached the airfield at Paulis eight days after the crash. A Belgian helicopter flew to the village, but one of its rotor blades struck a tree and it crash-landed. None of the crew or passengers was hurt, and a second helicopter landed successfully the next day. By this time, Holm was near death, unable to eat, unconscious most of the time, and suffering from delusions. After the rescue, Holm was flown to Paulis, then Leopoldville, and finally to the National Burn Center in Texas, where he underwent twenty-eight months of treatment before returning to duty. In gratitude for the care that had saved Holm's life, the CIA air-dropped a planeload of medications, tools, bicycles, and clothing to the village.

The Cuban pilot of the other T-28 on the mission, Juan Tunon, met a far worse fate. Peron and the village chief found his crashed T-28 near the village, but there was no trace of Tunon. It was not until several months later that reports from missionaries confirmed that Tunon had been captured by the Simbas, then killed and *eaten.* The Simbas believed that if they ate the skin and internal organs of a foe, they would gain his courage, strength, and wisdom. Another Cuban pilot, Fausto Gomez, was also cannibalized. When his body was found, it had been butchered.

It was not until June 1965 that the mercenaries launched Operation Imperial Violets, which cleared the last two towns of Simba troops. The CIA T-28s and B-26Ks supported the final drive. This included air strikes on villages across the border in the Sudan, where the Simbas had taken refuge. This broke the Simbas as an organized military force, although some sporadic action continued through 1966. The covert war for the Congo had attracted little public or press attention.

By the time *Thunderball* appeared in theaters, in late December 1965, the war in the Congo was effectively over. As the Intermountain Aviation B-17 made the pickup of the two stand-in dummies at the end of the film, the audiences did not know that the airplane really belonged to the CIA, or that three years before, it had performed a similar recovery from a Soviet ice station. *Thunderball* represented a fantasy covert operation. The brutal reality of covert operations was something very different.

IV
The Longest War

9

Air America

Anything, Anywhere, Anytime—Professionally.

— Air America motto

What would become the longest war in U.S. history started in early 1947, in what was then called French Indochina. It began as a guerrilla war between the French colonial authorities and the Communist-dominated Viet Minh. Initially, the United States stood aside from what it saw as a distasteful colonial war. With the start of the Korean War, this attitude changed. In the fall of 1950, the United States began supplying the French with weapons, supplies, and money. Despite this assistance, the French were unable to make any headway against the Viet Minh. President Dwight D. Eisenhower in April 1953, however, was unwilling to commit U.S. forces and rejected a French request for U.S. Air Force C-119 transports and crews. A covert operation, on the other hand, could provide a means to assist the French without direct commitment of American forces.

Eisenhower approved the use of pilots from CIA-owned CAT, and Air Force C-119s were repainted in French markings. CAT pilots made airdrops to French outposts and provided training for French C-119 crewmen. The CAT pilots' initial stay in Vietnam was brief. The resupply and training missions were flown between May and July 1953, and the CAT pilots were then withdrawn. They were soon back, however.

CAT chief pilot Paul Holden and some twenty-two C-119 crewmen returned to Vietnam on 13 March 1954 to fly resupply missions to the besieged French camp at Dien Bien Phu. The French were surprised by their brightly colored Hawaiian shirts, as well as by their pistol belts. On their first missions over Dien Bien Phu on the afternoon of 14 March, the CAT pilots were met with intense 37-mm antiaircraft fire. The lead C-119 was hit several times and jettisoned its cargo. The other two aircraft aborted their runs and returned to base.

The ground fire damaged several more aircraft over the following weeks. On 27 March, one of the CAT C-119s was hit in its left wing by a 37-mm shell, and several .50-caliber rounds struck another. Holden's aircraft was hit by several 37-mm bursts on 23 April. Shrapnel tore into Holden's hip and ripped muscle from his arm. Copilot Wallace Buford was able to stop the bleeding with a tourniquet, make the drop, and then fly the damaged aircraft back to a landing. American doctors were able to save Holden's arm, and he later returned to flight duty.

A C-119, flown by James B. McGovern, better known as "Earthquake Magoon," was also hit during April. After making the drop, the elevator control was shot away. McGovern had to fly the aircraft using the trim tab, which he said was "like a jolly kangaroo." Despite his bravura, which included parachuting beer and cigarettes to the French troops, the long flight hours and heavy ground fire were taking a toll. McGovern would sometimes lie on his bunk, staring up at the ceiling, lost in his own thoughts.

McGovern was scheduled for a six-plane drop mission on the afternoon of 6 May 1954, as the Viet Minh closed in on the last French defenders. McGovern and Buford were the pilots aboard the C-119, tail number 149. In the back of the plane were three colonial paratroopers—Bataille, Rescouriou, and Moussa. The observer was 2nd Lt. Jean Arlaux, a twenty-four-year-old newly commissioned French officer. He had arrived in Indochina on 27 April, and this was his first combat mission.

Arriving over Dien Bien Phu, the C-119s were greeted by heavy ground fire. McGovern's plane was hit in the left wing's leading edge by a 37-mm shell, causing the engine to leak oil. A second round then hit its right boom. The cargo was dropped, and McGovern flew toward a small landing strip, his aircraft dropping lower and lower. Finally, with the airplane skimming just above the ground, he radioed, "Looks like this is it, son." The C-119's wingtip snagged a hilltop, then cartwheeled, and exploded in a fireball. The following evening, 7 May 1954, the last French outpost fell to the Communists. CAT had flown a total of 682 missions.

McGovern and Buford died in the crash, the first Americans killed in Vietnam. In the back of the plane, Rescouriou and Bataille were also killed. Moussa and Arlaux survived, but were soon captured by the Viet Minh. Moussa died within a few days from his injuries; Arlaux was released in October, among the last prisoners to be freed.

The Geneva Convention ending French rule of Indochina was signed on 21 July 1954. Vietnam was divided at the 17th parallel between the Communist Democratic Republic of Vietnam in the north and the Republic of Vietnam in the south. It also gave independence to the French protectorates of Laos and Cambodia. Between mid-May and mid-August, CAT C-119s dropped supplies to isolated French garrisons. CAT C-46s also evacuated civilians from North Vietnam. Between 22 August and 4 October, CAT moved a total of 19,808 men, women, and children south, out of Communist-controlled areas.

Air America in Laos

CAT first established a permanent presence in Laos on 1 July 1957, when Bruce B. Blevins flew a C-47 into the Laotian capital of Vientiane in support of a contract with the U.S. embassy. The political situation in Laos deteriorated between 1957 and 1959, and the United States increased its aid and military presence in the country. CAT (Air America after March 1959) provided the logistics support for this expanding role. C-47s and C-46s made airdrops and landings throughout the country to isolated Royal Laotian Army (FAR) posts. The summer of 1959 saw both the introduction of a U.S. Army training unit and the outbreak of fighting between FAR troops and the Communist Pathet Lao forces.

As the fighting increased, Air America expanded its airlift capability with aircraft better suited to the conditions in Laos, conditions that included dense jungles, mountains reaching seven thousand feet in elevation, and rugged landing strips. C-7 and C-123 twin-engine transports supplemented the older C-46s, while Air America also began using helicopters and light aircraft.

In August 1959, Air America's President, Hugh L. Grundy, called Vice President of Operations Robert E. Rousselot to his office in Taiwan and showed him an order from the CIA to train two helicopter pilots. Rousselot recalled that it had "come out of the blue." He initially thought the CIA had a special operation in mind that required a helicopter, and that it would be "a one-time deal." Four Air America pilots were trained on Air Force H-19A helicopters in Japan and the Philippines. The Air America helicopters did not reach Laos until March 1960, and the pilots soon found the underpowered H-19s could fly only at lower elevations. Despite the shortcomings, by June 1960 it was clear that helicopters would be critical to Air America's future operations in Laos. Rousselot and the CIA decided to "hire" experienced military helicopter pilots. Rousselot made arrangements for four U.S. Marine Corps pilots to obtain their discharges in Okinawa and fly the H-19s. Later in 1960, the CIA arranged for the transfer of four Marine Corps H-34 helicopters to Air America.

At the same time, Air America introduced the Helio Courier, a single-engine light aircraft, into its inventory. It could land in about 50 feet and take off in 150 feet. The first Helio Courier was supplied to Air America in the fall of 1959, but it was problematic: the airplane's engine was subject to vapor locks on starting; the landing gear could be blocked by mud, rocks, and gravel; and the rudder had to be modified to prevent jamming. The pilots initially selected to fly the Helio Courier were all multiengine transport pilots and did not receive sufficient training in the special techniques needed to fly the demanding aircraft.

Air America was about to abandon the Helio Courier, but Maj. Harry Aderholt and Rousselot then stepped in and saved the effort. Aderholt believed the aircraft was ideal for operations from the short, unimproved airstrips in Laos. Rousselot, on the other hand, thought the CIA would give the light aircraft mission to a rival private company, Bird and Son, if Air America proved incapable of doing it. Rousselot assigned Ronald J. Sutphin, an experienced light airplane pilot, to the Helio Courier project in early 1960. Sutphin demonstrated the airplane's ability and convinced the CIA to expand the program.

In August 1960, a full-scale civil war broke out in Laos, which pitted the neutralist forces of paratroop commander Kong Le, who had the backing of Pathet Lao, against a right-wing general named Phoumi Nosavan, who received assistance from the U.S. military, the CIA, and Thai forces, with Air America flying in supplies. The civil war in Laos now became a major East/West confrontation, as it shared borders with six countries—North and South Vietnam, China, Cambodia, Thailand, and Burma.

Adm. Harry D. Felt, commander in chief of the Pacific Fleet, sent a cable to the JCS on 29 December 1960. He stated, "With full realization of the seriousness of the decision to intervene, I believe strongly that we must intervene now or give up northern Laos." Chief of Naval Operations Adm. Arleigh Burke added his support, telling the JCS on 31 December: "If we lose Laos, we will probably lose Thailand and the rest of Southeast Asia. We will have demonstrated to the world that we cannot or will not stand when challenged."

For his part, President Eisenhower was no more willing to commit U.S. ground troops to Laos than he had been at Dien Bien Phu nearly six years earlier. The alternative was for the CIA to equip and train Hmong tribesmen, who were led by Lt. Col. Vang Pao, the commander of the FAR 10th Infantry Battalion on the Plain of Jars. When fighting broke out in 1959, Vang Pao expressed concern that if Laos fell to the Communist Pathet Lao, the Hmong would face reprisals because of their previous ties with the French. CIA paramilitary specialist James W. "Bill" Lair met with Vang Pao in late December 1959. Vang Pao told Lair that if the United States supplied weapons, he could raise an army of ten thousand. Lair's proposal received the approval of the CIA, Admiral Felt, and the State Department. Eisenhower authorized a test program to arm and train an initial group of a thousand Hmong.

In January 1961, Air America made an arms drop at Pa Dong, a mountaintop base south of the Plain of Jars, where the first Hmong trainees waited. Lair realized from the beginning that Air America would be critical to maintaining communications between the Hmong villages in the mountains surrounding the Plain of Jars. In early 1961, however, Air America lacked the capability for such operations. It had but a few helicopters and Helio Couriers, whereas the villages lacked even rudimentary landing strips. The future of Laos, the Hmongs, and Air America's role also awaited decisions by the new administration.

Newly elected President John F. Kennedy faced a worsening situation in Laos. In March 1961, the Pathet Lao, backed by some twelve thousand North Vietnamese "advisors" and "volunteer" troops, threatened Vientiane and the royal capital of Luang Prabang. President Kennedy was alarmed by these developments, and on 21 March 1961, he approved "Mill Pond," a plan for covert air strikes by sixteen B-26s against Pathet Lao targets on the Plain of Jars.

The aircraft to be used in Mill Pond were sanitized—they had no national insignias or serial numbers and were in either bare metal or all-black finishes. The Air Force pilots selected for the missions were described as American "civilians" employed by Bangkok Contract Air Service, a CIA front company. The aircraft and crews were at the Royal Thai Air Base at Takhi. The unit was commanded by now Lieutenant Colonel Aderholt, assisted by his brother, Capt. Warren Aderholt. Early in April, the Pathet Lao launched attacks in northern and central Laos, as well as in the southern panhandle, which bordered part of South Vietnam. As the situation worsened, President Kennedy approved launching the Mill Pond strikes.

The aircraft were fueled and armed with bombs, rockets, and .50-caliber ammunition on 16 April 1961. The U.S. ambassador to Laos, Winthrop Brown, imposed a political restriction that banned the use of napalm on the strikes. Warren Aderholt gave the crews their target folders and a final briefing. At dawn, four cells of four B-26s would each take off on the strikes. An Air America pilot would lead each cell to the targets. Two of the cells would attack the Pathet Lao airfield at Xieng Khouang and crater the runway, destroy any aircraft on the ground, and hit targets of opportunity. The third cell would attack Pathet Lao forces in the Ban Ban Valley, and the fourth cell would hit targets in the southern Plain of Jars. Harry Aderholt gave the "employees" of the Bangkok Contract Air Service commissions in the Royal Laotian Air Force "blood chits," which were multilingual documents promising rewards for safely returning the pilots to friendly hands, and gold sovereigns.

Early the next morning, Harry Aderholt awoke the pilots to tell them that the attack had been called off at the last minute. Half a world away, the Bay of Pigs was unfolding. With one political humiliation on his hands, Kennedy had no desire to read more headlines about a "private company" starting a war in Laos.

The same events that set the abortive Mill Pond into motion also resulted in an expansion of Air America activities in Laos. President Kennedy authorized the transfer of fourteen H-34 helicopters from the Marine Corps to Air America, which were flown by Marine, Army, and Navy volunteers. Air America pilot Clarence J. Abadie led a flight of sixteen H-34 helicopters from Bangkok to an airbase at Udorn, Thailand, on 29 March 1961. This new forward base was merely forty miles from Vientiane.

The Air America helicopters were soon in action, as Pathet Lao troops launched attacks on Vang Pao's headquarters at Pa Dong. The helicopters flew supply missions to the Hmong. Flight time by Air America crews was soon totaling two thousand hours per month. The Pathet Lao troops finally forced the Hmong out of Pa Dong. Despite the setback, the Hmong forces regrouped at Pha Khao, some ten miles away, and now numbered in excess of nine thousand guerrillas, with another four thousand recruits available.

As the Hmong forces grew, so did the need to supply food to their scattered villages. Having arrived in Vientiane in April 1961 to oversee the Helio Courier program, William L. Andersevic was put in charge of construction of landing sites throughout Hmong territory for use by the Helio Couriers. Andersevic located suitable sites and then arranged for local Hmong to cut down trees and level the ground as best they could. Flying in and out of the fields, which were called "Lima Sites," was demanding. The Hmongs had just simple tools, and the rough terrain meant that the landing strips were on top of a mountain or ridge, or carved out of the side of a hill. By the summer of 1961, work had started on what would eventually become an extensive network of these rough airstrips.

The battles against the Pathet Lao, the pace of operations, the rugged terrain, and the unpredictable weather claimed a toll on Air America pilots and crews. Charles Mateer and Walter Wizbowski were killed on 30 May 1961 when their helicopter crashed in bad weather while trying to land supplies. They were the first Air America helicopter pilots to die in action.

President Kennedy was unwilling either to directly commit U.S. troops or to undertake politically risky covert operations like Mill Pond. Instead, the president opted for a diplomatic solution. The "Declaration on the Neutrality of Laos" was signed in Geneva on 23 July 1962. The agreement provided for a coalition government of neutralist, rightist, and Pathet Lao representatives, and the withdrawal of all foreign troops by 7 October 1962.

The Geneva Accords made it politically impossible for the United States to cut off the flow of supplies down the Ho Chi Minh Trail through Laos. Assistant Secretary of State Averill Harriman, who had negotiated the Geneva Accords, was determined to ensure that the United States complied with the agreement. He blocked any activities that might embarrass the Laotian government or cause problems with the Soviets. He ordered that only two CIA case officers remain in Laos to monitor Communist activities, and also restricted Air America to food drops to the Hmong.

Despite the agreement on Laos and the restrictions on Air America operations, losses continued. In November 1962, an Air America C-123 flown by Fred Reilly was on final approach to Xieng Khouang on the Plain of Jars. North Vietnamese troops opened fire, and Reilly was hit in the legs by machine-gun rounds. The plane crashed at the end of the strip, and Reilly and the copilot were both killed. The loadmaster was the only survivor, with a severe wound in his leg.

Air America's operations did not show a decline until the first part of 1963. Flight time, which had been some two thousand hours per month before the Geneva Accords, dropped to merely six hundred hours. Helicopter pilot Harry Casterlin summed up the situation in a letter to his parents on 24 January 1963. "There are 37 of us over here and not enough work.... We are doing virtually no flying in Laos anymore." By May 1963, the number of H-34 helicopters at Udorn had been reduced from eighteen to six, aircraft were being stored, and people were being laid off. In the summer, only about forty tons of food was being dropped per month to the Hmong villages.

Although Laos seemed peaceful, an estimated seven thousand North Vietnamese troops had remained in Laos. In addition to working on the Ho Chi Minh Trail, they also attacked both the neutralist and Hmong troops. William Colby, chief of the CIA's Far East Division, pleaded with Harriman to allow weapons drops to resume. Despite the North Vietnamese violations, Harriman reluctantly approved an Air America arms drop, on the condition that the weapons would be used strictly in self-defense. More drops soon followed, but Colby recalled that Harriman would personally approve "each and every clandestine supply flight and its cargo."

Kennedy did authorize the CIA to expand the Hmong force, and by the end of 1963 it had reached some twenty thousand men. They fought as guerrillas, blowing up North Vietnamese supply dumps, ambushing the growing numbers of truck convoys, planting mines in roads, among other such harassing actions. The expansion of the Hmong reversed the near-halt in Air America activities. Casterlin wrote to his parents on 11 November 1963, "The war is going great guns now," then added, "Don't be misled [by news reports] that I am only carrying rice on my missions as wars aren't won by rice."

Air America to the Rescue

Although its primary function remained moving supplies and personnel in support of the Hmong forces, Air America crews often found themselves flying combat missions. In March 1964, North Vietnamese and Pathet Lao troops launched attacks throughout the Plain of Jars. By mid-May, the Communist forces had control of the area, and the coalition government had collapsed. In response, President Lyndon B. Johnson ordered reconnaissance flights over the Communist-controlled areas to provide intelligence and to send the North "a message of U.S. resolve." Code-named "Yankee Team," the missions were flown by Navy RF-8As and RA-3Bs and Air Force RF-101s. There was little coordination between the Air Force and Navy, and rescue capability was minimal. The Navy flights were by two unarmed RF-8s, without fighter escorts, flying at high speed and at low altitude.

Lt. Charles E. Klusmann's RF-8 was hit by ground fire on 6 June 1964, and he was forced to bail out deep inside Pathet Lao–controlled territory. As a military rescue attempt was being organized, the Navy was given a direct order by Secretary of Defense Robert S. McNamara that there would be no "round eye" rescue attempt. Adm. Harry Felt was told that, for political reasons, the State Department did not want identifiable Americans in Laos. Admiral Felt then asked to speak with President Johnson. McNamara replied that it was after midnight in Washington. Felt insisted and was put through, waking up the president. After Admiral Felt explained the situation, the president gave his approval for a rescue.

While official Washington debated, a rescue attempt by Air America was already under way. When Klusmann bailed out, his wingman, Lt. Jerry Kuechman, sent a Mayday call. An Air America C-123 pilot heard it and radioed, "Where are you and what do you need?" Kuechman gave the position of the downed pilot and then headed back to the carrier because of low fuel. Klusmann had hurt his right leg in the landing and had trouble walking. After about an hour on the ground, he saw a Helio Courier and popped a smoke flare. Soon after, the sun came out and Klusmann began signaling with a mirror. In response, the Helio Courier pilot rocked his wings and revved its engine. The C-123 and an Air America C-7 joined him.

The aircraft circled over Klusmann for several hours. Despite the passage of time, there were no signs of Pathet Lao troops. Finally, Klusmann heard the distant sounds of approaching helicopters. He signaled his position with the mirror, and then crawled up a small hill to a clearing in the ridgeline. A pair of Air America H-34 helicopters appeared and one, piloted by Tom Moher, began its approach. When it was about a quarter mile from Klusmann's position, the H-34 came under heavy ground fire. Moher's H-34 took more than eighty hits, and his copilot was badly wounded. Moher pulled up and struggled to clear the area.

The C-7 made a low pass for ground fire suppression. Gunfire poured from every window on the twin-engine transport, while other crewmen threw hand grenades from the aircraft. One of the grenades exploded barely fifteen to twenty feet from Klusmann. Despite the pass, the ground fire remained heavy. The second H-34, flown by Bill Cook, began its run, but it also began to take hits, and a crewman was badly wounded. Klusmann waved off Cook's helicopter. Klusmann wrote later, "It just seemed the right thing to do at the time, and there were never any regrets." He was surrounded by Pathet Lao troops and was taken prisoner. Klusmann was able to escape three months later and reach a friendly outpost.

The same day that Klusmann was captured, Washington authorized armed escorts for the RF-8s. The following day, one of the escorts for a Yankee Team mission, an F-8D flown by Comdr. Doyle W. Lynn, was shot down. His wingman reported that Commander Lynn's parachute had opened, and gave his position. Air America H-34 helicopters took off, escorted by Royal Laotian T-28s. They searched an area three miles on either side of the downed pilot's reported position. The search proved unsuccessful, as the position was wrong. The search team also did not know that the Navy homing beacon transmitted on a frequency different from that used by the Air Force, and that their receiving equipment was incompatible. The Air America C-7s, on the other hand, were equipped to pick up the Navy frequency, and several took off. They were able to locate Commander Lynn, but darkness was falling, and the rescue had to be postponed until daybreak.

As the sun rose the next morning, a low overcast covered much of northern Laos. The Air America C-7s took off and were able to detect Lynn's homing beacon. He was about forty miles south of the reported position. With the overcast, they could not see him on the ground. Lynn, however, could hear the drone of their engines and fired a signal flare through the fog. An Air America H-34 helicopter descended below the clouds and rescued Lynn.

The twin rescue attempts in June 1964 showed the weaknesses of the Air Rescue Service. Having focused on peacetime rescue, their crews lacked the long-range helicopters, armed escorts, equipment, and training needed for combat rescue. Air America crews also lacked the training and equipment for search and rescue, but they were based in Laos, were familiar with the terrain, and were the only group available on short notice. Between June 1964 and June 1965, Air America helicopters picked up twenty-one downed crewmen in Laos. The Air Rescue Service, in contrast, had recovered only five pilots from Laos.

As the rescues continued, a rumor began to spread among U.S. military personnel about Air America's motives. This apparently originated with a U.S. Air Force captain in the air attaché's office in Vientiane, who briefed U.S. pilots on rescue capabilities in Laos. He said that pilots shot down over Laos had nothing to worry about, as the Air America pilots would compete to pick them up, in order to get a $1,500 bonus. The claim was completely false and caused resentment among military pilots toward the "mercenaries." The story eventually reached Air America and also caused resentment. Casterlin wrote in a note titled "For Posterity" that "The AF doesn't, I'm sure, appreciate what we are doing for them at great risk to ourselves. . . . What makes us mad is that the AF thinks we get $1,500 for a pickup. We get nothing—but ulcers."

In the summer of 1965, the first Air Force HH-3 helicopters began arriving in Thailand. These had a long range, as well as armor plating, and could make rescues in areas that formerly only Air America could cover. With the new helicopters also came dedicated A-1 escorts, and better training and equipment. These were later joined by the larger HH-53 helicopters. As a result, Air America's role in rescue missions diminished, but did not end.

The continued Air America involvement in recovering downed pilots was reflected in an escape-and-evasion training film called *Here There Be Dragons*. In the unclassified version, the crewman being lowered down the helicopter hoist to rescue the pilot was an American. In the classified version, which was shown to the pilots, the man on the hoist was Asian. Air America crewmen were often Laotians, and it was important that the downed pilots not shoot them because they believed them to be hostile.

Air America played a hidden part in one of the most difficult rescues in Laos. An Air Force F-4 was shot down near Ban Phanop, Laos, on 5 December 1969. Pilot Capt. Benjamin Danielson and weapons systems officer Lt. Woodrow Bergeron Jr. were able to eject, but they were in a desperate situation. Tchepone, a major North Vietnamese staging area in Laos along the Ho Chi Minh Trail, was nearby. The bowl-shaped valley where they had landed was covered with low grass and shrub trees, which gave scant cover, and was surrounded by sheer cliffs. They were just two hundred yards apart, but they were separated by a river and could not reach each other.

When the first HH-3 arrived to pick up the two crewmen, ground fire struck the helicopter. It was driven off and A-1s dropped cluster bombs and strafed the area to silence the guns. When the next helicopter arrived, it too was damaged by ground fire. The same story was repeated all day. Despite heavy attacks by F-4s, F-100s, and F-105s, each time an HH-3 or HH-53 tried to make a pickup, it was hit by heavy ground fire. When night fell, the attempts were halted. An hour after the Air Force and Navy air strikes began the next morning, Bergeron radioed that he had heard voices across the river, then a burst of AK-47 fire, and a scream. Danielson had been found and killed by the North Vietnamese.

The rescue attempts continued. To keep the Communist troops away from Bergeron, the A-1s built a smoke screen around his position by dropping tear gas bombs. The situation was a standoff. The North Vietnamese troops could not reach Bergeron, but every time the helicopters tried to reach him, they were met with a hail of fire. This damaged a total of twelve helicopters and five A-1 escorts, and one of the helicopter crewmen was hit and died before he could reach a hospital.

Finally, on 7 December 1969, prolonged bombing was made, and then an Air America–operated HH-3 helicopter was able to slip through the smoke screen and tear gas and recover Bergeron. His relief soon turned to confusion, however. The Air America HH-3 pilot did not turn west, toward Thailand, but rather flew northwest. Based on the time the flight took, and the helicopter's approximate speed and heading, Bergeron estimated they were somewhere in the vicinity of the Chinese border. The Air America crew explained that they had pressing business elsewhere, and they would have to drop him off in a jungle clearing. Bergeron was reassured that an Air Force helicopter would be along shortly to pick him up. He soon found himself in the Laotian jungle, watching the Air America HH-3 fly off. Soon after, an Air Force helicopter did arrive and picked him up. The operation was over, a crewman was saved, and Air America was not mentioned.

Fly the Friendly Skies of Southeast Asia

As the secret war in Laos grew in the mid-1960s, Air America also expanded. It soon became one of the largest operators of H-34 and S-58T helicopters in the world. (The latter was a turbine-powered modification of the H-34.) The airline also used Bell 204 and 205 helicopters, which were the civilian versions of the Army UH-1B and UH-1D Huey helicopters.

The Helio Courier was the initial short takeoff and landing light aircraft used by Air America. The aircraft was demanding to fly, and with the added problems

240 The Longest War

of overloading, bad weather, and the short, rough Lima Site runways, its accident rate was high. The Pilatus PC-6 Porter largely superseded the Helio Courier in the late 1960s. A long-nose, turboprop-powered aircraft, it was originally built by a Swiss company for operating in the Alps and for takeoffs from and landings on glaciers. A landing speed of fifty knots, and a reversible prop to slow down, also made it ideal for operations in the Laotian jungle airstrips. The Porter was a much easier airplane to fly, but it was not as crashworthy as the Helio Courier.

Air America also operated several types of light twin-engine transports. These included a limited number of DO-28s, a West German airplane with an unusual configuration. The engine nacelles were mounted on either side of the nose on stub wings. Attached to these was the main gear in spat housings that would not have been out of place on a 1930s' aircraft. The DO-28s were not popular with most Air America pilots. An exception was Jesse Markham, who flew it after joining the company in December 1965 and called it "a noble steed." The DO-28 continued to be used into the late 1960s. Air America also bought the first of four Twin Otters in 1971. For operations from paved runways, Air America used Beech 18s and twin turboprop conversions called the Beech Volpar. These had a cruising speed of 202 knots and could hold ten passengers.

In terms of large fixed-wing, twin-engine aircraft, Air America was still operating C-46s and a few C-47s, many dating from CAT's days in China. These were limited to operations from established airfields, however. The newer C-123 and C-7 twin-engine transports could carry payloads larger than those of the Porters or Couriers to the rugged Lima Sites. The C-7s flew for as long as eight hours a day, and made twelve to fourteen takeoffs and landings. The C-123s were considered less suited to operating from the rough strips, but the aircraft's wider fuselage could carry cargos larger and heavier than those of the narrow C-7s.

Whatever they flew, the Air America pilots had several traits in common: they shared a love of adventure and of flying; they took pride in being able to do what no other pilots—civilian or military—could do; and they believed in an old-fashioned kind of patriotism. Ed Dearborn, who headed the Helio Courier program in 1964, recalled: "They were wild. . . . You don't find a normal citizen who's willing to go fly a slow plane and let people shoot at you. . . . The guts-to-brains ratio must reach infinity for someone to do this crap for a living."

The pilots and aircrews reported for duty early each morning to receive their assignments. Wild or not, Air America expected them to observe a twelve-hour "bottle to throttle" rule. That is, no drinking of alcohol within the twelve hours before a flight. Although the pilots were always American, the loadmasters and airfreight specialists, also called "kickers" (so named because they literally kicked cargo off the airplane), were a varied group. In the spring of 1961, eight Forest Service smoke jumpers were assigned to Air America as PDOs. That summer, however, a C-46 hit a mountain, killing three of them: Dave Bevan, John "Tex" Lewis, and Darrel "Yogi" Eubanks. (This was one of several C-46s that were also lost during this time period because of engine fires or flying into hillsides, killing most or all of their crews.) By the end of the year, most of the PDOs had moved on, and Air America began hiring their own kickers. Although some were American, most were Laotian, Filipino, Thai, or some other Asian nationality.

A crewman's day was a long one. At its peak in 1970, Air America made nearly a thousand flights *per day*, and a total of twenty-eight to thirty thousand flights per month. The average flight was about twenty minutes long, and some fixed-wing pilots flew as many as sixty-eight flights a day. The Air America facility at Long Tieng, which was Vang Pao's headquarters, was one of the busiest airports in the world. Some long-time CAT/Air America pilots had as many as ten thousand flight hours, while a few had more than fifteen thousand hours of flight time.

Air America was primarily a cargo airline, and the "anything" in its motto was not an idle boast. The airline was the sole contact with the outside world for many Laotian villages. Most of the drops to these villages were of rice. Air America could deliver enough rice in a single morning to feed five thousand people for a month. Rice drops did not use parachutes, but rather were free fall. About eighty pounds of rice would be put into a two-hundred-pound-capacity bag. This was then placed inside two more empty rice bags. Pallets of these multilayer bags would be loaded aboard a C-46, and once over the drop zone, the kickers simply pushed the bags out of the airplane. The rice was loose in the bags, so when dropped from about eight hundred feet from a slow-flying C-46, the bags slowed and were able to absorb the impact. The first or second bag would sometimes break, but rarely was the third bag holding the rice torn open.

Other drops were of "hard rice," which was the term for weapons and ammunition. This was parachuted in or unloaded at a Lima Site. Hard rice could range from boxes of 81-mm mortar rounds up to 155-mm howitzers. Other flights brought in medicine, spare parts, and any other supplies that might be needed. Jim Rhyne recalled that his very first Air America flight in July 1962 was to drop boxes of toothbrushes into a Lima Site. He remembered that there was no toothpaste with them. Other missions carried live animals, which were strapped down in the airplanes. An American kicker recalled that chickens were the least favorite cargo because of their smell.

Whatever the cargo, and wherever the destination, there remained the everyday risks of flying in Laos. The monsoon season, which lasted from early June to mid-October, brought heavy rain, thick clouds, and fog. Pilots had to use dead-reckoning navigation under these conditions. One procedure was to fly at exactly 120 knots (two nautical miles per minute) and use a stopwatch to time each leg. When time was up, the pilot would then turn onto the next heading. Rhyne described the process as "heading, time, distance, and luck." When a pilot neared his destination, he made a blind descent through the clouds. Once below the clouds, he would spot a landmark, if lucky, and correct his heading to the Lima Site.

When the monsoons ended, the weather improved but still remained difficult. The dry season lasted from late October into the end of May. As the dry season was ending, around March, an unusual problem appeared. The Hmong were slash-and-burn farmers, and as they prepared their fields, great clouds of smoke would obscure the landscape. Visibility often dropped to a mile, with no ceiling. Air America pilots said there were three seasons in Laos—wet, dry, and smoky.

The problems posed by weather were made worse by enemy action. Air America's operations center provided warnings of "hot" areas to the pilots. To avoid them, the pilots would have to improvise a dead-reckoning course, literally on the fly. Over the drop zone, no such evasions were possible. Ground fire could range from AK-47s and 23-mm cannons up to 85-mm antiaircraft guns. There was no predicting where or when a pilot might come under attack.

The final risk came from operating out of the improvised Lima Sites. Often positioned on the tops of hills, they were not level or straight, and they had dips and/or humps. Some resembled a wide dirt road running up a slope, rather than an airport. The steepest Lima Site was LS-213, with a 13-degree slope. A four-hundred-foot-long strip was needed for the Porters, whereas a C-123 or a C-7 required about sixteen hundred feet of landing strip.

The landing technique was for the airplane to approach the Lima Site from below, flying up the slope. This meant that the pilot could not go around if the airplane was caught in a wind gust or thermal. The Porters and Helio Couriers touched down, bounced, and then rolled to a stop. A landing by one of the large transports, such as a C-7, was more spectacular. As it rolled up the rough hill, its wings rocked back and forth. At the end of the runway, the airplane would stop and turn around. It was hurriedly unloaded, and new passengers and cargo were taken aboard. The pilot then ran the engines up to full power and released the brakes. The airplane rolled down the runway and launched itself off the edge, into thin air.

Combat in Laos was seasonal. Because of the mobility that Air America provided, the Hmong went on the offensive during the monsoons. They struck deep into Communist-held territory in the Plain of Jars. When the monsoons ended, the situation was reversed. The North Vietnamese and Pathet Lao went on the offensive. They were able to push back the Hmong from the areas they had taken during the monsoons. Air America aircraft and helicopters transported young Hmong or Royal Laotian soldiers to the battlefield, then brought the wounded out for medical treatment.

The fluid situation in Laos meant a pilot often found his schedule abruptly changed in the course of a day. Typical was the experience of H-34 pilot Ben A. Van Etten in March 1972. His original assignment was to fly several crewmen from Udorn, Thailand, to Pakse, Laos, for a crew rotation. During the flight, Van Etten was asked to assist in a rescue, and he agreed. As the rescue effort continued, an A-1 was hit and its pilot was forced to bail out. Van Etten and his crew flew at treetop altitude to the site. Once over the site, copilot B. J.

Ruck kept watch for enemy troops with an Uzi submachine gun on his lap, while flight mechanic Jim Nakamoto operated the hoist. After several tries, they were able to recover the A-1 pilot. Finally arriving at Pakse airport, Van Etten landed and turned the pilot over to the Air Force representative. By this time, the rumored bonus for a rescued pilot had grown to $10,000, rumors also being subject to inflation. Van Etten had a little fun with the A-1 pilot and told him he had not gotten the bonus for his last rescue, so he was going to make sure the pilot was turned over to the right person. Van Etten wrote, "He bought it all, hook, line and sinker."

Van Etten's busy day was not yet over. He and his crew were ordered to immediately report to the briefing room, where Van Etten and two other H-34 crews were told to pick up wounded Royal Laotian troops about thirty miles away. Van Etten was the flight leader, and CIA case officer Jim Lewis would ride in his helicopter. Arriving over the site, Van Etten landed and dropped off Lewis, who began organizing the wounded. Van Etten took off again and waited for Lewis's signal to return. After about five minutes, Van Etten saw the signal, and landed.

Several litters and walking wounded were lined up at the helicopter. As they were being loaded aboard Van Etten's H-34, a shell exploded about a thousand feet behind the helicopter. Within seconds, another round exploded, this time amid the wounded. Van Etten recalled: "The concussion and noise from the impact were instantaneous, but the resulting mass of bodies being thrown in all directions seemed to happen in slow motion. Just like a 'spaghetti western.'"

Lewis was able to climb aboard the H-34 before it took off despite having been wounded by shrapnel. Then Van Etten saw a wounded Laotian soldier hanging onto the wheel strut, with the back of his shirt covered with blood. By now, the H-34 was several hundred feet in the air. Nakamoto reached out of the cargo door, grabbed the soldier's shirt, and pulled him aboard. The soldier later recovered from his wounds. The three helicopters landed back at Pakse at about sunset. Van Etten and his crew inspected their H-34, but found only a few minor holes.

For many Air America pilots and crewmen, the end of the day brought the final irony of the secret war in Laos. Having flown off to war in the morning, they now returned to their wives and children that night. Many of the Air America crews had been with the airline since the days of CAT. In that decade or more, they had married and raised families. So many Air America personnel had families that the company had a dependents school at its main base in Udorn. Felix Smith, who had joined CAT before the fall of mainland China to Mao's forces and remained with Air America into the late 1960s, wrote about those children: "Raised overseas, outside the insulation of military bases, they played and attended school with children of diverse cultures.... Like me, they feel at home almost anywhere, yet outsiders everywhere."

Their school was seemingly like any other American school. As one student recounted decades later, however, if a special alarm went off, they were to take cover, as it meant that Udorn was under sapper attack. Their school had recesses, like any other American school. During one recess, though, the children watched a damaged F-4 make an emergency landing with its nose gear still retracted. The fighter touched down, and the pilot held its nose up as long as he could, then he eased it down. The F-4 skidded down the runway in a shower of sparks.

Sometimes, what their fathers did became clear to the children in a way that even they could understand. A son remembered that one evening his father came home wearing his Air America uniform. The left side of his uniform was splattered with blood. During a flight earlier that day, the aircraft's pilot had been hit by ground fire, and it was the pilot's blood that had soaked into his father's clothing.

Air America and Covert Operations

While covert operations inside North Vietnam were the responsibility of the U.S. military, such operations in Laos were the domain of the CIA. Because of the 1962 agreement on Laotian neutrality, foreign military forces were prohibited from being in the country. In practice, this meant only U.S. forces, as the North Vietnamese had never observed the ban, and had deployed massive numbers of their troops in Laos. The U.S. embassy in Laos insisted that the fiction of the Geneva Accords be observed. As a result, the embassy tightly controlled the secret war in Laos.

The most politically sensitive of Air America's covert activities were combat missions in armed T-28 trainers. These were both escorts for rescue missions and close air support. In March 1964, an Air Force unit had been established at Udorn under the designation "Water Pump" to train Royal Laotian Air Force T-28 pilots. Soon, Water Pump was expanded to include the training of Thai, Hmong, and Air America pilots. On 20 May 1964, the State Department gave its approval to use the Air America T-28 pilots on offensive missions in Laos.

To hide such direct U.S. involvement, the Air America pilots had their employment "terminated" with the airline. They were then issued papers giving them the status of "civilian technicians," hired by the Royal Laotian Air Force. (The process was called "sheep dipping.") The Air America T-28 pilots served as a private air force, controlled by the U.S. ambassador to Laos and used for missions the Laotian pilots were unable to handle. This combat role also brought the history of Air America back to its roots with the Flying Tigers of World War II.

In August 1964, approval was sought for the use of Air America T-28s to be extended to support of rescue missions. Secretary of State Dean Rusk and President Johnson discussed the request, and approval was given on 26 August. The Air America T-28s could be used when it was absolutely necessary for a successful rescue. Combat missions by Air America pilots continued until 1967. By this time, sufficient numbers of Hmong, Laotian, and Thai T-28 pilots were available, and there was no longer a need for the politically risky use of American pilots.

Beyond the T-28 combat activities, there were also "special project missions." As with the covert missions flown by CAT a decade earlier, most Air America pilots participated in them at one time or another. They were flown not only by Air America, however, but also by several other airlines under contract with the CIA. These included Bird and Son, which had been set up by William Bird, the owner of a heavy construction company in Laos. By January 1961, Bird and Son was undertaking missions for the CIA, such as cargo drops. The airline operated C-46s, PV-2s, DO-28s, and the first Porter used in Laos.

The primary covert missions flown by Air America and the other airlines were in support of Laotian "roadwatch" teams. These reported on movements of trucks and supplies along the Ho Chi Minh Trail. The normal procedure was for the team to be inserted and then to establish a rear operating camp well away from the trail. The team would then find a forward observation post overlooking the trail, from which observations of troop and supply movements could be radioed. With regular airdrops of food and other supplies, a team could remain in the field for six months.

The initial roadwatch resupply missions were flown by another contract airline. Boun Oum Airways (BOA) was owned and named for a pro-Western prince from southern Laos, and had been established to provide an "independent" airline flown by Asian pilots. Air America loaned BOA a Helio Courier and provided maintenance, while Bird and Son provided both a DO-28 and financial services. BOA's mission was to fly night resupply missions to the roadwatch teams. When the roadwatch effort began in 1965, it was crude. In 1967, the CIA greatly expanded the roadwatch program. Additional teams were established in the area of Laos stretching from the Mu Gia Pass to Tchepone.

One unique aircraft used for supply drops was Air America's "Blue Goose." This was a much-modified B-26, with a long, murky history. The aircraft, serial number 44-34415, was taken from the storage area at Davis-Monthan AFB on 13 October 1960 for use in an Asian classified project. It was reregistered as N5002X on 12 July 1962, now under the ownership of Intermountain Aviation. The B-26 was then sold to On-Mark Engineering in July 1963 for conversion into a hybrid B-26K, with features of both the B-26K and On-Mark's "Marketeer" business aircraft. These features included wing tip tanks, copilot controls, an enlarged rudder, antiskid brakes, a door on the starboard side of the aircraft, and more powerful engines. The bomb bay doors were removed and replaced with a compartment with a large couch and several chairs, as in the Marketeer. The aircraft also had a small cargo ramp from which to drop supplies.

The conversion was completed in early 1964, and the B-26K was sold back to Intermountain Aviation. It was then sent to LTV Temco Aerosystems in Greenville, Texas, for the addition of terrain-following radar. Fitted in an elongated nose, this was the same radar used in the F-111 fighter-bomber. The radar was connected to the B-26's autopilot, allowing the aircraft to fly automatically over hills at low altitude in total darkness and in nearly any weather. The work was completed by November 1964. Atlantic General Enterprises in Washington, D.C. (which was probably a CIA proprietary), now owned the aircraft. The B-26K was then sold back to Intermountain Aviation. By early 1966, the B-26 was owned by Pan Aero Investment Corporation of Reno, Nevada. They, in turn, sold it to Air America in April 1967. By this time, the B-26K, now reregistered as N46598, was actually in Laos.

The Blue Goose got its name from its overall dark blue paint finish and white trim, which proved an effective night camouflage. With its extensive equipment load, the B-26K was also called the "Blivit," referring to something stuffed with more than it could hold. Intermountain Aviation pilot Don Gearke, electronic technician Paul Byrne, and mechanic Leonard Billotee were sent to Laos to conduct the ground school for the Blue Goose crews. After seven takeoffs and landings, then a check ride, the crews made daytime practice drops to a Thai border police camp outside Udorn. These exercises were followed in the night by practice drops to roadwatch teams training in Laos. Some of these practice missions proved more realistic than others. Frank Bonansinga, one of the pilots checked out in the B-26K, recalled that he and copilot Berl King were making a training drop when suddenly " 'practice' tracers were coming our way." They aborted the drop and returned to Udorn. That night, at the Club Rendezvous, they learned that the roadwatch team had been attacked by enemy troops and had successfully fought them off.

By May 1967, the Blue Goose was in operation. The roadwatch teams would radio a list of supplies they needed, along with the drop zone location, and would then be given a time and signal to use. The Blue Goose was towed to the "customer's warehouse" at Udorn, called the "AB-1 ramp." The kicker supervised the loading of a five-hundred-pound pallet of food, hard rice, and other supplies, while the two pilots and the navigator worked on the flight plan. The aircraft took off after dark. Once over Laos, it would descend to low altitude. The navigator, sitting behind the pilots, would operate the terrain-following radar.

The initial point for the drop was about seven miles from the drop zone. The airplane's speed was reduced to 140 knots, and the kicker lowered the ramp. As they closed in on the drop zone, both the pilots and the navigator tried to spot the signal. This was usually an "L" or "T" made with flashlights, and was turned on just before the planned drop time or when the team heard the aircraft's engines. The crews found that the airplane's long nose reduced forward visibility during a drop. Rather than a run straight in, the Blue Goose had to fly in a slight left turn to keep the signal lights in sight. Over the drop zone, the kicker would push the pallet out the ramp. The ramp was retracted, and the B-26K would return either to Udorn or to Savannakhet, Laos. It was then reloaded for another drop that night.

In the course of the drop missions, some incidents occurred. Several times, an engine had to be shut down in flight, and there was also an in-flight electrical fire. During one drop, the pallet came off the rails and the kicker nearly fell out of the airplane. Other times, no light signal was seen in the drop zone, presumably because of enemy troops nearby. There was no communication between the aircraft and the team on the ground, and if no signal was seen, the drop was not made. A single pass was made over any given drop zone for each scheduled mission.

As the Blue Goose flew its nighttime missions during the summer of 1967, a major shortcoming became apparent. The airplane's minimum drop speed of 140 knots was too fast. This cut down on the time the crew had to line up on the drop zone and on their ability to maneuver. By the fall of 1967, Air America concluded that other drop planes could do the job better.

What was probably the Blue Goose's last drop mission was flown on the night of 7 October 1967 with Frank Bonansinga (pilot), Terry Luther (copilot), Ray Feind (navigator), and Cliff Hamilton (kicker) as the crew. Soon after, the project was canceled. The B-26K was listed in March 1968 as being owned by Overseas Aeromarine, Inc., of Seattle, Washington. The Federal Aviation Administration (FAA) was then notified on 30 April that the aircraft had been scrapped. Subsequently, missions to resupply the roadwatch teams were flown by both Air America and Continental Air Services, which had bought out Bird and Son in August 1965.

Another element in the expanded roadwatch effort was a new communications system. The forward observer carried a special radio. Rather than a microphone, it had buttons with drawings of a truck, troops, cannon, and other items. The observer simply had to press the correct button each time he saw a particular piece of equipment moving down the trail. This was simple to operate and eliminated any language difficulties. The radios were low power, and their signals were picked up by aircraft and relayed to Nakhon Phanom Air Base in Thailand. To provide full coverage, several aircraft had to fly racetrack patterns over the trail throughout the night.

Air America initially proposed use of its new Beech Volpars modified with extra tanks, which would allow the airplanes to stay aloft from dusk till dawn. The planned use of Beech Volpars was soon dropped, however, and Beech 18s were substituted in the Air America proposal. Continental Air Services proposed using its U.S. pilots (many of whom were ex–Air America) flying DO-28s belonging to BOA. (By this time, the distinction between Continental Air Services and BOA was very blurred.) The CIA liked the Continental/BOA proposal and awarded it the contract in the spring of 1967.

The Continental/BOA effort proved short-lived, however. Continental pilot Carl Stone, exhausted after flying all night over the trail, crashed his DO-28 into a hangar at Savannakhet on 12 March. Three days later, Air America took over the contract, using the Beech Volpars. Within a few months, Continental Air Services completely absorbed BOA's remaining aircraft and Thai pilots. Despite the problems, the roadwatch teams proved a highly effective means of gathering intelligence on the trail. The effort continued throughout the rest of the war in Laos, involving both Air America and Continental Air Services.

In addition to supporting the roadwatch teams, Air America was involved with other covert operations. One of these, Lima Site 85, was one of the most important and secret U.S. facilities in Laos. It was at the base of Phou Pha Thi, the Sacred Mountain. To the Hmong, this 5,600-foot ridgeline with steep rocky cliffs was the home of spirits who had supernatural control over their lives and fates. To the U.S. Air Force, it was one of the few places in the rugged terrain of northern Laos that was within radio and radar range of targets in North Vietnam. This included Hanoi, only 160 miles to the east of Phou Pha Thi. At its top was a small flat area, just large enough to hold a few buildings and a helicopter landing pad.

A tactical air navigation (TACAN) station was built atop the mountain in August 1966. This was a radio station that transmitted range and bearing data to aircraft attacking North Vietnam. The site was upgraded with a Sky Spot bombing control radar in November 1967 to improve the accuracy of air strikes in bad weather. Because of the Geneva Accords, the Air Force technicians who maintained and serviced the facility were sheep dipped and posed as civilian employees of Lockheed Aircraft. Their position was very dangerous, as LS-85 was deep inside Communist-controlled territory. The Pathet Lao capital of Samneua was a mere twenty-five miles away. Because of its vulnerable position, LS-85 was guarded by three hundred Thai mercenaries and about a thousand local Hmong troops. Phou Pha Thi could have been the creation of a Hollywood scriptwriter, but it was critical to the air war over the North.

The North Vietnamese knew about the Americans on Phou Pha Thi, knew what they were doing, and were determined to take the mountain. Probing attacks began in December 1967, and by early January 1968, it was clear that a major attack was imminent. Plans were made to evacuate the site—should it be about to fall—using Air Force and Air America helicopters. William Sullivan, the U.S. ambassador to Laos, was the sole person with authority to order the evacuation. When the attack came, however, it was not by land, but by air.

The strike was made on 12 January. Lookouts spotted four airplanes flying toward Phou Pha Thi. They were AN-2s, the largest single-engine biplane in the world. Two of the North Vietnamese aircraft headed away, while the two others attacked the TACAN station. Normally used to haul cargo, they had been fitted with rockets, guns, and a hydraulically operated dispenser that dropped mortar rounds. The AN-2's top speed of about 120 knots made it an unlikely ground attack aircraft. To hide their origin, their North Vietnamese insignias were partially covered with green-gray paint. The biplanes made several attack runs, using rockets, guns, and the mortar bombs, and killed several Hmong. The CIA officers and an Air Force forward air controller (FAC) fired back at the AN-2s. They also called for help from an Air America Model 204 Huey.

The helicopter crew sighted the two biplanes, and, according to one account, the copilot said, "We can go faster than those things." The pilot replied, "So let's go." The engineer grabbed his personal weapon, an Uzi submachine gun, smiled, and then yelled over the intercom, "Charge!" The helicopter soon caught up with one of the AN-2s and pulled alongside. The engineer fired into the biplane's cockpit, killing or wounding the crew. The AN-2 peeled off and crashed into the jungle. The Air America crew had just scored the first helicopter versus biplane kill. The other AN-2 had been damaged by ground fire, ran out of fuel, and crashed before it was able to reach safety. A section of the fuselage from one of the downed AN-2s was recovered. Bearing the number 665, it was displayed as a trophy at the Air America facility at Long Tieng.

The success against the North Vietnamese biplanes was only a brief respite. During the night of 10–11 March, three battalions of North Vietnamese troops attacked up the southwest face of Phou Pha Thi. At the same time, a twenty-man sapper team silently made its way up the cliff on the northeast side of the mountain. By 3:00 A.M. the sappers had slipped through the defenses and begun throwing hand grenades at the buildings. Several of the Air Force technicians were killed outright. (Because of the Geneva Accords, they were unarmed.)

Sullivan ordered an evacuation at 7:15 A.M. When the Air America helicopters sent to rescue the personnel arrived at Phou Pha Thi, they came under ground fire. The CIA site commander, a former Green Beret named Howard Freeman, ordered Air Force A-1s to bomb the facility. This silenced the ground fire, and the Air America helicopters were able to rescue Freeman and another CIA officer, the Air Force FAC, five Air Force technicians (one of whom died during the flight to Udorn), and a number of wounded Hmong. Of the other eleven Air Force technicians, the bodies of eight were recovered or accounted for, and three were missing. By mid-morning, the recovery attempt was abandoned, and the facility was bombed for eight days to destroy the classified equipment and documents.

The End of Air America

The capture of Phou Pha Thi marked a major change in the war for Laos. The North Vietnamese had become impatient with the Pathet Lao and took over the 1968 dry season offensive. Besides eliminating the LS-85 site, by mid-March, the North Vietnamese had taken a strategic valley north of Luang

Prabang and were threatening to drive the Hmong from their strongholds around the Plain of Jars. The North Vietnamese offensive ended with the start of the monsoons in May 1968. The Hmong had lost more than a thousand men since January, including several senior commanders. A recruiting drive turned up only three hundred replacements. Of these, 30 percent were between the ages of ten and fourteen, another 30 percent were fourteen or fifteen years old, and the remaining 40 percent were over thirty-five years of age. All those between fifteen and thirty-five were already dead or fighting.

With the Hmong now a waning force, the United States tried to even the odds by use of airpower. Since 1965, about ten to twenty missions had been flown against targets in Laos. In 1969, this increased to some three hundred strikes per day. Vang Pao decided to abandon guerrilla tactics, and the remaining Hmong forces launched an offensive during the 1969 monsoon season called Operation About Face. The Hmong forces retook the whole of the Plain of Jars for the first time since 1960. The attack captured 1,700 tons of food, 2,500 tons of ammunition, 640 heavy weapons, and 25 Soviet-built PT-76 light tanks. In response, the North Vietnamese added two divisions in January 1970 and quickly took back the lost territory, and even threatened Long Tieng. It took the first use of B-52s in Laos to finally blunt the Communist drive.

To bolster the Hmong, large numbers of Thai volunteer battalions were committed to Laos. These were trained and paid by the CIA. With the start of the 1971 monsoon season, Vang Pao launched what would be the last Hmong offensive. By July, the Plain of Jars was retaken, and a network of artillery strongpoints was established, manned by Thai gunners. These were to hold the Plain of Jars during the dry season.

In response, North Vietnamese troops launched a coordinated attack in December 1971 using 130-mm guns, which could outrange the Thai gun batteries. The strongpoints were quickly rolled back, and the Plain of Jars was retaken once more. At the end of 1971 and early in 1972, the North Vietnamese were again threatening Vang Pao's base at Long Tieng. At the same time, in the southern panhandle, North Vietnamese troops were advancing against government forces. The Communist goal was to establish a wider buffer zone to protect the Ho Chi Minh Trail. Also by year's end in 1971, the North Vietnamese had taken the town of Paksong, which was only twenty-five miles from the Air America facility at Pakse.

The intense action took a heavy toll on Air America crewmen. In December 1971 alone, twenty-four of its aircraft were hit by ground fire and three went down. Between December 1971 and April 1972, six Air America crewmen were killed in Laos. The number of Air America crewmen injured was also high; among them was Jim Rhyne. He had been aboard a Beech Volpar on 15 January 1972 when the aircraft was damaged by an 85-mm antiaircraft round. Rhyne lost his leg. Air America's vice president for flight operations sent a telex message on 24 April to all flight crews. In it he stated, "the past few months have produced an appalling toll in lives and serious injuries," and he urged all crewmen and supervisors to exercise extreme caution when flying over Laos.

Enemy action and bad weather were no longer the only threats to Air America. The airline now faced attacks from politicians, from the antiwar movement, and from within the CIA itself. Congressional appropriations committees had been briefed on the Laotian operations, and Senator Stuart Symington and other congressmen had visited Laos. They indicated their approved of the CIA's activities, believing, as DCI Richard Helms later noted, that "it was a much cheaper and better way to fight a war in Southeast Asia than to commit American troops." When the war in Laos finally came to public attention in 1969–70, those same politicians were now "shocked" at what was taking place.

Air America was also accused of direct involvement in the shipping and processing of opium. Alfred W. McCoy made the charge in his 1972 study, *The Politics of Heroin in Southeast Asia.* McCoy's charge was that Air America helicopters collected the 1970 and 1971 opium harvests and then transported them to Vang Pao's headquarters at Long Tieng, where they were turned into heroin at his drug laboratory.

William M. Leary, a professor of history at the University of Georgia, spent more than twenty years researching the history of CAT, Air America, and the other CIA proprietaries. In the course of his research, he talked with some three hundred people—CIA officers, pilots, kickers, and ground crewmen who cleaned the aircraft—and investigated every accusation against Air America. He never found any evidence to back up any of the charges that Air America had knowingly been involved with the drug trade.

The reality was that the CIA did little about the drug trade in the 1960s. As drug use later became a problem among American troops in Southeast Asia, the CIA began to take action against the traders, although the focus was always on the war itself. To prevent smuggling, Air America established a fifteen-man team with drug-sniffing dogs at Udorn to inspect aircraft and personnel. Despite the lack of evidence, the charges have lingered in the public's mind a quarter of a century later, largely because of the 1990 Mel Gibson film *Air America.*

The end of Air America and the other proprietaries came from within the CIA. At its peak in 1970, Pacific Corporation had eleven thousand employees and operated the largest cargo airline fleet in the world. Air America alone accounted for some two-dozen twin-engine transports, a similar number of light aircraft, about thirty helicopters, and more than three hundred crewmen in Laos. Its helicopters logged more than four thousand hours per month in 1970, whereas a total of twenty-three thousand tons of food was delivered during the same year. In addition to supply missions, Air America transported both troops and refugees; flew medevac and rescue missions; inserted, supported, and extracted the roadwatch teams; monitored sensors on the Ho Chi Minh Trail and taps on North Vietnamese telephone lines; and flew photoreconnaissance missions.

Within the CIA, a long-standing debate over the future of the air proprietaries had grown more intense. In the political environment of the Vietnam War, many in the CIA saw them as unwieldy, expensive, easily exposed, and no longer needed. To preserve plausible deniability, the fact that the CIA owned Air America was known only to a handful of its officials. The crewmen in the field were well aware, however, that the agency was deeply involved in its activities. The willingness of the U.S. military to "loan" the company helicopters, aircraft, and pilots also marked it as something more than just an airline. By the late 1960s, many in the airline industry had begun to suspect the truth.

CAT, the first of the CIA proprietaries, was also the first to go. Following the crash of a CAT 727 on 16 February 1968, the Nationalist Chinese government had canceled the airline's charter. They had wanted to get rid of CAT for some time, and the crash offered an excuse. The government-owned China Airlines replaced CAT as Taiwan's flag carrier. Pacific Corporation sold off Southern Air Transport in 1971. This was followed by the sale of Intermountain Aviation to Evergreen Helicopters. The deal included not only its base at Marana Air Park, but also the B-17 used both for the mission to NP8 and in the movie *Thunderball.* The aircraft was converted to a fire tanker and carried the tail numbers C71, 71, and 22. Evergreen International Aviation restored the B-17 to its wartime configuration, and the aircraft is now part of its air museum at McMinnville, Oregon.

DCI Helms ended the long debate; on 21 April 1972 he ordered Air America to phase out its operations in Laos. Ironically, the heaviest period of losses for Air America was between April 1972, when the decision was reached to dispose of the company, and June 1974, when it closed down Laotian operations. A total of twenty-three crewmen died in Laos during this period. This was nearly a quarter of the Air America crewmen lost. This period was also a time of intense activities. A coalition government had been established in Laos with a cease-fire agreement in February 1973. The surviving Hmong were vulnerable to retribution, and Air America evacuated some 150,000 Hmong to the safety of refugee camps. Once the airlift was complete, it was time for Air America itself to leave.

The final Air America aircraft left Laos on 3 June 1974. The Air America operations office in Vientiane reported to CIA headquarters: "The departure of [Air America] from Laos was without incident, although some lumps are visible in the throats of those who put so much of themselves into the operation over the years.... We grieve for those missing and dead in Laos and regret that they too could not have enjoyed today." By the end of June, Air America's base at Udorn was also closed down. The last remnant of Air America was its Saigon operation. Pacific Corporation was down to merely eleven hundred employees by the spring of 1975. Air America was too closely identified with the CIA to be sold off as a unit. Instead, its aircraft and other assets were to be liquidated.

Before that was to occur, however, Air America had one last mission to fly.

10

The Covert War against North Vietnam

Every quantitative measurement we have shows that we're winning this war.
—Secretary of Defense Robert S. McNamara, May 1962

Although the 1954 Geneva Convention ended French colonial rule, it also began the next phase of the war for Southeast Asia. This began as a covert operation—designed by Ho Chi Minh and intended to overthrow the government of South Vietnam while providing plausible deniability for North Vietnam. As the first step, Ho Chi Minh ordered ten thousand Viet Minh troops to remain in South Vietnam, as the basis of an "indigenous" Communist guerrilla force. In 1957, these ex-Viet Minh troops began a campaign of propaganda, sabotage, and assassinations of South Vietnamese officials, teachers, and village leaders. This quickly spread, and in 1959 some twenty-five hundred killings took place, more than double that of the previous year. Sabotage, which had been localized, now became widespread.

To support the expanded guerrilla activities, North Vietnamese soldiers and supplies began to flow down the newly constructed Ho Chi Minh Trail. To conceal North Vietnam's involvement, the troops being infiltrated into South Vietnam were originally southerners who were equipped with captured French weapons. The North Vietnamese also established the "Liberation Army of South Vietnam," better known as the Viet Cong (VC). Despite wartime claims that the VC was independent, it was always a "subordinate component" of the North Vietnamese army.

President John F. Kennedy's involvement with Vietnam policy began at his first National Security Council meeting on 28 January 1961. He was told that the situation was grim, and that reforms by the South Vietnamese government were needed. Kennedy then asked DCI Allen Dulles whether a guerrilla movement could be established in North Vietnam. Dulles replied that the CIA's efforts were minimal. The president was dissatisfied with this, saying that he "want[ed] guerrillas to operate in the North." Kennedy and many of his advisers believed that the United States had to meet situations like the guerrilla war in South Vietnam through "counterinsurgency." It was the concept of using guerrilla tactics against the guerrillas. This was to be combined with "nation building," which was to attack the root social and political causes behind the insurgency.

Among those supporting counterinsurgency activities was Secretary of Defense Robert S. McNamara. The prototype of the postwar manager, his decisions were reached logically and rationally, based solely on numbers, with no room for intuition or emotion. McNamara took a top-down approach as secretary of defense, bringing in a very small group of like-minded, confident, young, rational civilians of superior education and intelligence. Called the "whiz kids," they came from think tanks like RAND or from universities, and had specialized in strategic theory, mathematics, or economic analysis. They evaluated and approved every action by the military, and they were given centralized control of all strategic, policy, budget, and program decisions.

McNamara and the whiz kids were openly contemptuous of the military, believing that traditional military strategy was outmoded. Instead, they proposed limited force be used to coerce an enemy into changing its policies. This would be tightly controlled from Washington. If the enemy failed to comply, the level of force would be "escalated" until they did. This would also be linked with political bargaining and negotiation in a process called "graduated response." Establishing a guerrilla force in the North, doing to Ho Chi Minh what he was doing in the South, would send a "message" that the United States did not accept the North's actions and would impress them with the cost of their support for guerrillas in South Vietnam and Laos.

At the same time, the CIA began a small-scale effort to establish both "singleton" (lone agents) and small agent networks inside North Vietnam. William

Colby, the CIA station chief in Saigon, directed the agent operations against the North. The first agent sent in was named Pham Chuyen. He said he was a mid-level party cadre who had become disaffected. Chuyen fled south in 1959 and was recruited the following year. Given the code name "Ares," he was to operate as a singleton. Ares was sent to North Vietnam in February 1961 by a thirty-eight-foot junk manned by Vietnamese refugees. When the junk reached the coastal town of Cam Pha, near the border with China, Ares went ashore in a small woven basket boat, which also carried his radio and provisions. Ares was soon in regular contact with a CIA radio station in the Philippines.

Team Atlas, a four-man group led by Tran Huu Quang, followed. They were flown to Thailand, where they boarded a helicopter. They were then flown to a landing zone in Laos, just across the border from North Vietnam. Once they were on the ground, a herdsman spotted them and reported their presence to a border security post. They were tracked by the North Vietnamese and ambushed on 5 April. Two of the agents were killed in the resulting firefight, and the others were captured.

Haylift—Airdrops into North Vietnam

Subsequent paramilitary teams would be sent into North Vietnam by C-47 aircraft flown by South Vietnamese crews, in an effort code-named "Haylift." Col. Harry Aderholt and Maj. Larry Ropka, both of whom had been involved with the Tibetan airdrops, planned the missions. The unit was led by Col. Nguyen Cao Ky, who would later become the head of the South Vietnamese air force, then the country's vice president. Ky decided that the best way to drop teams into North Vietnam would be to fly in from the sea at a very low level to evade the coastal radar stations. Once across the coast, the C-47 would follow a river valley until it reached the mountainous and sparsely populated areas near the Laotian border. Here the agents would be dropped.

Ky and the other crewmen began their low-level night training with U.S. instructors. The route was from Saigon to a point in the mountains about a hundred miles to the northeast. The South Vietnamese did so well that the Americans let them continue training on their own after a few days. The

C-47 pilots divided the route into five-minute segments, which were flown at a specific speed. The copilot and navigator stood behind the pilot, calling out the time in one-minute intervals and alerting the pilot to upcoming course changes. No lights could be used in the cockpit, even to read a map, so the crew had to memorize every detail of the route. The only illumination was the full moon.

Several weeks before the first drop was to be made, the aircrews' training intensified. They spent upward of twelve hours a day practicing the mission in a closed hangar, memorizing the route, the elevation of the surrounding terrain, the speed and heading of each leg, and the location of each obstacle. To assist, the CIA built a scale model of the complete flight route.

The first South Vietnamese agent drop was scheduled for 27 May 1961 in far northwestern North Vietnam. Colonel Ky was to fly the C-47. This was a violation of security, but he had said, "I'm the commander. I'll fly the first mission." Also aboard was Team Caster, which consisted of four South Vietnamese army sergeants. All had been born in Son La province, where they were being dropped. The team leader was Ha Van Chap. Team Caster was briefed to set up a resistance base and to establish networks of agents deep inside North Vietnam. Additional teams would follow them.

After nightfall, Ky and the crew made a preflight check of the C-47. With this completed, the crew and the members of Team Caster boarded the aircraft, and the equipment and parachutes were loaded. Both the aircrew and the agents were dressed in black cotton pajamas like those worn by Vietnamese peasants. This was intended to hide their identities should the C-47 crash. They also carried North Vietnamese money, cigarettes, and matches in their pockets. Each person also carried $100 in U.S. currency for bribes. Ky had no illusions about their chances, noting, "If we went down, we would be very lucky to have any use for currency or cigarettes."

The C-47 took off from Danang, climbed to several thousand feet, and headed out to sea. Once out of sight of land, Ky descended until the airplane was at a very low level and he could see the individual white caps on each wave. After heading east for a few minutes, he turned the C-47 to the north–northwest, directly toward the mouth of the Red River. He hoped that the coastal radar stations would not be able to detect the low-flying aircraft.

The C-47 crossed the North Vietnamese coastline at Than Hoa and followed the Red River. A nearly full moon illuminated the ground, and the copilot and navigator called off the time and turn points, just as they had during the hangar practice sessions. Ky pulled the aircraft up just enough to avoid bridges and power lines. The roar of the twin engines could be heard for miles, but the C-47 was flying too low and too fast for the defenses to react in time. Once past the coastline, they did not have to worry about the radar, but as the C-47 continued inland, the ground rose. Soon, the river valley narrowed and moonlit mountains surrounded the C-47. Finally, shortly after midnight, the crew spotted the drop zone.

As the C-47 flew low over the tree-covered hills, the four men jumped from the airplane. As far as Ky and the other crewmen could tell, all of the chutes opened. The C-47 continued heading west until it crossed into Laos. Ky then climbed to twelve thousand feet and turned south. The crew could now relax; they turned on the autopilot and smoked cigarettes. The dawn was breaking as the C-47 landed back at Saigon and taxied to the unit's hangar. To Ky's surprise, Colby was inside waiting for the plane. With him were several U.S. and South Vietnamese officials, and two cases of French champagne. Soon after, Team Caster's radio operator transmitted a message announcing their safe arrival. As far as the CIA knew, they had an operational team inside North Vietnam.

The apparent success of Team Caster proved to be the last good news for some time. Team Echo parachuted into the coastal province of Quang Binh on 2 June. The three men were captured along with three radio sets. The team's radio operator sent the signal that he was under hostile control. That same month, Team Dido also parachuted into northwestern North Vietnam. Two more agents joined the four sergeants, but they were all later captured. The team's radio operator was also able to send a warning signal.

The next Haylift mission was scheduled for the night of 1 July 1961. Ky recalled that he was originally to make the flight, which was to be his third drop mission. As Ky was heading home to get ready for the 8:00 P.M. departure, however, he met Lt. Phan Thanh Van, who was one of the unit's best pilots. Van was renowned for his bravura, and often did not wear either a seat belt or a shirt in flight. Van offered Ky a drink, but Ky refused and explained that he was flying that night. Van responded, "I'll go in your place. I'd like to fly that mission tonight." Ky replied, "If you want to take it, then go." Ky received a call at a nightclub later that night at about 1:00 A.M. from the duty officer, who reported that the C-47 was overdue and was presumed to have gone down in North Vietnam.

Van's C-47 had successfully crossed the North Vietnamese coastline and was over Ninh Binh province. Aboard were seven South Vietnamese crewmen and three agents. As the airplane flew toward the drop zone, Gun Crew 40 opened fire. The C-47 was hit and crashed. Lieutenant Van was thrown through the windshield on impact, cutting his face badly. The C-47 burst into flames. Along with Van, the airplane's flight engineer and one of the agents were the only survivors. All three were captured the following day.

In December 1961, the North Vietnamese army published an account of their trial. Rather than mention the CIA, the Americans involved with the drops were described as belonging to the FBI. Van spent a decade in the Hoa Lo Prison, known to American POWs as the Hanoi Hilton. Although Van survived his imprisonment, both the flight engineer and the agent died in captivity.

The loss of Van's C-47 was not the only setback for the covert war in North Vietnam. In addition, two more singleton agents were infiltrated by sea in June and September 1961, but they were captured. Thus, by the end of 1961, three teams, one reinforcement group, and three singletons had been sent into North Vietnam. Of these, only the singleton Ares and Team Caster were still considered operational. All of the others had been captured, and a C-47, its crew, and an agent team had been lost.

As the agent operations were beginning, the governments of both the United States and North Vietnam were making policy decisions that edged them closer to a direct military confrontation. The Politburo of the Vietnamese Communist Party held a series of meetings between 31 January and 25 February 1961. They ordered a shift from political action to a "military struggle." District- and province-level local forces were to be built up, and ten to fifteen main-force infantry regiments would be organized in South Vietnam. At the start of 1961, there were fifteen thousand full-time Communist troops in South Vietnam, of which only three thousand were in Communist main-force units. Under this plan, the main-force units would number between twenty-five and forty-five thousand troops.

A similar expansion of infiltration efforts on the Ho Chi Minh Trail also took place. During 1961, a total of 7,664 North Vietnamese officers and enlisted men were sent to the South. This was more than twice the total of 1959 and 1960 combined. In addition, the 317 tons of weapons sent to the South in 1961 were four times the total infiltrated in 1960. In September 1961, the North Vietnamese Politburo approved army plans to send thirty to forty thousand North Vietnamese regulars into South Vietnam between 1961 and 1963. Despite this increase, North Vietnam still wanted to hide its involvement. The North Vietnamese army troops were still limited to ex-Southerners carrying captured French weapons.

Running in parallel were actions by the U.S. government. In early March 1961, President Kennedy had asked what action had been taken by the CIA to carry out his instructions to start covert actions within North Vietnam. When he learned little had been done, he quickly issued National Security Action Memorandum (NSAM) 28. This ordered the CIA to carry out the "President's instructions that we make every possible effort to launch guerrilla operations in North Vietnam territory." The failure of the Bay of Pigs invasion the following month soured Kennedy on the CIA's ability to plan and carry out such operations. A review panel headed by U.S. Army Gen. Maxwell Taylor recommended that the military undertake future large-scale covert paramilitary operations.

President Kennedy signed NSAM 52 on 11 May 1961, which stated that "The U.S. objective [was] . . . to prevent Communist domination of South Vietnam; to create in that country a viable democratic society, and to initiate, on an accelerated basis, a series of mutually supporting actions of a military, political, economic, psychological, and covert character designated to achieve this objective." Kennedy acted on General Taylor's recommendations and transferred authority for such activities to the military in June 1961. The CIA operations in North Vietnam were included in his order. In the fall of 1961, after a year of continued bad news from South Vietnam, President Kennedy approved a major expansion of U.S. forces to some fifteen thousand troops. Although described as "advisers" for political reasons, the United States was taking an increasingly direct combat role, which was also subject to tight political controls.

The CIA agent program continued in early 1962, but with little to show for the effort. Ares had sent a message that he needed supplies, including radios. A fishing boat was loaded with twenty-seven crates and headed north. The crew, code-named "Nautilus-1," had landed Ares nearly a year before. On the night of 14 January 1962, after a two-day voyage, the boat was just off the beach, and the crew was preparing to unload the cargo. Without warning, a North Vietnamese patrol boat approached, blocked their escape, and ordered the Nautilus-1 crew to surrender. The loss of the ship and its crew caused Adm. Harry D. Felt, commander in chief of the Pacific Fleet, to later say that the CIA's poor maritime record indicated that it was not up to the task.

The CIA was also looking at the loss of the South Vietnamese C-47 on the 1 July 1961 Haylift mission. This was blamed on the poor performance of the twin-engine transport. As a replacement, the South Vietnamese were provided with a C-54. An Air America instructor pilot and navigator conducted the conversion training, and the South Vietnamese crew was soon qualified on the aircraft. The unmarked C-54's first drop mission was made on 20 February 1962. The five members of Team Europa successfully parachuted into Hoa Binh province. The use of the C-54 was brief because before a second mission could be flown, the aircraft flew into a mountain during bad weather, killing everyone aboard.

The loss of the airplane meant that a replacement was needed to prevent a backlog of agents. As an interim measure, an Air America C-46 was used to drop Team Remus on 16 April. The drop zone was near the ill-fated village of Dien Bien Phu. The six men, commanded by Dieu Chinh Ich, were able to make contact with local relatives and arranged supply drops over the next two months. Despite the apparent success of the Team Remus drop, it was clear that use of Air America was not a long-term option because of the lack of deniability. It was the Nationalist Chinese Air Force that provided the solution.

In August 1955, the Nationalist Chinese had taken over many of the intelligence activities against mainland China that had been conducted by the United States. This included overflights as well as agent and leaflet drops. Selected crews from the 8th Bombardment Group flew PB4Y Privateers on missions code-named "Hunting Wolf." They proved very successful, and the United States loaned the Nationalists B-26s, B-17s, and RB-69s (the latter the Air Force/CIA version of the P2V). Although the B-17s and RB-69s were occasionally used for agent and supply drops, their primary mission was overflights. They were fitted with receiving equipment to pick up emissions from air defenses and high-voltage power lines. The United States got the intelligence data it wanted, while the airplanes kept alive the Nationalists' hopes of returning to the mainland.

The agent drops made by the Nationalists were no more successful than those by the CIA in the early 1950s. At a meeting in Manila in 1959, the CIA's Hong Kong station chief Peter Sichel complained to Richard Bissell, the CIA's deputy director of plans, about the dropping of Nationalist "boy scouts into China to blow up railway cars." Sichel called the missions "a complete waste of life." So few of the agents returned, he added, "We may as well just shoot them." Bissell listened to his complaints, and the missions were soon reduced. These covert missions also took a toll on the aircraft during 1960-61. Several B-17s were lost over the mainland. The RB-69 was still operational, but it was fitted for electronic missions.

The Nationalists were also suffering losses farther afield. In a separate operation, supplies were airlifted to Nationalist troops in northern Burma using PB4Ys. In late 1960, the Burmese government finally moved to rid itself of the Nationalist forces, and began several weeks of ground and air attacks. After a bloody battle on 26 January 1961, the Nationalists were routed. The Nationalists began a major airlift in response. A PB4Y on one of these supply flights was intercepted by a Burma Air Force Sea Fury and shot down on 14 February 1961. The Burmese aircraft was also lost. Killed in the Sea Fury crash was Pilot Officer Noel Peters. The PB4Ys were retired following the loss over Burma, and the remaining Nationalist forces were driven into Thailand.

Only five days later another aircraft was lost. Starting in December 1960, a pair of Nationalist C-46s had been making airdrops in Laos. One of the C-46s was making a supply drop to a government outpost on 19 February 1961 when it was hit by ground fire. Only the Laotian kicker was able to bail out before the plane crashed. He was captured by the Pathet Lao and told them the dead crew had been Nationalist Chinese. The crash ended participation by the Nationalists in the Laotian drops.

To replace the lost aircraft, the Nationalist Chinese Air Force established a new unit in 1961 for covert operations—the 34th Squadron. It was built around a C-54G provided by the United States the previous year. In early 1962, with the need for airdrops into North Vietnam, the unit provided a deniable means to fly the missions. Two Air America navigators, Jim Keck and Ken Rockwell, went to Taiwan and trained the Nationalist crewmen. They flew practice missions around the offshore islands. Rockwell recalled: "We basically wanted to show them what it looked like on the radar when you approached a terrain feature taller than your own altitude." The training was successful, and a crew was assigned to Tan Son Nhut Air Base. The C-54 was registered to Vietnam Air Transport, which was a CIA front company, and each Nationalist crewman carried a false South Vietnamese identity card.

The first group of agents they were to carry was also completing its training. The eight men of Team Tourbillon were to parachute into Son La province as reinforcements for Team Caster. Vang A Giong, Tourbillon's radio operator, was told that Caster had established a base and had recruited a lot of agents. Caster was too small a group to train the force they had assembled, however, so they had radioed Saigon and asked for more men. Tourbillon was to serve as their training cadre, as well as to scout Route 41 and attack the bridges leading to Laos.

Team Tourbillon boarded the Nationalist C-54 on 16 May 1962. The aircraft took off and headed toward the drop zone in North Vietnam. At about midnight, the eight men jumped from the airplane. Eleven days later, radioman Vang A Giong reported their safe arrival. He included his personal five-digit code group in the message to indicate he was not under North Vietnamese control.

Despite the apparently successful drops of Remus and Tourbillon, the results continued to be bleak in 1962. The five men of Team Eros parachuted into North Vietnam on 20 May, but they were quickly captured. Team Lyre was dropped into North Vietnam on Christmas Eve to scout a radar site they were to destroy. This was the third attempt, as the earlier tries were aborted when the Nationalist crew was forced back by heavy ground fire. Within a few days, the eight men were tracked down by troops of the North Vietnamese Ministry of Public

Security and were captured or killed. In addition, a number of singleton agents were also captured. The maritime covert operations fared no better. The Nautilus-2 crew and three frogmen were lost on 28 June 1962 during a raid on Swatow-class patrol boats anchored in the Gianh River. Only one South Vietnamese crew member escaped capture after the sinking and was picked up by friendly forces.

Operation Switchback

By the end of 1962, the CIA concluded that the agent operations were simply not working. As a result, plans were made to shift operations against North Vietnam during 1963 to psychological warfare. Colby later observed, "It was my thesis that if we worked reasonably hard on psychological operations . . . you could have an impact because the Communists are so hyper about the danger of resistance that if you suggest that there was any opposition group within their ranks, it would drive them crazy." Herb Weisshart was sent to Saigon to direct the new efforts. He found almost nothing had been done and set about developing a program. This entailed increased leaflet drops, clandestine radio broadcasts, and the creation of a bogus internal North Vietnamese resistance movement called the Sacred Sword of the Patriots League. The goal, Weisshart later explained, was "to see what we could do to force North Vietnam to take some of their assets and divert them to worrying about what we were doing in their backyard."

At the same time, plans for the military to take over CIA covert operations against the North were taking form. In July 1962, McNamara held a meeting in Hawaii with officials of the Defense Department, Pacific Command, the CIA, the State Department, and the head of the U.S. Military Assistance Command, Vietnam (MACV), Gen. Paul Harkins, to discuss the transfer, called "Operation Switchback." The transfer was to be completed on 1 November 1963, and would include the agent, maritime, and psychological warfare operations.

The overall mood about Vietnam at the meeting was very upbeat. MACV commander Harkins said, "If our programs continue, we can expect VC actions to decline." This optimism was based on statistical data McNamara and the whiz kids used to track the war's progress. This included body counts, kill rates, and numbers of weapons captured. The data indicated heavy North Vietnamese and VC losses during 1962.

However, contrary to what the numbers indicated, the key was not in the rice paddies of South Vietnam, but in the jungles of Laos. The Ho Chi Minh Trail had originally been a small network of jungle paths, unable to handle large-scale infiltration. With most of the Laotian panhandle under Communist control following the Pathet Lao's 1961 offensive, work began on a road suitable for truck traffic, which was completed in December 1961. This supported the North's expanded war in the South. North Vietnamese trucks were now making regular runs to warehouses at Tchepone, Laos. Porters and bicyclists then carried the supplies into South Vietnam.

This meant that despite their heavy losses during 1962, the North was able to not only retain the military initiative, but also to expand their forces. This became clear at the battle of Ap Bac. The South Vietnamese army's Seventh Division, equipped with automatic weapons and armored personnel carriers and backed by U.S. helicopters and aircraft, attacked a group of three hundred VC. Despite being outnumbered, the VC was able to hold off the South Vietnamese forces before finally slipping away on 2 January 1963. The South Vietnamese defeat at Ap Bac highlighted its lack of leadership and motivation. In contrast, the North Vietnamese forces in the South grew from fifteen thousand at the start of 1961 to seventy thousand by the end of 1963.

CIA covert operations in the North during 1963 were an almost complete failure. Not until 13 April 1963 and Team Pegasus did the missions resume; however, the six men were captured soon after landing. The same fate also befell Team Jason, dropped on 14 May. Because of a backlog of teams, a second Nationalist C-54 was added to the effort. On 4 June, three teams—code-named "Dauphine," "Bell," and "Becassine"—were dropped into North Vietnam. Only the seven men of Team Bell reported that they had successfully landed. The other teams were, like their predecessors, captured soon after reaching the ground.

Three nights later, Teams Bart and Tellus parachuted from one of the Nationalist C-54s. They had originally been a single team, commanded by Nguyen Van Ngo, which was to be infiltrated by sea. When this proved impractical, they began parachute training. With this completed, they were split into two groups, with Nguyen Van Ngo in command of Team Tellus. The standard procedure was that the drop zone was to be at least six miles from any known habitations. The French maps of Vietnam the crew was using were inaccurate, however, and Team Tellus jumped over a large village. The four men landed in front of the village cooperative office. Its staff was working late, and they saw the agents as they descended. The team was captured before they could even draw their guns. Team Bart came down in a more isolated location, but was spotted by local inhabitants, and the five men were also soon captured.

In July 1963, a pair of Nationalist C-123B Providers was sent to South Vietnam to continue the agent drops. They were painted gray overall and were fitted with extra fuel tanks and radar detection and electronic countermeasures (ECM) equipment. One of the C-123s and the remaining C-54 (the other had already been sent back to Taiwan) were scheduled to make several drops on 4 July. The C-54 crew made the first drop, but then the aircraft flew into a mountain, killing all aboard. The C-123 successfully completed its drop.

In all, sixteen teams, totaling ninety-five men, parachuted into North Vietnam during 1963. In addition to Team Bell, only Team Easy, an eight-man group dropped on 9 August, and two men sent in on 12 August as reinforcements for Team Remus reported success. The CIA listed the other thirteen teams and seventy-eight men as "captured soon after landing." In addition, radio contact with Team Caster was lost in July 1963 when they were believed to be in Laos. The risks posed to the drop planes by North Vietnamese air defenses also remained.

On 10 August, the ECM operator on a C-123 making a resupply mission detected radar signals as it began its run toward the lighted drop zone. Then three antiaircraft rounds exploded close to the C-123, followed by tracer rounds passing in front of the windshield. The crew took evasive action, causing the cargo to shift. Once it was secured, the crew dove for the ground. After the crew reached Tan Son Nhut, they reported the incident and their suspicions that the team had been compromised. Upon inspection, they found that none of the shells had hit the aircraft. First Officer T. T. Chen recalled, "Our jamming worked well. Otherwise, we would have never survived the attack."

Despite the lack of results, plans went ahead for Operation Switchback. McNamara held a meeting at Pacific Command headquarters on 6 May 1963 to discuss the covert war in the North. Later in May, the JCS ordered Admiral Felt to develop a plan for covert operations in the North. The draft of Operational Plan (OPLAN) 34A was sent to the JCS on 17 June. OPLAN 34A proposed seventy-two different categories of actions, which during the course of a year would result in a total of 2,062 separate operations. OPLAN 34A was intended to cause the leadership of North Vietnam to divert resources and ultimately stop their war in the South.

The draft plan was sent to General Taylor, who had become the JCS chairman. General Taylor did not approve OPLAN 34A until 9 September 1963. Buddhist protests against South Vietnamese President Ngo Dinh Diem caused further action on OPLAN 34A to be delayed for another two months. A coup by South Vietnamese generals was launched against Diem with tacit U.S. approval on 1 November. The following day, Ngo Dinh Diem and his brother, the head of the secret police, were both murdered.

In the aftermath of the coup, a special meeting was held on 20 November 1963 in Honolulu to discuss policy on Vietnam. The atmosphere at the meeting was gloomy. Despite the year's setbacks, McNamara was confident that OPLAN 34A would produce results. The military had the men, aircraft, ships, and special warfare doctrine to launch a massive covert effort in the North. This would pressure Ho Chi Minh into halting the insurgency in the South.

Colby responded that operations against the North would fail, no matter the size of the effort. He remembered standing up and saying: "We in CIA had come to the conclusion that the agent operation in North Vietnam just wasn't going to work. My Deputy Chief of the Far East Division bugged me on the subject, saying, 'Look, this is just nonsense.' We went back and took a look at our experience in North Korea, in the Soviet Union in the late 1940s–early 1950s, in China, and in none of these cases had any of the operations really proved successful." When McNamara continued to express support for covert operations in the North, Colby replied: "Mr. Secretary, I hear what you are saying, but it's not going to work. It won't work in this kind of society."

Two days later, on 22 November 1963, while on a political trip to Dallas, Texas, President Kennedy was assassinated by Lee Harvey Oswald. The future of both OPLAN 34A and overall Vietnam policy was now in the hands of the new president, Lyndon B. Johnson. Four days after Kennedy's death, Johnson approved NSAM 273, which called for a joint MACV/CIA plan to escalate the covert war against the North. The plan called for "progressively escalating pressure to inflict increasing punishment upon North Vietnam and to create pressures, which may convince the North Vietnamese leadership, in its own self-interest, to desist from its aggressive policies." This reflected the whiz kids' doctrine of coercing an enemy to force him to change his actions.

After the plan was delivered to President Johnson, he decided on 21 December to establish an interdepartmental study committee to review OPLAN 34A and "select from it those actions of least risk." The interdepartmental study committee provided a list of low-risk operations from the overall OPLAN 34A on 2 January 1964, and recommended that the first four-month phase of operations begin on 1 February.

McNamara, DCI John McCone, Secretary of State Dean Rusk, and presidential adviser McGeorge Bundy each reviewed OPLAN 34A as part of their duties with the 303 Committee, which oversaw all intelligence operations. They submitted their separate report to Johnson on 3 January. Although all the members supported the plan, there were critical differences in their assessment. McNamara was "highly enthusiastic"; DCI McCone commented, "no great results are likely from this kind of effort"; Rusk felt that it "will help to persuade Hanoi that we have no intention of quitting," although he also noted "98% of the problem is in South Vietnam." Bundy was supportive, but insisted that the entire program be closely monitored by the 303 Committee.

As the Johnson administration was debating the scale of covert actions they were to undertake, the North Vietnamese government was reaching a fateful decision of its own. The fall of the Diem government had left South Vietnam in chaos, and the North Vietnamese Politburo saw an opportunity not to be missed. They ordered Col. Bui Tin and a dozen military and civilian cadres on a fact-finding mission down the Ho Chi Minh Trail. They were to determine whether the VC was strong enough, on its own, to win in the South, or whether large numbers of regular North Vietnamese troops were needed.

By early 1964, they concluded that only massive numbers of regular North Vietnamese army troops could defeat South Vietnam and the Americans. The North began expanding both its army and the Ho Chi Minh Trail. Trucks would now be used to move supplies, as speed was more important than either secrecy or deniability. The decade-old captured French weapons that had been sent into South Vietnam were now replaced by modern Soviet and Chinese weapons, such as AK-47s.

The Studies and Observation Group

In mid-January 1964, President Johnson approved the start of covert operations against North Vietnam. Of the original seventy-two categories of operations, thirty-three were approved for implementation during Phase I. MACV was assigned responsibility for undertaking the covert operations. Despite the nearly two years that Operation Switchback had been under way, there was still no organization in place at MACV to conduct the operations that it had inherited from the CIA. MACV issued General Order 6 on 24 January 1964, which created the "Studies and Observation Group" (SOG). It was to undertake covert operations against North Vietnam, which were given the overall code name "Footboy."

The first chief of SOG was Col. Clyde Russell, who was an experienced Green Beret officer. He had assumed that he would be taking over a large-scale, ongoing effort. In fact, only the singleton Ares and Teams Bell, Remus, Tourbillon, and Easy were still operational. (Team Europa had gone off the air on 27 January 1964.) Despite this, Colonel Russell was under pressure from McNamara to increase the number of operations. SOG's difficulties were compounded by its staff's lack of experience. Green Beret training was in counterinsurgency and behind-the-lines operations, not running spy networks, which had been the responsibility of the CIA.

Lt. Col. Edward Partain, who ran SOG's agent operations (code-named "Timberwork") in 1964, later noted, "I was familiar with the terminology, but as far as agent handling or covert-type operations experience, I had nothing." His deputy had been involved with unconventional warfare in Korea, but not agent handling. Partain said that the officers assigned to him were "dedicated, hard working, and willing to learn," but had no training at all in agent handling. Also, they were rotated out at the end of a one-year tour, meaning there was a constant influx of inexperienced personnel.

SOG also had to cope with the restrictions imposed by Washington. Senior policy makers wanted to use SOG's operations to pressure the North into abandoning their war in the South, but fretted over the possible consequences. A key element of OPLAN 34A was the establishment of an internal resistance movement within North Vietnam. However, if the Communist government seemed on the verge of being overthrown by this resistance group, the Chinese might intervene, as they had in the Korean War. If the resistance forced Ho Chi Minh out, someone worse might take his place. OPLAN 34A was approved, but any references to a resistance force inside North Vietnam were removed.

Colonel Russell was told to continue the blind drops of agents into North Vietnam. The agents were ordered not to contact the local population. Their mission was to be strictly psychological warfare and intelligence collection. To Colonel Russell, this made no sense. He later wondered how an agent could "collect much intelligence when you're hiding in the hills and trying to protect your life." He also could not understand what good it would do "running around in the woods dropping a few hand-printed leaflets." Russell thought the blind drops of agents should be abandoned and replaced by attempts to build up a resistance movement among the tribal groups along North Vietnam's border. His proposal was rejected.

The first SOG team of agents was air-dropped into North Vietnam on 23 April 1964. The team consisted of three men to reinforce Team Remus. Although this drop was apparently successful, of the next eleven drops, made between April and November 1964, five teams were listed as "captured, tried by North Vietnam." Of the other six drops, five were of reinforcements for Teams Tourbillon (two drops), Easy, Remus, and Bell. The other was Team Eagle, a six-man group parachuting into an area on the northeastern border with China. Although the agent drops had resumed under SOG control, the Nationalist crews of the two C-123Bs were quick to notice a change in their missions.

T. T. Chen commented: "When the CIA was running the operation, drop missions were the focus. When SOG took over, we were often being asked to go into North Vietnamese airspace and use our electronic equipment to gather radar emissions." Being asked to serve as bait for North Vietnam's radar network did not appeal to the C-123 crews. They also lost confidence in the SOG briefings. After SOG had assured them a drop zone was safe, a CIA officer would take them aside and warn them not to believe what they had just been told.

As the drops were being made in mid-1964, the original pair of Nationalist Chinese C-123Bs began to be replaced by six C-123Bs that had been modified under Project Duck Hook and fitted with Doppler navigation radar and improved ECM equipment. The original C-123s were retired after a final leaflet drop mission on 23 November 1964. The Duck Hook C-123 crews were given a different cover story. If shot down, they were not to pretend to be South Vietnamese, but to admit they were Nationalist Chinese citizens and claim they had flown off course while flying to Taiwan.

The first Duck Hook C-123 mission over the North was made on 20 January 1965. Soon after, one of the C-123s was nearly lost in the first air-to-air engagement of the Vietnam War. Crew C-3 was heading toward a drop zone on the night of 14 February 1965. Team Dog, which was assigned to reinforce Team Bell, was aboard. A North Vietnamese Air Force-operated T-28 ambushed the airplane when it was about two and a half miles away from the drop zone. The North Vietnamese pilot attacked from below and behind the transport, firing at least two bursts of .50-caliber machine-gun fire. He then broke off the attack, claiming a kill. The C-123 was merely damaged and was able to land back at Nakhon Phanom Air Base in Thailand. Four crewmen and one member of Team Dog had been wounded in the attack. When examined, the aircraft was found to have 234 bullet holes in it.

The Nationalist kickers thought another aircraft—possibly a helicopter—had attacked them. The U.S. investigators initially thought a propeller aircraft might have been used in the attack. This possibility was rejected, however, because the North Vietnamese were not known to have any such aircraft. As a result, it was concluded that the C-123 had happened to fly near a group of North Vietnamese troops that happened to be on a hilltop near its flight path. In reality, a disgruntled Royal Laotian Air Force T-28 pilot, Lt. Chert Saibory, had defected to North Vietnam in September 1963. Lieutenant Chert was thrown in prison, and the T-28 was refurbished to become North Vietnam's first fighter. (Its tail number was "963" after the date of its arrival.) That Chert had successfully reached the North was not known, however. The airplane had simply disappeared, and it was thought to have crashed.

Soon after the near loss of crew C-3, the nature of the Vietnam War changed, making such covert operations increasingly irrelevant. With the commitment of large numbers of North Vietnamese regular troops in 1964, the situation in South Vietnam deteriorated. The chief concern of American officials was the political consequences to U.S. interests should South Vietnam fall to the Communists, rather than any specific importance of Vietnam itself.

President Johnson approved use of U.S. ground forces. In early March 1965, U.S. Marines landed in South Vietnam. At the same time, U.S. Air Force and Navy airplanes began air strikes against North Vietnam. As with the covert operations, these air strikes were subject to "rules of engagement" about what targets were off-limits. As with the covert actions, the intent of the bombing was to put psychological pressure on North Vietnam.

As the U.S. commitment in South Vietnam grew rapidly, Col. Donald Blackburn replaced Colonel Russell as chief of SOG in May 1965. Like his predecessor, Blackburn could not understand the point. He had run guerrilla networks in the Philippines during World War II and was one of the few U.S. Army officers who understood such operations. Blackburn also tried to get a resistance movement approved, but the 303 Committee again turned the proposal down. In October 1965, SOG was given new operational orders for the agents. They were now to "conduct intelligence, sabotage, psychological, and escape and evasion operations." The agents were allowed to make limited contacts with the local population, in order to "recruit and support local agents." It was a change without meaning.

Blackburn wanted to halt the drops, saying later, "I think that they had a misdirected purpose because you go and take a team of South Vietnamese and drop them in an area that they know nothing about or very little about and where they weren't able to gather the support of the people, and they were going to be captured right away." He could not understand why, if the U.S. government was unwilling to organize the local population into a resistance movement, the agents were being dropped in the first place. Blackburn commented, "This thing always stuck in my mind out there, and that is why I was never very enthusiastic about the agent teams."

Although just six agent teams were dropped during Colonel Blackburn's tour, the means were greatly improved. As North Vietnamese air defenses increased, SOG looked for a replacement for the C-123s. Helicopters allowed a more precise insertion than by parachute. Team Romeo was successfully landed on 19 November 1965 from two helicopters. The landing zone was near the Laotian border and north of the Demilitarized Zone (DMZ). The ten men were to conduct reconnaissance, road watch, and sabotage activities against supplies moving south.

After a year as the head of SOG, Col. Jack K. Singlaub replaced Blackburn in May 1966. He had extensive covert experience, having been in the OSS during World War II and the CIA in the late 1940s, conducting operations in Manchuria. After the outbreak of the Korean War, he had been a member of JACK, which attempted to set up guerrilla units behind the Communist lines. When Singlaub was briefed about Timberwork at the Pentagon, he recalled: "I was surprised they thought that they could get away with parachuting agents into that territory. The territory of Vietnam, as I found earlier in Korea, was not like parachuting agents into occupied France or Yugoslavia. . . . I expressed some negative views about this way of getting them in, but I saw right away they didn't appreciate my insights, so I didn't make an issue of it in the briefing."

In fact, the JCS ordered SOG to greatly expand the number of teams. The orders continued that the agents should place their "maximum emphasis . . . upon intelligence collection and the establishment of civilian contacts." Their mission was "intelligence collection by road watch, rail watch, and river watch" of the supply lines from North Vietnam into Laos. To start the expansion, twenty-five agents were to be trained over the next few months, and then dropped into the North. Over a period of fifteen months, several hundred agents were to be inserted.

Team Hadley was inserted by helicopter into Laos on 26 January 1967, and then hiked across the border to take a position north of Team Romeo. Team Red Dragon was air-dropped to a location near the Chinese border on 21 September 1967, at the far northern border of North Vietnam. Drops of supplies and reinforcements were also made to several of the existing teams. Starting in 1966, these supply drops used high-speed aircraft, such as South Vietnamese A-1Gs, which reduced the risk of interception and loss.

The agent drop aircraft were also improved, with the arrival in October 1966 of four modified U.S. Air Force C-130E Blackbirds. These had originally been built to rescue U.S. bomber crews in SAFE areas within the USSR. Each aircraft was fitted with Fulton recovery equipment on its nose, and extensive navigation and ECM equipment. The Blackbirds were painted in a special green and black finish, as camouflage on low-level night missions. One of the C-130E Blackbirds was lost on 29 December 1967. To this day, it is not known whether it crashed, was hit by a surface-to-air-missile, or was shot down by a MiG. The Communist government in Vietnam claims to have no information as to the crew's fate. Between the helicopters, fast supply aircraft, and the C-130E Blackbirds, there was little role for the Nationalist Chinese C-123s, and they soon were relegated to transport missions for SOG.

The Failure of Timberwork

Colonel Singlaub had been doubtful about the Timberwork agent operations against North Vietnam when he received his assignment as SOG chief in May 1966. By October 1967, a total of nine agent teams had parachuted into North Vietnam, had been landed by helicopter or infiltrated by sea. Despite the orders by the JCS that massive numbers of agents be infiltrated into North Vietnam, only the singleton agent Ares and Teams Tourbillon, Easy, Remus, Eagle, Romeo, Hadley, and Red Dragon were still operational.

The lack of results did nothing to improve Colonel Singlaub's low opinion of the blind drops. However, unlike his two predecessors, he decided to take a closer look at the reasons for the failures. Singlaub brought in Lt. Col. Robert Kingston as the head of Timberwork. "Barbed Wire Bob," as he was known, was the first in that position to have case officer training and actual experience in running agents. Kingston made a quick review of the communications from the teams, which made it clear nothing had been accomplished—a few claims of agents being recruited, a few claims of sabotage operations, but no significant intelligence. Next, Kingston called in the case officers and told them to brief him on their teams. He recalled, "They couldn't tell me what the [team] composition was, what the mission was, when the team went in, how they went in, what communications were with their teams."

After a few weeks, Kingston was ready to brief Singlaub. He began by asking the SOG chief, "What do you want me to tell Ho Chi Minh?" When Singlaub asked when he meant, Kingston told him that all the teams had been captured and he could contact Ho through them. "Singlaub went right through the roof," Kingston recalled.

Kingston's conclusion was based on several clues. The most obvious, in retrospect, was the pattern of losses. Only about one team was being "successfully" inserted per year. All the other teams were captured at the drop zone or soon after. The reverse was true of the agents sent as reinforcements to the established teams. Team Tourbillon received new agents twice in 1964, and again in 1965 and 1966. Team Easy was reinforced three times, and Team Remus four times. The infiltration of these reinforcement teams was always successful, although the drops often had one or more agents killed because of parachute accidents. This was far higher than the training loss rate. The final element was the failure to exfiltrate any agents. Each time SOG would issue orders for agents to move to a pickup point, the team would make excuses. The patterns were too consistent to be accidental.

Singlaub decided to have an outside assessment of Timberwork by a team of counterintelligence specialists from the CIA and Defense Intelligence Agency. When they reported back in early 1968, the conclusion was that every single team or singleton agent had been caught, killed, turned, or been a double agent from the start. This amounted to nearly seventy separate missions, involving some four hundred agents. The North Vietnamese had been running a "double cross system" against first the CIA and then SOG for seven years. Lt. Col. Robert McKnight, who took over Timberwork in January 1968, also shared this assessment. Although he lacked agent experience, McKnight read through the files for two or three weeks and came to the same conclusion.

Singlaub and McKnight now faced the question of what to do. Would it be better to shut down Timberwork, or was there still some way to salvage the operation? As they reviewed the reports, Singlaub and McKnight kept running across something odd about the North Vietnamese response to the agents. The Communist authorities had increased internal security measures. Large-scale security sweeps were also being made in areas where no agents existed. Villagers were being rounded up and interrogated, while anyone who had been suspected of anti-Communist actions in the past was also being brought in.

Singlaub and McKnight realized that North Vietnamese officials had not yet realized that they already controlled all of SOG's teams. The Communists were obsessed with the belief that agents were still operating freely. Singlaub and McKnight decided to deceive the deceivers. Gen. William Westmoreland, commander of U.S. forces in South Vietnam, verbally approved their plan, code-named "Forae," on 14 March 1968. To all but a few, Forae was simply a new version of the Timberwork long-term agent program. In reality, it was a triple cross, intended to exploit the North Vietnamese belief that the captured teams were only the tip of a far larger network of agents. The intention was to divert the North Vietnamese into launching witch hunts for these nonexistent agents.

The first element in Forae was code-named "Borden" and involved the recruitment of North Vietnamese POWs as low-level agents. SOG did not care whether they were trustworthy or not, as it was intended that they would reveal their "mission" to the Communist authorities. The "agents" were to unwittingly convince the Ministry of Public Security that they were part of a much larger spy network and resistance movement. Once a POW was selected, he was told that he was to make contact and deliver a message to a team inside North Vietnam. During his training, the agent would be given lists of contacts or dead drops that were to be used to communicate with the team. The agent would also hear stories about other agents who had already been sent into the North and about possible resistance movements that were active.

Once the agent's training was completed, he would be scheduled for a drop from a C-130E into North Vietnam or Communist-controlled territory in Laos or Cambodia. The Borden agent and several others would board the aircraft. Because of his excellent training record, the agent was told, he would be the first to jump, with the rest to follow. As the C-130E Blackbird neared the drop zone, the agent and the other team members lined up, and at the jump signal, the agent went out the door. Other parachutes soon followed him into the darkness.

What the agent did not know was that as soon as he left the airplane, the other "team members" unhooked their parachutes and sat down. The parachutes that were dropped from the airplane did not carry agents, but blocks of ice. The unwitting agent either surrendered immediately or was captured. Either way, he would describe his mission and provide the clues he had picked up in conversations. Combined, this information would point to large-scale agent operations in the North. As final proof that what the agent had said was true, when Ministry of Public Security personnel searched the drop zone, they found empty parachutes hanging from trees. There were no traces of the other agents, however. They had melted away, so to speak, into the jungle.

To add credibility to the Borden deception, agents who "washed out" of the training were returned to the POW camps. They had been primed with information that SOG wanted them to tell the other POWs. Events were also staged for the benefit of POWs who were not recruited. A U.S. interrogation team would arrive at a camp and begin shining an ultraviolet light at each POW's forehead. Eventually, the forehead of one POW would glow. The Americans would crowd around him, shake his hand, and hug him before taking him out of the room. The other POWs would believe he was an American agent who had returned. (In reality, he had been marked the day before during a physical examination.) SOG expected that word of these incidents would soon reach the Ministry of Public Security.

The second element of the Forae deception was code-named "Urgent." One part of this was similar to Borden, but the unwitting agents were North Vietnamese fishermen. This was a continuation of the Sacred Sword of the Patriots League (SSPL) operation. As part of this bogus resistance movement, in May 1964 unmarked gunboats flying the SSPL flag headed north. The gunboat crews then intercepted North Vietnamese fishing boats and abducted their crews, in a project code-named "Plowman." The captives were blindfolded, tied up, and taken below. The crewmen, each of whom spoke a northern or a central Vietnamese dialect, told the captives that they were being taken to an SSPL "liberated area" on the coast. After several hours, the captives arrived at a North Vietnamese coastal village.

They were actually at Cu Lao Cham Island, which was off the coast of South Vietnam, near Danang. "Paradise Island," as SOG referred to it, was intended to create the illusion that the fishermen really were in an SSPL-controlled area of North Vietnam, and that there really was a resistance movement against the Communist government. The kidnapped fishermen spent three weeks on Paradise Island, during which time they were fed, their medical conditions were treated, their information was collected, and they were indoctrinated. As their stay neared an end, the fishermen were told about SSPL cells inside North Vietnam and how to contact them. Finally, they would be given "gift kits" containing cloth, soap, and other items in short supply in North Vietnam. The kit also contained a small radio pre-tuned to the Voice of the SSPL radio. The fishermen then boarded the gunboat, were blindfolded, and taken back to North Vietnam. In four years, 1,003 detainees passed through Paradise Island.

In early 1968, the Paradise Island operation became part of the Urgent deception. As with the POWs in Borden, fishermen would be recruited as low-level agents. During their training, they were surrounded by role players and were fed disinformation about existent agent networks. As with Borden, it did not matter to SOG whether they were genuine, as either way, it was intended that the information reach the Ministry of Public Security. The training process was elaborate and ended with the new agent being inducted into a secret brotherhood. He was then loaded aboard a gunboat and sent back into North Vietnam.

The other part of Urgent dealt with North Vietnamese who were hard-core Communists, such as party cadres or militia members, and who were POWs or Paradise Island detainees. They were true believers and totally uncooperative, but SOG had a special use for them too. As with the other deception agents, these individuals were fed disinformation and were then sent back into North Vietnam.

The agent would go running to the authorities, but when his clothing was searched, the Ministry of Public Security interrogators found materials identifying other agents and spy activities carefully sown into the seams. This had been planted without the agent's knowledge. When confronted with the incriminating material, SOG expected that the agent would deny knowing about the items and that the interrogators would not believe him. The more the framed agent tried to explain away the planted materials, the more he protested his innocence and proclaimed his loyalty, the rougher the interrogations would become. McKnight was quite blunt, "We were hoping they'd all be killed or give false information that we planted."

Borden and Urgent agents were also used for offensive operations against North Vietnamese government officials. The agents were given letters that had easily discovered invisible ink messages, which implicated the targeted official as a U.S. agent. SOG described the letters as having "the specific objectives of diverting NVN [North Vietnamese] security to apprehend, detain, interrogate, and investigate innocent officials and their agencies." The information in the messages was also used to provide false confirmation of the disinformation given to the Borden and Urgent agents.

The final element of Forae was code-named "Oodles." This was to be the finishing touch on SOG's deception operation against the Ministry of Public Security. If, as the North Vietnamese believed, agent teams were really still active, there would have to be radio traffic back and forth between the teams and their controllers, as well as drops of supplies and reinforcements. Oodles was "designed to portray an apparently extensive and successful agent network in selected areas of North Vietnam. To this end, fourteen phantom teams [were] activated." To be credible to the North Vietnamese, the bogus teams would have to be run exactly as if they were real, because from the captured teams, the North Vietnamese had become familiar with U.S. tradecraft.

This began with the radio messages sent to the "teams." They had to use call signs and formats similar to those of real messages. Different messages were sent to each team, including operational instructions and intelligence targets they were to cover, the activities of the other teams, and the schedule of airdrops of supplies and reinforcements. Beyond the operational aspects, Project

Oodles added a human touch to give each team "personality." On each agent's "birthday," he would receive greetings from his parents, wife, and children. On his "wedding anniversary," he would be sent a very personal message from his "wife," referring to past events.

As with the messages, the supply drops to the bogus teams had to be made at the same intervals and to include the same equipment as had been done with the real teams. The drops were made into the same areas as the bogus teams were "operating." Of course, when the Ministry of Public Security troops arrived at the drop zone, they would find only the empty packages. It would seem that they had just missed the team. "Reinforcements" were also dropped to the teams, or so the North Vietnamese were intended to believe. In addition to the parachuted ice blocks, Borden and Urgent agents were told that they would be met by existing team members. After they were captured or surrendered, they would tell this to their interrogators.

The final link in the chain was accomplished through air-dropping radios into North Vietnam. These would then transmit prerecorded messages "from" the teams. This completed the communications circuit. As far as the Ministry of Public Security knew, orders were being transmitted to the teams, and intelligence information was being sent back.

Borden got off to a quick start following General Westmoreland's approval. SOG records noted that by late 1968 "98 detainees had been collected for this project. Fifty of them were returned to detention facilities, 44 were inserted as agents into NVN or NVN-controlled territory. . . . Four were scheduled for insertion in January 1969." Project Urgent recruited eleven low-level agents, two false agents who were given disinformation, and numerous other individuals who were framed with planted evidence. The ultimate goal was to insert a few hundred agents per year.

Those involved with Forae believed that the deception operations were having an impact on the North Vietnamese. Since 1965 it had been clear that Hanoi feared internal unrest and resistance activities. In 1968, with the start of Forae, these fears grew. The North Vietnamese claimed that the United States was trying to "agitate the counterrevolutionary clique in the North to rebel against our regime. They are trying to create disorder in our rear sections."

North Vietnamese press and radio statements in 1968 were more extensive and more alarmist than they had been in the past. An indication of Forae's success was a private statement made by a former North Vietnamese security official in March 1997. He said that Hanoi believed that SOG had sent one thousand to two thousand agents into the North. In reality, the actual CIA/SOG total was around four hundred agents. Forae had made a good start at disrupting the North, but it was about to end.

Neither Peace nor Honor

In late 1967, the North Vietnamese decided to launch a massive attack throughout South Vietnam, with the intention of sparking a mass popular uprising and forcing a quick end to the war. The North Vietnamese army and VC launched the Tet Offensive on 31 January 1968, with attacks by eighty-four thousand troops against thirty-six provincial capitals, sixty-four district capitals, and fifty villages. In Saigon, sappers attacked the U.S. embassy, the Presidential Palace, South Vietnamese army headquarters, and the national radio station. Despite achieving surprise, the North Vietnamese were pushed back with heavy losses, the VC was destroyed as a fighting force, the South Vietnamese army held, and the population did not rise up. However, in the end, this did not matter.

The American public perceived the Tet Offensive to be a North Vietnamese victory. Having committed hundreds of thousands of U.S. troops to avoid being seen as weak, a demoralized Johnson administration now prepared to walk away from South Vietnam. President Johnson announced a bombing halt over most of North Vietnam on 31 March 1968, and that he would not seek reelection. He also proposed that the United States and North Vietnam begin talks to end the war. The North Vietnamese, battered by their Tet losses, agreed.

When meetings began in Paris on 13 May, the North Vietnamese made clear the price they required for the talks to continue. They demanded the "unconditional cessation of the U.S. bombing raids and all other acts of war." The latter included halting the Forae agent operations, the SSPL efforts, and all other covert operations against the North (another indication of their fear of internal subversion). Although demanding a U.S. capitulation, the North

Vietnamese refused American demands for reciprocity. They would not halt VC activities, remove their troops from South Vietnam, or recognize the South Vietnamese government.

The U.S. negotiator, Averell Harriman, found Hanoi was unwilling to bend on the issue of reciprocity. By early fall, Harriman was able to negotiate an "understanding" with the North Vietnamese. Harriman told them that the United States would halt all bombing without conditions. Harriman continued that he presumed that the North would then cut back on rocket attacks against South Vietnamese cities and the infiltration of North Vietnamese troops into the South. The North Vietnamese delegation made no formal commitment to the understanding, but Harriman felt they gave him a "wink and a nod." On the basis of this wink and a nod, President Johnson announced on 31 October 1968 that the United States was halting all bombing missions over North Vietnam. The presidential elections were also only a few days away, and the Democratic Party nominee, Hubert H. Humphrey, was trailing Richard M. Nixon. Despite the last-minute action, Nixon was elected president in a narrow victory.

The "understanding" was akin to the agreement on Laotian neutrality Harriman had negotiated six years earlier. The United States was restricted from taking action, while the North Vietnamese were free to do whatever they wished. They did not even have to admit they had troops in the South, and their fiction of an independent VC was maintained. There was no slowdown in rocket attacks in the South or in the infiltration of northern troops. Harriman's wink and a nod also meant the end of covert operations inside North Vietnam.

Col. Steve Cavanaugh had replaced Singlaub as chief of SOG in September 1968. Only a few weeks after taking command, Cavanaugh was ordered to close down his operations in the North. Those involved with Forae could not understand the reasons behind giving up a potentially valuable asset even before negotiations actually began. The United States could simply deny any involvement with the Forae agents and the SSPL, just as the North Vietnamese denied that the VC was under their control. Officials in the Johnson administration, in contrast, had always directed that covert actions had to conform to their policy. As it was U.S. policy that all war-like acts had to be halted against North Vietnam, the covert operations also had to stop.

In the end, radio contact was maintained with Ares and Teams Tourbillon, Eagle, Hadley, and Red Dragon as late as March and April 1969 for deception purposes. The drops of "agents" and supplies to the bogus teams were halted. The only part of Oodles that continued was the sending of radio messages to the fourteen teams "operating" in the North. This amounted to about two messages a week. Without the airdrops and return of Paradise Island detainees, however, these efforts soon lost any credibility.

It was not until January 1973 that the Paris Peace Agreement was finally signed, ending direct U.S. involvement in the Vietnam War. The following month, a separate cease-fire agreement was signed in Laos, providing for yet another coalition government in Vientiane. Although President Nixon spoke of "peace with honor," the agreement meant that North Vietnamese forces were allowed to remain in the territories they had captured in South Vietnam and Laos, while all U.S. forces had to be removed. The North Vietnamese began moving troops, armor, artillery, and surface-to-air missiles into South Vietnam during 1973 and 1974 to rebuild their forces for the eventual showdown.

The North Vietnamese army launched its final offensive on 10 March 1975. Within a month, the North had committed more than 300,000 troops, and South Vietnamese forces were in full retreat. Air America crews were called in to assist with the evacuation of refugees fleeing the advancing Communist forces on 6 April. The Air America crews met a scene akin to that experienced by CAT crews a quarter century before, as mainland China was about to fall to the Communists. Panic-stricken refugees and South Vietnamese soldiers tried to force their way aboard the Air America aircraft. As the North Vietnamese troops encircled Saigon in late April, the situation became one of total chaos.

The final group of fixed-winged aircraft to take off from Saigon on 28 April 1975 had to taxi around debris-littered aprons. South Vietnamese Air Force pilots stole four Air America helicopters. Air America personnel were carrying weapons and several operational personnel had tense face-offs with armed South Vietnamese troops trying to flee. As Air America Capt. Ed Adams was boarding his C-46 to take off, a South Vietnamese soldier tried to force his way aboard. Air America pilot Fred Walker recalled: "Ed stopped him and the guy started to swing an M-16 around to point at him. The soldier got the gun about half way around when Ed knocked him on his ass (busting his hand in the process) and disarmed him."

The last day of the refugee airlift was 29 April 1975. The situation in Saigon was too dangerous to use fixed-wing aircraft, so some thirty Air America helicopter crews made pickups of U.S. and South Vietnamese personnel from six locations around the city. One of these was the Pittman Building in downtown Saigon. The Air America helicopters joined in the steady procession of U.S. Air Force, Navy, and Marine helicopters shuttled back and forth between the besieged city and Seventh Fleet ships standing off the coast. Fuel was short, and communications and cooperation with the Navy ships offshore, which did not initially know that the Air America helicopters were part of the official evacuation, were minimal. South Vietnamese helicopters were also flying out to the ships, and they attempted to land without authorization. As the carrier flight decks began to fill up, helicopters were pushed overboard to make room, while others were told to off-load their passengers, then ditch into the sea.

One of those told to ditch was Air America pilot Dave Kendall. As with other CAT/Air America pilots, he was an individualist. While off duty he wore bib overalls and brightly colored shirts. Flying out of uniform was forbidden, but as Saigon collapsed around him, Kendall thought that the comfort of the overalls was more important than company rules. He landed with a load of refugees on the USS *Blue Ridge* and was ordered to ditch the Huey helicopter. He took off and flew a short distance from the ship. Rather than landing the helicopter in the water, which was the normal procedure, Kendall took a different approach. As he hovered twenty feet above the South China Sea, he trimmed the helicopter nose down, and then jumped overboard. The loss of his weight caused the helicopter's center of gravity to change. It reared up, its tail boom hit the water, and the helicopter rolled over. The rotors nearly hit Kendall as he floated in the water.

A boat from the *Blue Ridge* picked Kendall up. After boarding the ship, he went below and changed into another shirt. He saw that another Air America pilot, Larry Stadulis, was about to fly back into Saigon and said he would go with him. They flew between Saigon and the fleet for the rest of the day. Their final trip was after nightfall. The long hours had left both Kendall and Stadulis mentally and physically exhausted. The night was dark, and a light rain had started. They were attempting to find the USS *Midway*, but the ship was blacked out. Their twenty-minute low-fuel light had been on for about fifteen minutes, and a night ditching would be fatal. Kendall called the ship and said he needed them to turn on a light. The carrier turned on every light and looked like a Christmas tree. The helicopter landed on fumes.

Between 6 and 29 April 1975, a total of 51,888 people were flown out of Saigon. Of these, 45,185, or 87 percent, were evacuated by Air America. On the last two days of the evacuation, 28 and 29 April, a total of 7,014 had escaped, with 80 percent being carried by Air America. The evacuations had given some the chance for a new life.

The CIA had made plans for a small stay-behind company in Thailand, staffed with a few selected helicopter and transport pilots. The plans fell through, however, and the handful of remaining Air America personnel were discharged. Air America went out of existence on 30 June 1976. The sale of its assets returned $23 million dollars to the U.S. Treasury. Between 1950 and 1976, 242 individuals working for CAT, Air America, and the other air proprietaries were killed or listed as missing in action.

Air America also provided the last, haunting image of the tragic end of U.S. involvement in Southeast Asia. It is the photo of an Air America Huey helicopter atop the Pittman Building in Saigon. A line of refugees is standing on the metal stairs leading up to the roof and the waiting helicopter. The line is too long for them to fit on this helicopter, however. It will take many trips to rescue them all. At the top of the stairs is the figure of a man, reaching out his hand to help the refugees into the helicopter and away from this nightmare, and from the greater nightmare about to descend. No one knows which helicopter crew is in the picture. Thus, they represent all of the Air America crews who flew in Southeast Asia. The man extending his hand to the refugees in the picture is O. B. Harnage, a CIA case officer. Years later, Harnage summed up that final, tragic day. "We kept telling them we would come back. And then we didn't."

Conclusion

The Darkness of the Future

Do you begin to see, then, what kind of world we are creating? . . . A world of fear and treachery and torment, a world of trampling and being trampled upon, a world which will grow not less but *more* merciless as it refines itself.

—George Orwell, *Nineteen Eighty-Four*

The reasons for the West's failures to establish agent networks and resistance movements inside the USSR and its allies were complex. In retrospect, however, these failures seemed preordained. These frantic Western efforts were driven by the fear of a Soviet surprise attack. This had begun with the March 1948 war scare and was fueled by the Berlin Blockade, the Soviet A-bomb test, the outbreak of the Korean War, and the Chinese intervention. Western intelligence had failed to anticipate any of these crises. CIA official Frank Lindsay recalled the belief in the early 1950s that "there was a fifty-fifty chance of war within a year." He continued, "That was the mood. The atmosphere was, my God, we're right back into the trenches."

The threats facing the West, and the actions needed to counter them, were seen in the darkest possible terms. A report by Gen. James H. Doolittle to President Dwight D. Eisenhower in the summer of 1954 reflected this. "It is now clear that we are facing an implacable enemy whose avowed objective is world domination by whatever means and at whatever cost. There are no rules in such a game. Hitherto accepted norms of human conduct do not apply. If the United States is to survive . . . we . . . must learn to subvert, sabotage and destroy our enemies by more clever, more sophisticated and more effective methods than those used against us."

New Wars—Old Tactics

This atmosphere generated intense pressure on the CIA and the British SIS. It seemed only logical to use the same covert methods—for example, underground movements like the French Resistance—that had proven so successful just a few years earlier. However, the World War II experience was not a reliable guide for conducting Cold War operations. The OSS, SIS, and Special Operations Executive had operated under wartime conditions. Supply drops to the resistance groups were on a massive scale, involving squadrons of aircraft. Along with the supplies, U.S. and British military personnel had parachuted into occupied Europe as training officers, radio operators, and liaisons with Allied intelligence. These had allowed large-scale attacks to be made on German supply lines, military forces, and Nazi officials, as well as provided a steady stream of intelligence reports.

For a resistance movement to survive, it must have the support of a significant number of the population. This did not have to be active support on the part of the population, but rather simply not reporting what they saw or heard. Although the Gestapo was able to break up many resistance networks, the Nazi secret police had not totally penetrated either German society or occupied Europe. The reprisals that German forces inflicted on the populations of Europe did not break their support for the resistance. The Gestapo also had to cope with deteriorating conditions as the war neared its close. These included air attacks on Gestapo headquarters within occupied Europe.

None of these factors applied to the early Cold War covert operations within Eastern Europe and the USSR. The need for plausible deniability meant that the agents and resistance movements had to be "sponsored" by independent anti-Soviet groups such as OUN, NTS, or WiN. Direct involvement by the West could not be apparent. This meant the supply drops were on a much smaller scale, using a handful of war-surplus C-47s flown by exiled Eastern European pilots. The weapons provided also had to be war surplus and untraceable to the West. The teams dropped into the Soviet bloc could not include CIA or SIS personnel, lest Western sponsorship be revealed if they were captured. The populations among whom the teams were trying to recruit agents viewed the absence of American or British personnel, as well as the meager supplies, as a lack of commitment. They were unwilling to risk their lives without the implied promise of direct Western military assistance.

The Soviet counterintelligence state was also far more effective than its Nazi counterpart had been. Within the USSR, the secret police had a generation to penetrate society. Informers lurked in every apartment building and every workplace. It simply was not possible for the Soviet or Eastern European populations to look the other way. The Soviet secret police could also operate with impunity, with no limits on its conduct and without the disruptions of operating under wartime conditions or direct attacks.

The scale of the Soviet police state controls became apparent to CIA officer Frank Lindsay in 1951 during a conversation with the leader of a Russian émigré group who was working for the CIA. Lindsay asked him how long an agent inside the USSR would have to know another person before the agent could attempt to recruit him. The émigré answered that if they worked together, it would take six months. Lindsay then asked the Russian what the odds were that a cell of ten or fifteen people would have an informant. The émigré replied that it would be fifty-fifty, and Lindsay concluded that long before a resistance movement could reach a size where it might be effective, it would have been infiltrated and destroyed.

Another factor behind the failure of the agent and guerrilla operations was the sheer ruthlessness of the Soviets. Troops would move from district to district in the central USSR, the Ukraine, and the Baltic states, wherever partisans were suspected. The troops would encircle the area and conduct sweeps. To destroy the support of the population, the Soviets conducted wholesale arrests, executions, and deportations, numbering in the hundreds of thousands. These efforts were already under way in 1945 and 1946, before the West made major efforts to support the anti-Soviet movements. Within Eastern Europe, the situation was much the same. "Class enemies" and anti-Soviet elements were rounded up and deported, while opposition political parties were purged, then forced to join the Communist Party. As a result, the number of prisoners in the Gulag reached its peak not during the purge years of 1937 and 1938, but between 1950 and 1953.

The final factor in the failure of Western covert operations was their betrayal by Kim Philby, Donald Maclean, Guy Burgess, and other, lower-level, double agents. Although most of the blame was placed on Philby for the failure of the Albanian operation, Lindsay believed the reasons went deeper. He said later, "I think the operation went down the drain because we couldn't maintain security in the DP [displaced persons] camps and because the Communist security apparatus was so damn strong." The net result of this was that the Western agents were often captured as soon as they landed. With the agents and resistance movements controlled by the Soviets, no leaks of information could reach the CIA or SIS. Double agents like Philby could provide "feedback" on how the deception was working—whether it was being accepted, or whether suspicions were developing.

The Rev. William Sloane Coffin, who had been recruited at Yale in 1949 to handle parachute drops, described the results of the miscalculations and failures this way: "It was all tragic, all lost. But it was war. You buried your buddies and kept fighting." (Coffin became famous in the late 1960s as a fierce opponent of the Vietnam War.) It was not only the agents who paid the price, however. In Poland, the WiN deception was used to flush out those who opposed Soviet control. In Albania, family members of the resistance fighters, as well as all those they had contacted, were rounded up. Thousands died as a result of these roundups of "enemies of the people." Tragically, these losses and sacrifices resulted in no reliable intelligence on Soviet activities and intentions.

Although the Soviets deceived, defeated, and humiliated the CIA and SIS, they also suffered their own losses because of their own fear, blindness, and carelessness. These losses, in retrospect, were far more severe than those of the West. In the 1930s and 1940s, Soviet intelligence had recruited a generation of agents that infiltrated the governments of the United States and Great Britain. These were ideological agents who were inspired by the propaganda image of the Soviet Union as the first worker-peasant state and of Stalin as its all-knowing leader.

Among these spies were State Department officials Laurence Duggan, Noel Field, and Alger Hiss; Treasury Department officials Harry Dexter White and Nathan Silvermaster; Congressman Samuel Dickstein; congressional staffer Charles Kramer; White House assistant Lauchlin Currie; and other agents in the Justice Department, Commerce Department, the National Advisory Committee for Aeronautics, the War Production Board, the OSS, and the Manhattan Project. They were able to provide intelligence on a whole range of U.S. political, diplomatic, military, intelligence, nuclear, scientific, aviation, and economic activities.

Starting at the end of 1945, these networks began to collapse because of defections, demobilization, the abolishment of the OSS, and, most important of all, the decoding of Soviet coded messages in the Venona project. Although few spy cases ever came to trial, the known and suspected agents found themselves being forced out of sensitive positions. Yet, although these moles could no longer provide intelligence, the Soviets had not yet totally lost their window into the U.S. government.

Philby, Maclean, and Burgess continued to operate undetected for several more years after the Soviet agent networks had been broken up. Through these British agents, the Soviets continued to receive high-grade intelligence about activities of both Great Britain and the United States. It was as if the Soviets were able to sit in on SIS/CIA discussions, British cabinet meetings, and talks between President Harry Truman and Prime Minister Clement Attlee. With the defection of Maclean and Burgess, and the subsequent exposure of Philby, this finally came to an end.

The Soviets themselves wrecked other attempts to gain intelligence on Western covert activities. The Baltic and Polish deception operations were golden opportunities for the Soviets. The United States lacked sources within the Soviet Union to double-check any "intelligence" the bogus underground was providing. Given the blindness of CIA and SIS officials to the growing evidence that the resistance networks were under Soviet control, there seemed little chance the deception would have been realized. Had the Soviets exploited the opportunity, they could have manipulated Western intelligence agencies. Had the Soviets done so, the damage to the West could have been great.

Instead, the Soviets were unwilling to undertake a serious "double cross" operation. This was primarily because of the fear among senior Ministry of State Security officials that giving even chicken feed to the West would result in their being "unmasked" as traitors. Ironically, the very fear used to control the Soviet population also controlled the controllers. As a result, the Soviets undertook only defensive measures to control the resistance movements, rather than exploiting them as a weapon. In the end, they were able to gain only an empty propaganda victory against the West.

A new international situation following the death of Stalin meant the USSR faced changing intelligence requirements. The success enjoyed by the Soviets against the West during the previous three decades caused the KGB to look to its past as the guide to its future. Agents ideologically committed to Communism would be recruited to reestablish networks within the U.S. and British governments. Communist-controlled front organizations would be used to influence Western populations to support Soviet positions on international issues. Finally, efforts to undermine, neutralize, and even assassinate the leaders of émigré groups would be continued.

The fact was that ideological agents like Philby, Maclean, and Burgess belonged to the past. The realities of Soviet rule were now apparent to all in the West but the dwindling number of Communist Party true believers and aging fellow travelers. Counterintelligence procedures had also been established to keep Communists out of sensitive positions. The successes of Soviet agents in the 1930s and 1940s had been largely due to the lack of any such screening. Even if an individual was forced out of a sensitive position because of Communist leanings, he had little trouble finding another job. There was no coordination between the FBI and military security efforts until after the start of the Cold War. Although the KGB continued to successfully recruit Westerners, they were less interested in Communist ideology than in Soviet money.

Front organizations faced similar difficulties in influencing Western public opinion. The U.S. Communist Party had enjoyed large-scale public support during the Depression and war years, while its control of front organizations was carefully concealed. By the mid-1950s, the U.S. Communist Party had been reduced to a few thousand members, and its role in the front groups was now obvious.

The KGB also continued to overestimate the threat from émigré groups. By the mid-1950s these groups were marginal, infiltrated, unreliable, and beset by personal and ideological rivalries. Although the Soviets were successful in assassinating NTS ideologist Lev Rebet in October 1957 and the OUN leader Stepan Bandera in October 1959, several failed attempts and the defections of the assassins embarrassed the Soviets. Even in the late 1960s, the KGB continued to play operational games against the émigré groups.

The Changing of the Guard

Under Eisenhower, covert operations were reviewed by the "Special Group," which consisted of the president, the national security adviser, the secretaries of state and defense, the chairman of the Joint Chiefs of Staff, and the Director of Central Intelligence. Based on their recommendations, Eisenhower himself made the final decision to approve or reject an operation. Eisenhower was seldom beset by second thoughts; he did not tinker with a plan, nor was he interested in those with doubts. He focused on removing leftist governments in the third world and, once committed, he followed through.

The Kennedy and Johnson administrations' policies were very different. For all the fashionable talk about covert warfare, below the surface were deep divisions over the issue. While Eisenhower centralized control, in the Kennedy and Johnson administrations authority over covert operations was fragmented, the chain of command was unclear, and the debates over their advantages versus political risk were never ending. With their administrations divided, both presidents split the differences. Kennedy approved the Bay of Pigs invasion, but cut the number of exile B-26s used in the first wave from sixteen to eight. With Johnson, agent teams were sent into North Vietnam to collect intelligence and to conduct psychological warfare, but they were not allowed to establish a resistance movement or to even make contact with the local population. For all the internal debates, the critical questions were never asked. Why would eight bombers be less of an indication of U.S. involvement than sixteen? How does an agent influence the thinking of a population when he is forbidden to speak with anyone?

The "rules of engagement" imposed on the military by President Johnson in Southeast Asia were an extension of these divisions. Johnson, McNamara, and the whiz kids minutely controlled the air war over the North in order to "signal" U.S. determination to the Communist government. These rules had little or nothing to do with a coherent military strategy. The results were exactly the reverse of what the whiz kids intended. The Johnson administration's on-again/off-again air strikes signaled to the North Vietnamese that the United States was weak.

Although the often-absurd rules of engagement for the air war were known at the time, those for the "secret war" in Laos were even worse in their nature and consequences. The Geneva Accords on Laos were sacred to the U.S. government, even after years of violations by North Vietnamese troops. Because of the ban on foreign troops in Laos, the Air Force technicians at Lima Site 85 had to be sheep-dipped and were forbidden to carry weapons, despite being deep inside enemy territory and surrounded by massive numbers of North Vietnamese troops. The Ho Chi Minh Trail through Laos was the key to North Vietnam's campaign in the South. Cutting the trail would not have ended the war in South Vietnam outright. It would, however, have made it far harder for the North to undertake large-scale actions, and far easier for the United States and South Vietnam to counter them. The U.S. government sought to preserve both South Vietnam and the Geneva Accords. In the end, neither survived.

The failures of the CIA's attempts to build spy networks inside the USSR, Eastern Europe, North Korea, and China in the late 1940s and early 1950s had taught the agency a bitter lesson. The experience made them understand the difficulties of operating inside denied areas under Communist control. North Vietnam was viewed by the CIA as being a tougher target than any of these countries. The rulers had popular support, social controls were exceptionally strong, there was no flow of refugees that could be recruited, and there were few travelers who could serve as contacts. Thus the CIA had little enthusiasm for the kind of large-scale effort President John F. Kennedy was seeking.

Kennedy was looking for quick action, and when the CIA proved unwilling to repeat the mistakes of the past, McNamara was eager to oblige. To him it was merely a matter of numbers. The military had the resources for a large effort, the doctrine for unconventional warfare had been developed, and U.S. Special Forces had been expanded. A major covert effort should convince the North Vietnamese to stop their war in the South. William Colby warned McNamara that it was not going to work, but he was not interested.

Some of the reasons for the failure of agent operations against North Vietnam were the same as those with the earlier efforts. These included the strength of North Vietnamese internal security, double agents such as Ares, and leaks from within South Vietnamese intelligence, government, and military. The North Vietnamese had agents at all levels; an Air Force pilot once said that he thought that a full third of the South Vietnamese working at his base were supplying information to the Communists. Another reason was the transfer to the military of a role that had been the exclusive domain of the CIA. The intelligence officers who had run the agent operations against the USSR and Eastern Europe at least had wartime experience. When SOG took over the CIA agent activities in 1964, none of their personnel had any experience, or even training, for their new role. SOG was conducting on-the-job training, whereas the North Vietnamese had decades of experience against the French.

Col. Nguyen Cao Ky, who led Operation Haylift into North Vietnam, pointed out another problem with the agent drops. Agents were selected because they had originally come from the North. They knew the areas in which they were to operate, had the proper accents to blend into the population, and had friends and relatives who could provide help. In the five years since the partition of Vietnam, however, Communist rule had produced subtle cultural changes. These included differences in vocabulary and how people spoke to each other. Northerners used different spices in their soup and different fingers to hold their spoons from those used by Southerners. The Northerners also wore sandals; when the agents were dropped, they were wearing shoes. Such differences attracted suspicion.

Ky described the results of the failed agent drops against North Vietnam in terms similar to those used by the Reverend Coffin in describing his experiences against the Soviet bloc. Ky wrote: "We made mistakes, and those cost men their lives or their liberty. Nevertheless, we were fighting a war. We had to get intelligence, even at the sacrifice of dozens of men. I think the agents understood this."

After Col. John Singlaub's review of Timberwork in early 1968 showed that the agent networks were all under North Vietnamese control, SOG responded with Forae. Its potential was clear. Forae exploited a totalitarian society's greatest weakness—the fear of internal subversion. The empty parachutes, captured agents, bogus radio messages, and discarded supply packages created the illusion of spy networks inside the North. When the Ministry of Public Security failed to uncover the agents, pressure was put on it to find them. The dragnets to capture suspects intensified, as did the interrogations of those suspects, but still without results. The framing of loyal Communists by Urgent showed that no one was above suspicion, no matter how spotless their party record. Suspicion built, the party and government turned on itself, and more and more effort was diverted to internal security.

By this time in the war, however, Forae's possible contributions were limited. Nevertheless, even though Forae could not defeat the enemy, it still could mess with their minds. Because of the halt in covert operations against the North in October 1968, however, what Forae might have accomplished will never be known. What Forae might have done had it been started in 1961 is also unknown.

That Was Then, This Is Now

It's uncertain just what lessons from Cold War covert operations can be applied to the world after September 11, 2001. The situation is too new for patterns to be clear and too much is yet to unfold. In many ways, we find ourselves in a time like that of 1948 and 1949. The Cold War had begun, and the battle was joined. At the same time, the means by which this struggle was to be fought, and where it would take place, were still unknown.

The differences between the Cold War and the early twenty-first century are both in the nature of the struggle and the changes in society and technology in the past five decades. These suggest that, just as the French Resistance was not a guide to Cold War covert operations, what happened in the USSR, China, and the Third World in the 1950s and 1960s may not be a forecast of what is to follow 9-11.

The twentieth century was the "Age of Ideologies." The wars and chaos of that era were the products of totalitarian ideologies—Soviet Communism, Italian Fascism, Japanese militarism, and German Nazism. The end of World War II in 1945 saw the destruction of three of the four, but left Soviet Communism in control of an empire stretching from Eastern Europe to the Pacific. The Cold War, the struggle that continued for the next forty-six years, pitted Soviet Communism against Western capitalist democracy.

The decade between the fall of the Soviet Union and 9-11 marked a dramatic change in the structure of totalitarianism. It lost a coherent ideological structure, becoming a chaotic mixture of extreme nationalism, ethnic and religious hatred, terrorism, nihilism, and the cult of the personality. The warlords, strongmen, and self-made deities who emerged seemed more intent on having their statue on every street corner than fitting into categories of "the Left" and "the Right." More significant is the rise of religious extremism in the Muslim world. With the possible exception of the "troubles" in Northern Ireland, religious wars have been absent from Europe since the battles between Catholics and Protestants during the Reformation of the sixteenth and seventeenth centuries.

A major difference between the Cold War era and now is access to information. By the end of the twentieth century, communications technology had reached the point that traditional censorship measures were rendered ineffective, and, at worst, pointless. In the mid-1970s the Soviets realized the threat posed by the development of communications satellites, a product of the Cold War space race, that allowed television images to be directly broadcast anywhere in the world, including a home television receiver. The Soviets demanded that no such broadcasts be made without the permission of the state receiving them, as this represented a violation of national sovereignty. To block any unauthorized broadcasts, the Soviet government demanded the right to destroy the satellite. Today, satellite receiving dishes sprout from rooftops around the world, and although the Soviet Union is gone, today's totalitarian states still try to ban satellite dishes and the images and ideas pouring down from the sky.

The Internet has become the ultimate expression of the late-twentieth-century communications revolution. Just as satellite television leaps over the barricades put up by totalitarian censors, the Internet allows anyone with a computer the possibility to reach beyond state controls to any place in the world about any subject in the world, however much their government may object. The central role the Internet has in the global economy and society makes it difficult for a totalitarian state to counter it. Radio Free Europe could be jammed and Western newspapers confiscated without interfering with the USSR's own internal or external communications links. With the Internet, it is different. A totalitarian state needs to communicate with the outside world for its own economic well-being. Thus, the Internet must be available on a large scale. But as the number of Internet connections grows, as more people have computers, cell phones, or other public means of Internet access, the control a totalitarian government has over information potentially diminishes.

However, although the means of the struggle have changed between 1947 and today, the nature of the enemy facing Western capitalist democracy has not. Now, as then, totalitarianism represents a rejection of modernism. Communism was a rejection of the industrial revolution. Italian Fascism and Japanese militarism represented longings for the Roman Empire and samurai traditions. Nazism was a return to Prussian militarism and discipline; it emphasized a pre-Christian time of Teutonic myths and followed a policy of purging "undesirables," especially Jews. Islamic fundamentalism reflects a traditional religious society that rejects the secular world, particularly the Western modern world, which is seen as corrupt and atheistic. Islamic fundamentalists seek a return to an earlier, pure era, when the Muslim world swept all before it.

Totalitarianism is defined by an ideological "truth," rather than by facts and analysis. Philip Gourevitch, in a profile of North Korean dictator Kim Jong Il in The New Yorker, noted: "[T]his so-called truth is a confection of outright lies—not merely false but, more perniciously, a form of unreality, imposed with such relentlessness and violence on a people hermetically sealed . . . that it has become their only reality. . . . To maintain a kingdom of lies is to live in perpetual fear of being exposed." The result is the extraordinary efforts by the secret police in totalitarian societies to crush any unapproved ideas and to block access to any information that might undermine the lies. As the guardians of the lies, the secret police understands that if people ever begin to think that black is not really white, despite what the Party tells them, they might one day also begin to shout "Down with Big Brother."

Part of the "truth" of a totalitarian society is the central role of enemies. Indeed, totalitarianism without political, religious, racial, economic, class, or social enemies would be impossible. The enemy's conspiracy is the justification for the original seizure of power; the enemy is to blame for all failures and setbacks; and the enemy secretly controls all those who doubt the state's truth, thus justifying police state controls and the government's mass murder of its people deemed to be in league with the enemy. That the enemies and their crimes are imaginary is irrelevant.

Just as the totalitarian state represents itself as absolute truth, its enemies are viewed as absolute evil. They must be wiped out as a group, not as individuals, and without regard to guilt or innocence. They are stripped of their humanity and are labeled "enemies of the people," "traitors," "liars," "subhumans," or "infidels." The logical conclusion of this cult of hate, revenge, and power was seen in the killing fields of Cambodia in the mid-1970s, and now in the widespread starvation in North Korea. The whole country becomes a prison camp in which anyone is a potential enemy of the people.

In the larger picture, the struggles during the Cold War were only one chapter in the historical struggle between the worth and rights of the individual and state tyranny. It is a story dating back to the struggle between the democratic society of Athens and the militaristic society of Sparta. Then, just as during the Cold War and just as now, the question is the future of humanity. Will humanity continue to strive for its highest aspirations, or is it to be condemned to the pessimism depicted in George Orwell's *Nineteen Eighty-Four,* a future of "a boot stamping on a human face—forever"?

Notes

For the reader interested in more information, the sources are listed by topic within each chapter. A bibliography is included as further reading.

Introduction

Communist Parties: Kenneth Lloyd Billingsley, *Hollywood Party* (Roseville, California: Forum, 2000); John Earl Haynes and Harvey Klehr, *Venona: Decoding Soviet Espionage in America* (New Haven: Yale University Press, 1999).

World War II Resistance Movements: Peter Tompkins, "The OSS and Italian Partisans in World War II," *Studies in Intelligence* (Spring 1998, Unclassified Edition).

Origins of U.S. Intelligence: Christopher Andrew, *For the President's Eyes Only* (New York: Harper Collins, 1995) p. 158–61, 163–66, 169–71.

Soviet Post-War Foreign Policy: William Taubman, *Stalin's American Policy* (New York: W.W. Norton and Co., 1982), chapters 6 and 7; James Chace, "The Day the Cold War Started," *MHQ* (Spring 1997), 6–11; Mikhail M. Narinsky, "The Soviet Union and the Marshall Plan" and Scott D. Parrish, "The Turn Toward Confrontation: The Soviet Reaction to the Marshall Plan, 1947," Cold War International History Project web page.

March 1948 Crisis: William R. Harris, "March Crisis Act I" and "March Crisis Act II," *Studies in Intelligence* (Fall 1966 and Spring 1967); Roger R. Miller, "Freedom's Eagles the Berlin Airlift, 1948–1949" *Air Power History* (Fall 1998), 7–9.

Chapter 1

Paper Mills: Stephen M. Arness, "Paper Mills and Fabrication," *Studies in Intelligence* (Winter 1958).

Intelligence on the Soviet A-bomb: Henry S. Lowenhaupt, "On the Soviet Nuclear Scent," *Studies in Intelligence* (Fall 1967) and "Chasing Bitterfeld Calcium," *Studies in Intelligence* (Spring 1973).

Agent Operations in the Baltic states: Christopher Andrew and Oleg Gordievsky, *KGB: The Inside Story* (New York: Harper Perennial, 1991), 384, 385; Georgi Martynov, "The KGB in Latvia," *War in Peace Vol. 1* (London: Marshall Cavendish, 1985).

Plausible Deniability: Andrew Christopher, *For the President's Eyes Only* (New York: Harper Collins, 1995), 172–75.

Agent Airdrops: Rositzke, Harry, *The CIA's Secret Operations* (New York: Reader's Digest Press, 1977), 18–33.

Albania: Nicholas Bethell, *Betrayed* (New York: Times Books, 1985), chapters 4, 7, and 8; Evan Thomas, *The Very Best Men* (New York: Touchstone, 1996), 38, 39; "Current Situation in Albania," Central Intelligence Agency, 15 December 1949.

Chapter 2

Post-War Purges: Peer de Silva, *Sub Rosa* (New York: Times Books, 1978), 23–30.

The Baltic States: Stephen Dorril, *MI 6* (New York: Free Press, 2000), 290–99, 511, 512, 515, 516; Andrew and Gordievsky, *KGB: The Inside Story*, 386, 387; Francis Gary Powers and Curt Gentry, *Operation Overflight* (New York: Holt, Rinehart and Wilson, 1970), 204–9; Priit J. Vesilind, "The Baltic Nations," *National Geographic* (November 1990), 10.

WiN: Dorril, *MI 6*, 256–67; Andrew and Gordievsky, *KGB: The Inside Story*, 387–89; Thomas, *The Very Best Men*, 66–68; Andrew, *For the President's Eyes Only*, 183; Intelligence Reports, "Poland—Czechoslovak—East Germany—Western Europe," 18 August 1950.

Albania: Bethell, *Betrayed*, chapters 8, 9, 10; Andrew and Gordievsky, *KGB: The Inside Story*, 395–402.

Agent Drops into the USSR: George, A.L., "Case Studies of Actual and Alleged Overflights, 1930–1953," Project RAND Research Memorandum RM-1349, 15 August 1955, 103–6, 118–21, 127, 129, 130, 204, 205, 217, 218, 223, 224, 293, 294; "Tass Reports 2 Russians Executed as Spies Flown to Soviet by U.S.," *New York Times* (19 December 1951); "Acheson Ridicules Soviet Spy Charge," *New York Times* (20 December 1951); Harrison E. Salisbury, "Soviet Says It Shot 4 U.S.-Trained Spies," *New York Times* (27 May 1953); "U.S. Dismisses as 'Fantastic' Soviet Charge That 4 Spies Were Parachuted into Ukraine," *New York Times* (28 May 1953); "Russians Report Shooting of Spy," *New York Times* (21 May 1954); "Soviet Say 2 Spies for U.S. 'Repented,'" *New York Times* (16 June 1954); William J. Jorden, "Soviet Assails U.S., Produce 4 'Spies,'" *New York Times* (7 February 1957); "Four 'Spies' Identified," *New York Times* (8 February 1957); de Silva, *Sub Rosa*, 55–57.

Chapter 3

The Korean War: Kathryn Weathersby, "To Attack, or Not to Attack? Stalin, Kim Il Sung, and the Prelude to War"; Evgueni Bajanov, "Assessing the Politics of the Korean War, 1949–51"; Alexandre Y. Mansourov, "Stalin, Mao, Kim, and China's Decision to Enter the Korean War, Sept. 16–Oct. 15, 1950: New Evidence from Russian Archives," Cold War International History Project web page; Andrew, *For the President's Eyes Only*, 184.

AVIARY: Michael E. Haas, *Apollo's Warriors: United States Air Force Special Operations during the Cold War* (Maxwell AFB: Air University Press, 1997), 15–39; Michael E. Haas, *In the Devil's Shadow: U.N. Special Operations during the Korean War* (Annapolis: Naval Institute Press, 2000), 14–30; Warren A. Trest, *Air Commando One: Heinie Aderholt and America's Secret Air Wars* (Washington, D.C.: Smithsonian Institution Press, 2000), 38–47.

Sabotage Operations: Haas, *Apollo's Warriors*, 44, 46, 56–65; Haas, *In the Devil's Shadow*, 58–61; Intelligence Reports, "Poland—Czechoslovak—East Germany—Western Europe," 15 December 1950.

JACK: Haas, *In the Devil's Shadow*, 177–89, 201–5; Richard P. Hallion, *The Naval Air War in Korea* (Baltimore: Nautical and Aviation Publishing Company, 1986), 126, 127; Haas, *Apollo's Warriors*, 42–45; Antonio J. Mendez and Malcolm McConnell, *The Master of Disguise: My Secret Life in the CIA* (New York: William Morrow and Company, Inc., 1999), 45; "Talkback: Mystery Missions by B-26," *Air Enthusiast* (February–May 1979).

Chapter 4

Civil Air Transport in China: William M. Leary, *Perilous Missions* (Washington, D.C.: Smithsonian Institution Press, 2002); Felix Smith, *China Pilot Flying for Chennault during the Cold War* (Washington, D.C.: Smithsonian Institution Press, 1995); Guang Qiu Xu, "U.S. Air Aid and the CCP's Anti-American Campaign, 1945–1949," *Air Power History* (Spring 2000), 26–39; Frédéric Lert, *Wings of the CIA* (Paris: Histoire and Collections, 1998), 37; Terry Love, *Wings of Air America: A Photo History* (Atglen, Pennsylvania: Schiffer Publishing Ltd, 1998), 4, 5.

PAPER: Smith, *China Pilot*, 193, 194; Thomas, *The Very Best Men*, 51, 53–56; Leary, *Perilous Missions*, 129–33; Lert, *Wings of the CIA*, 41–43.

Western Enterprises Incorporated: Frank Holober, *Raiders of the China Coast: CIA Covert Operations during the Korean War* (Annapolis: Naval Institute Press, 1999), 5–7, 22, 23, 28–31, 44, 45, 81, 85–87, 120–22, 125–33; Mendez and McConnell, *The Master of Disguise*, 85, 86.

Agent Drops: Leary, *Perilous Missions,* 133–37; Love, *Wings of Air America,* 98; Sterling Seagrave, *Soldiers of Fortune* (Alexandria, Virginia: Time-Life Books, 1981), 149, 151; Holober, *Raiders of the China Coast,* 176–94.

TROPIC: Leary, *Perilous Missions,* 137–142; Smith, *China Pilot,* 215–19; W. David Lewis and William F. Trimble, *The Airway to Everywhere: A History of All American Aviation, 1937–1953* (Pittsburgh: University of Pittsburgh Press, 1988); "Remarks of the Director of Central Intelligence George J. Tenet on Presentation of the Director's Medal to John T. "Jack" Downey and Richard G. Fecteau," 25 June 1998, CIA web page; Wagner, Angie, "CIA Honors Heroes of Long-Secret Air America," *San Diego Union-Tribune* (3 June 2001); "China Authorizes Search for U.S. MIAs," *Aerotech News and Review* (12 July 2002); "Breaking News from China—Norm Schwartz and Bob Snoddy," Air America Association web page.

Chapter 5

Carpetbaggers: Orr Kelly, *From a Dark Sky* (Novato, California: Presidio Press, 1996); Haas, *Apollo's Warriors,* 2–9.

ARCW: Haas, *Apollo's Warriors,* 95–109, 111–19, 123–29; R.W. Koch, "The CIA's Death Valley Albatross," *Air Classics* (April 1979); Jack Watson, "Search for the CIA Albatross," *Air Progress Warbirds International* (Summer 1987); Alwayn T. Lloyd, *B-29 Superfortress in Detail and Scale* (Summit, Pennsylvania: Blue Ridge/Tab Books, 1987), 44; Gordon L. Rottman, *U.S. Army Special Forces 1952–84* (London: Osprey Publishing Limited, 1985); Memorandum for the Secretary, Subject: Oral Presentation of the Annual Report of the Net Evaluation Subcommittee, November 25, 1958.

ARCW in Korea: Haas, *In the Devil's Shadow,* 114–24; A. Timothy Warnock, *The USAF in Korea: A Chronology, 1950–1953* (Washington, D.C.: Air Force History and Museums Program, 2000), 81, 83; "Red China Jails Americans," undated clipping (ca. November 1954) provided by R.W. Koch; Document TFR 37–23, "S. Ignatyev to Malenkov, Beria, and Bulganin, January 29, 1953"; Document TFR 55–65, "List of USAF aircrew members participating in combat in North Korea, 1950–1953, information about whom was found in documents of the 64th Aviation Corps." This included the crew of the 581st ARCW B-29. It lists all fourteen crewmen, with the notation beside three names, "Killed (under what circumstances not specified)"; Iris Chang, *The Thread of the Silkworm* (New York: Basic Books, 1995).

SAFE Areas: Martin Middlebrook, *The Berlin Raids: R.A.F. Bomber Command Winter 1943– 44* (New York: Viking, 1988), 307, 352; Haas, *In the Devil's Shadow,* 103, 104; Thomas A. Julian, "The Origins of Air Refueling in the United States Air Force," in

Technology and the Air Force: A Retrospective Assessment (Washington, D.C.: Air Force History and Museum Program, 1997), 86, 98; Thomas, *The Very Best Men*, 71; R.W. Koch, "Operation Armageddon," *Air Classics* (October 1979); John F. Welch, *RB-36 Days at Rapid City or Rapid City Free Style* (Rapid City: Silver Wings Aviation, 1994), 182–85.

Chapter 6

CIA Domestic Contact Service: Anthony F. Czajkowski, "Techniques of Domestic Intelligence Collection," *Studies in Intelligence* (Winter 1959); Max Holland, "The Lie That Linked CIA to the Kennedy Assassination," *Studies in Intelligence* (Fall/Winter 2001); Rositzke, *The CIA's Secret Operations,* 57–60; Information Report, "Captured U.S. Balloons Shown to Tourist/Popular Attitudes and Morale," August 1956; Kenneth E. Bofrone, "Intelligence Photography," *Studies in Intelligence* (Spring 1961); Gerald Posner, *Case Closed Lee Harvey Oswald and the Assassination of JFK* (New York: Random House, 1993), 46–51; Charles R. Ahern, "The Yo-Yo Story: An Electronic Analysis Case Study," *Studies in Intelligence* (Winter 1961).

William Lear in the USSR: Richard Rashke, *Stormy Genius* (New York: Houghton Mifflin, Co., 1985), 180–86.

Russell UFO Sighting: Joel Carpenter, "The Senator, the Saucer, and Special Report 14," *International UFO Reporter* (Spring 2000); Air Intelligence Information Report, 13 October 1955; Report No. 193–55, Subject: Observations of Travelers in USSR; Memorandum for Information, Subject: Reported Sighting of Unconventional Aircraft, 19 October 1955.

U-2 Support: Henry S. Lowenhaupt, "The Decryption of a Picture," *Studies in Intelligence* (Summer 1967); "Mission to Birch Woods," *Studies in Intelligence* (Fall 1968); "Somewhere in Siberia," *Studies in Intelligence* (Winter 1971); "Visual-Talent Coverage of the USSR in Relation to Soviet ICBM Deployment January 1959–June 1960."

Arrests of Tourists: Vladislav M. Zubok, "Spy vs. Spy: The KGB vs. the CIA, 1960–1962," Cold War International History Project web page; "Tale of a Tourist," *Newsweek* (18 September 1961); "Espionage: How the Deadly Game Is Played," *Newsweek* (11 December 1961).

Chapter 7

Ajax and PBSuccess: Andrew, *For the President's Eyes Only*, 202–11; Thomas, *The Very Best Men*, 107–23. The rebel air force used in PBSuccess was the first use of offensive air power in a covert operation by the U.S.

Tibetan Background: John Kenneth Knaus, *Orphans of the Cold War: America and the Tibetan Struggle for Survival* (New York: Public Affairs, 1999), chapters 4, 6, 7; Haas, *Apollo's Warriors*, 137–40.

Airdrops into Tibet: William M. Leary, "Secret Missions to Tibet," *Air and Space* (December 1997/January 1998), 62–68; Knaus, *Orphans of the Cold War*, chapters 8, 9, 12; Memorandum for: Brigadier Andrew J. Goodpaster, Subject: U-2 Overflights of Soviet Bloc, 18 August 1960; Pocock, Chris, *The U-2 Spyplane: Toward the Unknown* (Atglen, Pennsylvania: Schiffer Military History, 2000); Thomas, *The Very Best Men*, 147–52, 160–65, 172.

C-130 Flights: Leary, "Secret Missions to Tibet," 66–71; Trest, *Air Commando One*, 83–98.

Tibet and Kennedy: Knaus, *Orphans of the Cold War*, chapters 13–16; Thomas, *The Very Best Men*, 275–78; Harold P. Ford, "Calling the Sino-Soviet Split," *Studies in Intelligence* (Winter 1998–1999).

Chapter 8

Thunderball: John Cork, "Inside Thunderball," *Goldeneye* (Issue 3, Vol 1), the Ian Fleming Foundation web page; "The Making of Thunderball," MGM/UA Home Videos, 1995; "Thunderball," MGM/UA Home Videos, 1995; Thomas, *The Very Best Men*, 384.

Bay of Pigs: White, Mark J., *The Kennedys and Cuba: The Declassified Documentary Record* (Chicago: Ivan R. Dee, 2002); Thomas, *The Very Best Men*, 241–51; Dan Hagedorn and Leif Hellström, *Foreign Invaders: The Douglas Invader in Foreign Military and US Clandestine Service* (Leicester, England: Midland Publishing Limited, 1994), 126–31; William M. Leary and Leonard A. LeSchack, *Project Coldfeet: Secret Mission to a Soviet Ice Station* (Annapolis: Naval Institution Press, 1996), 113–19; Lert, *Wings of the CIA*, 111, 112; Haas, *Apollo's Warriors*, 148–61; William Manchester, *The Glory and the Dream: A Narrative History of America–1931–1972* (New York: Bantam Books, 1975), 905; Michael Warner, "The CIA's Internal Probe of the Bay of Pigs Affair," *Studies in Intelligence* (Winter 1998–1999).

COLDFEET: Leary, and LeSchack, *Project Coldfeet*, chapters 4–6, 8, 9; William M. Leary, "Robert Fulton's Skyhook and Operation Coldfeet," *Studies in Intelligence* (1995); "For Sale Boeing B-17G," Intermountain Aviation Inc. flyer (ca. January 1969). (This flyer gives the B-17G's serial number as being 44–83875. Checks with three different references confirm it was actually 44–83785.); Frederick A. Johnsen, *Flying Fortress: The Symbol of Second World War Air Power* (New York: McGraw-Hill, 2000).

The Congo: Ted Gup, *The Book of Honor: The Secret Lives and Deaths of CIA Operatives* (New York: Anchor Books, 2001), 133–54; Lert, *Wings of the CIA*, 240–54; Hagedorn and Hellström, *Foreign Invaders*, 148–55; Richard L. Holm, "A Close Call in Africa," *Studies in Intelligence* (Winter 1999–2000); "CIA Secrets–Secret Wars," The Discovery Channel, 2001.

Chapter 9

CAT and Dien Bien Phu: Albert Grandolini, "French 'Packets' Fairchild C-119 Boxcars in French Indochina," *Air Enthusiast* (November/December 1996); Murray, Williamson, "Dien Bien Phu," *MHQ* (Spring 1997); Martin Windrow and Mike Chappell, *French Foreign Legion Since 1945* (London: Osprey Military, 1996), 17–19; Dominique Chao-Arlaux and Jean Arlaux, "The Battle of Dien Bieu Phu, May 6th, 1954, Air Mission," Air America Association web page.

Laos: William M. Leary, "CIA Air Operations in Laos, 1955–1974," *Studies in Intelligence* (Winter 1999–2000); Haas, *Apollo's Warriors*, 167–72; Trest, *Air Commando One*, 104–6, 109–16; Hagedorn and Hellström, *Foreign Invaders*, 132–36.

Air America Rescue Missions: Earl H. Tilford, Jr., *Search and Rescue in Southeast Asia* (Washington, D.C.: Center for Air Force History, 1992), 47–49, 62; Chuck Klusmann, "The Price of Freedom," Air America Association web page; Peter Mersky, *RF-8 Crusader Units Over Cuba and Vietnam* (Botley, England: Osprey Combat Aircraft, 1999), 22–26; Earl H. Tilford,, Jr., "Rescue at Ban Phanop," *Air Enthusiast* (December 1980–March 1981). (The details of Air America's involvement are from a private source.); Van Etten, Ben A., "Rescue," Air America Association web page.

Air America Operations: Leary, "CIA Air Operations in Laos, 1955–1974"; Love, *Wings of Air America*, "Air America: The CIA's Secret Airline" (The History Channel, 2000). (Air America pilot Jesse Markham was the brother of Monte Markham, the television actor and producer.); Donald V. Courtney, "Ration of Luck," *Air and Space* (October/November 2002).

Covert Projects: Haas, *Apollo's Warriors*, 176–83; Tilford, *Search and Rescue in Southeast Asia*, 52, 53; Peter R. Arnold and Ken Ellis, "Burmese Lions British Fighter Exports to Burma," *Air Enthusiast* (September/October 1997); Ken Conboy, "Wings Over the Land of a Million Elephants: Military Aviation in Laos 1949–1975," *Air Enthusiast* (March/April 1998); Ken Conboy and James Morrison, "Alternate Airlines CIA Airlift Contracts In Laos," *Air Enthusiast* (September/October 1999); Ken Conboy and Simon McCouaig, *The War in Laos 1960–1975* (London: Osprey Publishing, 1989); Frank Bonansinga, "Air America's B-26 Night Drop Project," Air America Association web page; Lert, *Wings of the CIA*, 189–91; James C. Linder, "The Fall of Lima Site 85," *Studies in Intelligence* (Unclassified Edition, 1995). (CIA officer Howard Freeman was given the pseudonym "Huey Marlow" in this article.)

The End of Air America: Leary, "CIA Air Operations in Laos, 1955–1974"; Love, *Wings of Air America*, 7, 20–22.

Chapter 10

Origins of the Vietnam War: Merle L. Pribbenow, "The Ho Chi Minh Trail's Early Years," *Vietnam* (August 1999); Merle L. Pribbenow, "North Vietnam's Master Plan," *Vietnam* (August 1999); Ken Conboy, Ken Bowra, and Simon McCouaig, *The NVA and Viet Cong* (London: Osprey Military, 1991), 8, 9, 15, 16; John A. Byrne, *The Whiz Kids: Ten Founding Fathers of American Business—And the Legacy They Left Us* (New York: Currency Doubleday 1993), 393–405.

Covert Operations in the North: Richard H. Shultz, Jr., *The Secret War Against Hanoi* (New York: Harper Collins, 1999), 1–3, 5–8, 16–49, 75–89, 310–29; Sedgwick Tourison, *Project Alpha* (New York: St. Martin's Paperbacks, 1995), 19–22, 29–34, 41–75, chapters 4–8, 11–13; Nguyen Cao Ky and Marvin Wolf, "Nights Over North Vietnam," *Air and Space* (August/September 2002); Ken Conboy and James Morrison, "Plausible Deniability," *Air Enthusiast* (November/December 1999).

Forae: Shultz, *The Secret War Against Hanoi*, 89–102, 108–27; John L. Plaster, *SOG* (New York: Simon and Schuster, 1997), chapter 7.

The Fall of South Vietnam: Leary, "CIA Air Operations in Laos, 1955–1974"; Fred Walker, Allen Cates, and E.G. Adams, "Memories of the Fall of Saigon–April 29, 1975," Air America Association web page.

Conclusion

The Reasons for Failure: Thomas, *The Very Best Men*, 60, 71–73, 134–35; Robert Louis Benson and Michael Warner, *Venona: Soviet Espionage and the American Response 1939–1957* (Washington, D.C.: National Security Agency/Central Intelligence Agency, 1996); Vladimir Pozniakov, "A NKVD/NKGB Report to Stalin: A Glimpse into Soviet Intelligence in the United States in the 1940s," Cold War International History Project web page; Anne Applebaum, *Gulag: A History* (New York: Doubleday, 2003); John Earl Haynes and Harvy Klehr, *Vernona: Decoding Soviet Espionage in America* (New Haven: Yale University Press, 1999); Allen Weinstein and Alexander Vassiliev, *The Haunted Wood* (New York: Random House, 1999); Raymond Garthoff and Amy Knight, "The KGB's 1967 Annual Report, with Commentary by Raymond Garthoff and Amy Knight," Cold War International History Project web page; Shultz, *The Secret War Against Hanoi*; Ky and Marvin Wolf, "Nights Over North Vietnam."

Modern Totalitarianism: Daniel Pipes, *Conspiracy: How the Paranoid Style Flourishes and Where It Comes From* (New York: The Free Press, 1997); Michael Nelson, *War of the Black Heavens: The Battles of Western Broadcasting in the Cold War* (Syracuse, New York: Syracuse University Press, 1997); Philip Gourevitch, "Letter from North Korea: Alone in the Dark," *The New Yorker* (3 September 2003); George Orwell, *Nineteen Eighty-Four* (New York: Signet Classic, 1981).

Bibliography

Books

Andrew, Christopher, and Oleg Gordievsky. *KGB: The Inside Story* (New York: Harper Perennial, 1991).

Andrew, Christopher. *For the President's Eyes Only* (New York: Harper Collins, 1995).

Andrew, Christopher, and Vasili Mitrokhin. *The Sword and the Shield: The Mitrokhin Archives and the Secret History of the KGB* (New York: Basic Books 1999).

Antonov-Ovseyenko, Anton. *The Time of Stalin* (New York: Harper and Row Publishers, 1981).

Applebaum, Anne. *Gulag: A History* (New York: Doubleday, 2003).

Benson, Robert Louis, and Michael Warner. *Venona: Soviet Espionage and the American Response 1939–1957* (Washington, D.C.: National Security Agency/Central Intelligence Agency, 1996).

Bering, Henrik. *Outpost Berlin* (Chicago: Edition Q, Inc., 1995).

Bethell, Nicholas. *Betrayed* (New York: Times Books, 1985).

Billingsley, Kenneth Lloyd. *Hollywood Party* (Roseville, California: Forum, 2000).

Brown, Anthony Cave [editor]. *Dropshot: The American Plan for World War III Against Russia in 1957* (New York: The Dial Press, 1978).

Byrne, John A. *The Whiz Kids: Ten Founding Fathers of American Business—And the Legacy They Left Us* (New York: Currency Doubleday 1993).

Chang, Iris. *The Thread of the Silkworm* (New York: Basic Books, 1995).

Churchill, Jan. *Classified Secret: Controlling Airstrikes in the Clandestine War in Laos* (Manhattan, Kansas: Sunflower University Press, 2000).

Conboy, Ken, and Simon McCouaig. *The War in Laos 1960–1975* (London: Osprey Publishing, 1989).

————, Ken Bowra, and Simon McCouaig. *The NVA and Viet Cong* (London: Osprey Military, 1991).

Davis, Larry. *Air War Over Korea* (Carrollton, Texas: Squadron/Signal Publications, 1982).

de Silva, Peer. *Sub Rosa* (New York: Times Books, 1978).

Dorril, Stephen. *MI 6* (New York: Free Press 2000).

Gup, Ted. *The Book of Honor: The Secret Lives and Deaths of CIA Operatives* (New York: Anchor Books, 2001).

Haas, Michael E. *Apollo's Warriors: United States Air Force Special Operations during the Cold War* (Maxwell AFB: Air University Press, 1997).

————. *In the Devil's Shadow: U.N. Special Operations During the Korean War* (Annapolis: Naval Institute Press, 2000).

Hagedorn, Dan, and Leif Hellström. *Foreign Invaders: The Douglas Invader in Foreign Military and US Clandestine Service* (Leicester, England: Midland Publishing Limited, 1994).

Hallion, Richard P. *The Naval Air War in Korea* (Baltimore: Nautical and Aviation Publishing Company, 1986).

Haynes, John Earl, and Harvy Klehr. *Vernona: Decoding Soviet Espionage in America* (New Haven: Yale University Press, 1999).

Holloway, David. *Stalin and the Bomb* (New Haven: Yale University Press, 1994).

Holober, Frank. *Raiders of the China Coast: CIA Covert Operations during the Korean War* (Annapolis: Naval Institute Press, 1999).

Johnsen, Frederick A. *Flying Fortress: The Symbol of Second World War Air Power* (New York: McGraw-Hill, 2000).

Kelly, Orr. *From a Dark Sky* (Novato, California: Presidio Press, 1996).

Klass, Philip J. *Secret Sentries in Space* (New York: Random House, 1971).

Knaus, John Kenneth. *Orphans of the Cold War: America and the Tibetan Struggle for Survival* (New York: Public Affairs, 1999).

Laurie, Clayton D. *Congress and the National Reconnaissance Office* (Washington, D.C.: NRO History Office, 2001).

Leary, William M. *Perilous Missions* (Washington, D.C.: Smithsonian Institution Press, 2002).

————, and Leonard A. LeSchack. *Project Coldfeet: Secret Mission to a Soviet Ice Station* (Annapolis: Naval Institution Press, 1996).

Lert, Frédéric. *Wings of the CIA* (Paris: Histoire and Collections, 1998).

Lewis, W. David, and William F. Trimble. *The Airway to Everywhere: A History of All American Aviation, 1937–1953* (Pittsburgh: University of Pittsburgh Press, 1988).

Lloyd, Alwayn T. *B-29 Superfortress in Detail and Scale* (Summit, Pennsylvania: Blue Ridge/Tab Books, 1987).

Love, Terry. *Wings of Air America: A Photo History* (Atglen, Pennsylvania: Schiffer Publishing Ltd, 1998).

Manchester, William. *The Dream and the Glory* (New York: Bantam Books, 1975).

Mendez, Antonio J., and Malcolm McConnell. *The Master of Disguise: My Secret Life in the CIA* (New York: William Morrow and Company, Inc., 1999).

Mersky, Peter. *RF-8 Crusader Units Over Cuba and Vietnam* (Botley, England: Osprey Combat Aircraft, 1999).

Middleton, Drew. *Air War–Vietnam* (New York: Arno Press, 1978).

Murphy, David E., Sergei A. Kondrashev, and George Baily. *Battleground Berlin: CIA vs. KGB in the Cold War* (New Haven: Yale University Press, 1997).

Nelson, Michael. *War of the Black Heavens: The Battles of Western Broadcasting in the Cold War* (Syracuse, New York: Syracuse University Press, 1997).

Ordway, Frederick I. III, and Mitchell R. Sharpe. *The Rocket Team* (New York: Thomas Y. Crowell, 1979).

Orwell, George. *Nineteen Eighty-Four* (New York: Signet Classic, 1981).

Peebles, Curtis. *The Corona Project* (Annapolis: Naval Institute Press, 1997).

———. *Shadow Flights: America's Secret Air War Against the Soviet Union* (Novato, California: Presidio Press, 2000).

Pipes, Daniel. *Conspiracy: How the Paranoid Style Flourishes and Where It Comes From* (New York: The Free Press, 1997).

Plaster, John L. *SOG* (New York: Simon and Schuster, 1997).

Pocock, Chris. *The U-2 Spyplane: Toward the Unknown* (Atglen, Pennsylvania: Schiffer Military History, 2000).

Posner, Gerald. *Case Closed: Lee Harvey Oswald and the Assassination of JFK* (New York: Random House, 1993).

Powers, Francis Gary, and Curt Gentry. *Operation Overflight* (New York: Holt, Rinehart and Wilson, 1970).

Rapoport, Louis. *Stalin's War Against the Jews* (New York: The Free Press, 1990).

Rashke, Richard. *Stormy Genius* (New York: Houghton Mifflin, Co., 1985).

Richelson, Jeffrey. *American Espionage and the Soviet Target* (New York: William Morrow and Company, 1987).

Rositzke, Harry. *The CIA's Secret Operations* (New York: Reader's Digest Press, 1977).

Ross, Steven T. *American War Plans 1945–1950* (London: Frank Cass, 1996).

Rottman, Gordon L. *U.S. Army Special Forces 1952–84* (London: Osprey Publishing Limited, 1985).

Seagrave, Sterling. *Soldiers of Fortune* (Alexandria, Virginia: Time-Life Books, 1981).

Shultz, Richard H., Jr. *The Secret War Against Hanoi* (New York: Harper Collins, 1999).

Smith, Felix. *China Pilot: Flying for Chennault during the Cold War* (Washington, D.C.: Smithsonian Institution Press, 1995).

Talbott, Strobe [editor]. *Khrushchev Remembers* (Boston: Little, Brown, 1974).

Taubman, William. *Stalin's American Policy* (New York: W.W. Norton and Co., 1982).

Thomas, Evan. *The Very Best Men* (New York: Touchstone, 1996).

Thompson, Wayne, and Bernard C. Nalty. *Within Limits: The U.S. Air Force and the Korean War* (Washington, D.C.: Air Force History and Museum Program, 1996).

Tilford, Earl H., Jr. *Search and Rescue in Southeast Asia* (Washington, D.C.: Center for Air Force History, 1992).

Tourison, Sedgwick. *Project Alpha* (New York: St. Martin's Paperbacks, 1995).

Trest, Warren A. *Air Commando One: Heinie Aderholt and America's Secret Air Wars* (Washington, D.C.: Smithsonian Institution Press, 2000).

Ulam, Adam B. *Expansion and Coexistence: Soviet Foreign Policy 1917–73* (New York: Holt, Rinehart and Winston, Inc., 1974).

Warnock, A. Timothy. *The USAF in Korea: A Chronology 1950–1953* (Washington, D.C.: Air Force History And Museums Program, 2000).

Weinstein, Allen, and Alexander Vassiliev. *The Haunted Wood* (New York: Random House, 1999).

Welch, John F. *RB-36 Days at Rapid City or Rapid City Free Style* (Rapid City: Silver Wings Aviation, 1994).

White, Mark J. *The Kennedys and Cuba: The Declassified Documentary Record* (Chicago: Ivan R. Dee, 2002).

Windrow, Martin, and Mike Chappell. *French Foreign Legion Since 1945* (London: Osprey Military, 1996).

Articles and Papers

"Tass Reports 2 Russians Executed as Spies Flown to Soviet by U.S.," *New York Times* (19 December 1951).

"Acheson Ridicules Soviet Spy Charge," *New York Times* (20 December 1951).

"U.S. Dismisses as 'Fantastic' Soviet Charge That 4 Spies Were Parachuted into Ukraine," *New York Times* (28 May 1953).

"Russians Report Shooting of Spy," *New York Times* (21 May 1954).

"Soviet Say 2 Spies for U.S. 'Repented,'" *New York Times* (16 June 1954).

"Red China Jails Americans," undated clipping (ca. November 1954) provided by R.W. Koch.

"Four 'Spies' Identified," *New York Times* (8 February 1957).

"Tale of a Tourist," *Newsweek* (18 September 1961).

"Espionage: How the Deadly Game Is Played," *Newsweek* (11 December 1961).

"Talkback: Mystery Missions by B-26," *Air Enthusiast* (February–May 1979).

"Germans Pay Dearly for Uranium," *San Diego Union* (24 November 1999).

"Penchant for Spies Came Early," *Antelope Valley Press* (28 December 2000). "John Le Carre" (a pseudonym which means "John the Square" in French) said in a BBC-TV interview that he first became interested in espionage as a teenage gofer for a British diplomat. He was subsequently recruited by British intelligence. He later became the best-selling author of such spy novels as *Tinker, Tailor, Soldier, Spy*.

"China Authorizes Search for U.S. MIAs," *Aerotech News and Review* (12 July 2002).

Ahern, Charles R. "The Yo-Yo Story: An Electronic Analysis Case Study," *Studies in Intelligence* (Winter 1961).

Arness, Stephen M. "Paper Mills and Fabrication," *Studies in Intelligence* (Winter 1958).

Arnold, Peter R., and Ken Ellis. "Burmese Lions: British Fighter Exports to Burma," *Air Enthusiast* (September/October 1997).

Bajanov, Evgueni. "Assessing the Politics of the Korean War, 1949–51," Cold War International History Project web page.

Bofrone, Kenneth E. "Intelligence Photography," *Studies in Intelligence* (Spring 1961).

Bonansinga, Frank. "Air America's B-26 Night Drop Project," Air America web page. In a postscript to the Blue Goose, two Air America Twin Otters (N774M and N5662) were fitted with terrain-following radar. N5662 crashed on 23 July 23 1972, but the other aircraft was photographed in 1973 in a night-flying scheme similar to that of the Blue Goose.

Brugioni, Dino A. "The Unidentifieds," *Studies in Intelligence* (Summer 1969).

———. "The Tyuratam Enigma," *Air Force Magazine* (March 1984).

Carpenter, Joel. "The Senator, the Saucer, and Special Report 14," *International UFO Reporter* (Spring 2000).

Chace, James. "The Day the Cold War Started," *MHQ* (Spring 1997).

Chao-Arlaux, Dominique, and Jean Arlaux. "The Battle of Dien Bien Phu, May 6th, 1954, Air Mission," Air America Association web page.

Conboy, Ken. "Wings Over the Land of a Million Elephants: Military Aviation in Laos 1949–1975," *Air Enthusiast* (March/April 1998).

———, and James Morrison. "Alternate Airlines: CIA Airlift Contracts in Laos," *Air Enthusiast* (September/October 1999).

———, and James Morrison. "Plausible Deniability," *Air Enthusiast* (November/December 1999).

Cork, John. "Inside Thunderball," *Goldeneye* (Issue 3, Vol 1). The Ian Fleming Foundation web page.

Courtney, Donald V. "Ration of Luck," *Air and Space* (October/November 2002).

Czajkowski, Anthony F. "Techniques of Domestic Intelligence Collection," *Studies in Intelligence* (Winter 1959).

Ford, Harold P. "Why CIA Analysts Were So Doubtful About Vietnam," *Studies in Intelligence* (Vol. 1, No. 1, 1997).

———. "Calling the Sino-Soviet Split," *Studies in Intelligence* (Winter 1998–1999).

Garthoff, Raymond, and Amy Knight. "The KGB's 1967 Annual Report, with Commentary by Raymond Garthoff and Amy Knight," Cold War International History Project web page.

Gourevitch, Philip. "Letter From North Korea: Alone in the Dark," *The New Yorker* (3 September 2003).

Grandolini, Albert. "French 'Packets' Fairchild C-119 Boxcars in French Indochina," *Air Enthusiast* (November/December 1996).

Haines, Gerald K. "CIA's Role in the Study of UFOs, 1947–90," *Studies in Intelligence* (Vol. 1, No.1, 1997).

Hall, R. Cargill. "The 14 April 1956 Overflight of Noril'sk, U.S.S.R.," National Reconnaissance Office, August 2003.

Holland, Max. "The Lie That Linked CIA to the Kennedy Assassination," *Studies in Intelligence* (Fall/Winter 2001).

Holm, Richard L. "A Close Call in Africa," *Studies in Intelligence* (Winter 1999–2000).

Jorden, William J. "Soviet Assails U.S., Produce 4 'Spies,'" *New York Times* (7 February 1957).

Julian, Thomas A. "The Origins of Air Refueling in the United States Air Force," in *Technology and the Air Force: A Retrospective Assessment*, Jacob Neufield, George M. Watson, Jr., and David Chenoweth [editors] (Washington, D.C.: Air Force History and Museum Program, 1997).

Klusmann, Chuck "The Price of Freedom," Air America Association web page.

Koch, R.W. "The CIA's Death Valley Albatross," *Air Classics* (April 1979).

———. "Operation Armageddon," *Air Classics* (October 1979).

Ky, Nguyen Cao, and Marvin Wolf. "Nights Over North Vietnam," *Air and Space* (August/September 2002).

Leary, William M. "Secret Missions to Tibet," *Air and Space* (December 1997/January 1998).

———. "Robert Fulton's Skyhook and Operation Coldfeet," *Studies in Intelligence* (1995).

———. "CIA Air Operations in Laos, 1955–1974," *Studies in Intelligence* (Winter 1999–2000).

Linder, James C. "The Fall of Lima Site 85," *Studies in Intelligence* (Unclassified Edition, 1995).

Lowenhaupt, Henry S. "The Decryption of a Picture," *Studies in Intelligence* (Summer 1967).

———. "On The Soviet Nuclear Scent," *Studies in Intelligence* (Fall 1967).

———. "Mission to Birch Woods," *Studies in Intelligence* (Fall 1968).

———. "Somewhere in Siberia," *Studies in Intelligence* (Winter 1971).

———. "Chasing Bitterfeld Calcium," *Studies in Intelligence* (Spring 1973).

Mansourov, Alexandre Y. "Stalin, Mao, Kim, and China's Decision to Enter the Korean War, Sept. 16–Oct. 15, 1950: New Evidence from Russian Archives," Cold War International History Project web page.

Martynov, Georgi. "The KGB in Latvia," *War in Peace Vol. 1* (London: Marshall Cavendish, 1985).

Murray, Williamson. "Dien Bien Phu," *MHQ* (Spring 1997).

Narinsky, Mikhail M. "The Soviet Union and the Marshall Plan," Cold War International History Project web page.

Parrish, Scott D. "The Turn Toward Confrontation: The Soviet Reaction to the Marshall Plan, 1947," Cold War International History Project web page.

Pozniakov, Vladimir. "A NKVD/NKGB Report to Stalin: A Glimpse into Soviet Intelligence in the United States in the 1940s," Cold War International History Project web page.

Pribbenow, Merle L. "The Ho Chi Minh Trail's Early Years," *Vietnam* (August 1999).

———."North Vietnam's Master Plan," *Vietnam* (August 1999).

Salisbury, Harrison E. "Soviet Says It Shot 4 U.S.-Trained Spies," *New York Times* (27 May 1953).

Tilford, Earl H., Jr. "Rescue at Ban Phanop," *Air Enthusiast* (December 1980–March 1981). The details of Air America's involvement are from a private source.

Tompkins, Peter. "The OSS and Italian Partisans in World War II," *Studies in Intelligence* (Spring 1998, Unclassified Edition).

Thompson, Michael. "Thoughts Provoked by the Very Best Men," *Studies in Intelligence* (1996 edition).

Van Etten, Ben A. "Rescue," Air America Association web page.

Veazey, G. Robert. "Pickup!! Action in World War II," *Friends Journal* (Spring 1994).

Vesilind, Priit J. "The Baltic Nations," *National Geographic* (November 1990).

Wagner, Angie. "CIA Honors Heroes of Long-Secret Air America," *San Diego Union-Tribune* (3 June 2001).

Walker, Fred, Allen Cates, and E.G. Adams. "Memories of the Fall of Saigon–April 29, 1975," Air America Association web page.

Warner, Michael. "The CIA's Internal Probe of the Bay of Pigs Affair," *Studies in Intelligence* (Winter 1998–1999).

Watson, Jack. "Search for the CIA Albatross," *Air Progress Warbirds International* (Summer 1987).

Weathersby, Kathryn. "To Attack, or Not to Attack? Stalin, Kim Il Sung, and the Prelude to War," Cold War International History Project web page.

Wolf, Thomas W. "Obstacle Course for Attaches," *Studies in Intelligence* (Summer 1960).

Xu, Guang Qiu. "U.S. Air Aid and the CCP's Anti-American Campaign, 1945–1949," *Air Power History* (Spring 2000).

Documents

"Current Situation in Albania," Central Intelligence Agency, 15 December 1949.

Intelligence Reports, "Poland—Czechoslovak—East Germany—Western Europe," 18 August 1950 and 15 December 1950.

Intelligence Report, "Yugoslavia—The Balkans—Turkey—Greece," 15 December 1950.

Document TFR 37–23, S. Ignatyev to Malenkov, Beria, and Bulganin, 29 January 1953. "TsK KPK" is the Russian language abbreviation for the Central Committee of the Communist Party of China.

Report by The National Security Council on Interim United States Objectives and Actions to Exploit the Unrest in the Satellite States, 29 June 1953.

Document TFR 55–65, List of USAF aircrew members participating in combat in North Korea, 1950–1953, information about whom was found in documents of the 64th Aviation Corps. This included the crew of the 581st ARCW B-29. It lists all fourteen crewmen, with the notation beside three names, "Killed (under what circumstances not specified)."

George, A.L. "Case Studies of Actual and Alleged Overflights, 1930–1953," Project RAND Research Memorandum RM-1349, 15 August 1955.

Air Intelligence Information Report, 13 October 1955, Report No. 193–55, Subject: Observations of Travelers in USSR.

Memorandum for Information, Subject: Reported Sighting of Unconventional Aircraft, 19 October 1955.

Information Report, "Captured U.S. Balloons Shown to Tourist/Popular Attitudes and Morale," August 1956.

Memorandum for the Secretary, Subject: Oral Presentation of the Annual Report of the Net Evaluation Subcommittee, 25 November 1958.

"Visual-Talent Coverage of the USSR in Relation to Soviet ICBM Deployment January 1959–June 1960."

Memorandum for: Brigadier Andrew J. Goodpaster, Subject: U-2 Overflights of Soviet Bloc, 18 August 1960.

"For Sale Boeing B-17G," Intermountain Aviation Inc. flyer (ca. January 1969). This flyer gives the B-17G's serial number as being 44-83875. Checks with three different references confirm it was actually 44-83785.

"Remarks of the Director of Central Intelligence George J. Tenet on Presentation of the Director's Medal to John T. "Jack" Downey and Richard G. Fecteau," 25 June 1998, CIA web page.

N-number Database Search Results—N207EV.

Joe Baugher's Home Page, USAAS/USAAC/USAAF/USAF Aircraft Serials: 1944 Serial Numbers 44-70255 to 44-83885.

Television Programs and Videos

"Stalin Part 3," Public Broadcasting Service, 1990.

"The Making of Thunderball," MGM/UA Home Videos, 1995.

"Thunderball," MGM/UA Home Videos, 1995.

"Air America: The CIA's Secret Airline" (The History Channel, 2000). Air America pilot Jesse Markham was the brother of Monte Markham, the television actor and producer.

"CIA Secrets–Secret Wars" The Discovery Channel, 2001.

"Escape from a Living Hell" The History Channel, 2001.

Index

About the Author

Curtis Peebles is an aerospace historian who has authored, edited, and co-written fourteen books, including *The Corona Project: America's First Spy Satellites,* published by the Naval Institute Press in 1997. He has a BA in History from California State University—Long Beach. A resource person in his field, the author has been interviewed for numerous television shows, such as "NOVA," "Unsolved History," "Tactical to Practical," and other television series.

The **Naval Institute Press** is the book-publishing arm of the U. S. Naval Institute, a private, nonprofit, membership society for sea service professionals and others who share an interest in naval and maritime affairs. Established in 1873 at the U. S. Naval Academy in Annapolis, Maryland, where its offices remain today, the Naval Institute has members worlwide.

Members of the Naval Institute support the education programs of the society and receive the influential monthly magazine *Proceedings* and discounts on fine nautical prints and on ship and aircraft photos. They also have access to the transcripts of the Institute's Oral History Program and get discounted admission to any of the Institute-sponsored seminars offered around the country.

The Naval Institute also publishes *Naval History* magazine. This colorful bi-monthly is filled with entertaining and thought-provoking articles, first-person reminiscences, and dramatic art and photography. Members receive a discount on *Naval History* subscriptions.

The Naval Institute's book-publishing program, begun in 1898 with basic guides to naval practices, has broadened its scope to include books of more general interest. Now the Naval Institute Press publishes about one hundred titles each year, ranging from how-to books on boating and navigation to battle histories, biographies, ship and aircraft guides, and novels. Institute members receive significant discounts on the Press's more than eight hundred books in print.

Full-time students are eligible for special half-price membership rates. Life memberships are also available.

For a free catalog describing Naval Institute Press books currently available, and for further information about subscribing to *Naval History* magazine or about joining the U. S. Naval Institute, please write to:

Customer Service
U. S. Naval Institute
291 Wood Road
Annapolis, MD 21402-5034

Telephone: (800) 233-8764
Fax: (410) 269-7940
Web address: www.navalinstitute.org